ARCHITECTURE
Drafting and Design

DONALD E. HEPLER

AND

PAUL I. WALLACH

McGraw-Hill Book Company
New York • St. Louis • San Francisco • Dallas
Toronto • London • Sydney

Cover photograph: The residence of Elliott Erwitt designed
by Roy Siguard Johnson; Courtesy of *Record Houses of 1961*,
annual publication of *Architectural Record*, a McGraw-Hill
magazine.

End paper map created by Hermann Bollmann for Pictorial
Maps, Inc.

ARCHITECTURE: DRAFTING AND DESIGN

28288

7 8 9 10-VH-75 74 73 72 71 70 69

CONTENTS

PREFACE   vi

INTRODUCTION   1

SECTION SIX. ELEVATION DRAWINGS

SECTION SEVEN. PICTORIAL DRAWINGS

PART III. Technical Architectural Plans

SECTION EIGHT. LOCATION PLANS

SECTION NINE. SECTIONAL DRAWINGS

SECTION TEN. FOUNDATION PLANS

SECTION ELEVEN. FRAMING PLANS

SECTION TWELVE. SCHEDULES AND SPECIFICATIONS

PREFACE

This textbook is designed for a first course in architectural drafting and design. Since a study of the basic principles and techniques of mechanical drawing normally precedes a course in architectural drafting and design, only the principles and practices that are essentially related to architectural drafting are presented in this book.

Architecture: Drafting and Design is divided into four parts: Part I, Area Planning; Part II, Basic Architectural Plans; Part III, Technical Architectural Plans; and Part IV, Creative Architectural Drafting and Design.

Part I, *Area Planning,* covers the basic elements of planning various areas of a structure and combining these areas into a composite, functional plan.

Part II, *Basic Architectural Plans,* includes the basic techniques and procedures used in preparing architectural floor plans, elevations, and pictorial drawings.

Part III, *Technical Architectural Plans,* shows how to prepare the many technical architectural plans that are necessary for a complete and detailed description of the basic design. This part covers in detail the preparation of location plans, sectional drawings, foundation plans, framing plans, specifications, electrical plans, air-conditioning plans, plumbing diagrams, and modular construction plans. A section also deals with building codes.

Part IV, *Creative Architectural Drafting and Design,* is organized to provide the student with an opportunity to express his creativity in the application of the fundamental principles, concepts, skills, and ideas he has developed in his study of the first three parts. In Part IV, the student is provided with exercises that will stimulate and develop creative architectural activities.

Architecture: Drafting and Design is organized to be presented consecutively from Part I through Part IV. When the basic emphasis is placed on developing fundamental architectural drafting skills and techniques, Part II may be studied first. Classes that are specifically oriented to the construction phase of architecture may find Part III a logical point of departure. For classes in which the main interest is surveying and developing an appreciation of the field of architectural drafting and design, Part IV would be the most appropriate juncture at which to begin.

All the illustrations have been selected and prepared to reinforce and amplify the principles and procedures described in the text. Whenever possible, each principle and practice has been reduced to its most elementary form and, for easy comprehension, directly related to the student's own environment.

Progression within each section and unit is from the simple to the complex, from the familiar to the abstract. The problems that appear at the end of each unit are organized to provide the maximum amount of flexibility. Each unit includes problems that range from the simplest, which can be completed in a few minutes, to the complex, which require considerable research and application of the principles of architectural drafting and design.

Since communication in the field of architectural drafting and design largely depends on understanding the vocabulary of architecture, new terms, abbreviations, and symbols are defined when they first appear and are reinforced throughout the rest of the text.

The practice of architecture functions through a utilization of the basic principles of mathematics and science. The correlation of basic scientific and mathematical concepts with architectural principles has been presented wherever appropriate.

The residence is used primarily throughout the book to illustrate the application of the various architectural plans and techniques, but other structures also are used as examples when suitable.

The authors wish to make grateful acknowledgment to Norma K. Pittard and Jay D. Helsel for much of the art work; to Albert P. Wittman, President of Home Planners, Inc., for his constant guidance, his recommendations, and his contribution of Home Planners' drawings; to Richard B. Pollman and Irving E. Kronquist for the use of many of their designs; to Shriver L. Coover for his professional inspiration; to the following teachers who participated in much of the basic organizational research: Dean S. Billik, Delbert R. Gottke, Kent S. Miller, Don Yost, Don Van Slyke, Carl F. Stoltenberg, Joseph Neumeier and Howard Mohan; and to Donna Hepler and Janet Wallach for their constant assistance and encouragement.

Donald E. Hepler completed his undergraduate work at California State College, California, Pennsylvania, and his graduate work at the University of Pittsburgh. In 1949 he joined Admiral Homes, Inc., as an architectural draftsman and later joined the architectural staffs of Rust Engineering; Patterson, Emerson, and Comstock, Engineers; and Union Switch and Signal Company. During the Korean conflict he served as an officer with the United States Army Corps of Engineers. He returned to civilian life as head of the Industrial Arts Department, Avonworth High School, Pittsburgh, Pennsylvania. He joined the faculty of California State College in 1957 as Associate Professor of Industrial Arts and remained there until 1961 when he became Senior Industrial Education Editor, Webster Division, McGraw-Hill Book Company. He is now editorial director, Technical and Vocational Division, McGraw-Hill Book Company.

Paul I. Wallach received his undergraduate education at the University of California at Santa Barbara and did his graduate work at Los Angeles State College. He has acquired extensive experience in the drafting, designing, and construction phases of architecture. He has traveled extensively in Europe and the Far East and has studied and taught for several years in Europe. For the last thirteen years he has been teaching architecture and drafting in the Los Angeles City Schools. He is now teaching drafting and design at San Carlos High School, San Carlos, California.

Steelways Magazine; American Iron and Steel Institute

introduction

When an architect designs a structure, he uses the cumulative knowledge of centuries. Architecture had its beginning when early man first fashioned a cave or lean-to shelter for his family. Architectural drafting and design began when man first drew the outline of this shelter in the sand or dirt and planned in advance how he would use existing materials.

▶ History

The history of architectural design can be traced through, and directly related to, the great movements of history. Throughout this historical development, the architect has relied heavily upon the advancements of science and mathematics. These advancements have precipitated the development of new building materials and methods. New developments in architectural engineering and new building materials have brought about more changes in architectural design in the last 30 years than occurred during the entire preceding history of architecture. Yet many of the basic principles of modern architecture, such as bearing-wall construction and skeleton-frame construction, have been known for centuries.

Even today architectural structures are divided into two basic types, the bearing wall and the skeleton frame. In the bearing-wall type of architecture, the walls are solid and support themselves and the roof. The log cabin shown is an example of bearing-wall construction.

▶ Bearing Wall

Most early architecture, such as the Egyptian and Grecian structures, were of the bearing-wall type. In fact, one of the first major problems in architectural drafting and design involved the bearing wall. The problem was simply how to provide an opening in a supporting wall without sacrificing the support. The first of many solutions to this problem resulted in the development of the post and the lintel. In this type of construction, posts large enough to support the lintel were used to support the rest of the wall and the roof.

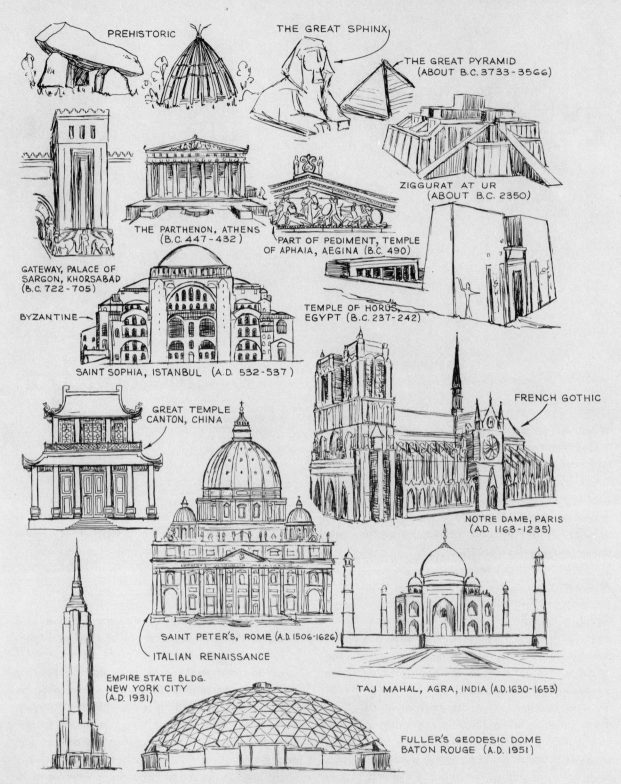

PREHISTORIC

THE GREAT SPHINX

THE GREAT PYRAMID (ABOUT B.C. 3733-3566)

ZIGGURAT AT UR (ABOUT B.C. 2350)

GATEWAY, PALACE OF SARGON, KHORSABAD (B.C. 722-705)

THE PARTHENON, ATHENS (B.C. 447-432)

PART OF PEDIMENT, TEMPLE OF APHAIA, AEGINA (B.C. 490)

BYZANTINE

TEMPLE OF HORUS, EGYPT (B.C. 237-242)

SAINT SOPHIA, ISTANBUL (A.D. 532-537)

GREAT TEMPLE CANTON, CHINA

FRENCH GOTHIC

NOTRE DAME, PARIS (A.D. 1163-1235)

SAINT PETER'S, ROME (A.D. 1506-1626)

ITALIAN RENAISSANCE

EMPIRE STATE BLDG. NEW YORK CITY (A.D. 1931)

TAJ MAHAL, AGRA, INDIA (A.D. 1630-1653)

FULLER'S GEODESIC DOME BATON ROUGE (A.D. 1951)

The historical development of architecture.

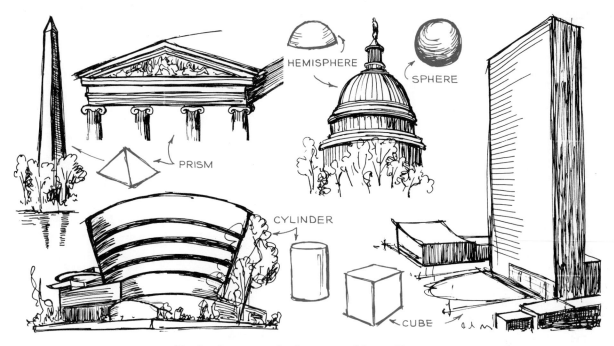

The basic geometric shapes used in architecture.

The ancient Greeks used post and lintel construction to erect many of their outstanding structures. Since most ancients, including the Greeks, used stone as their primary building material, the great weight of the stone considerably limited the application of post and lintel construction. Furthermore, stone post and lintel construction could not support wide openings. Therefore, many posts were placed close together to provide the needed support. The Greeks developed many styles of columns and gave names to the parts. The various styles of column designs were known as *orders*. These orders of architecture developed by the Greeks were known as the *Doric*, the *Ionic*, and the *Corinthian* orders. Later the Romans developed the *Composite* and the *Tuscan* orders.

Since the Greek climate was particularly suited to open-air construction, the Greeks used this post and lintel technique to great advantage. The Parthenon, a classic example of Greek use of the post and the lintel, for centuries has been considered one of the most beautiful buildings in the world.

A log cabin is an example of bearing-wall construction.

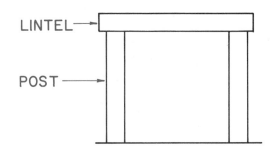

Post and lintel construction.

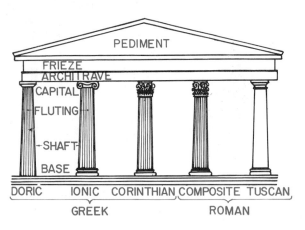

The basic orders of architecture.

An early oriental application of post and beam construction.

The Orientals also made effective use of the post and lintel. They were able to construct buildings with larger openings under the lintel because of the use of lighter materials. The use of lighter materials resulted in the development of an oriental style of architecture which was extremely light and graceful. The oriental post and lintel technique was used in building construction and was also used extensively for gates and entrances.

The arch. The Romans began a new trend in the design of wall openings when they developed and popularized the use of the arch. The arch differs from the post and lintel primarily in that it can span greater areas without support. This advantage of the arch is due to the fact that it

can be made of small pieces of stone, whereas the post and lintel construction is limited by the size of the stone used for the lintel.

The principle of the arch is that each stone is supported by leaning on the keystone in the center. The great disadvantage in the use of the early arch was that the weight of the stone caused the sides to spread. To counteract this spreading, the walls had to be thick and heavy at the bottom.

Post and lintel construction was used in the Parthenon.

Wide World Photo

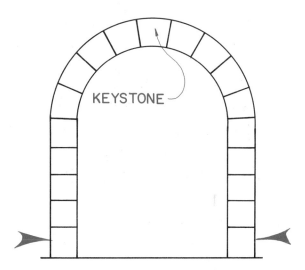

A keystone supports both sides of an arch. An arch must also be supported at its base.

The vault. The simple arch was the forerunner of the vault. The *vault* is simply a series of arches which form a continuous covering. This development allowed the use of the arch as a passageway rather than just as an opening in a wall. The barrel vault and the cross vault were popular Roman construction devices. The cross vault is the intersection of two barrel vaults. The intersections make additional strength possible with less foundational support. The Romans combined the use of the vault and the column very extensively in their architecture.

The barrel vault is a series of arches.

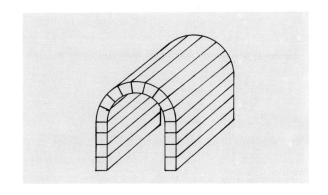

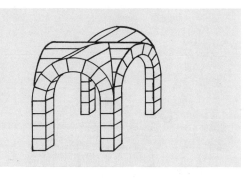

The cross vault is the result of the intersection of two barrel vaults.

The dome. The dome is a further refinement of the arch. The *dome* is made of arches so arranged that the bases make a circle and the tops meet in the middle of the ceiling. The Romans felt that the dome developed a feeling of power and omnipotence. Hence domes were used extensively on religious and governmental structures. In fact, the word *dome* comes from the Italian word *duomo,* meaning "cathedral," and is derived from the Latin word *domus,* meaning "house."

A dome is comprised of a series of intersecting arches.

The dome has become a symbol of power and piety.

The pointed arch was used extensively in Gothic cathedrals.

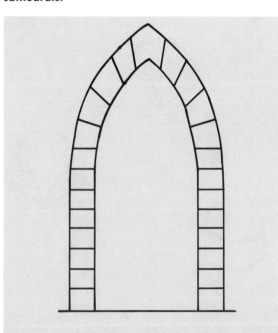

The flying buttress helps support thin walls and arches.

Gothic architecture originated in France and spread throughout Western Europe between 1160 and 1530. With its development came another variation of the arch—the pointed arch. The pointed arch became very popular in Gothic cathedrals because it created a sense of reaching and aspiring by its emphasis on vertical lines. Construction of the pointed arch posed the same problem as did conventional arches, that of spreading at the bottom. But instead of just supporting the arch at the bottom, a new device known as a *buttress* was developed. Buttresses were gradually moved up the walls and resulted in the development of the *flying buttress,* which supported the tops of the walls. The buttress helped maintain the support without adding weight to the wall. The use of buttresses made possible thinner walls and more windows.

Bearing-wall construction is still used extensively in modern architecture, but the use of more massive building materials, such as reinforced and prestressed concrete, enables the architect to span greater areas and develop greater flexibilities with his design.

▶ **Skeleton Frame**

The skeleton-frame type of architecture has open frame walls to which some covering is attached. The frame provides the primary support, and the covering provides the needed shelter. The use of the skeleton frame allows the structure to be much lighter and yet provides the needed support. Although the skeleton frame was used extensively by African natives and Indians, formal and permanent architectural use of the skeleton frame is a rather recent historical development.

The development of stronger and more diversified framing materials and wall coverings has led to the popularization of the skeleton frame in modern architecture. The skeleton-frame type of architecture is most commonly used in family dwellings today, and it is also the most popular method employed in the construction of commercial buildings. When steel is used for the skeleton, the skeleton framing is known as *steel-cage construction*.

▶ Cantilever Construction

A specialized type of skeleton-frame construction is cantilever construction. In this type the beams which carry the load are supported only at one end. Cantilever construction is uniquely suited to steel. It was impossible before lighter, stronger

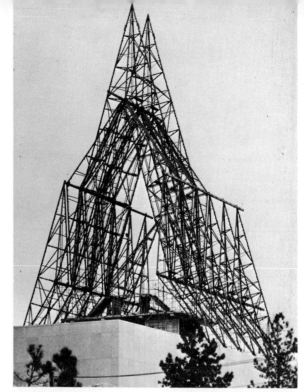

Republic Steel Corporation

Steel-cage construction is used on many large structures.

Skeleton-frame construction is used in most homes.

American Sisalcraft Company

Frank Lloyd Wright utilized cantilever construction in the design of "Falling Waters."

building materials were devised. Frank Lloyd Wright's Kauffman House is an outstanding example of a cantilever construction. Although this house was designed almost thirty years ago, its appearance and function have not become dated.

▶ Today and Tomorrow

Designing a structure that will endure through the ages is the supreme challenge to an architect. As new advancements are made in architectural engineering and in materials design, the architect, designer, or builder must keep abreast of technological changes and advancements, whether he is designing a residence based on the post and lintel principle or Manhattan's largest building utilizing steel-cage construction. Today's architect must understand people, their habits, their needs, their activities, and their desires. The architect, designer, or draftsman must be capable of manipulating shapes, materials, colors, and proportions into aesthetically pleasing structures. He must understand the science and engineering of architecture in order to produce buildings that are structurally sound, and he must be able to arrange and balance space in order to create buildings that are functionally appropriate.

pART 1

Area Planning

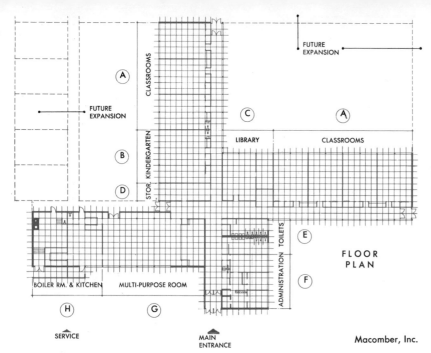

A school may be divided into many functional areas.

FLOOR PLAN

Macomber, Inc.

When an architect designs a building, he first divides it into various areas according to their function. A school would be divided into such areas as the administrative area, the classroom area, the service area, and the physical-activity area. A hospital would be divided into patient areas, administrative areas, surgical suites, and service areas.

In the same way a residence is divided into three major areas for planning purposes: the living area, the service area, and the sleeping area. *The living area* of the house is where the family meets friends, relaxes, dines, entertains. *The service area* is that part of the house in which the maintenance and servicing functions are performed, and the *sleeping area* is the area of the home designed for sleeping or resting.

To design effectively each area of a building, the designer must become extremely familiar with the activities that will occur in each area. Each area should be specifically designed to perform its

A residence is divided into three basic areas—sleeping, living, and service areas.

Home Planners, Inc.

SLEEPING   LIVING   SERVICE

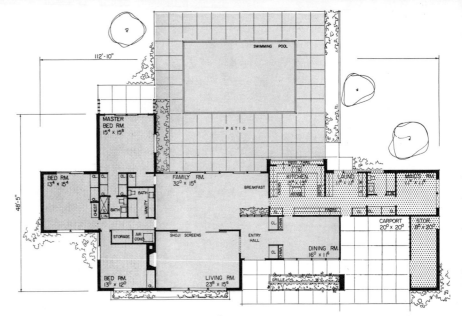

The location of the living, service, and sleeping areas.

Home Planners, Inc.

unique function; the function should not be adapted to the area design. The basic rule of design, *form follows function,* applies most stringently here.

Areas constitute the main subdivisions of a structure, but areas are also broken into subdivisions called *rooms.* These subdivisions contained in an area are related to the basic function of the area.

Many devices are used to separate the areas of a building. Areas are separated by their location in different ends of a building on the same level

with connecting corridors. They are separated by location in separate structures connected by covered walkways, and they are often separated by location on different levels. Areas are often referred to as parts of a building or as centers for some particular work, such as the "classroom wing" and the "administrative suite."

In Part I you will learn how to plan each area of a residence. You will learn about the function, location, decor, size, and shape of each room.

Areas are often separated by levels.

Home Planners, Inc.

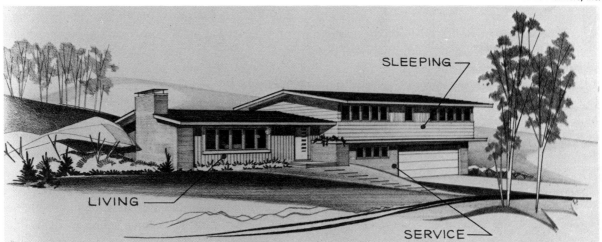

SECTION ONE. LIVING AREA

Your first impression of a home is probably the image you retain of the living area. In fact, this is the only area of the home that most strangers observe. The living area is just what the name implies, the area where most of the "living" occurs. It is here the family entertains, relaxes, dines, listens to music, watches television, enjoys hobbies, and participates in other recreational activities.

The living area is often referred to as the "show place" of the home. However, it is much more. A well-designed living area is a functional, useful, and integral part of the home. The living area is designed to accommodate practically all the activities of the household except those associated with sleeping, working, or servicing the home.

The total living area is divided into smaller areas (rooms) which are designed to perform specific living functions. The subdivisions of most living areas may include the living room, dining room, recreation or game room, family room, patio, entrance foyer, den or study, and guest lavatories. Other specialized rooms, such as the library, music room, or sewing room, are often included as part of the living area of large houses that have the space to devote to such specialized functions. In smaller homes many of the standard rooms combine two or more rooms. For example, the living room and dining room are often combined. In extremely small homes the living room constitutes the entire living area and provides all the facilities normally assigned to other rooms in the living area. Although the subdivisions of the living area are called *rooms*, they are not always separated by a partition or a wall. Nevertheless, they perform the function of a room, whether there is a complete separation, a partial separation, or no separation.

When rooms are completely separated by partitions and doors, the plan is known as a *closed plan*. When partitions do not divide the rooms of an area, the arrangement is called an *open plan*. The illustrated living room and dining room are examples of the open plan. Notice that as you enter the foyer and go to the living room, then to the dining room, there are no doors or partitions to restrict you.

In most two-story dwellings the living area is normally located on the first floor. However, in split-level homes or one-story homes with functional basements, part of the living area may be located on the lower level. In the plan shown, part of the living area, the family room and study, is located directly under the living and dining areas.

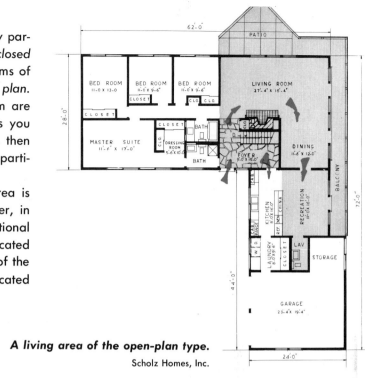

A living area of the open-plan type.

Scholz Homes, Inc.

Unit 1. The Living Room

The living room is the center of most living areas, and in small homes it may represent the entire living area. Hence, its function, location, decor, size, and shape are extremely important and affect the design, functioning, and appearance of the other living area rooms.

▶ **Function**

The living room is designed to perform many functions. The exact function depends on the living habits of the occupants. For example, it is often the entertainment center of the home, the recreation center, the library, the music room, the TV center, the reception room, the social room, the study, and occasionally the dining center. In small dwellings the living room often becomes a guest bedroom. If the living room is to perform all or any of these functions, then it should be designed

accordingly, and facilities, location, decor, size, and shape should be planned to provide for each of these activities. For example, if the living room is to be used for television viewing, it will be planned differently from a living room without television. Figure 1–1 shows some of the considerations in planning a room to function in this way.

Many of the facilities normally associated with the living room can be eliminated if a separate, special-purpose room exists for that activity. For example, if television viewing is restricted to a recreation room, then this aspect of the plan can be eliminated. If a den or study is provided for reading and for storing books, facilities for the use of books can be eliminated. Regardless of the exact activities anticipated, the living room should always be planned as a functional, integral part of the home. The living room is planned for the comfort

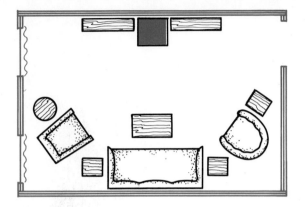

Fig. 1–1. A living room specifically planned for television viewing.

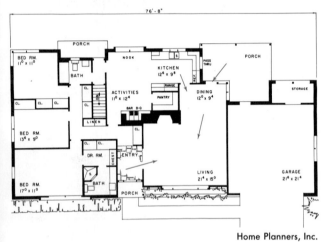

Home Planners, Inc.

Fig. 1–2. The living room should be centrally located.

and convenience of the family and guests, and not just as a place to observe or a room to enter only when guests are entertained. The maximum amount of utilization can be designed into the living room by providing the facilities that the family will need and use in this room.

▶ **Location**

The living room should be centrally located. It should be adjacent to the entrance, but the outside entrance should not lead directly into the living room. In smaller residences the entrance may open into the living room, but whenever possible this arrangement is to be avoided since the living room should not be a traffic access to the sleeping and service areas of the house. Since the living room and dining room function together, the living room should also be adjacent to the dining room. Figure 1–2 shows the central location of a living room and its proximity to other rooms of the living area.

Open plan. In a living area that utilizes the open plan, the living room, dining room, and entrance may be part of one open area, such as the living area shown in Fig. 1–3. Or the living room may be divided from other rooms in the living area by means of a divider without doors, such as the storage wall shown in Fig. 1–4. In Fig. 1–5, the living room is separated from the foyer by a

Fig. 1–3. An open-plan living room.

Home Planners, Inc.

14

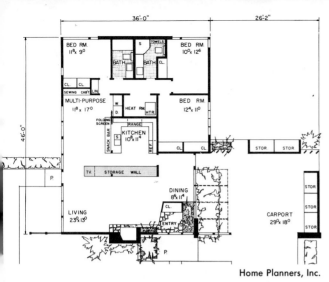

Fig. 1–4. The storage wall separates the living room from the kitchen without enclosing the room.

Fig. 1–6. The living room may be divided from other rooms by elevating it or by sinking it.

closet, from the dining room by the fireplace. Often a separation is accomplished by use of furniture placement or screens, or by placing the living room on a different level, as shown in Fig. 1–6. This feature does not separate the rooms visually, but does effect a functional separation.

When an open plan is desired and yet the designer wants to provide some means of closing off the room completely, sliding doors, or folding doors such as those shown in Fig. 1–7, can be used effectively.

Closed plan. In a closed plan, the living room would be completely closed from the other rooms by means of doors, arches, or relatively small openings in the partitions (Fig. 1–8).

Fig. 1–5. A fireplace is often used to divide the living room from the dining room.

Fig. 1-7. In the open plan folding doors provide privacy when needed.

Fig. 1-10. The living room should appear inviting, comfortable, and spacious.

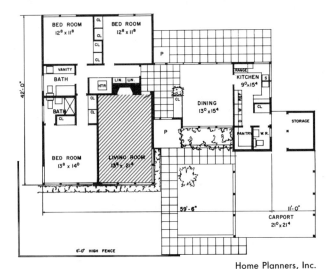

Fig. 1-8. A living room of the closed-plan type.

Fig. 1-9. A contemporary living room.

Rendering by George A. Parenti for the Masonite Corporation

▶ Decor

There is no one way to design and decorate a room. The decor depends primarily on the tastes, habits, and personalities of the people who will use the room. If the residents' tastes are modern, the wall, ceiling, and floor treatments should be consistent with the clean, functional lines of modern architecture and modern furniture, as shown in Fig. 1-9. If the residents prefer colonial or period-type architecture, then this theme should be reflected in the decor of the room. In either case, since the living room is usually the most handsomely decorated room in the home, it is often referred to as the "showplace of the home."

The living room should appear inviting, comfortable, and spacious. This appearance can be accomplished by an effective use of color and lighting techniques; by the tasteful selection of wall, ceiling, and floor covering materials; and by the selection and placement of functional, well-designed furniture. All these techniques have been combined to create a most desirable total impression in the living room shown in Fig. 1-10. Decorating a room is much like the selection of clothing. The color, style, and materials should be selected to minimize faults and to emphasize good points. Figure 1-11 shows how the use of mirrors and floor-to-ceiling drapes and the proper furniture

Fig. 1-11. Mirrors can help create a spacious effect.

Fig. 1-13. The outdoors can become part of the living-room decor.

placement can create a spacious effect in a relatively small room.

Walls. The design and placement of wall-covering materials, doors, windows, and chimneys along the walls of the living room can change the entire appearance of the room. Wall coverings are selected from a variety of materials, including plaster, sheetrock, wood paneling, brick, stone, and glass. Sometimes furniture is built into the walls. Fireplaces, windows, doors, or openings to other areas should be designed as integral parts of the room and should not appear as afterthoughts. Notice the difference between the two designs in Fig. 1-12. Figure 1-12A shows a wall, fireplace, and opening designed as a functional part of the room. Figure 1-12B shows the same room with door openings, fireplaces, and wall treatments

placed on the wall without reference to other parts of the room.

Orientation. The living room should be oriented to take full advantage of the position of the sun and the most attractive view. Since the living room is used primarily in the afternoon and evening, it should be located to take advantage of the position of the sun in the afternoon.

Windows. When a window is placed in a living room wall, it should become an integral part of that wall. The view from the window or windows becomes part of the living room decor, especially when landscape features are near and readily observable, as in Fig. 1-13. In considering the view from the window, consider also the various seasonal landscapes, as the position and window placement is planned.

Fig. 1-12A. A functionally-designed living room wall.

Fig. 1-12B. A living room wall with independent features.

OPEN PLAN

CLOSED PLAN

Fig. 1–14. Translucent glass admits only light, not images.

Fig. 1–15. This fireplace design is an integral part of the wall.

Fig. 1–16. A corner fireplace.

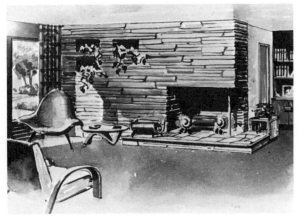

Although the primary function of a window is twofold, to admit light and to provide a pleasant view of the landscape, there are many conditions under which only the admission of light is desirable. If the view from the window is unpleasant or is restricted by other buildings, translucent glass, which admits only light, as shown in Fig. 1–14, can be incorporated into the plan.

Fireplace. The primary function of a fireplace is to provide heat, but it should be more than just that. The fireplace and accompanying masonry should maintain a clean, simple line consistent with the decor of the room and of the wall where it is placed. Figure 1–15 shows a fireplace in which the masonry is used on the entire wall rather than restricted to the immediate fireplace and chimney area. The corner fireplace in Fig. 1–16 is used to divide the library area of the living room from the conversational area, and the fireplace used in Fig. 1–17 is used as the major separation between the living room and the dining room.

Fig. 1–17. A fireplace used as a divider between the living room and the dining room.

Fig. 1–18. An open beam ceiling.

The external appearance of the house must be considered in locating the fireplace, because the location of the fireplace in the room determines the position of the chimney on the roof. This fact does not mean that the outside of the house should be designed first. But it does mean that the outside appearance must be considered in designing and locating features of the house that appear also on the outside, such as fireplaces, doors, and windows.

Floors. The living room floor should reinforce and blend with the color scheme, textures, and overall style of the living room. Exposed hardwood flooring, room-size carpeting, wall-to-wall carpeting, throw rugs, and occasionally polished flagstone are appropriate for living room use.

Ceilings. Most conventional ceilings are flat surfaces covered with plaster. New building materials, such as laminated beams and arches, and new construction methods, such as the post and beam, now enable architects to design ceilings that

Allan J. Gelbin, architect

Fig. 1–20. General lighting and local lighting should be used to illuminate the living room.

conserve building materials and utilize previously wasted space. The open beam ceiling shown in Fig. 1–18 is an example of the use of this technique. Figure 1–19 shows several optional methods of producing cathedral ceilings either in double-pitch or in single-pitch style. The cathedral ceiling makes a room appear more spacious, through the addition of more cubage, than another room which has the same amount of square feet.

Lighting. Living-room lighting is divided into two types, general lighting and local lighting. General lighting is designed to illuminate the entire room through the use of ceiling fixtures, wall spots, or cove lighting, as shown in Fig. 1–20. Local lighting is provided for a specific purpose, such as reading, drawing, or sewing. Local lighting can be supplied by table lamps, wall lamps, pole lamps, or floor lamps.

Furniture. Furniture for the living room should reflect the motif and architectural style of the home. If the architectural style of the home is modern, the furniture should be modern. If the home is colonial, the furniture should be colonial. If the home is of some period style, the furniture should reflect the furniture style of this period. Figure 1–21 shows the relationship between the various furniture styles and architectural styles. The mixing of modern and period furniture styles should be avoided.

Fig. 1–19. A cathedral ceiling helps make the room look more spacious.

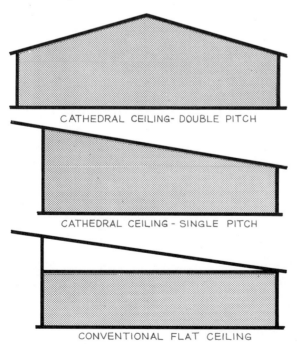

CATHEDRAL CEILING- DOUBLE PITCH

CATHEDRAL CEILING - SINGLE PITCH

CONVENTIONAL FLAT CEILING

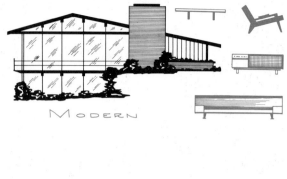

MODERN

ELIZABETHAN

COLONIAL

Fig. 1–21. Furniture styles should be related to the type of architecture used.

Figure 1–22 shows families of furniture selected with maximum emphasis on consistency in style and texture.

A special effort should be made to have built-in furniture maintain lines consistent with the remaining wall treatment. Notice how the built-in music center in Fig. 1–23 eliminates the need for other pieces of furniture in the room, and blends functionally into the total decor of the room.

The furniture for the living room is chosen to fit the living needs of the residents, and the size, shape, and layout of the room should be designed to accommodate the furniture. Figure 1–24A shows a living room of adequate proportions for function-

Fig. 1–22. Furniture should be consistent in style.

Fig. 1–23. Built-in furniture units can save much space.

Furniture should not only be consistent in period and style but should also be related in texture and design. All the furniture in the living room should be of the same type of wood. If walnut is used on built-in furniture, in the paneling, and in the trim, walnut should be repeated in the other furniture in the room. Avoid mixing furniture of different types of wood, such as oak, walnut, and mahogany. Wood furniture should be finished in the same type of finish throughout the room—either all glossy, all semiglossy, or all flat or satin finish.

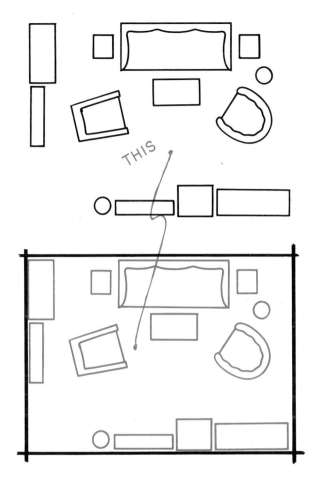

Fig. 1–24A. A living room planned to accommodate the necessary furniture.

Fig. 1–24B. A living room of inadequate size for the furniture needed.

ing well with the necessary furniture. Figure 1–24B shows a room in which the size and shape are not adequate for the furniture.

Sometimes an outstanding piece of furniture or fixture may affect the design of the entire room. For example, the room in which the stereophonic speaker cabinet shown in Fig. 1–25 is to be housed should be designed to take full advantage of this speaker system. Figure 1–26 shows a living room layout designed for maximum listening enjoyment.

▶ **Size and Shape**

One of the most difficult aspects of planning the size and shape of a living room, or any other room, is to provide sufficient wall space for the effective placement of furniture. Continuous wall space is

Fig. 1–25. One piece of furniture may become the focal point of the entire room.

James B. Lansing Sound, Inc.

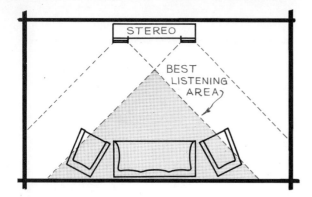

Fig. 1-26. A living room designed for maximum listening enjoyment.

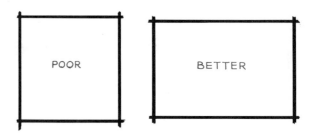

Fig. 1-28. Rectangular rooms provide more flexibility than square rooms.

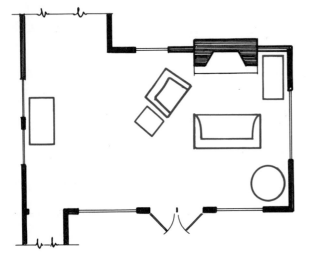

Fig. 1-27A. A living room with inadequate wall space.

Fig. 1-27B. A living room with ample wall space for furniture placement.

needed for the placement of many articles of furniture, especially musical equipment, bookcases, chairs, and couches. The placement of fireplaces, doors, or openings to other rooms should be planned to conserve as much wall space for furniture placement as possible. Figure 1-27A shows a living room with practically no wall space for furniture placement. Figure 1-27B shows the same room with the wall space adjusted to provide the needed space for furniture placement.

Rectangular rooms are generally easier to plan and to place furniture in than are square rooms (Fig. 1-28). However, the designer must be careful not to establish a proportion that will break the living room into several conversational areas, as shown in Fig. 1-29A. This design has actually resulted in the merging of two separate rooms into

Fig. 1-29 A and B. Avoid breaking the room into several isolated conversation areas.

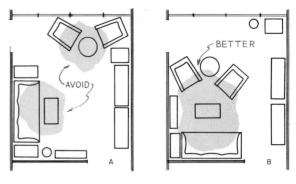

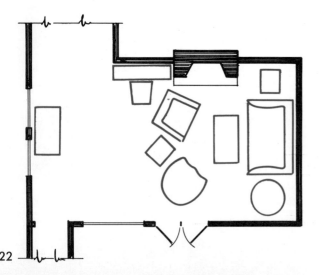

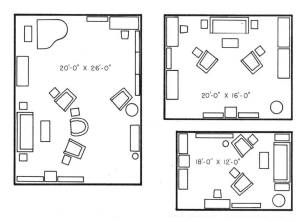

Fig. 1–30. Living rooms vary greatly in size.

one. The arrangement shown in Fig. 1–29B is much more desirable, since it integrates the total activities of the room without separation.

Living rooms vary greatly in size. A room 12 by 18 feet (12′ × 18′) would be considered a small or minimum-sized living room. A living room of average size would be approximately 16′ × 20′, and a very large or optimum-sized living room would be 20′ × 26′ or more, as shown in Fig. 1–30.

Problems

1. Sketch an open-plan living room. Indicate the position of windows, fireplace, foyer, entrance, and dining room.

2. Sketch a closed-plan living room. Show the position of adjacent rooms.

3. Sketch one wall of the living room you designed for Problem 2. Use Fig. 1–12 as a guide.

4. List the furniture you would include in your living room. Cut out samples of this furniture from catalogs or newspapers. Be consistent in style, choosing either contemporary or period-style furniture.

5. Determine the best size for a living room to accommodate these pieces of furniture: a couch, a television set, a stereo, a baby grand piano, a bookcase, a chaise longue, a coffee table, a fireplace, two chairs.

6. Identify the following terms: *closed plan, open plan, decor, living area, living room, local lighting, general lighting.*

Unit 2. The Dining Room

The dining facilities designed for a residence depend greatly on the dining habits of the occupants. The facilities may be rather large, elaborate, and formal, as shown in the dining room in Fig. 2–1. Or they may consist of only a modest dining alcove in the living area, or a breakfast nook in the kitchen. Large homes may contain dining facilities in all these areas.

▶ **Function**

The function of a dining area is to provide a place for the family to gather for breakfast, lunch, or dinner in both casual and formal situations. When possible, a separate dining area potentially capa-

Fig. 2–1. A large, formal dining area.

Armstrong Cork Company

Fig. 2-2. An informal dining area.

Scholz Homes, Inc.

ble of seating from eight to twelve persons for dinner should be provided in addition to breakfast or dinette facilities. Contrast the formal dining area shown in Fig. 2–1 with the informal atmosphere and casual dining facilities shown in the dining area in Fig. 2–2.

▶ **Location**

Figure 2–3 shows dining facilities located in the kitchen, in a dining room, in an area in the living area, and on a patio.

Relation to kitchen. Regardless of the exact position of the dining area, it must be placed adjacent to the kitchen. The ideal dining location is one that requires few steps from the kitchen to the dining table. However, the preparation of food and other kitchen activities should be baffled from direct view from the dining area.

Relation to living room. If dining facilities are not located in the living room, they should be located adjacent to the living room. The reason for this situation is that family and guests normally enter the dining room from the living room and use the facilities jointly.

The proximity of the dining room to the kitchen, and of the dining room to the living room, requires the dining room to be placed between the kitchen and the living area. The dining room in the closed plan shown in Fig. 2–4 is located in this manner.

Fig. 2-3. Dining facilities can be located in many different areas.

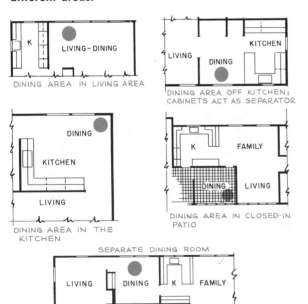

Fig. 2-4. The dining room is located between the living room and the kitchen.

Home Planners, Inc.

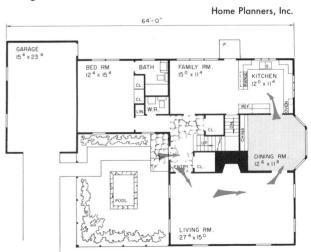

Fig. 2–5. The look-through fireplace divides the dining area from the living room.

Separation. Complete separation should be possible between the kitchen and the dining room, but the area between the living room and the dining room may be entirely open, partially baffled, or completely closed off. In Fig. 2–1, the separation is accomplished by sinking the dining room and dividing the rooms with a common fireplace. A partial separation is accomplished in Fig. 2–5 by means of a common fireplace. Compare this arrangement with the completely open dining area shown in Figs. 2–6 and 2–7.

Fig. 2–6. An open-plan dining room.

Fig. 2–7. A dining corner in the living area.

Armstrong Cork Company

Fig. 2–8. Dining facilities located adjacent to the patio.

Anderson Window Corporation

Fig. 2–10. Consider the view when locating the dining area.

Outside dining facilities. There is often a need for dining facilities on or adjacent to the patio, as shown in Fig. 2–8. In either case the porch or patio should be near the kitchen and directly accessible to it. Locating the patio or dining porch directly outside the dining room or kitchen wall provides maximum use of the facilities. This arrangement minimizes the inconvenience of using the outside dining facilities (Fig. 2–9).

▶ **Decor**

The decor of the dining room should be consistent with the rest of the house and specifically relate in style to the other parts of the living area. This relationship is especially desirable in the open plan, in which the dining area is integrated with the re-

mainder of the living area. Floor, wall, and ceiling treatment should therefore be the same in the dining area as in the living area.

If a dining porch or a dining patio is used, its decor must also be considered part of the dining room decor, since the outside view is projected to the inside. Notice how the view of the courtyard in Fig. 2–10 is brought to the inside by the use of window walls directly above the dining area.

Dividers. If semi-isolation is desired, the use of partial divider walls consisting of planter walls, glass walls, half walls of brick or stone, paneled walls, and even fireplaces and grillwork can function to provide partial separation. Figure 2–11 shows the effective use of grillwork to provide semi-isolation for the dining room.

Fig. 2–9. Dining facilities may be moved to a dining porch in fair weather.

Bethlehem Steel Company

Fig. 2–11. Grillwork provides semi-isolation for the dining area.

Southern California Gas Company

Fig. 2–12. Local lighting is needed for the dining table.

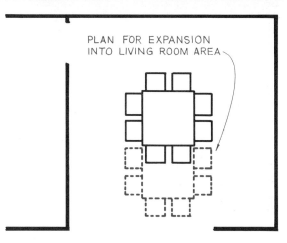

Fig. 2–13. A dining area planned for maximum expansion.

Lighting. Controlled lighting can greatly vary the decor of the dining room. General controlled illumination which can be subdued or intensified by means of a rheostat can provide the right atmosphere for almost any occasion.

In addition to general illumination, local lighting should be provided for the table either by a direct ceiling spot or by a hanging lamp (Fig. 2–12). A hanging lamp can sometimes be used for both general illumination and local lighting, according to the position of the lamp.

▶ Size and Shape

The size and shape of the dining area are determined by the size of the family, the size and number of pieces of furniture, and the clearances and traffic areas between furniture.

Maximum planning. The dining area should be planned for maximum utilization. It should be planned for the largest group that will dine in this area regularly. There is little advantage in having a dining room table that expands, if the room is not large enough to accommodate the expansion. One advantage of the open plan is that the dining facilities can be expanded in an unlimited manner into the living area, as shown in Fig. 2–13.

Furniture. The dining room should be planned to accommodate the furniture. Dining room furniture may include an expandable table, side chairs, armchairs, buffet, server or serving cart, china

closet, and serving bar. In most situations where a rectangular table is used, or even where a square or round table is expandable, a rectangular dining room will accommodate the furniture better than a square room. Figure 2–14 shows a typical furniture placement for a dining room.

Clearance. Regardless of the furniture arrangement, a minimum space of 2' should be allowed between the chair and the wall or furniture when the chair is pulled to the out position. This allowance will permit serving traffic behind chairs, and will permit entrance and exit to the table without difficulty. A distance of 27 inches (27") per person should be allowed at the table. This spacing is

Fig. 2–14. Typical furniture placement in a dining room.

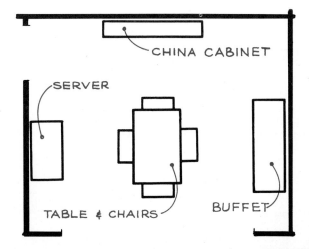

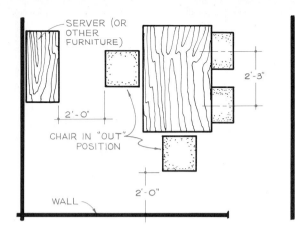

Fig. 2–15. Dining room clearances.

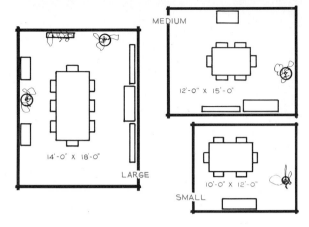

Fig. 2–16. Dining room sizes.

accomplished by allowing 27″ from the center line of one chair to the center line of another, as shown in Fig. 2–15.

Recommended sizes. A dining room that would accommodate the minimum amount of furniture—a table, four chairs, and a buffet—would be approximately 10′ × 12′. A minimum-sized dining room which would accommodate a dining table, six or eight persons, a buffet, a china closet, and a server, would be approximately 12′ × 15′. A more nearly optimum-sized dining room would be one 14′ × 18′ or larger. A room of this size would accommodate, or at least expand to accommodate, practically any size of gathering (Fig. 2–16).

Problems

1. Sketch a dining room to include the following furniture: dining table to accommodate 6, buffet, china closet. Indicate the relationship to the living room and provide access to a patio.

2. Sketch a plan for an informal dining area directly adjacent to the kitchen.

3. Sketch an open-plan dining area. Show the relationship of this area to the living room.

4. Sketch a separate dining room. Indicate the position of adjacent rooms.

5. Add a dining porch to the plan shown in Fig. 2–4.

6. Sketch a plan of the dining area shown in Fig. 2–7. Convert this to a closed plan.

7. Redesign the dining area of your own home.

8. Indicate the position of local lighting and general lighting on one of the plans you have designed.

9. Sketch a dining room to scale, showing the position of all furniture you would like to include in the dining room of a house of your own design.

10. Identify the following terms: *buffet, china closet, server, rheostat, dining porch, dining patio, formal dining, casual dining.*

Unit 3. The Family Room

Several years ago the term *family room* did not exist in the architectural vocabulary. The trend toward more informal living and more leisure time has influenced the growth and popularity of the family room. Today the majority of homes are designed to include a family room.

Fig. 3-1. A children's area in the family room.

Fig. 3-2. Sewing, knitting, and television viewing are popular family-room activities.

▶ Function

The purpose of the family room is to provide facilities for family-centered activities. It is designed for the entire family, children and adults alike.

Only in extremely large residences is there sufficient space for a separate sewing room, children's playroom, hobby room, or music room. The modern family room performs the functions of all of these rooms. For example, the children's area in the family room shown in Fig. 3-1 provides facilities for a variety of children's activities. The area of the family room shown in Fig. 3-2 is planned primarily for sewing, knitting, and television watching. Care must be taken in the design of the family room to ensure that it does not become just another living room. It should be activity-centered and therefore activity-equipped.

▶ Location

The family room is designed for many activities which result in the accumulation of hobby materials and clutter. It is therefore often located in an area not visible from the rest of the living area, but accessible from these rooms.

It is quite common to locate the family room adjacent to the kitchen, as shown in Fig. 3-3. This location revives the old country kitchen in which most family activities were centered.

When the family room is located adjacent to the living room or dining room, it becomes an

Fig. 3-3. A family room located adjacent to the kitchen.

extension of these rooms for social affairs. In this location, the family room is often separated by folding doors, screens, or sliding doors that separate the rooms when they are not being used in combination. The family room shown in Fig. 3-4 is located next to the kitchen and yet is accessible from the living room when the folding door is open.

Another popular location for the family room is between the service area and the living area. The family room shown in Fig. 3-5 is located between the garage and the kitchen and the entrance

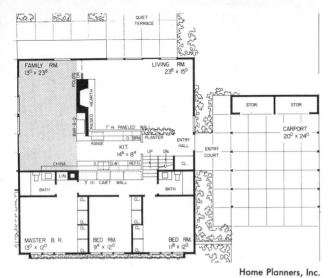

Home Planners, Inc.

Fig. 3–4. A family room accessible from the kitchen and living room.

and the living room. This location is especially appropriate when some service functions, such as home workshop facilities, are assigned to the family room.

▶ Decor

The family room is also known as the *activities room* or *multi-activities room*. Decoration of this room should therefore provide a vibrant atmosphere. Ease of maintenance should be one of the chief considerations in decorating the family room.

Fig. 3–5. A family room located in the service area.

Home Planners, Inc.

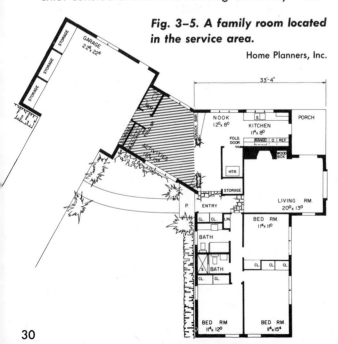

Furniture. Family-room furniture should be informal and suited to all members of the family. The use of plastics, leather, and wood provides great flexibility in color and style and promotes easy maintenance.

Floors. Floors should be resilient. Linoleum, asphalt, rubber, or vinyl tile will best resist the abuse normally given a family-room floor. If rugs are used, they should be fiber rugs that will stand up under rough treatment, and they should be reversible and washable.

Walls. Soft, easily-damaged materials such as wallpaper and plaster should be avoided for the family room. Materials such as tile and paneling are most functional. Chalkboards, built-in cupboards, toy-storage cabinets, and bulletin boards should be used when appropriate. Work areas that fold into the wall when not in use conserve space and may perform a dual function if the cover wall can also be used as a chalkboard or a bulletin board. Figure 3–6 shows the use of storage cabinets, bulletin boards, and chalkboards in the family room.

Ceilings. Acoustical ceilings are recommended to keep the noise of the various activities from spreading to other parts of the house. This feature is especially important if the family room is located on a lower level.

Storage. Since a variety of hobby and game materials will be used in the family room, sufficient space must be provided for the storage of these materials.

▶ Size and Shape

The size and shape of the family room depend directly on the equipment needed for the activities the family will pursue in this room. The room may vary from a minimum-sized room, as shown in Fig. 3–7, to the more optimum-sized family room shown in Fig. 3–8. This room contains practically all the equipment almost any family would need in the family room. Included are a sewing machine, a hobby table, bulletin boards, drawing boards, easels, a television set, a studio couch, chalk boards, a bookcase, a desk, a children's desk, a

Fig. 3–6. Plan for adequate storage in the family room.

children's play table, a children's toy box, storage cabinets, a motion picture screen, and a serving bar. Most family-room requirements lie somewhere between the two extremes shown.

Problems

1. Sketch a family room you would like to include in a home of your own design. Include the location of all furniture and facilities.
2. Determine the size and shape of a family room to accommodate the following activities: television viewing, sewing, knitting, model-building, slide-viewing, dancing, eating.
3. Design a family room primarily for children's activities.
4. Design a family room that doubles as a guest bedroom.
5. Define the following terms: *sewing room, children's playroom, hobby room, music room, family room, multi-activities, linoleum, asphalt tile, rubber tile, vinyl tile, acoustical ceiling.*

Fig. 3–7. A minimum-sized family room.

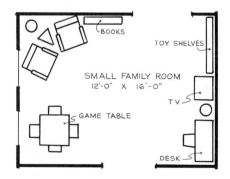

Fig. 3–8. An optimum-sized family room.

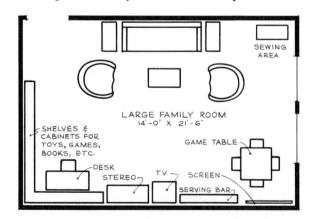

Unit 4. The Recreation Room

The recreation room (game room, playroom) is exactly what the name implies. It is a room for play and recreation. It includes facilities for participation in recreational activities.

▶ Function

The design of the recreation room depends on the number and arrangement of the facilities needed for the various pursuits. Activities for which many recreation rooms are designed include billiards, chess, checkers, ping-pong, darts, television watching, eating, and dancing. For example, the recreation room shown in Fig. 4–1 has been designed around three activity areas: the ping-pong area, the chess area, and the television and conversation area. Shuffleboard and other floor-pattern games such as the one shown in Fig. 4–2 are also quite popular recreation-room activities.

American Olean Tile Company

Fig. 4–2. Floor-pattern games are popular among recreation-room activities.

The function of the recreation room often overlaps that of the family room. Overlapping occurs when a multipurpose room is designed to provide for recreational activities such as ping-pong and billiards and also includes facilities for more sedentary family activities such as sewing, knitting, model-building, and other hobbies.

Fig. 4–1. The design of the recreation room depends on the number of activities planned.

Armstrong Cork Company

Fig. 4–3. The recreation-room fireplace is located directly below the living-room fireplace.

Fig. 4–5. A recreation room located adjacent to the patio.

▶ Location

The recreation room is frequently located in the basement because this arrangement utilizes space that would otherwise be wasted. Basement recreation rooms often provide more space for the placement of large equipment such as ping-pong tables, billiard tables, and shuffleboard. Figure 4–3 shows a basement recreation room with a fireplace located directly beneath the living room fireplace on the upper level. The most important reason why recreation rooms are often located in the basement of older homes, however, is the fact that the basement can be converted into a recreation room, as shown in Fig. 4–4.

When the recreation room can be located on the ground level, its function is expanded to the patio or terrace, as shown in Fig. 4–5. But regardless of the level of placement, the recreation room should be located away from the quiet areas of the house.

Often the recreation room can actually be separated from the main part of the house. This separation is possible when the recreation room is included as part of the garage or carport design, as shown in Fig. 4–6. When a separate location such as this is selected, some sheltered access should be provided from the house to the recreation area.

Fig. 4–6. A recreation room included as part of the garage design.

Fig. 4–4. The basement can often be converted into a recreation room.

Fig. 4–7. A quiet, restful recreation room.

▶ Decor

Designers take more liberties in decorating the recreation room than any other room. They do so primarily because the active, informal atmosphere which characterizes the recreation room lends itself readily to unconventional furniture, fixtures, and color schemes. Gay, warm colors can reflect a party mood. Furnishings and accessories can accent a dramatic central theme. The designer of the recreation room shown in Fig. 4–7 has developed a restful, quietly dignified atmosphere through the use of an oriental decor. The designer of the recreation room shown in Fig. 4–8 has created a festive yet casual atmosphere through the development of a Western theme.

Regardless of the central theme, recreation-room furniture should be comfortable and easy to maintain. The same rules apply to recreation room walls, floors, and ceilings as apply to those of the family room. Floors should be hard-surfaced and easy to maintain. Walls should be paneled or covered with some easily maintained material. Acoustical (soundproofed) ceilings are recommended if the recreation room is located in the basement or on a lower level.

Fig. 4–8. A recreation room decorated in a Western theme.

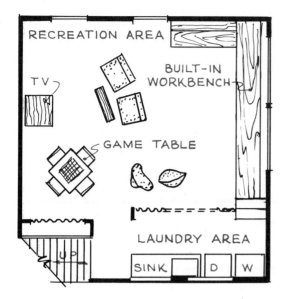

Fig. 4-9. A recreation room occupying a large area.

Fig. 4-10. A small recreation room.

room located on the main level of the house. The size of most recreation rooms ranges between these two extremes.

▶ Size and Shape

The size and shape of the recreation room depend on whether the room occupies an area on the main level or whether it occupies basement space. If basement space is utilized, the only restrictions on the size are the other facilities that will also occupy space in the basement, such as the laundry, workshop, and garage. Figure 4-9 shows a recreation room which occupies a rather large basement area which would otherwise be wasted space. Figure 4-10 shows a relatively small recreation

Problems

1. Sketch a plan of a recreation room you would include in a house of your own design.
2. Sketch a plan for a recreation room including facilities for billiards, chess, shuffleboard, television watching.
3. Determine the size and shape of a recreation room to accommodate the following furniture: television set, stereo, chaise longue, studio couch, two lounge chairs, soft-drink bar and stools, bookcase, billiard table.
4. Define the following terms: *game room, playroom, recreation room.*

Unit 5. Porches

A porch is a covered platform leading into an entrance of a building. Porches are commonly enclosed by glass, screen, or post and railings. A porch is not the same as a patio, but is attached structurally to the house, whereas a patio is placed directly on the ground. This difference is shown by the porch and patio in Fig. 5-1. Notice that the

screened porch comprises a structural part of the house and the attached patio does not.

▶ Function

Porches serve a variety of functions. Some are basically dining porches. Others are furnished and function like patios for outdoor living and recrea-

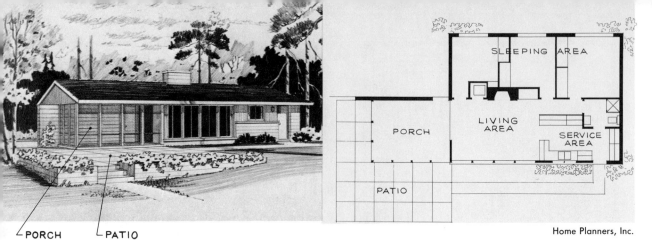

Home Planners, Inc.

Fig. 5–1. A screened porch and patio.

tion. Still others provide only a shelter for the entrance to a house.

Verandas. Southern colonial homes such as the one shown in Fig. 5–2 were designed with large porches extending around several sides of the home. These large porches were known as *verandas.* Outdoor plantation life centered in the veranda, which therefore was very large.

Balconies. A balcony is a porch suspended from an upper level of a structure. It usually has no access from the outside. Balconies often pro-

Fig. 5–2. A Southern colonial home with a veranda.

United Airlines, Photo

vide an extension to the living area or a private extension to bedrooms.

The house shown in Fig. 5–3 is distinguished by several types of balconies. The living-area balcony in the center is supported by cantilevered beams and provides an extension to the living area through its entire length. The deck of this same balcony provides the shelter for the main entrance and drive underneath. The bedroom balcony on the right has wing walls which provide privacy and shelter from each side, and a roof which shelters it from above. The deck provides shelter for the garage entrance below.

Spanish and Italian architecture is characterized by numerous balconies. However, the return of the balcony to popularity has been influenced and accelerated by new developments in building materials which permit an increase in areas to be suspended. The balconies in the house shown in Fig. 5–4 are supported by steel beams and columns. In fact, the entire structure is supported by steel columns.

The principle of *cantileverage,* or suspension in space, can also be utilized with wood construction, as shown in the balcony which overhangs the patio in Fig. 5–5.

Stoop. The stoop is a projection from a building similar to a porch. However, a stoop does not provide sufficient space for any activities. It provides only shelter and an access to the entrance of the building.

Fig. 5–3. Balconies are a distinguishing feature of this house.

The modern porch. Only in the last several years has the porch been functionally designed and effectively utilized for outdoor living. The classic front porch and back porch which characterized most homes built in this country during the 1920s and 1930s were designed and utilized merely as places in which to sit. Little effort was made to utilize the porch for any other activities. Any porch designed to function in today's homes should be designed for the specific activities anticipated for it. The form of the porch should be determined by its function.

▶ Location

Since the porch is an integral part of the total house design, it must be located where it will function best. The screened porch in Fig. 5–6A becomes a functional extension of the living area when in use. It is made consistent with the rest of the house by

Fig. 5–4. The balconies of this house are supported by steel beams and columns.

Fig. 5–5. This balcony also provides protection for the patio below.

Fig. 5–6A. This screened porch can become part of the living room.

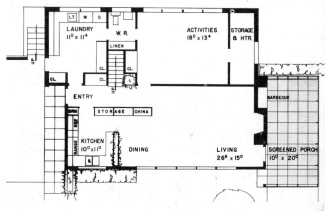

Fig. 5–6B. The porch should be an integral part of the exterior design.

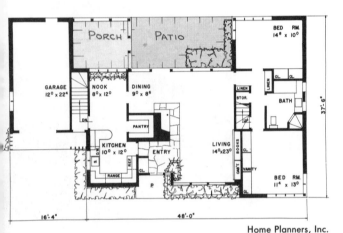

Fig. 5–7. Location of a dining porch.

Fig. 5–8. This dining porch can also be utilized as a sun deck.

extending the lines of the roof to provide sufficient *overhang* (projection), as shown in Fig. 5–6B.

A dining porch should be located adjacent to either the dining room or the kitchen. The dining porch shown in Fig. 5–7 can be approached from the dining room through the terrace. This arrangement makes possible the use of the nook, dining room, patio, or porch for dining purposes with little traffic difficulty. Locating the porch between two walls of the house in this manner is also economical since only two sides must be enclosed. This position also eliminates the "tacked-on" look so objectionable in some porches.

The porch should be located to provide the maximum in flexibility. A porch which can function for dining and other living activities is desirable. Notice how the dining porch shown in Fig. 5–8 can be utilized as a sun deck and is large enough to perform many of the functions of the patio. The primary functions of the porch should be considered when orienting the porch with the sun. If much daytime use is anticipated and direct sunlight is desirable, a southern exposure should be planned for. If little sun is wanted during the day, a northern exposure would be preferable. If morning sun is desirable, an eastern exposure would be best, and for the afternoon sun, a western exposure.

▶ **Decor**

The porch should be designed as an integral and functional part of the total structure. A blending of roof styles and major lines of the porch roof

Fig. 5–9. The lines of the porch should be consistent with the major lines of the house.

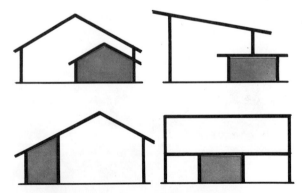

Electromode

Fig. 5–10. Porch furniture should be durable and waterproof.

California Redwood Association

Fig. 5–11. A large porch.

and house roof is especially important (Fig. 5–9). A similar consistency should characterize the vertical columns or support members of the porch. Figure 5–9 shows some relationships that can be established to prevent the "tacked-on" look and to ensure uniformity in design.

Porch furniture should withstand deterioration in any kind of weather. Covering material should be waterproof and completely stain-resistant and washable. Redwood and wrought-iron furniture is excellent for porch use. It is essential that the structure and furnishings of the porch be consistent with the rest of the house (Fig. 5–10).

Home Planners, Inc.

Fig. 5–12. A small porch.

▶ Size and Shape

Porches range in size from the very large veranda to rather modest-sized stoops, which provide only shelter and a landing surface for the main entrance. Figure 5–11 shows a large porch which extends across the entire front of the house. Figure 5–12 shows a minimum-sized porch. A porch approximately 6′ × 8′ is considered a minimum size. An 8′ × 12′ porch is about average. Porches larger than 12′ × 18′ are considered rather large.

The shape of the porch depends greatly upon how the porch can be integrated into the overall design of the house. Figure 5–13 shows various shapes of porches, depending on the position of the porch and the shape of the house.

Fig. 5–13. Some basic porch shapes.

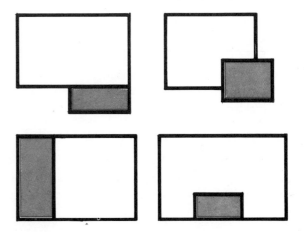

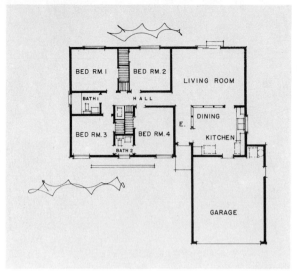

Fig. 5–14. Add a porch to this plan.

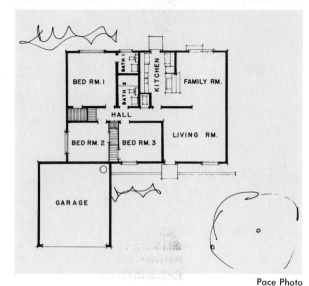

Fig. 5–15. Select the best location for a porch on this plan.

Pace Photo

Problems

1. Add a porch to the floor-plan sketch shown in Fig. 5–14. Show the exact width and length, and list the materials you recommend for the deck, roof, and enclosure.
2. Add a porch to the sketch shown in Fig. 5–15.
3. Add a porch to a floor plan of your own design.
4. From catalogs, newspapers, and magazines, cut out pictures of porch furniture you would choose for your own porch.
5. Define the following terms: *veranda*, *balcony*, *cantileverage*, *stoop*.

Unit 6. Patios

A *patio* is a covered surface adjacent or directly accessible to the house. The word *patio* comes from the Spanish word for "courtyard." Courtyard living was an important aspect of Spanish culture, and courtyard design an important part of early Spanish architecture.

▶ **Function**

The patio at various times may perform outdoors all the functions that the living room, dining room, recreation room, kitchen, and family room perform indoors.

The patio is often referred to by other names, such as *loggia*, *breezeway*, and *terrace*.

Patios can be divided into three main types according to function: living patios, play patios, and quiet patios. The home shown in Fig. 6–1 contains all three kinds of patios.

▶ **Location**

Patios should be located adjacent to the area of the home to which they relate. They should also be somewhat secluded from the street or from neighboring residences.

Living patio. Living patios should be located in close proximity to such rooms in the living area as the living room and the dining room. When dining is anticipated on the patio, access should be provided from the kitchen or dining room.

Play patio. It is often advantageous to provide a play patio, or terrace, for use by children and for activities of a more physical type than those normally associated with the living terrace. The play terrace sometimes doubles as the service terrace and can conveniently be placed adjacent to the service area. Notice the location of the play terrace in Fig. 6–1. It is related directly to the service area and also to the family room in the living area.

Quiet patio. The quiet patio can actually become an extension of the bedroom and can be used for relaxation or even sleeping. The quiet terrace shown in Fig. 6–1 can be entered from the bedrooms or the living area. This type of patio should be secluded from the normal traffic of the home. Often the design of the house will allow these separately functioning patios to be combined in one large, continuous patio. This type of patio is shown in Fig. 6–2. Here the playroom, living room, and master bedroom all have access to the various parts of the patio.

Placement. Patios can be conveniently placed at the end of a building, as the living terrace is placed in Fig. 6–1; between offsets of the house, as in the play terrace and quiet terrace in Fig. 6–1;

Home Planners, Inc.

Fig. 6–1. This plan includes three types of patios.

wrapped around the side of the house, as in Fig. 6–2; or placed in the center of the U-shaped house, as shown in Fig. 6–3. This last type of patio is a revival of the old Spanish courtyard design. This placement affords practically complete privacy from all sides with a minimum amount of baffle.

Separate patios. In addition to the preceding locations, the patio is often located completely apart from the house. When a wooded area or a particular view or terrain feature merits it, the patio can be placed away from the house. When it is

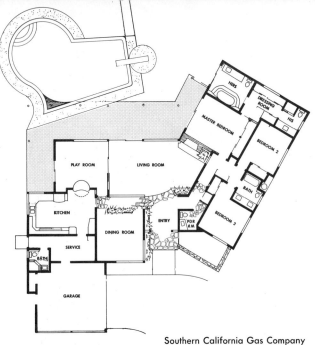

Fig. 6–2. A continuous patio.

Fig. 6–3. A courtyard patio.

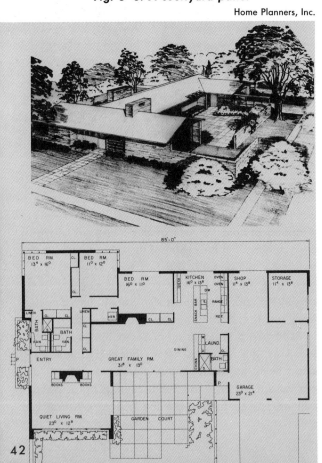

Fig. 6–4. A patio separated from the house.

located in this manner, it should be readily accessible and sheltered as shown in Fig. 6–4.

Orientation. When the patio is placed on the north side of the house, the house itself can be used to shade the patio. If sunlight is desired, the patio should be located on the south side of the house. The planner should take full advantage of the most pleasing view and should restrict the view of undesirable sights.

▶ **Decor**

The materials used in the deck, cover, baffles, and furniture of the patio should be consistent with the lines and materials used in the rest of the home. Patios should not appear to be designed as an afterthought but should appear and function as an integral part of the total design.

Patio deck. The deck (floor) of the patio should be constructed from materials that are permanent and maintenance-free and that drain easily. Flagstone, redwood, concrete, ceramic tile, and brick are among the best materials for use on patio decks. Wood slats such as those shown in Fig. 6–5 provide for drainage between the slats and also create a warm appearance. However, they do require some maintenance.

Flagstone patio decks are very popular because they can be placed in a variety of arrangements to adapt to practically any shape or space. The area between the flagstones is sometimes filled with concrete, gravel, or even grass (Fig. 6–6).

Fig. 6–5. A wood-slat patio deck.

Fig. 6–7. A concrete patio deck.

A concrete deck is effective when a smooth, unbroken surface is desired. Patios where bouncing ball games are played, or where poolside cover is desired, can use concrete advantageously (Fig. 6–7).

Patio cover. Patios need not be covered if the house is oriented to shade the patio during the times of the day when shade is normally desired. Since a patio is designed to provide outdoor living, too much cover can defeat the purpose of the patio. Coverings can be an extension of the roof overhang, as shown in Fig. 6–8. They may be graded to allow light to enter when the sun is high and to block the sun's rays when the sun is lower, as shown in Fig. 6–9. The graded effect can be ob-

Fig. 6–8. A roof overhang used as a patio cover.

Fig. 6–6. A flagstone deck.

Fig. 6–9. A louvered patio cover.

Nestlé Alimentana (Nestle's Headquarters, Switzerland)

Fig. 6-10. A cantilevered patio cover.

tained with straight, flat louvers or with an intricate design.

Fiberglas and other translucent materials used to cover patios admit sunlight and yet provide protection from the direct rays of the sun and from precipitation. When this translucent type of covering is used, it is often desirable to have only part of the patio covered. This provides sun for part of the patio and shade for other parts.

If the placement of support posts for a patio cover interferes with the function of the patio, a cantilevered (suspended) cover can be provided, such as the one shown in Fig. 6-10.

Walls and baffles. Patios are designed for outdoor living, but outdoor living need not be public living. Some privacy is always desirable. Solid walls can often be used effectively to baffle the patio from a street view, from wind, and from the low rays of the sun (Fig. 6-11). Baffling devices include solid fences, slatted fences, concrete blocks, post and rails, brick or stone walls, and hedges or other shrubbery.

A solid baffle wall is often undesirable because it restricts the view, eliminates the circulation of air, and makes the patio appear smaller. Figure 6-12 shows a baffle wall used to provide privacy for the patio without restricting circulation of air. The baffle wall in Fig. 6-13 is used to separate the patio from the service entrance without restricting the view.

In mild climates, completely enclosing a patio by solid walls can help make the patio function as another room. In such an enclosed patio, some opening should be provided to allow light and air

Fig. 6-11. A patio with solid walls.

Masonite Corporation

Fig. 6-12. A slatted baffle wall.

Simpson Timber Company

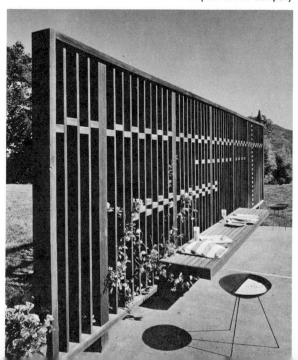

Fig. 6–13. A baffle wall used to separate the patio from the service entrance.

to enter. The grillwork openings on the wall shown in Fig. 6–14 provide an effective and aesthetically pleasing solution to this problem.

Occasionally nature provides its own baffle through a rise in the landscape, as shown in Fig. 6–15. This condition is highly desirable and should be taken advantage of, if sufficient drainage away from the house and patio can be maintained.

Day and night decor. To be totally effective, the patio should be designed for both daytime and nighttime use. Figure 6–16 shows a typical midday use of the patio. Figure 6–17 shows some of the possibilities for nighttime utilization. Correct use of general and local lighting can make the patio useful for many hours each day. If the walls between the inside areas of the house and the patio are designed as in Fig. 6–17, much light from the inside can be utilized on the patio. Figure 6–18 shows some of the specific types of lights and lighting that can be used to illuminate patios at night.

Fig. 6–14. A semi-isolated patio.

Home Planners, Inc.

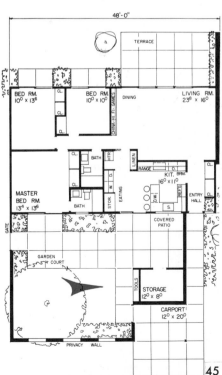

Paul J. Peart, landscape architect
Fig. 6–15. A natural patio baffle.

West Coast Lumbermen's Association
Fig. 6–16. Midday use of the patio.

Fig. 6–17. The patio should also be designed for nighttime use.

Scholz Homes, Inc.

New Homes Guide
Fig. 6–18. Types of patio lighting.

▶ **Size and Shape**

Patios may be as minute as the Japanese garden terrace shown in Fig. 6–19 or as spacious as the courtyard type of patio shown in Fig. 6–20. The primary function will largely determine the size. The Japanese garden has no furniture and is designed primarily to provide a baffle and a beautiful view. The courtyard type of patio is designed for a multiplicity of uses.

Activities should be interpreted into the amount of space needed for equipment. Equipment and

Fig. 6–19. A small Japanese garden terrace.
House Beautiful

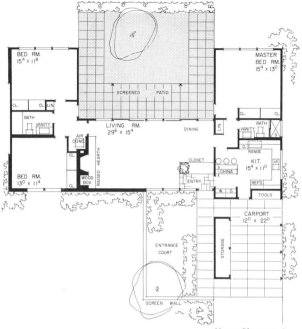

Fig. 6–20. A large courtyard terrace.

Home Planners, Inc.

Southern California Gas Company

Fig. 6–22. The patio and pool design can be blended together.

furnishings normally used on patios include picnic tables and benches, lounge chairs, serving carts, game apparatus, and barbecue pits. The placement of these items and the storage of games, apparatus, and fixtures should determine the size of the patio. Patios vary more in length than in width since patios may extend over the entire length of the house. A patio 12' × 12' is considered a minimum-sized patio. Patios with dimensions of 20' × 30' or more are not uncommon but are

certainly considered large. When a pool is designed for a home, it becomes an integral part of the patio. The poolside and the entire area around the pool function as a patio (Fig. 6–21).

Many pool shapes now available allow the designer to blend the pool into the size and shape of the patio. Notice how the shape of the pool in Fig. 6–22 extends to the patio and continues around it. Other pool shapes are shown in Fig. 6–23.

Fig. 6–21. The poolside area functions as a patio.

Scholz Homes, Inc.

Fig. 6–23. Common pool shapes.

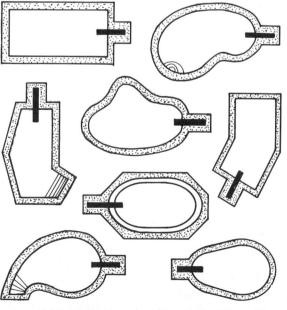

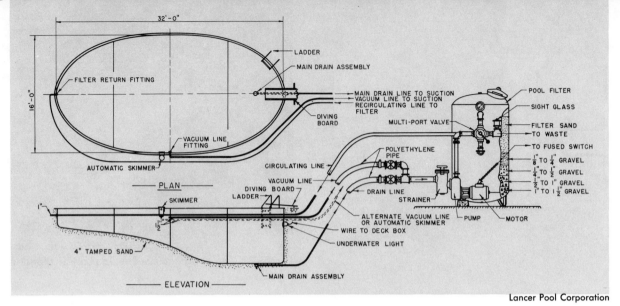

Lancer Pool Corporation

Fig. 6–24. The filtering system and apparatus necessary for a pool.

When a pool is designed, other facilities must accompany it. A cabana or some facility for dressing, and a filtering system are mandatory. Figure 6–24 shows a filtering system necessary to accommodate a 16′ × 32′ pool.

Problems

1. Sketch a baffle wall for the exposed patio shown in Fig. 6–25.
2. What type of covering would you recommend for the patio shown in Fig. 6–25?
3. Design a covering for the patio shown in Fig. 6–25. Sketch a top view of your solution.
4. Choose one of the pool shapes shown in Fig. 6–23 and incorporate it in the patio design shown in Fig. 6–20.

Fig. 6–25. Sketch a baffle wall for this exposed patio.

Home Planners, Inc.

5. Add a patio design to the floor plan layout shown in Fig. 6–26.
6. Plan a patio for a house of your own design. Sketch the basic scheme and the facilities.
7. Define the following terms: *patio, port side, loggia, breezeway, terrace, play patio, quiet patio, living patio, flagstone, redwood, concrete, patio deck, patio cover, translucent covers, patio baffles.*

Fig. 6–26. Add a patio to this floor plan.

Signature Homes

Unit 7. Lanais

Lanai is the Hawaiian word for "porch." However, the word *lanai* is used to refer to a covered exterior passageway.

▶ Function

Large lanais are often used as patios, although their main function is to provide shelter for the traffic accesses on the exterior of the house. Lanais are actually exterior hallways. For example, the lanai shown in Fig. 7–1A provides shelter and a surface needed for access from the garage to the living area without passage through the interior of the house.

Fig. 7–1A. This lanai provides shelter from the garage to the living area.

▶ Location

Lanais are commonly located between the garage and the kitchen; the patio and the kitchen or the living area; the sleeping area and the living area; and the living area and the service area (Fig. 7–1B).

When lanais are carefully located, they can function as access for traffic and as patio and poolside shelters, as shown in Fig. 7–2. When lanais are used to connect the building with the street, they actually function as *marquees* (Fig. 7–3).

Bethlehem Steel Company

Fig. 7–1B. A lanai provides external access between several areas.

Fig. 7–2. A large lanai can function as a sheltered patio.

Southern California Gas Company

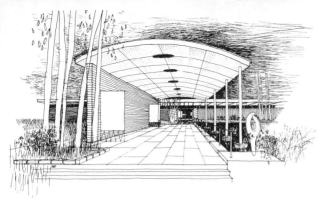

Rendering by George A. Parenti for the Masonite Corporation

Fig. 7–3. A marquee is a type of lanai.

Libbey-Owens-Ford Glass Company

Fig. 7–6. This lanai provides access from one end of the building to the other.

Allan J. Gelbin, architect

Fig. 7–4. The roof overhang may provide a lanai cover.

Fig. 7–5. Columns support this large lanai cover.

Rendering by George A. Parenti for the Masonite Corporation

▶ Decor

The lanai should be a consistent, integral part of the design of the structure. The lanai cover may be an extension of the roof overhang, as shown in Fig. 7–4, or may be supported by columns, as shown in Fig. 7–5. If glass were placed between the columns in the lanai shown in Fig. 7–5, this lanai would become an interior hallway rather than an exterior one. This separation is sometimes the only difference between a lanai and an interior hall.

It is often desirable to design and locate the lanai to provide access from one end of a building to the other end, as shown in Fig. 7–6. The

Fig. 7–7. Lighting must be provided if the lanai is to be used at night.

Rendering by George A. Parenti for the Masonite Corporation

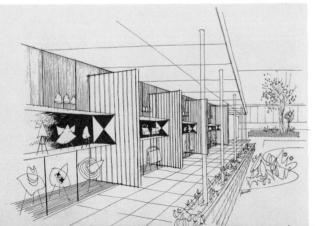

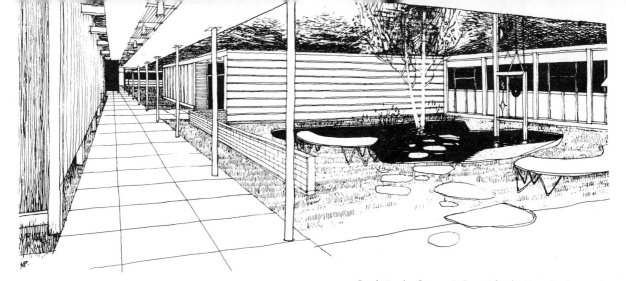

Fig. 7–8. A large lanai.

lines of this kind of lanai strengthen and reinforce the basic lines of the building. Notice how this line reinforcement was accomplished in Fig. 7–6 by intersecting the lanai cover with the end wall and roof to provide additional shade for the upper level.

If a lanai is to be utilized extensively at night, effective lighting must be provided. Figure 7–7 shows one method of lighting lanais. The lanai shown in Fig. 7–7 is equally well lit at night and during the day. The cover is hung from beams supported on the outside of the lanai, thus letting light pass between the building and the lanai. This feature eliminates the closed-in, dark-corridor appearance which some lanais produce.

▶ Size and Shape

Lanais may extend the full length of a building and may be designed for maximum traffic loads, as shown in Fig. 7–8. They may be as small as the area under a two- or three-foot roof overhang (Fig. 7–9). However, a lanai at least 4' wide is desirable. The length is limited only by the location of the areas to be connected.

Problems

1. Draw the outline of a lanai you would plan for a home of your own design.
2. Add a lanai to the plan shown in Fig. 1–2.
3. Add a lanai to the plan shown in Fig. 1–4.
4. Resketch the plan shown in Fig. 2–4. Using dotted lines, sketch the outline of a lanai you would add to this plan.
5. Sketch the floor plan shown in Fig. 2–6. With a colored pencil indicate where you would plan a lanai to connect the sleeping area with the living area.
6. Sketch a floor plan of your own home. Add a lanai to connect two of the areas of your home.
7. Define the following terms: *lanai cover, roof overhang, exterior hallways.*

Fig. 7–9. A small lanai.

Unit 8. Traffic Areas

The traffic areas of the home provide passage from one room to another and from one area to another. The main traffic areas of a residence include the halls, entrance foyers, stairs, lanais, and areas of rooms that are used for access to other parts of the house.

▶ Traffic Patterns

Traffic patterns of a residence should be carefully considered in the design of the room layout. A minimum amount of space should be devoted to traffic areas. Extremely long halls and corridors should be avoided. They are difficult to light and actually provide no living space. Traffic patterns that require passage through one room to get to another should also be avoided, especially in the sleeping area.

The traffic pattern shown in the plan in Fig. 8–1 is efficient and functional. It contains a minimum amount of wasted hall space without creating a boxed-in appearance. It provides access to each of the areas without passing through other areas. The arrows clearly show that the sleeping area, living area, and service area are accessible from the entrance without passage through other areas. In this plan the service entrance provides access to the kitchen from the carport and other parts of the service area.

One method of determining the effectiveness of the traffic pattern of a house is to move through the house vicariously by placing your pencil on the floor plan and tracing your route through the house as you perform your daily routine. If you trace through a whole day's activities, including those of other members of the household, you will be able to see graphically where the heaviest traffic occurs and whether the traffic areas have been planned effectively. Figure 8–2 shows the difference between a poorly designed traffic pattern and a well-designed traffic pattern.

Fig. 8–1. An efficient traffic pattern.

Home Planners, Inc.

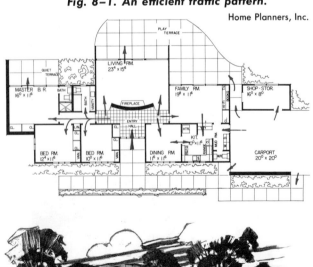

Fig. 8–2. The difference between a poorly designed and a well-designed traffic pattern.

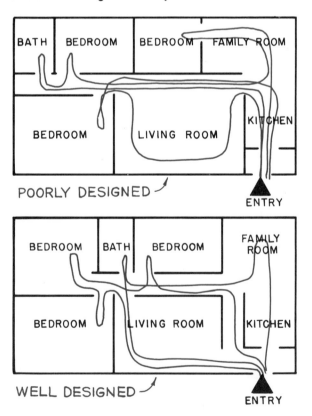

Fig. 8–4. The use of movable partitions to separate traffic areas.

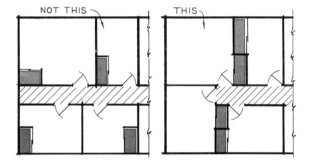

Fig. 8–3. The use of furniture components in separating traffic areas.

Fig. 8–5. Principles of efficient hall design.

▶ Halls

Halls are the highways and streets of the home; they provide a controlled path which connects the various areas of the house. Halls should be planned to eliminate or to keep to a minimum the passage of traffic through rooms. Long, dark, tunnel-like halls should be avoided. Halls should be well lighted, light in color and texture, and planned with the decor of the whole house in mind.

One method of channeling hall traffic without the use of solid walls is the use of dividers. Planters, half walls, louvered walls, and even furniture can be used as dividers. Figure 8–3 shows the use of furniture components in dividing the living area from the hall. This arrangement enables both the hall and the living room to share ventilation, light, and heat.

Another method of designing halls and corridors that are an integral part of the area design is the use of movable partitions. The Japanese scheme of placing these partitions between the living area and a hall is shown in Fig. 8–4. In some Japanese homes this hall actually becomes a lanai when the partition between the living area and the hall is closed and the outside wall is opened. Figure 8–5 shows some of the basic principles of efficient hall design.

▶ Stairs

Stairs are inclined hallways. They provide access from one level to another. Stairs may lead directly from one area to another without a change of direction, or they may turn 90 degrees (90°) by means of a landing, or they may turn 180° by means of landings. Figure 8–6 shows four basic

53

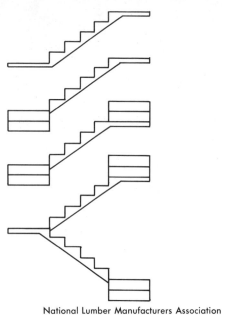

National Lumber Manufacturers Association

Fig. 8–6. Basic types of stairs.

Armstrong Cork Company

Fig. 8–9. These stairs have supports without complete separation.

Fig. 8–7. Center-supported stairs.

Fig. 8–8. Stairs anchored into a stone wall.

types of stairs and the amount of space utilized by each type.

With the use of newer, stronger building materials and new techniques, there is no longer any reason for enclosing stairs in walls that restrict light and ventilation. Stairs can now be supported by many different devices. The stairs in Fig. 8–7 are center-supported and therefore do not need side walls or other supports. In Fig. 8–8 side supports are eliminated by tying the stairs into the fireplace wall. Even when vertical supports are necessary or desirable, completely closing in the wall is not mandatory. Figure 8–9 shows stairs supported by exposed supports which maintain the open plan without sacrificing support or safety. A similar device is employed in the stairs in Fig. 8–10. These stairs are supported by hanging one side of the tread from steel rods. Combining open stair assemblies with windows provides the maximum amount of light, especially when the windows in the open area extend through several levels, as shown in Fig. 8–11.

Armstrong Cork Company

Fig. 8-10. These stairs are hung from steel rods.

Robert C. Cleveland Photo

Fig. 8-11. Use natural light to illuminate stairwells when possible.

Fig. 8-12. Correct tread and riser design is important.

▶ Space Requirements

There are many variables to consider in designing stairs. The *tread* width, the *riser* width, the width of the stair opening, and the headroom all help to determine the total length of the stairwell.

The *tread* is the horizontal part of the stair, the part upon which you walk. The average width of the tread is 10″. The *riser* is the vertical part of the stair. The average riser height is 7¼″. Figure 8-12 shows the importance of correct tread and riser design.

The overall width of the stairs is the distance across the treads. A minimum of 3′ should be allowed for the total width. However, a width of 3′-6″ or even 4′ is preferred (Fig. 8-13).

Headroom is the vertical distance between the top of each tread and the top of the stairwell ceil-

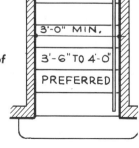

Fig. 8-13. Minimum width of stairs.

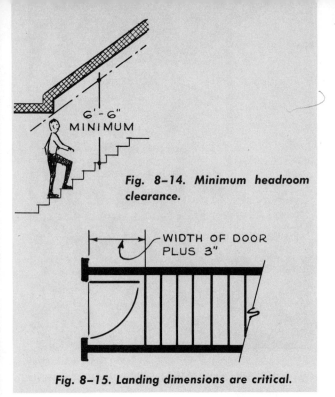

Fig. 8-14. Minimum headroom clearance.

Fig. 8-15. Landing dimensions are critical.

ing. A minimum headroom distance of 6'-6" should be allowed. However, distances of 7' are more desirable (Fig. 8-14).

Landing dimensions are also critical. Figure 8-15 shows some allowances for landings when used to turn a stairway 90° and 180°. More clearance must be allowed where a door opens on a landing, as shown in Fig. 8-15.

Problems

1. Sketch the floor plan shown in Fig. 5-1. Redesign the traffic pattern to eliminate passing directly through the living room to get to the sleeping area.
2. Sketch the plan shown in Fig. 5-7. Move the entrance to another location to provide more central access to each of the areas without passing through the others.
3. Resketch the plan shown in Fig. 6-1 in order to shorten the long hall in the bedroom area.
4. Sketch the floor plan of your own home. Redesign the entrance and halls to make this pattern more efficient.
5. Define the following terms: *traffic pattern, halls, corridors, main traffic areas, movable partitions, center-supported stairs, tread, riser, minimum stair width, headroom, landing.*

Unit 9. Entrances

Entrances are divided into several different types: the main entrance, the service entrance, and special-purpose entrances. The entrance is composed of the outside waiting area (porch, marquee, lanai), a separation (door), and an inside waiting area (foyer, entrance hall).

▶ Function

The function of all entrances is to provide for and control the flow of traffic into and out of a building. However, the different types of entrances have somewhat different functions.

Main entrance. The main entrance provides access to the house through which guests are welcomed and from which all major traffic patterns radiate. The main entrance should be readily identifiable by the stranger. It should provide shelter to anyone awaiting entrance. Figure 9-1 shows a sheltered entrance which directly connects with the driveway. This arrangement provides complete protection from the car to the door.

Some provision should be made in the main entrance wall for the viewing of callers from the inside. This can be accomplished through the use of side panels (Fig. 9–2), through *lights* (panes) in the door, or through windows which face the side of the entrance.

The main entrance should be planned to create a desirable first impression. A direct view of other areas of the house from the foyer should be baffled, but not completely sealed off. This result is often accomplished by placing the access to the other rooms at the rear or side of the entrance foyer, as shown in Fig. 9–3.

The entrance foyer should include a closet for the storage of outside clothing and bad-weather gear. This foyer closet should have a capacity which will accommodate both family and guests. The foyer closet shown in Fig. 9–3 is located at a convenient distance from the entrance door.

Service entrance. The service entrance provides access to the house through which supplies can be delivered to the service areas without going through other parts of the house. It should also provide access to parts of the service area (garage, laundry, workshop) for which the main entrance is inappropriate and inconvenient.

Special-purpose entrances. Special-purpose entrances and exits do not provide for outside traffic but provide for movement from the inside living area of the house to the outside living areas. A sliding door from the living area to the patio is a special-purpose entrance. It is not an entrance

Fig. 9–2. Side panels provide a view of the entrance from the inside.

Fig. 9–3. A direct view from the foyer of other rooms should be baffled.

Fig. 9–1. A sheltered entrance.

Kimble Glass Company; Hedrich-Blessing Photo

57

Scholz Homes, Inc.

Fig. 9–4. The basic types of entrances.

through which street, drive, or sidewalk traffic would have access. Figure 9–4 shows the difference between special-purpose entrances, main entrance, and service entrances.

▶ Location

The main entrance should be centrally located to provide easy access to each area. It should be conveniently accessible from driveways, sidewalks, or street.

The service entrance should be located close to the drive and garage. It should be placed near the kitchen or food-storage areas.

Special-purpose entrances and exits are often located between the bedroom and the quiet patio, between the living room and the living patio, and between the dining room or kitchen and the dining patio. Figure 9–4 shows the functional placement of all these entrances.

▶ Decor

The entrance should be designed to create a desirable first impression. The entrance should be easily identifiable but should be an integral part of the architectural style.

Consistency of style. The total design of the entrance should be consistent with the overall design of the house. The design of the door, the side panel, and the deck and cover should be directly related to the lines of the house. The entrance shown in Fig. 9–5A is designed as an integral part of the exterior. The lines of the entrance are part of the major building lines of the house. The entrance shown in Fig. 9–5B is unrelated to the major building lines of the house.

Whenever existing features of the house, such as the chimney, the roof, and planters can be incorporated in the entrance design, consistency

Fig. 9–5A. An entrance related to the lines of the structure.

Fig. 9–5B. An entrance unrelated to the lines of the structure.

Robert C. Cleveland Photo

Scholz Homes, Inc.

Fig. 9–7. The entrance should create an open and inviting impression.

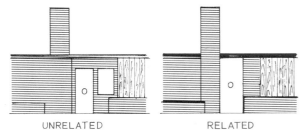

UNRELATED   RELATED

Fig. 9–6. Clean, consistent lines are a feature of this entrance.

and simplicity of design are more easily attained. The massive chimney in Fig. 9–6 provides a side wall for the entrance, and the roof of the house extends to provide the shelter without breaking the eave line of the roof. The door and side panel completely fill the entrance opening, with a minimum of intersecting lines. The importance of reducing the number of intersecting lines and simplifying this design is shown in Fig. 9–6.

Open planning. The view from the main entrance to the living area should be baffled without creating a boxed-in appearance. The foyer should not appear as a dead end. The extensive use of glass, effective lighting, and carefully placed baffle walls can create an open and inviting impression. This is accomplished in the entrance shown

in Fig. 9–7 by the use of window walls, double doors, roof-overhang extension, and baffle walls which extend the length of the foyer. Open planning between the entrance foyer and the living areas can also be accomplished by the use of louvered walls or planter walls. These provide a break in the line of sight but not a complete separation. Sinking or elevating the foyer (Fig. 9–8) also provides the desired separation without isolation.

Fig. 9–8. The foyer may be divided from other areas by placing it on a different level.

Fig. 9-9. Foyer floors should be hard-surfaced and easily maintained.

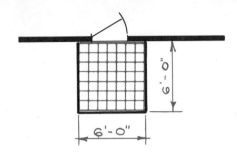

Fig. 9–11A. Minimum outside-entrance dimensions.

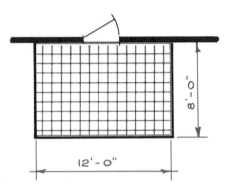

Fig. 9–11B. Optimum outside-entrance dimensions.

Fig. 9–10. The entrance must be designed to function at all hours.

Flooring. The outside portion of the entrance should be weather-resistant stone, brick, or concrete. If a porch is used outside the entrance, a wood deck will suffice. The foyer deck should be easily maintained and resistant to mud, water, and dirt brought in from the outside. Asphalt, vinyl or rubber tile, stone, flagstone, marble, and terrazzo are most frequently used for the foyer deck. The use of a different material in the foyer area helps to define the area when no other separation exists (Fig. 9–9).

Foyer walls. Paneling, masonry, planters, murals, and glass are used extensively for entrance foyer walls. The walls of the exterior portion of the entrance should be consistent with the other materials used on the exterior of the house.

Lighting. An entrance must be designed to function at all hours of the day and night. General lighting, spot lighting, and all-night lighting (Fig. 9–10) are all effective for this purpose. Lighting can be used to accent distinguishing features, or to illuminate the pattern of a wall which actually provides more light by reflection and helps to identify and accentuate the entrance at night.

▶ Size and Shape

The size and shape of the areas inside and outside the entrance depend on the budget and type

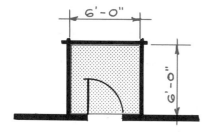

Fig. 9–12A. A minimum-sized foyer.

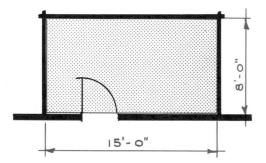

Fig. 9–12B. An optimum-sized foyer.

of plan. Foyers are not bounded by solid walls in the open plan.

The outside. The outside, covered portion of the entrance should be large enough to shelter several people at one time. Sufficient space should be allowed on all sides, exclusive of the amount of space needed to open storm doors which open to the outside. Outside shelter areas range in size from the minimum arrangement shown in Fig. 9–11A to the more generous size shown in Fig. 9–11B.

The inside. The inside of the entrance foyer should be sufficiently large to allow several people to enter at the same time, remove their coats, and store them in the closet. A 6′ × 6′ foyer, as shown in Fig. 9–12A, is considered minimum for this function. A foyer 8′ × 10′ is average, but a more desirable size is 8′ × 15′ as shown in Fig. 9–12B.

Figure 9–12B also shows a foyer arrangement which allows for the swing of the door, something which must be taken into consideration in determining the size of the foyer. If the foyer is too shallow, passage will be blocked when the door is open, and only one person may enter at

Scholz Homes, Inc.

Fig. 9–13. A large foyer.

a time. Figure 9–13 shows a foyer that is near the optimum size. It is not extremely deep, but does extend a great distance on either side. This allows sufficient traffic to pass. It also allows sufficient movement around the doors when they are opened. Notice how the planter area in Fig. 9–13 occupies space behind the door that would otherwise be wasted. You may also have noticed that this foyer is the inside view of the entrance shown in Fig. 9–7.

Foyers are normally rectangular because they lead to several areas of the home. They do not need much depth in any one direction.

Home Planners, Inc.

Fig. 9–14. Redesign this entrance.

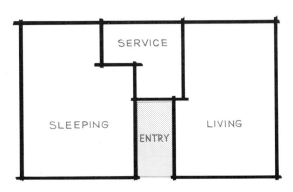

Fig. 9–16. Sketch this foyer. Locate a foyer closet.

Armstrong Cork Company

Fig. 9–15. List the good features of this foyer.

Problems

1. Redesign the entrance shown in Fig. 9–14, adding sufficient shelter space that will be consistent with the main lines of the house.

2. List the characteristics of good foyer design in the foyer shown in Fig. 9–15.

3. Sketch the foyer layout for the plan shown in Fig. 9–16, showing the position of the foyer closet.

4. Plan a partial divider for the wall dividing the foyer from the living room shown in Fig. 1–2. Label the materials you select for the outside deck, overhang, access walk, foyer floor, and foyer walls.

5. Define the following terms: *main entrance, service entrance, foyer, special-purpose entrances, open planning.*

Unit 10. The Den

The den or study can be designed for many different purposes depending on the living habits of its occupants.

▶ Function

The den may function basically as a reading room, writing room, drafting room, hobby room, or professional office. For the teacher, writer, or clergyman the study may be basically a reading room, such as the one shown in Fig. 10–1. For the engineer, architect, draftsman, or artist the den or study may function primarily as a studio and may include such facilities as those shown in the study in Fig. 10–2.

Armstrong Cork Company

Fig. 10–1. This study is basically a reading room.

United States Plywood Corporation

Fig. 10–3. This study doubles as a bedroom.

The den or study often doubles as a guest room, and quite often the children's bedroom must provide facilities normally included in a study, such as desk, bookcase, and typewriter (Fig. 10–3).

The den is often considered part of the sleeping area since it may require placement in a quiet part of the house. But it may function primarily in the living area, especially if the study is used as a professional office by a physician or an insurance agent whose clients call on him at his residence. Figure 10–4 shows a professional study or office located near the main entrance hall and accessible from the main entrance and also from a side entrance directly from the garage.

Fig. 10–2. This study was planned for drawing and designing activities.

Louis Rens Photo; Interiors Magazine

▶ **Location**

The den or study is often located in the basement in order to utilize space that otherwise might be wasted. Figure 10–5 shows a basement study, and Fig. 10–6 shows the utilization of otherwise wasted attic space as a study.

Fig. 10–4. A study used as a professional office.

Home Planners, Inc.

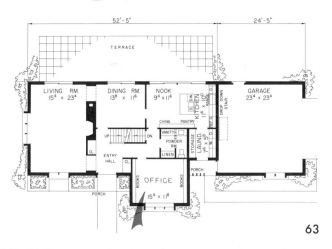

Fig. 10–5. A den or study located adjacent to the patio.

▶ Decor

The decor of the study should reflect the main activity and should have well-diffused general lighting and glareproof local lighting. Notice how the skylight in Fig. 10–7 provides natural diffused light for the use of books, whereas the study designed for a variety of activities such as designing and drawing can be more gaily and vibrantly decorated. Notice the open effect achieved in Fig. 10–8 by the row of windows above the eye level. These admit the maximum amount of light without exposing distracting eye-level images from the outside.

As in the recreation room, a central theme can permeate the decoration of the study. The person who uses the study shown in Fig. 10–9 obviously has some interest in boats and boating. Notice how not only the decorations reflect this interest, but also the paneling and furniture suggest the rough-textured appearance of a cabin.

Fig. 10–6. An attic study.

American-Saint Gobain Corporation

Fig. 10–7. A skylight provides natural diffused light for reading.

Rendering by George A. Parenti for the Masonite Corporation

Fig. 10–8. High windows admit light but block the view.

Fig. 10–9. A nautical decor.

United States Plywood Corporation

Armstrong Cork Company

Fig. 10–10. A small study-corner.

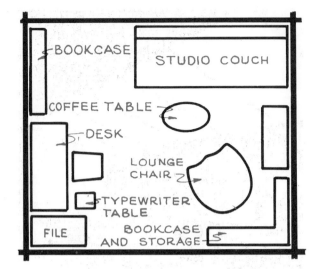

BOOKCASE

STUDIO COUCH

COFFEE TABLE

DESK

LOUNGE
CHAIR

TYPEWRITER
TABLE

FILE

BOOKCASE
AND STORAGE

Fig. 10–11. An optimum-sized study.

▶ Size and Shape

The size and shape of the den or study · or office will vary greatly, depending on whether one person expects to use the room or two; or whether it should provide a meeting place for business clients. Studies range in size from just enough space for a desk and chair in a small corner, as shown in Fig. 10–10, to a large amount of space with a diversity of furnishings, such as the study shown in Fig. 10–8. Figure 10–11 shows a study with the maximum number of furnishings, including a desk and chair, lounge chair, studio couch, drafting table, file cabinets, bookcases, typewriter tables, storage space, and coffee table. Obviously this study is designed to provide facilities for working, relaxing, and conversing intermittently.

Problems

1. Sketch a plan for a den in a home of your own design.

2. Sketch a plan for a den for your own home.

3. Sketch a plan for a den to accommodate the following facilities: desk, chair, bookcases, drafting table, lounge.

4. Sketch a plan for a den which will double as a guest bedroom.

5. Sketch the floor plan of your present home. List the furniture you would like to include in a den. Redesign the floor plan to include a den or study of sufficient size to accommodate this furniture.

6. Identify the following terms: *den, study, living area, sleeping area, guest room, professional office, central theme.*

Hotpoint Division, General Electric Company

SECTION TWO. SERVICE AREA

The service area includes facilities for the maintenance and servicing of the other areas of the home. The functioning of the living and the sleeping areas is greatly dependent upon the efficiency of the service area.

The service area includes the kitchen, laundry, garage, workshop, storage centers, and utility room. Since a great number of different activities take place in the service area, it should be designed for the utmost efficiency.

Unit II. The Kitchen

A well-planned kitchen is efficient, attractive, and easy to maintain. To design an efficient kitchen, the designer must consider the function, basic shape, decor, size, and location of equipment.

▶ Function
The preparation of food is the basic function of the kitchen. However, the kitchen may also be used as a dining area and sometimes as a laundry.

▶ Designing for Efficiency
The proper placement of appliances, storage cabinets, and furniture is important in planning efficient kitchens. Locating appliances in an efficient pattern eliminates much wasted motion for the homemaker (Fig. 11–1).

The finest appliances cannot be used well if they are not arranged in a pattern which is convenient to the homemaker. An efficient kitchen is

Formica Corporation

Fig. 11-1. A well-planned kitchen should be efficient for the homemaker.

divided into three areas: the storage and mixing center, the cleaning and preparation center, and the cooking center.

Storage and mixing center. The refrigerator is the major appliance in the storage and mixing center. The refrigerator may be free-standing, built-in, or suspended from a wall. The storage and mixing center also includes cabinets for the storage of utensils and ingredients used in cooking and baking, and a counter-top work area.

Preparation and cleaning center. The sink is the major appliance in the preparation and cleaning center. Sinks are available in one- and two-bowl models with a variety of cabinet arrangements, counter-top and drainboard areas. The preparation and cleaning center may also include a waste-disposal unit; an automatic dishwasher; and cabinets for storing brushes, towels, and cleaning supplies.

Cooking center. The range and oven are the major appliances in the cooking center. The range and oven may be combined into one appliance, or the burners may be installed in the counter top and the oven built into the wall. The cooking center should also include counter-top work space and storage space for minor appliances, and cooking utensils that will be used in the area. This area

must have an adequate supply of electrical outlets for the many minor appliances used in cooking.

Figure 11-3 shows the size requirements for the storage or installation of many minor appliances that may be located in the various centers.

Work triangle. If you draw a line connecting the three centers of the kitchen, a triangle is formed (Fig. 11-2). This is called the *work triangle.* If the three sides of the work triangle total more than 22', the kitchen is inefficient. The work triangle of an efficient kitchen is from 12' to 22'.

▶ Basic Shapes

The position of the three areas on the work triangle may vary greatly. However, the most efficient arrangements usually fall into the following categories.

U-shaped kitchen. The U-shaped kitchen, as shown in Figs. 11-4 and 11-5, is a very efficient arrangement. The sink is located at the bottom of the U, and the range and the refrigerator are on the opposite ends. In this arrangement, traffic passing through the kitchen is completely separated from the work triangle. The open space in the U between the sides may be 4' or 5'. This arrangement produces a very efficient but small kitchen.

Fig. 11-2. The total length of the work triangle should be between 12' and 22'.

Southern California Gas Company

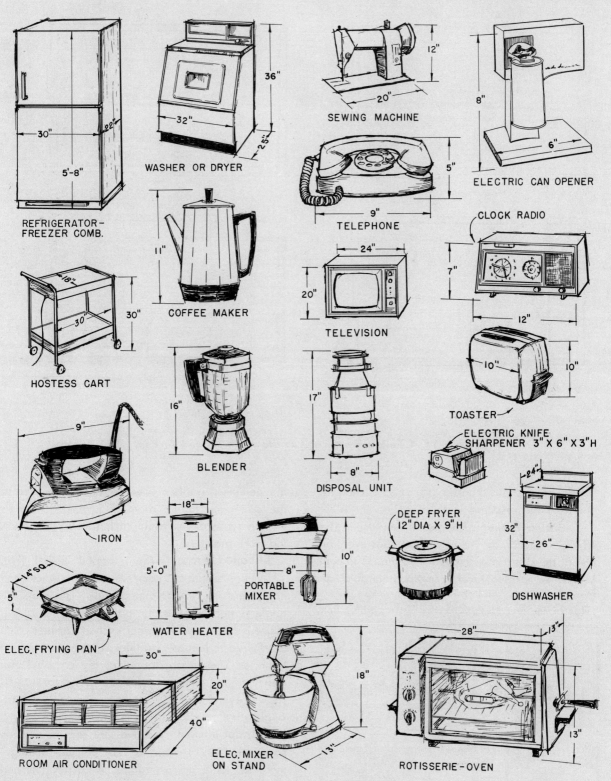

Fig. 11–3. Sizes of common appliances.

REFRIGERATOR-FREEZER COMB.
30"
22"
5'-8"

WASHER OR DRYER
36"
32"
25"

SEWING MACHINE
12"
20"

ELECTRIC CAN OPENER
8"
6"

TELEPHONE
5"
9"

CLOCK RADIO
7"
12"

COFFEE MAKER
11"

TELEVISION
24"
20"

HOSTESS CART
18"
30"
30"

BLENDER
16"

DISPOSAL UNIT
17"
8"

TOASTER
10"
10"

ELECTRIC KNIFE SHARPENER 3" X 6" X 3"H

IRON
9"

WATER HEATER
18"
5'-0"

PORTABLE MIXER
8"
10"

DEEP FRYER 12" DIA X 9"H

DISHWASHER
24"
32"
26"

ELEC. FRYING PAN
14" SQ.
5"

ROOM AIR CONDITIONER
30"
20"
40"

ELEC. MIXER ON STAND
18"
13"

ROTISSERIE-OVEN
28"
13"
13"

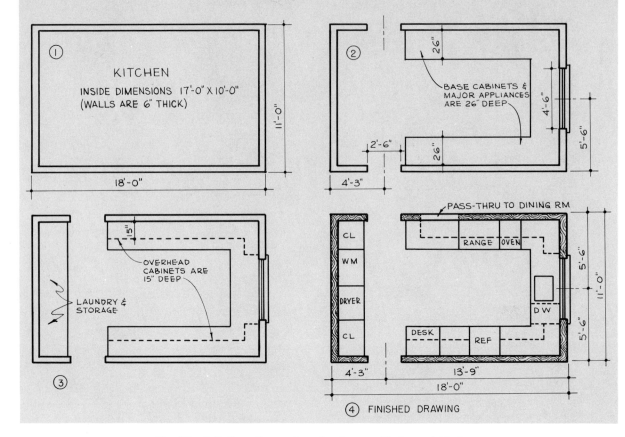

Fig. 11–4. Follow these steps to draw a U-shaped kitchen.

Figure 11–6 shows various U-shaped kitchen layouts and the resulting work triangles.

Peninsula kitchen. The peninsula kitchen (Fig. 11–7) is similar to the U kitchen. However, one end of the U is not enclosed with a wall. The cooking center is often located in this peninsula, and

Fig. 11–5. Four elevations of a U-shaped kitchen.

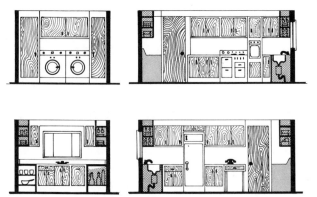

the peninsula is often used to join the kitchen to the dining or family room. Figure 11–8 shows various types of peninsula kitchens and the resulting work triangles.

L-shaped kitchen. The L-shaped kitchen (Fig. 11–9) has continuous counters and appliances and equipment on two adjoining walls. The work triangle is not in the traffic pattern. The remaining space is often used for other kitchen facilities, such as dining or laundry facilities. If the walls of an L-shaped kitchen are too long, the compact efficiency of the kitchen is destroyed. Figure 11–10 shows several L-shaped kitchens and the work triangles that result from these arrangements.

Corridor kitchen. The two-wall corridor kitchen shown in Fig. 11–11 is a very efficient arrangement for long, narrow rooms. A corridor kitchen is unsatisfactory, however, if considerable traffic

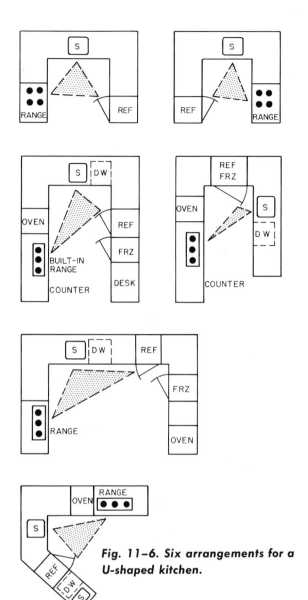

Fig. 11-6. Six arrangements for a U-shaped kitchen.

Fig. 11-7. A peninsula kitchen.

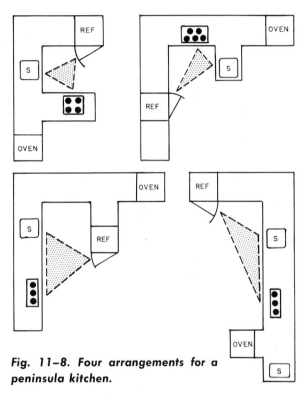

Fig. 11-8. Four arrangements for a peninsula kitchen.

Fig. 11-9. L-shaped kitchens permit a large area of open floor space.

passes through the work triangle. A corridor-type kitchen produces one of the most efficient work triangles of all the arrangements.

One-wall kitchen. A one-wall kitchen is an excellent plan for small apartments, cabins, or houses in which little space is available. The work centers are located in one line and produce a very efficient arrangement. However, in planning the one-wall kitchen, the designer must be careful

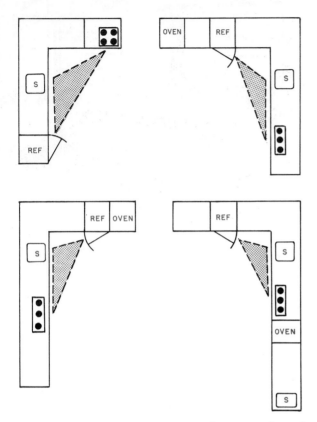

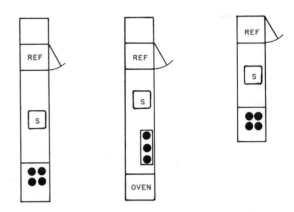

Fig. 11–12. *Three arrangements for one-wall kitchens.*

Fig. 11–10. *Four arrangements for an L-shaped kitchen.*

Fig. 11–11. *Four arrangements for a corridor kitchen.*

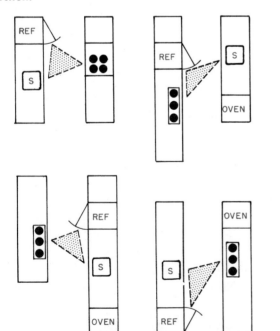

to avoid having the wall too long and must provide adequate storage facilities. Figure 11–12 shows several one-wall kitchen arrangements.

Island kitchen. The island, which serves as a separator for the different parts of the kitchen, usually has a range top or sink or both, and is accessible on all sides, as shown in Fig. 11–13. Other facilities that are sometimes located in the island are the mixing center, buffet counter, extra sink, and snack center, as shown in Fig. 11–14.

Fig. 11–13. *This island kitchen has a sink in the island.*

Hotpoint Division, General Electric Company

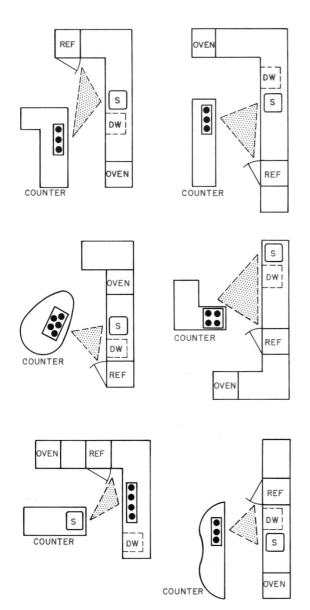

Fig. 11-14. Island-kitchen arrangements.

Family kitchen. The family kitchen is an open kitchen using any of the basic plans. Its function is to provide a meeting place for the entire family in addition to providing for the normal kitchen functions. Family kitchens are normally divided into two sections. One section is for food preparation, which includes the three work centers; the other section includes a dining area and family-room facilities, as shown in Fig. 11-15.

Fig. 11-15. This family kitchen is designed for a variety of activities.

Family kitchens must be rather large to accommodate these facilities. An average size for a family kitchen is 15 feet square. Figure 11-16 shows several possible arrangements for family kitchens.

▶ **Decor**

Even though kitchen appliances are of contemporary design, some homemakers prefer to decorate kitchens with a period or colonial motif. The design of the cabinets, floors, walls, and accessory furniture must therefore be accented to give the desired effect. Compare the colonial kitchen shown in Fig. 11-17 with the modern kitchen shown in Fig. 11-18. You will notice that it is somewhat easier to design the lines of the modern kitchen in harmony with the lines of the major appliances.

Regardless of the style, kitchen walls, floors, counter tops, and cabinets should require a minimum amount of maintenance. Materials that are relatively maintenance-free include stainless steel, stain-resistant plastic, wall tile, washable wall coverings, washable paint, asphalt vinyl tile, plastic upholstery, and formica or micarta counter tops.

▶ **Location**

Since the kitchen is the core of the service area, it should be located near the service entrance and

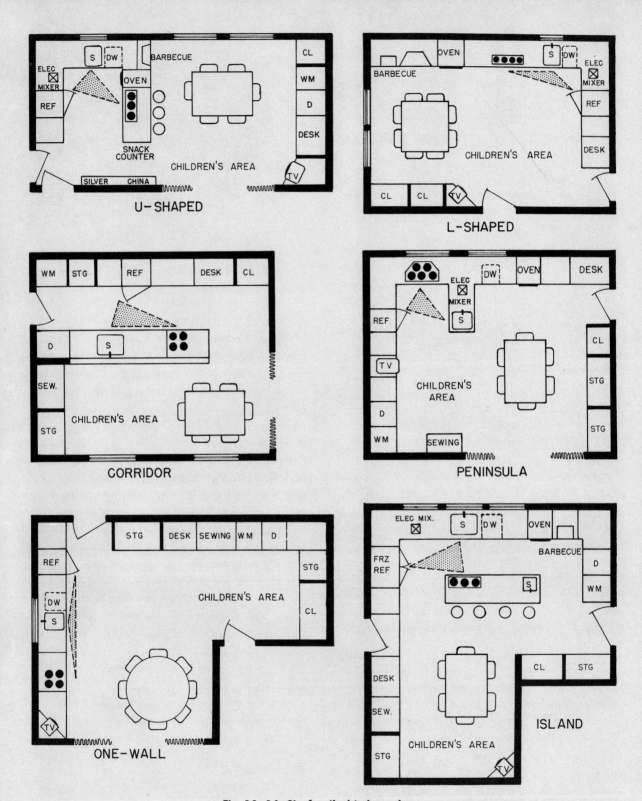

Fig. 11–16. Six family-kitchen plans.

Formica Corporation.

Fig. 11–17. A U-shaped kitchen in early American decor.

near the waste-disposal area. The children's play area should also be visible from the kitchen (Fig. 11–19), and the kitchen must be adjacent to the dining area and outdoor eating areas.

▶ Kitchen Planning Guides

The following guides for kitchen planning provide a review of the more important factors to consider in designing efficient and functional kitchens:

1. The traffic lane is clear of the work triangle.

2. The work areas include all necessary appliances and facilities.

Fig. 11–18. A modern kitchen with clean, simple lines.

Southern California Edison Company

Fig. 11–19. A kitchen designed with a view of the play area.

Home Planners, Inc.

3. The kitchen is located adjacent to the dining area.

4. The kitchen is located near the children's play area.

5. The view from the kitchen is cheerful and pleasant.

6. The centers include (1) the storage center, (2) the preparation and cleaning center, and (3) the cooking center.

7. The work triangle measures less than 22'.

8. Electrical outlets are provided for each work center.

9. Adequate storage facilities in base and wall cabinets are available in each work center.

10. Shadowless and glareless light is provided and is concentrated on each work center.

11. Adequate counter space is provided for meal preparation.

12. Ventilation is adequate.

13. The oven and range are separated from the refrigerator by at least one cabinet.

14. Doors on appliances swing away from the work counter area (Fig. 11–20).

15. Lapboard heights are 26" (Fig. 11–21).

16. Working heights for counters are 36" (Fig. 11–22).

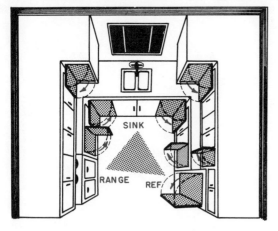

Fig. 11–20. Cabinet doors should open away from the work area.

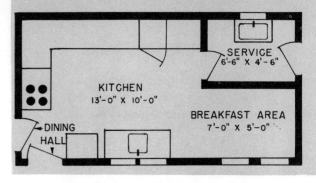

Fig. 11–23. Remodel this kitchen.

17. Working heights for tables are 30″ (Fig. 11–21).

18. The combination of base cabinets, wall cabinets, and appliances provides a consistent standard unit without gaps or awkward depressions or extensions.

Problems

1. Sketch a floor plan of the peninsula kitchen shown in Fig. 11–7. Use the scale $\frac{1}{4}'' = 1'\text{-}0''$.
2. Sketch an elevation drawing of the two walls of the L-shaped kitchen shown in Fig. 11–9. Use the scale $\frac{1}{4}'' = 1'\text{-}0''$.
3. Sketch a floor plan of the island kitchen shown in Fig. 11–13. Show the position of the dining area in relation to this kitchen. Use the scale $\frac{1}{4}'' = 1'\text{-}0''$.

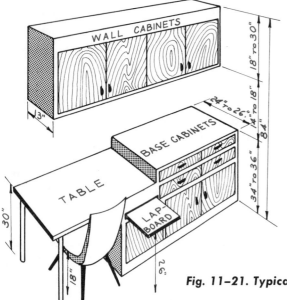

Fig. 11–21. Typical heights of kitchen working surfaces.

Fig. 11–22. Typical heights of kitchen cabinets.

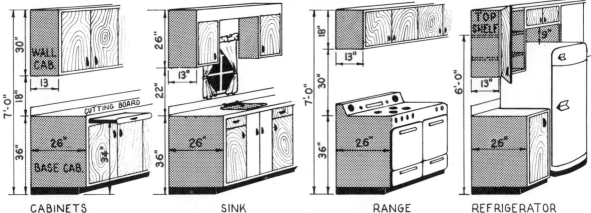

CABINETS   SINK   RANGE   REFRIGERATOR

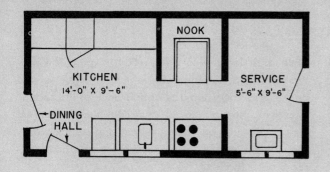

Fig. 11–24. Improve this plan.

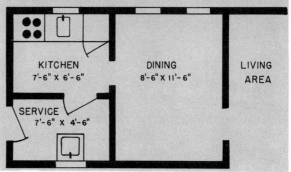

Fig. 11–25. Redesign this arrangement.

4. Sketch a floor plan and elevation of the kitchen shown in Fig. 11–18. Use the scale ¼″ = 1′-0″. Remodel the kitchen shown in Fig. 11–23. Alter the walls and work area positions as desired.

5. Remodel the kitchen shown in Fig. 11–24. Change door arrangements and dining facilities as needed.

6. Redesign the kitchen and dining room as shown in Fig. 11–25. Prepare a floor plan and one elevation of your revised design.

7. Redesign the kitchen and service entrance shown in Fig. 11–26. Combine these facilities into an open-plan kitchen.

8. Sketch a floor plan of the kitchen in your own home. Prepare a revised sketch to show how you would propose to redesign this kitchen. Make an attempt to reduce the size of the work triangle.

9. Sketch a floor plan of a kitchen you would include in a house of your own design. Use the scale ¼″ = 1′-0″.

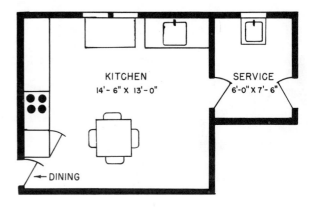

Fig. 11–26. Redesign this plan.

10. Define the following terms: *work triangle, U-shape, peninsula, L-shape, corridor, island, family kitchen, storage and mixing center, planning and preparation center, cooking center, major appliances, minor appliances, base cabinet, wall cabinet, lapboard, counter top, service area.*

Unit 12. The Utility Room

The utility room may include facilities for washing, drying, ironing, sewing, and storing household cleaning equipment. It may contain heating and air-conditioning equipment or even a pantry for storing foods. Other names for this room are *service room, all-purpose room,* and *laundry room* (Fig. 12–1).

▶ **Shape and Size**

The shapes and sizes of utility rooms differ, as shown in Fig. 12–2. The average floor space required for appliances, counter, and storage area is 95 square feet. However, this size may vary according to the budget or needs of the homemaker.

Fig. 12–1. A finished utility room.

▶ Style and Decor

Style and decor in a utility room depend on the function of the appliances, which are themselves an important factor in the appearance of the room. Simplicity, straight lines, and continuous counter spaces produce an orderly effect and permit work to progress easily. Such features also make the room easy to clean.

An important part of the decor is the color of the paint used for walls and cabinet finishes. Colors should harmonize with the colors used on the appliances. All finishes should be washable. The walls may be lined with sound-absorbing tiles or wood paneling.

The lighting in a utility room should be carefully planned so that it will be 48″ above the equipment used for washing, ironing, and sewing (Fig. 12–3). However the lighting fixtures placed above the preparation area and laundry sinks can be further from the work top area as shown in Fig. 12–3.

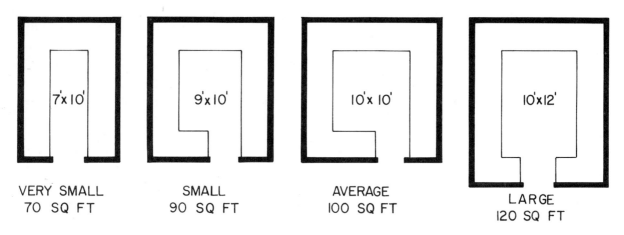

7'x10'	9'x10'	10'x10'	10'x12'
VERY SMALL 70 SQ FT	SMALL 90 SQ FT	AVERAGE 100 SQ FT	LARGE 120 SQ FT

Fig. 12–2. The size of a utility room varies according to the budget and needs of the homemaker.

Fig. 12–3. The lighting for a utility room must be carefully planned.

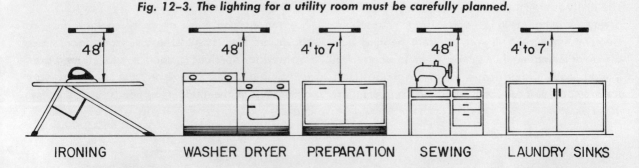

IRONING WASHER DRYER PREPARATION SEWING LAUNDRY SINKS

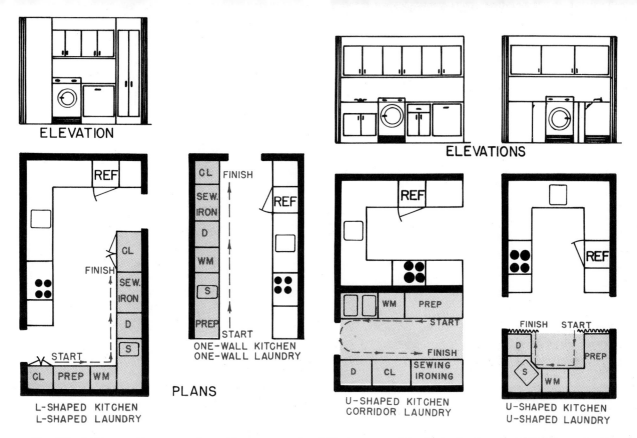

ELEVATION

ELEVATIONS

REF

CL FINISH

SEW.
IRON

D

WM

S

PREP START

REF

ONE-WALL KITCHEN
ONE-WALL LAUNDRY

REF

CL

FINISH

SEW.
IRON

D

S

START

CL PREP WM

L-SHAPED KITCHEN
L-SHAPED LAUNDRY

PLANS

REF

WM PREP

START

FINISH

D CL SEWING IRONING

U-SHAPED KITCHEN
CORRIDOR LAUNDRY

REF

FINISH START

D

S

PREP

WM

U-SHAPED KITCHEN
U-SHAPED LAUNDRY

Fig. 12-4. The appliances and working spaces should be arranged in the order in which they are used.

▶ The Laundry Area

The laundry area is only one part of the utility room, but it is usually the most important center. Its function is to serve the homemaker in the work of keeping clothing and other washable materials clean.

To make this work as easy and effective as possible, the appliances and working spaces in a laundry area should be located in the order in which they will be used. Such an arrangement will save time and effort. There are four steps in the process of laundering. The equipment needed for each of these steps should be grouped so that the homemaker can proceed from one stage to the next in an orderly and efficient way (Fig. 12-4).

Receiving and preparing laundry. The first step in laundering—receiving and preparing the items—requires hampers or bins, and counters on which to collect and sort the articles. Near this

equipment there should be storage facilities for detergents, bleaches, and stain removers (Fig. 12-5).

Washing. The next step, the actual washing, takes place in the area containing the washing machine and laundry tubs or sink. Figure 12-6 shows the equipment used in this area.

Drying. The equipment needed for this stage of the work includes a dryer, indoor drying lines, and space to store clothespins and a laundry cart (Fig. 12-7).

Ironing and storage. For the last part of the process, the required equipment consists of an iron and a board or an automatic ironer, a counter for sprinkling and folding, a rack on which to hang finished ironing, and facilities for sewing and mending. If a sewing machine is included, it may be portable, or it may fold into a counter or wall (Fig. 12-8).

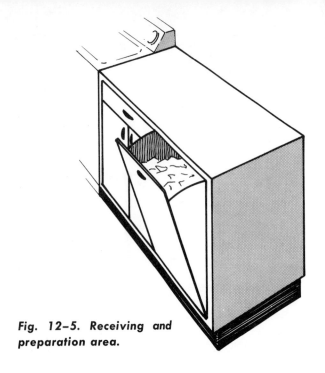

Fig. 12–5. Receiving and preparation area.

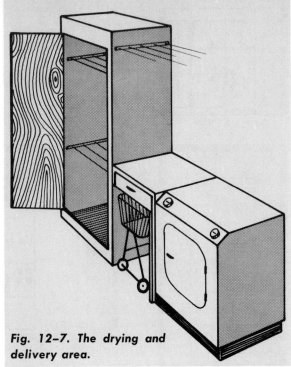

Fig. 12–7. The drying and delivery area.

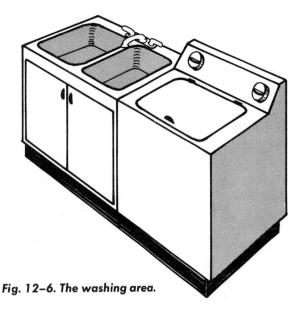

Fig. 12–6. The washing area.

▶ Separate Laundry Area

The location of the laundry area in a utility room is desirable because all laundry functions, including repairs, are centered in one place. A further advantage of the separate room is that laundering is kept well apart from the preparation of foods (Fig. 12–9).

Space is not always available for a utility room, however, and the laundry appliances and space for washing and drying may need to be located in some other area (Fig. 12–10). Wherever it is placed, the equipment in the laundry unit should be arranged in the order in which the work must be done.

The kitchen. Placing the laundry unit in the kitchen has some advantages. The unit is in a central location and is near a service entrance. Plumbing facilities are near. The sink may be used as a laundry tub, and the drain boards may be used as counters for sprinkling and folding.

Other locations. Laundry appliances may be located in a closet, on a service porch, in a basement, or in a garage or carport. The service porch, basement, garage, or carport provides less expensive floor space than other parts of the house. However, when the laundry unit is located in one of these four places, the homemaker has the problem of heating the area for winter laundering. Another problem may arise if the location is far from the water heater. If this problem is acute, an additional water heater may be required.

Reichhold Chemicals, Inc.

Fig. 12-8. A sewing area in a utility room.

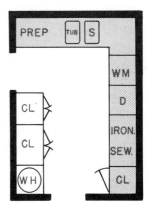

Fig. 12-9. A laundry room located in a separate area.

Fig. 12-10. An alternate location for the washer and dryer.

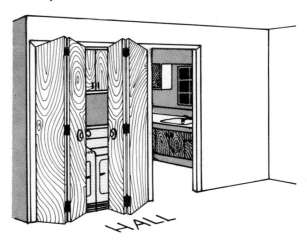

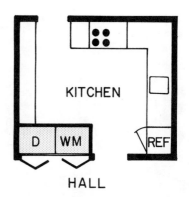

▶ The Water Heater

Hot water is essential to every modern household. The size of the family determines the amount needed, and therefore the size of the water heater. This should be installed near the kitchen, the utility room, and the baths. If the heater is too far from a point at which it is used, long plumbing lines will be required, time will be lost in waiting for hot water to reach the outlet, and hot water left in the plumbing lines will be wasted.

Problems

1. Sketch the laundry area shown in Fig. 12-1. Show the position of all appliances and equipment.
2. Design a utility room with a complete laundry within an area of 100 square feet.
3. Consult gas and electric companies in your community to secure information about appliances and design for laundry areas.
4. Explain the following terms: *utility room, laundry area, hamper.*

Unit 13. Garages and Carports

Storage of the automobile occupies a large percentage of the available space of the house or property. Garages and carports must therefore be designed with utmost care to ensure maximum utilization of space.

▶ Garage

A garage is a structure designed primarily to shelter an automobile. However, it may be used for many secondary purposes, as a workshop or storage space, for example. A garage may be connected with the house (integral) or it may be a separate building (detached). Figure 13–1 shows several possible garage locations.

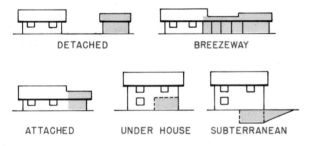

Fig. 13–1. Possible locations for the garage.

▶ Carport

A carport is a garage with one or more of the exterior walls removed. It may consist of a free-standing roof completely separate from the house (Fig. 13–2), or it may be built against the existing walls of the house (Fig. 13–3). Carports are most acceptable in mild climates where complete protection from cold weather is not needed. A carport offers protection primarily from sun and precipitation.

The garage and the carport both have distinct advantages. The garage is more secure and provides more shelter. However, carports lend themselves to open-planning techniques and are less expensive than garages.

▶ Design

The lines of the garage or carport should be consistent with the major building lines of the remainder of the house. The style of the garage should be consistent with the style of architecture used in the house (Fig. 13–4).

The garage or carport must never appear as an afterthought. Often a patio, porch, or breezeway is planned between the garage and the house to integrate a detached garage with the house

Fig. 13–2. A carport provides overhead protection.
Kaiser Aluminum and Chemical Corp.

Fig. 13–3. A combination garage and carport.
Samuel Cabot, Inc.

Home Planners, Inc.

Fig. 13-4. Garage style must be integrated with the total decor.

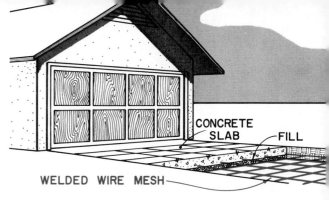

Fig. 13-7. Steel wire mesh in the concrete will stop the pavement and garage floor from cracking.

(Fig. 13-5). A covered walkway from the garage or carport to the house should be provided if the garage is detached.

The garage floor must be solid and easily maintained. A concrete slab 3" or 4" thick provides the best deck for a garage or carport. The garage floor must have adequate drainage either to the outside or through drains located inside the garage (Fig. 13-6). A vapor barrier consisting of waterproofing materials under the slab should be provided.

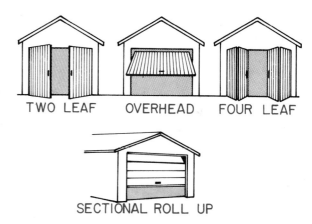

Fig. 13-8. Four common types of garage doors.

Fig. 13-5. A covered walkway or breezeway provides protection for the access.

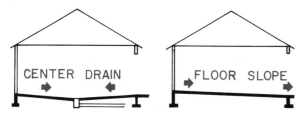

Fig. 13-6. Proper drainage is important for the garage.

The driveway should be of asphalt or concrete construction, preferably with welded wire fabric to maintain rigidity (Fig. 13-7). In cold climates, heating pipes laid under the driveway help melt snow and ice.

The design of the garage door greatly affects the appearance of the garage. Several types of garage doors are available. These include the two-leaf outswinging, overhead, four-leaf inward-swinging, and sectional roll-up doors (Fig. 13-8). Several electrical devices are available for opening the door of the garage from the car (Fig. 13-9).

▶ Size

The size and number of automobiles and the additional facilities needed for storage or workshop use should determine the size of the garage (Fig. 13-10).

Berry Door Corporation

Fig. 13–9. Garage door controlled with a push-button.

Crawford Garage Door Company

Fig. 13–11. Utilize wasted space when possible.

The dimensions of a single-car garage range between 11' × 19' and 13' × 25'. A 16' × 25' garage is more desirable if space is needed for benches, mowers, tools, and the storage of children's vehicles. A full double garage is 25' × 25'.

A two-car garage does not cost twice as much as a one-car garage. However, if the second half is added at a later date, the cost will more than double. It is therefore advisable to design a two-car garage even though there may not be two cars in the family at the time. The other half of the garage will provide space for a play area, a workshop, and a laundry; also storage space for boats, bicycles, wagons, and garden tools; and it may be utilized at a later date for a second car.

▶ **Storage**

Storage is often an additional function of most garages. The storage space over the hood of the car should be utilized effectively (Fig. 13–11). Cabinets should be elevated from the floor several inches to eliminate moisture and to facilitate cleaning the garage floor. Garden-tool cabinets can be designed to open from the outside of the garage (Fig. 13–12).

Fig. 13–10. Typical garage sizes.

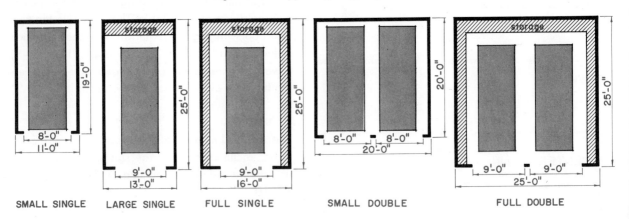

| SMALL SINGLE | LARGE SINGLE | FULL SINGLE | SMALL DOUBLE | FULL DOUBLE |

EXTERIOR   INTERIOR

Fig. 13-12. Plan for storage space in a garage.

▶ Driveway

A driveway can be planned for purposes other than providing access to the garage and temporary parking space for guests. By adding a wider space to an apron at the door of the garage, an area can be provided for car washing and polishing and for a hard, level surface for children's games. Aprons are often needed to provide space for turning the car in order to eliminate backing out onto a main street (Fig. 13-13).

The driveway should be accessible to all entrances, and the garage should provide easy access to the service area of the home. Sufficient space in the driveway should be provided for parking of guests' cars.

Driveways should be designed at least several feet wider than the track of the car (approximately 7'). However, slightly wider driveways are desirable (Fig. 13-14).

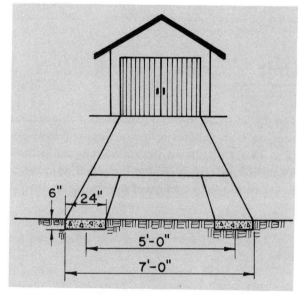

Fig. 13-14. Driveway width.

Fig. 13-13. Apron arrangements for parking and turning.

Crawford Garage Door Company

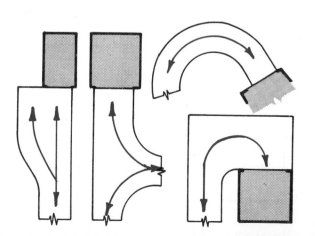

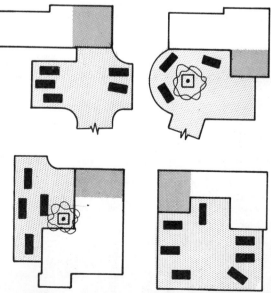

Problems

1. Sketch the floor plans shown in Fig. 13–10 and design a garage, apron, and driveway for each.
2. Sketch a front elevation for a small single garage, using the scale 1/4'' = 1'-0''.
3. Sketch a full double garage and draw in storage, laundry, and workbench.
4. Convert a large double garage to a recreation and entertainment area. Sketch the layout.
5. Sketch a two-car garage plan. Show the following storage facilities: storage wall, outside storage, boat slung from ceiling, laundry area, gardening equipment, over-hood storage.
6. Know these architectural terms: *garage*, *carport*, *breezeway*, *subterranean*, *apron*, *integral garage*, *detached garage*.

Unit 14. Home Work Area

The home work area is designed for activities ranging from hobbies to home maintenance work (Fig. 14–1). The home work area may be located in part of the garage, in the basement, in a separate room, or in an adjacent building (Fig. 14–2).

Fig. 14–1. The home work area is often used for hobby work.

Delco Appliance Div., General Motors Corporation.

▶ Layout

Power tools, hand tools, workbench space, and storage should be systematically planned. A workbench complete with vise is needed in every home work area. The average workbench is 36'' high. A movable workbench is appropriate when large projects are to be constructed. A *peninsula workbench* provides three working sides and storage compartments on three sides. A dropleaf workbench is excellent for work areas where a minimum amount of space is available (Fig. 14–3).

Fig. 14–2. The home workshop may be located in the garage, basement, or in a separate building.

SEPARATE SHOP

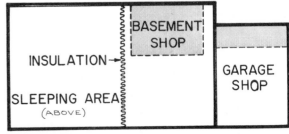

INSULATION→

BASEMENT SHOP

SLEEPING AREA (ABOVE)

GARAGE SHOP

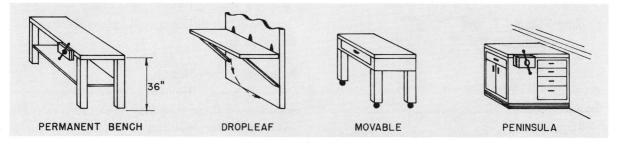

Fig. 14–3. Types of workbenches.

PERMANENT BENCH   DROPLEAF   MOVABLE   PENINSULA

Hand tools. Some hand tools are basic to all types of hobbies or home maintenance work. These basic tools include a claw hammer, files, carpenter's squares, hand drills, screwdrivers, planes, pliers, chisels, scales, wrenches, saws, a brace and bit, mallets, and clamps.

If hobbies are in specialized fields, special tools and storage facilities for these tools should be provided in the basic plans for the work area.

Power tools. Although power tools are not absolutely necessary for the performance of most home workshop activities, they do make the performance of many tasks easier and quicker. Some of the more common power tools used in home workshops include electric drills, band saws, circular saws, jointers, belt sanders, radial-arm saws, lathes, jigsaws, and drill presses. Placement of this equipment should be planned to provide the maximum amount of work space. Figure 14–4 shows the clearances necessary for the safe and efficient operation of these machines.

Multipurpose machines. Multipurpose machines are machines that can perform a variety of operations. The multipurpose tool shown in Fig. 14–5 has many attachments which are used to convert the function. Multipurpose equipment is popular for use in the home workshop since the purchase of only one piece of equipment is necessary and the amount of space needed is relatively small, compared with the amount of space needed for a variety of machines. The greatest disadvantage in the use of multipurpose equipment for home workshops is the amount of time it takes to change over the machine from one function to another.

Tools and equipment needed for working with large materials should be placed where the material can be easily handled. Separate-drive motors can be used to drive more than one piece of power equipment, in order to conserve motors (Fig. 14–6).

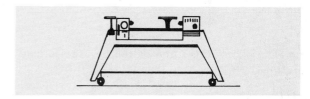

Fig. 14–5. A multipurpose tool.

Fig. 14–4. Proper spacing of machinery.

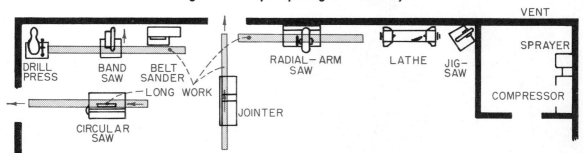

DRILL PRESS   BAND SAW   BELT SANDER   —LONG WORK   RADIAL–ARM SAW   LATHE   JIG-SAW   VENT   SPRAYER   COMPRESSOR   CIRCULAR SAW   JOINTER

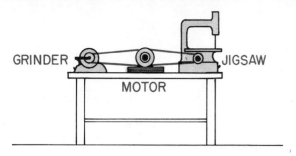

Fig. 14–6. One motor can drive several machines.

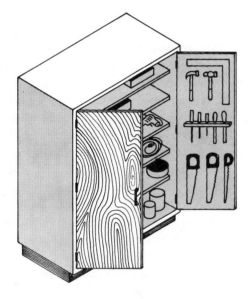

Fig. 14–7. Closed storage facilities are the safest for tools.

Fig. 14–8. Perforated boards can be used to hold tools.

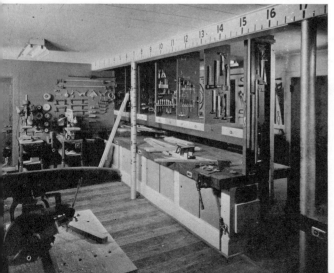

Separate electrical circuits for lights and power tools should be included in the plans for the home workshop area.

▶ Storage Facilities

Maximum storage facilities in the home work area are essential. Hand tools may be stored in cabinets which keep them dust-free and safe (Fig. 14–7), or hung on perforated wallboard, as shown in Fig. 14–8. Tools too small to be hung should be kept in special-purpose drawers, and any inflammable finishing material, such as turpentine or oil paint, should be stored in metal cabinets.

▶ Size and Shape

The size of the work area depends on the size and number of power tools and equipment, the amount of workbench area, and the amount of tool and material storage facilities provided. The size of the work area should be planned for maximum expansion, even though only a workbench or a few tools may be available when the area is first occupied. Therefore, space for the maximum amount of facilities should be planned and located when the area is designed. As new equipment is added, it will fit appropriately into the basic plan (Fig. 14–9).

The designer must anticipate the type and number of materials for which storage space will be needed and design the storage space accordingly. If a relatively small amount of space is available the use of multipurpose tools, rolling tool chests, tool panels, and folding workbenches can help conserve space. If large projects are anticipated, more area will be needed for laying out and storing materials. Often a two-car garage can double as a layout area for large projects when the cars are removed.

▶ Decor

The work area should be as maintenance-free as possible. Glossy paint or tile retards an accumulation of shop dust on the walls. Exhaust fans eliminate much of the dust and the gasses produced in the shop. The shop floor should be of concrete or linoleum for easy maintenance. Abrasive strips around machines will eliminate the possibility of slipping. Do not locate noisy equipment near the children's sleeping area. Interior walls and ceilings should be soundproofed by offsetting studs and adding adequate insulation to produce a sound barrier (Fig. 14–10).

Light and color are most important factors in designing the work area. Pastel colors, which reduce eye strain, should be used for the general color scheme of the shop. Extremely light colors that produce glare, and extremely dark colors that reduce effective illumination, should be avoided. Adopting one of the major paint manufacturers' color systems for color coding will help to create a pleasant atmosphere in the shop and will also help to provide the most efficient and safest working conditions.

General lighting of 10 to 15 candlepower should be provided in the shop, and the local lighting on machines and worktable tops should be 100 candlepower.

If the work area is in a basement with any tendency to be damp, a dehumidifier should be provided to keep tools and machine tops from accumulating an excess of oxidation.

Problems

1. Design a small work area to fit into a single garage that will also house a car (Unit 13).

2. Design a work area to fill one side of a double garage (Unit 13).

3. Design a work area in a double garage for an activity other than woodworking (ceramics, jewelry, metalworking, automotive repairs, for example). Show what tools and work areas are necessary.

4. Know the following architectural terms: *dehumidifier, workbench, perforated wallboard, flammable, hand tools, power tools, multipurpose tools.*

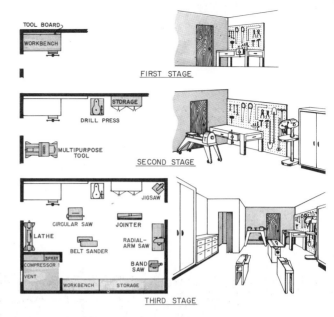

Fig. 14-9. A three-stage development of a workshop.

Fig. 14–10. Insulation stops disturbing noises from entering other parts of the house.

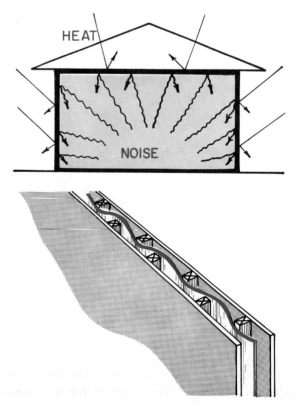

Unit 15. Storage Areas

Storage areas should be provided for general storage and for specific storage within each room (Fig. 15–1). Areas that would otherwise be considered wasted space should be utilized as general storage areas. Parts of the basement, attic or garage often fall into this category (Fig. 15–2). Effective storage planning is necessary to provide storage facilities within each room that will create the least amount of inconvenience in securing the stored articles. Articles that are used daily or weekly should be stored in or near the room where they will be used (Fig. 15–3). Articles that are used only seasonally should be placed in more permanent general storage areas.

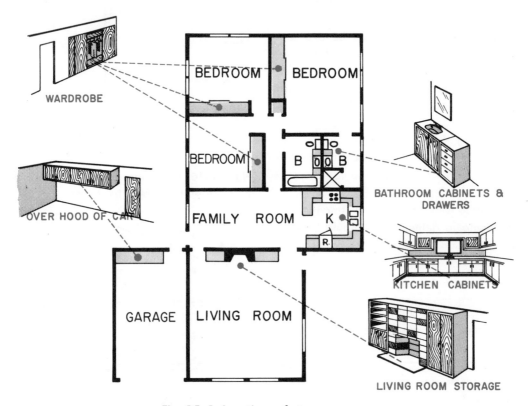

Fig. 15–1. Locations of storage areas.

Fig. 15–2. A typical storage area in most homes.
Masonite Corporation

Fig. 15–3. Room storage must be provided for objects used every day.

Home Planners, Inc.

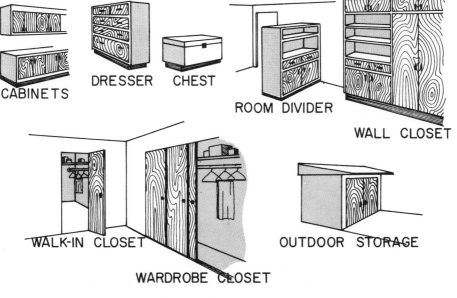

CABINETS DRESSER CHEST ROOM DIVIDER WALL CLOSET

WALK-IN CLOSET WARDROBE CLOSET OUTDOOR STORAGE

Fig. 15–4. Types of storage facilities.

▶ Storage Facilities

Storage facilities, equipment, and furniture used for storage within the various rooms of the house are divided into the following categories (Fig. 15–4).

Wardrobe closets. A *wardrobe closet* is a shallow clothes closet built into the wall. The minimum depth for the wardrobe is 24''. If this closet is more

Fig. 15–5. Dimensions for wardrobe closets.

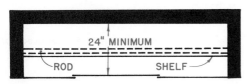

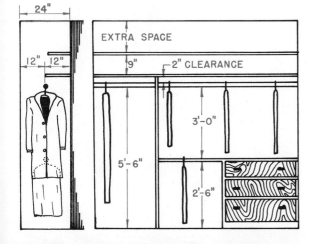

than 30'' deep you will be unable to reach the back of the closet. Swinging or sliding doors should expose all parts of the closet to your reach. A disadvantage of the wardrobe closet is the amount of wall space needed for the doors (Fig. 15–5).

Walk-in closets. *Walk-in closets* are closets large enough to walk into. The area needed for this type of closet is an area equal to the amount of space needed to hang clothes plus enough space to walk and turn. Although some area is wasted in the passage, the use of the walk-in closet does provide more wall area for furniture placement since only one door is needed (Fig. 15–6).

Fig. 15–6. Dimensions for walk-in closets.

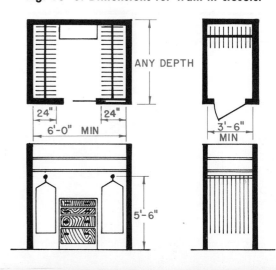

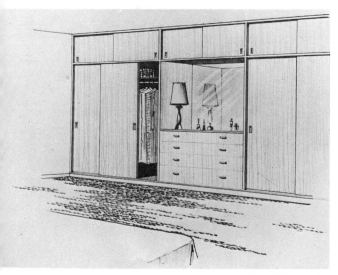

Home Planners, Inc.

Wall closets. A *wall closet* is a shallow closet in the wall holding cupboards, shelves, and drawers. Wall closets are normally 18" deep, since this size provides access to all stored items without using an excessive amount of floor area (Fig. 15–7).

Protruding closets that create an offset in a room should be avoided. Often by filling the entire wall between two bedrooms with closet space it is possible to design a square or rectangular room without the use of offsets (Fig. 15–8). Doors on closets should be sufficiently wide to allow easy accessibility. Swing-out doors have the advantage of providing extra storage space on the back of the door. However, space must be allowed for the swing. For this reason, sliding doors are usually preferred. All closets, except very shallow linen closets, should be provided with lighting.

Chests and dressers. Chests and dressers are free-standing pieces of furniture used for storage, generally in the bedroom. They are available in a variety of sizes usually with shelves and drawers.

Room dividers. A room divider often doubles as a storage area, especially when a protruding closet divides several areas. Room dividers often extend from the floor to the ceiling or may only be several feet high. Many room dividers include shelves and drawers that open from both sides (Fig. 15–9).

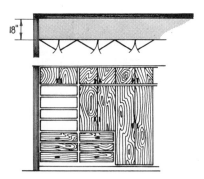

Fig. 15–7. Wall storage uses a minimum of floor space.

Fig. 15–8. Avoid closets that create offsets.

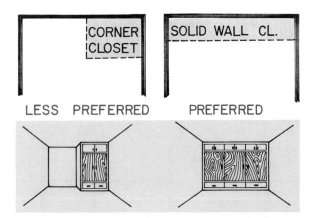

Fig. 15–9. Room dividers can be used for storage.

Douglas Fir Plywood Association

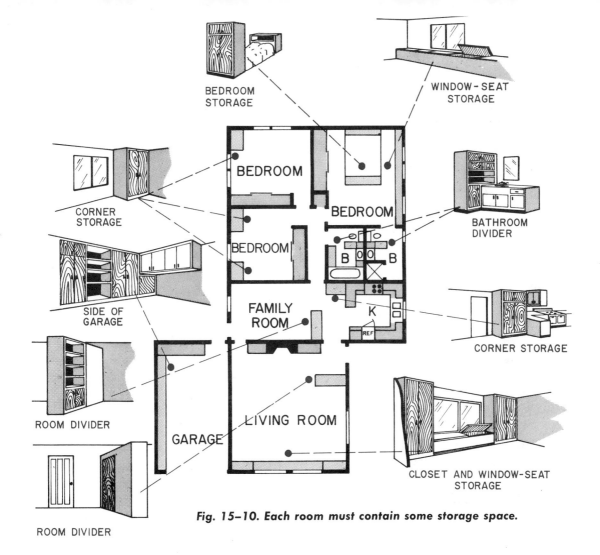

Fig. 15-10. Each room must contain some storage space.

BEDROOM STORAGE

WINDOW-SEAT STORAGE

CORNER STORAGE

BATHROOM DIVIDER

SIDE OF GARAGE

CORNER STORAGE

ROOM DIVIDER

CLOSET AND WINDOW-SEAT STORAGE

ROOM DIVIDER

BEDROOM

BEDROOM

BEDROOM

FAMILY ROOM

LIVING ROOM

GARAGE

► Location

Different types of storage facilities are necessary for areas of the home, depending on the type of article to be stored. The most appropriate types of storage facilities for each room in the house are as follows (Fig. 15-10).

Living room: room divider, built-in wall cabinets, bookcases, window seats (Fig. 15-11)

Dining area: room divider, built-in wall closet

Family room: built-in wall storage, window seats

Recreation room: built-in wall storage (Fig. 15-12)

Porches: under porch stairs, walk-in closet

Patios: sides of barbecue, separate building

Fig. 15-11. Continuous storage walls.

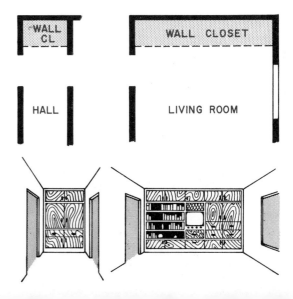

WALL CL

WALL CLOSET

HALL

LIVING ROOM

93

Fig. 15–12. Built-in wall storage.

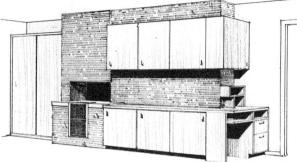

Fig. 15–15. Kitchen storage.

Outside: closets built into the side of the house (Fig. 15–13)

Halls: solid built-in wall closets, ends of blind halls (Fig. 15–14)

Entrance: room divider, wardrobe, walk-in closet

Den: built-in wall closet, window seats, bookcases.

Kitchen: wall and floor cabinets, room divider, wall closets (Fig. 15–15)

Utility room: cabinets on floor and walls

Garage: cabinets over hood of car, wall closets along sides, added construction on the outside of the garage (Fig. 15–17)

Work area: open tool board, wall closets, cabinets

Bedroom: walk-in closet, wardrobe closet, under bed, foot of bed, head of bed, built-in cabinets and shelves, dressers, chests

Bathroom: cabinets on floor and ceiling, room dividers

Problems

1. Draw the floor plan in Fig. 15–16, using the scale ¼″ = 1′-0″. Add all needed storage space.
2. Draw the floor plan in Fig. 15–18, using the scale ¼″ = 1′-0″. Add all the needed storage space.
3. Draw the floor plan in Fig. 15–19, using the scale ¼″ = 1′-0″. Add all needed storage space.

Fig. 15–13. Outside storage.

Fig. 15–14. Hall storage.

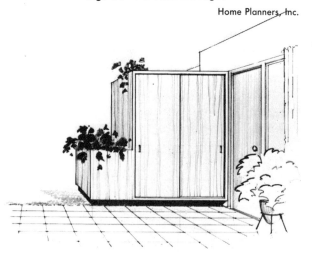

Fig. 15–16. Add storage facilities to this plan.

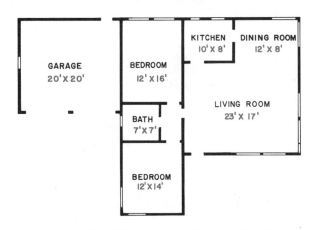

Fig. 15–18. Add storage facilities to this plan.

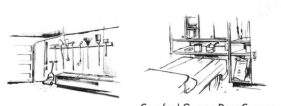

Crawford Garage Door Company

Fig. 15–17. Garage storage.

Fig. 15–19. Add storage facilities to this plan.

4. How many square feet of storage area are there in Fig. 15–19? Is this at least 7 percent of the area of the house?

5. Add storage facilities to the first floor and basement of the house shown in Fig. 15–20. Sketch your solution and label each storage area.

6. Plan lighting and dust-free design for all your closets. Sketch your proposals.

7. Know these architectural terms: *wardrobe closet, walk-in closet, wall closet, room divider, cabinets.*

Fig. 15–20. Sketch and label storage areas on this plan.

Home Planners Inc.

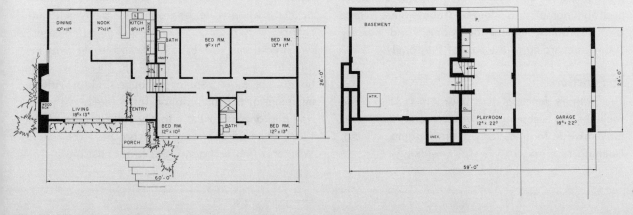

SECTION THREE. SLEEPING AREA

One-third of our time is spent in sleeping. Because of its importance the sleeping area should be planned to provide facilities for maximum comfort and relaxation. The sleeping area is usually located in a quiet part of the house and contains bedrooms, baths, dressing areas, and nurseries.

Unit 16. Bedrooms

Houses are usually classified by size according to the number of bedrooms; for example, a "three-bedroom home" or a "four-bedroom home." There are bedrooms, master bedrooms, and nursery rooms, according to the size of the family.

▶ Function

The primary function of a bedroom is to provide facilities for sleeping. However, some bedrooms may provide facilities for writing, reading, sewing, listening to music, or generally relaxing.

▶ Number of Bedrooms

Ideally, each member of the family should have his or her own private bedroom. A family with no children may require only one bedroom. However, two bedrooms are usually desirable, to provide one for guest use (Fig. 16–1). Three-bedroom homes are most popular because they provide a minimum of accommodation for a family with one boy and one girl. As the family enlarges, boys can share one bedroom and girls can share the other. With only two bedrooms, this is not possible.

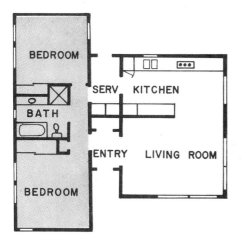

Fig. 16-1. *The sleeping area should be away from the activity area of the home.*

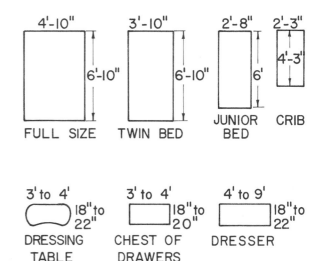

Fig. 16-3. *Bedroom furniture sizes.*

Often a fourth bedroom is included in the plan, even though it may not be needed. If it is not used immediately as a bedroom, it may be converted into a den or study and still double as a guest bedroom.

▶ Sizes and Shapes

The size and shape of a bedroom depend upon the amount of furniture needed. A minimum-sized bedroom would accommodate a single bed, bed-side table, and dresser. In contrast, a complete master bedroom might include a double bed or twin beds, bedside stands, dresser, chest of

Fig. 16-2. *A dressing area adjacent to the master bedroom.*

Masonite Corporation

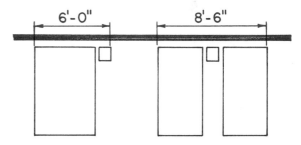

Fig. 16-4. *Wall space is needed for bedroom furniture.*

drawers, lounge chair, dressing area, and adjacent master bath (Fig. 16-2).

Space requirements. The type and style of furniture included in the bedroom should be chosen before the size of the bedroom is established. The size of the furniture should determine the size of the room, and not the reverse. Average bedroom furniture sizes are shown in Fig. 16-3. The wall space needed for twin beds is 8'-6''. A full bed with a night stand requires 6' wall space (Fig. 16-4).

A small bedroom would average from 90 to 100 square feet, (Fig. 16-5), an average bedroom from 100 to 150 square feet, (Fig. 16-6), and a large bedroom over 200 square feet (Fig. 16-7).

Fig. 16-5. A small bedroom.

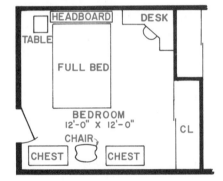

Fig. 16-6. An average-sized bedroom.

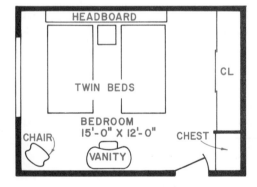

Fig. 16-7. A large bedroom.

Wall space. Since wall space is critical in the placement of furniture in the bedroom, the designer must plan for maximum wall space. One method of conserving wall space for bedroom furniture placement is the utilization of high windows which allow the location of furniture underneath. High ribbon-type windows also provide some privacy for the bedroom.

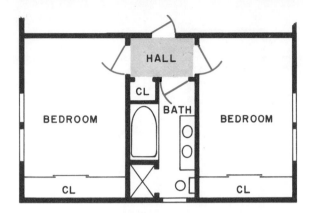

Fig. 16-8. Doors should not open into halls.

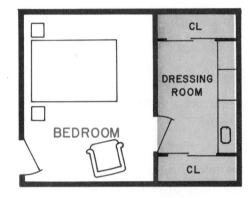

Fig. 16-9. A dressing area.

Bedroom doors. Unless it has doors leading to a patio, the bedroom will normally have only one access door from the inside. Entrance doors, closet doors, and windows should be grouped to conserve wall space whenever possible. Separating these doors slightly will spread out the amount of unusable wall space by eliminating long stretches of unused wall space. Sliding doors for closets and for entrance doors help to conserve valuable wall space in bedrooms. If swinging doors are used, the door should always swing into the bedroom and not into the hall (Fig. 16-8).

▶ **Dressing Areas**

Dressing areas are sometimes separate rooms or an alcove or a part of the room separated by a divider (Fig. 16-9).

▶ Noise Control

Since noise contributes to fatigue, it is important to plan for the elimination of as much noise as possible from the bedroom area (Fig. 16–10). The following guides for noise control will help you design bedrooms that are quiet and restful:

1. The bedroom should be in the quiet part of the house, away from major street noises.

2. Carpeting or soft cork helps absorb many noises.

3. Rooms above a bedroom should be carpeted.

4. Floor-to-ceiling draperies help to reduce noise.

5. Acoustical tile in the ceiling is effective in reducing noise.

6. Trees and shrubbery outside the bedroom help deaden sounds.

7. The use of Thermopane glass in windows and sliding doors helps to seal off the bedroom.

8. The windows of an air-conditioned room may be kept closed even during hot weather. Air conditioning eliminates much noise and aids in keeping the bedroom free from dust and pollen.

9. Air is a good insulator; therefore, closets provide additional buffers which eliminate much noise coming from other rooms.

10. In extreme cases when complete sound-proofing is desired, fibrous materials in the walls may be used, and studs may be offset to provide a sound buffer.

11. Placing rubber pads under appliances such as refrigerators, dishwashers, washers, and dryers often eliminates much vibration and noise throughout the house.

▶ Storage Space

Storage space in the bedroom is needed primarily for clothing and personal accessories. Storage areas should be easily accessible, easily maintained, and adequate in volume. Walk-in closets or wardrobe closets should be built-in for hanging clothes (Fig. 16–11). Care should be taken to eliminate offset closets. Balancing offset closets from one room to an adjacent bedroom helps solve

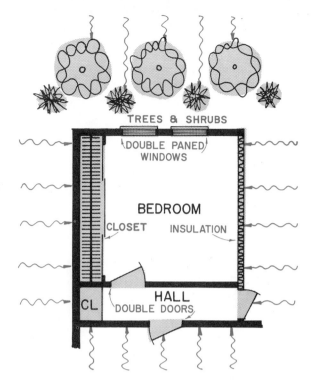

Fig. 16–10. Bedroom noise control.

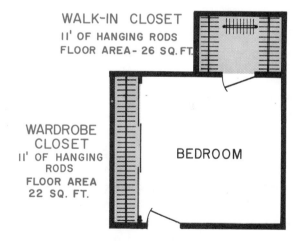

Fig. 16–11. Hanging rods are best for storing clothing.

this problem. Except for the storage space provided in dressers, chests, vanities, and dressing tables, most storage space in the bedroom should be provided for by the closet. Adequate hanging space and shelf storage (Fig. 16–12) should be provided.

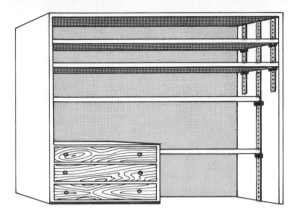

Fig. 16-12. Adequate shelf storage is needed.

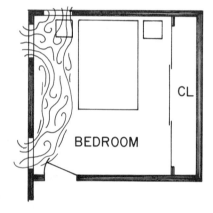

Fig. 16-13. Cross-ventilation is desirable.

▶ Ventilation

Proper ventilation is necessary and is conducive to sound rest and sleep. Central air conditioning and humidity control provide constant levels of temperature and humidity and are the best method of providing ventilation and air circulation. When air conditioning is available, the windows and doors may remain closed. Without air conditioning, windows and doors must provide the ventila-

Fig. 16-14. Louvered or jalousie windows direct air circulation upward.

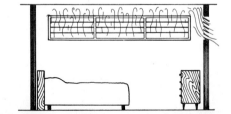

100

BABY'S BEDROOM
11'-0" x 9'-0"

CHILD'S BEDROOM
11'-0" x 9'-0"

TEEN AGER'S BEDROOM
11'-0" x 9'-0"

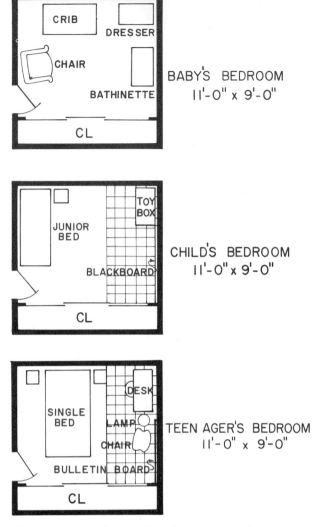

Fig. 16-15. Bedroom furnishings must change as children grow older.

tion. Bedrooms should have cross-ventilation. However, the draft must not pass over the bed (Fig. 16-13). High ribbon windows provide light, privacy, and cross-ventilation without causing a draft on the bed (Fig. 16-14). Jalousie windows are also very effective, since they direct the air flow upward.

▶ Nurseries

Children's bedrooms and nurseries need special facilities. They must be planned to be comfortable, quiet and sufficiently flexible to change as the

Southern California Edison Company

Fig. 16–16. Study facilities must be provided for school-age children.

child grows and matures (Fig. 16–15). Storage shelves and rods in closets should be adjustable so that they may be raised as the child becomes taller. Light switches should be placed low, with a delay switch which allows the light to stay on for some time after the switch has been thrown.

Chalkboards and bulletin boards help make the child's room usable. Adequate facilities for study and some hobby activities should be provided, such as a desk and work table (Fig. 16–16). Storage space for books, models, and athletic equipment is also desirable. Figures 16–17 and 16–18 show a room that has been converted from a nursery to a room for teen-agers.

▶ Decor

Bedrooms should be decorated in quiet, restful tones. Matching or contrasting bedspreads, draperies, and carpets help accent the color scheme. Uncluttered furniture with simple lines also helps to develop a restful atmosphere in the bedroom.

Armstrong Cork Company

Fig. 16–17. A few changes can convert a child's room into a room for a teen-ager.

Fig. 16–18. A room converted for teen-age use.

Armstrong Cork Company.

Problems

1. Design a bedroom, 100 square feet in size, for a very young child.
2. Design a bedroom, 150 square feet in size, for a teen-ager.

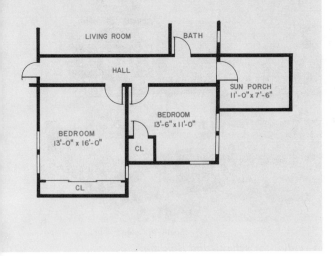

Fig. 16–19. Redesign the sleeping area for a family of four.

3. Design a master bedroom which is 200 square feet in size.

4. List five things which make a bedroom comfortable for you. Draw the furniture and show its placement to illustrate your list.

5. How could you make your own bedroom more comfortable?

6. A family composed of a mother, a father, and a baby bought a home with the bedroom area shown in Fig. 16–19. The family has expanded and now consists of the mother, the father, and two teen-agers. Redesign their bedroom area to fit their needs. Additional area may be added to the exterior of the house.

7. Define these architectural terms: *alcove, insulation, acoustical tile, cross-ventilation, weather stripping.*

Unit 17. Baths

The design of the bathroom requires careful planning, as does every other room in the house. The bath must be planned to be functional, attractive, and easily maintained.

▶ Function

In addition to the normal functions of the bath, facilities may also be included for dressing, exercising, sunning, and laundering (Fig. 17–1). Design-

Fig. 17–1. A bath may be designed for many functions.

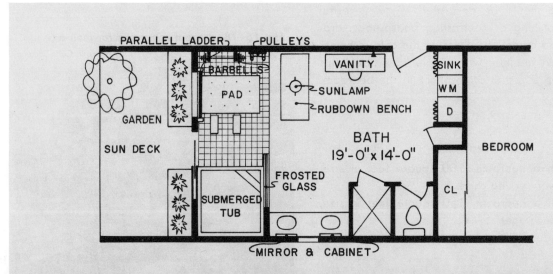

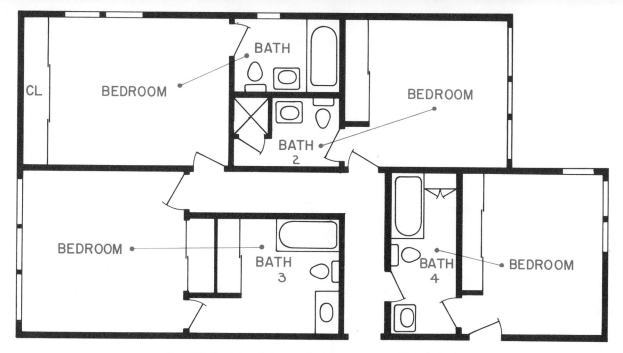

Fig. 17–2. A bath for each bedroom would be ideal.

ing the bath involves the appropriate placing of fixtures; providing for adequate ventilation, lighting, and heating; and planning efficient runs for plumbing pipes.

Ideally it would be advisable to provide a bath for each bedroom, as in Fig. 17–2. Usually this provision is not possible, and a central bath is designed to meet the needs of the entire family (Fig. 17–3). A bath for general use and a bath adjacent to the master bedroom are a most desirable compromise (Fig. 17–4). When it is impossible to have a bath with the master bedroom, the general bath should be accessible from all bedrooms in the sleeping area. A bath may also function as a dressing room (Fig. 17–5). In this case, a combination bath and dressing room with space for clothing storage can be placed between the bathroom and the bedroom.

Fixtures. The three basic fixtures included in most bathrooms are a lavatory, water closet, and tub or shower (Fig. 17–6). The efficiency of the bath is greatly dependent upon the effectiveness of the arrangement of these three fixtures. Mirrors should be located a distance from the tub to pre-

Fig. 17–3. A central bath serves the entire family.

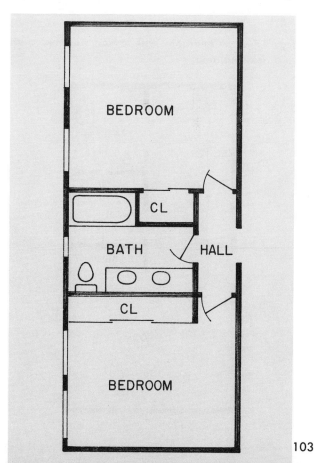

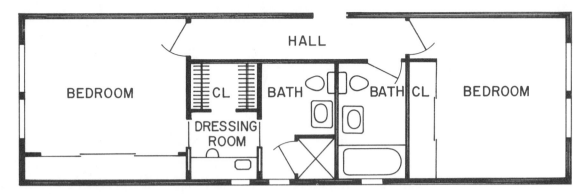

Fig. 17–4. A bath for the master bedroom and another bath for other bedrooms is a convenient arrangement.

vent fogging. Sinks should be well lighted and free from traffic. If sinks are placed 18″ from other fixtures, they need no separate plumbing lines. The water closet needs a minimum of 15″ from the center to the side wall or other fixtures (Fig. 17–7). Tubs and showers are available in a great variety of sizes and shapes. Square, rectangular, or

sunken-pool types of tubs allow flexibility in fixture arrangement.

Ventilation. Baths should have either natural ventilation from a window or forced ventilation from an exhaust fan. However, care should be taken not to place windows in a position where they will cause a draft on the tub or interfere with privacy.

Lighting. Lighting should be relatively shadowless in the area used for grooming (Fig. 17–8).

Fig. 17–5. A bedroom with a compartment bath and dressing area.

Fig. 17–6. The three basic bathroom fixtures.
Eljer Plumbing Company

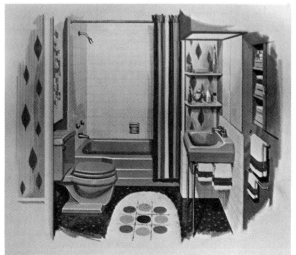

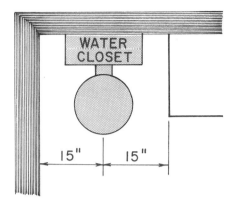

Fig. 17–7. Water-closet spacing.

Shadowless general lighting can be achieved by the use of fluorescent tubes on the ceiling, covered with plastic panels, as shown in Fig. 17–9.

Heating. Heating in the bath is most important to prevent chills. In addition to the conventional heating outlets, an electric heater or heat lamp is often used to provide instant heat. It is advisable to have the source of heat under the window to eliminate drafts. All heaters should be properly ventilated.

Fig. 17–8. Shadowless lighting is desirable.

Eljer Plumbing Co.

C. R. Campbell Home

Fig. 17–9. Continuous fluorescent tubes under frosted glass help to diffuse light.

Plumbing lines. The plumbing lines that carry water to and from the fixtures should be concealed and minimized as much as possible. When two bathrooms are placed side by side, placing the fixtures back to back on opposite sides of the plumbing wall results in considerable reduction of the length of plumbing lines (Fig. 17–10). In multiple-story dwellings, the length of plumbing lines can be reduced and a common plumbing wall used if the baths are placed directly above each

Fig. 17–10. Fixture arrangements that compact plumbing lines.

The Mosaic Tile Company

Fig. 17–11. Compartment-type bath.

Fig. 17–13. A minimum-sized bath.

4'-0" x 5'-0"

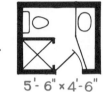

Fig. 17–14. A small bath.

5'-6" x 4'-6"

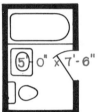

Fig. 17–15. An average-sized bath.

other, with the plumbing walls aligned. When a bath is placed on a second floor, a plumbing wall must be provided through the first floor for the soil and water pipes.

Layout. There are two basic types of bathroom layout, the compartment type and the open-plan type. In the *compartment plan,* partitions (sliding doors, glass dividers, louvers, or even plants) are used to divide the bath into several compartments, one housing the water closet, another the lavatory area, and the third the bathing area (Fig. 17–11). In the *open plan,* all fixtures are visible.

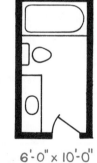

Fig. 17–16. A large bath.

6'-0" x 10'-0"

Fig. 17–12. Typical fixture sizes.

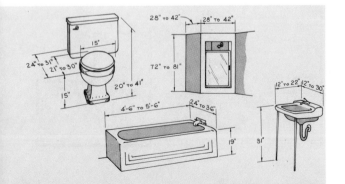

A bath designed for, or used partially by, children should include a low or tilt-down mirror, benches for reaching the lavatory, low towel racks, and shelves for personal items and bath toys.

▶ Size and Shape

The size and shape of the bath are influenced by the spacing of basic fixtures, the number of auxiliary functions requiring additional equipment, the arrangement or compartmentalization of areas, and the relationship to other rooms in the house.

Fig. 17–17. Waterproof materials should be used in the bath.

Furniture. Typical fixture sizes, as shown in Fig. 17–12, greatly influence the ultimate size of the bath. Figure 17–13 shows a minimum-sized bath. Figure 17–14 shows the dimensions of a small bath. Figure 17–15 is an average bath, and Fig. 17–16 is considered a rather large bath. Regardless of the size, these baths contain the three basic fixtures: lavatory, tub, and water closet.

The sizes given here refer to complete baths and not to half-baths, which include only a lava-

Fig. 17–18. Use light to create a spacious effect.

tory and water closet and are used in conjunction with the living area and therefore not designed for bathing.

Accessories. In addition to the three basic fixtures, the following accessories are most desirable in a bath designed for optimum use:

  combination exhaust fan
  sunlamp
  heat lamp or instant wall heater
  medicine cabinet, preferably with a lock to
    keep children from opening it
  extensive use of mirrors above the lavatory
  magnifying mirror and steamproof mirrors
  extra counter space for personal items
  dressing table
  whirlpool bath
  foot-pedal control for water
  single-mixing, one-control faucets

  facility for linen storage
  clothes hamper

▶ Decor

The bath should be decorated and designed to provide the maximum amount of light and color. Materials used in the bath should be water-resistant, easily maintained, and easily sanitized (Fig. 17–17). Tiles, linoleum, marble, Formica, and glass are excellent materials for bathroom use. If wallpaper or wood paneling is used, it should be waterproof. If plastered or dry wall construction is exposed, a gloss or semi-gloss paint should be used on the surface.

Fixtures and accessories should match in color. Fixtures are now available in a variety of pastel colors. Matching counter tops and cabinets are also available. An extensive use of mirrors, glass blocks, and large windows is effective in creating the impression of more space in the bath (Fig. 17–18).

Towels, colored decanters, and tiles can help accent or contrast the basic color scheme of the bath.

Problems

1. Make a plan for adding fixtures to the drawings in Fig. 17–19.
2. Draw a plan for remodeling the bathroom in Fig. 17–20 and make it more efficient.
3. Draw a plan for remodeling the bathroom in Fig. 17–21 and make it more efficient.
4. Sketch a plan for remodeling and make the bathroom in Fig. 17–22 into two separate baths, one accessible from the hall and the other adjoining the bedroom.
5. Make a plan for arranging the rooms in Fig. 17–23 to form a two-bathroom home. Add hall space as needed.
6. Design one bedroom and bath in an area of $12' \times 17'$.

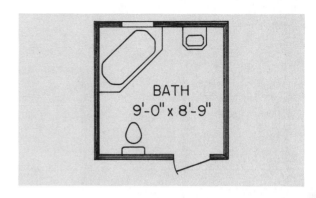

Fig. 17–21. Remodel this bath.

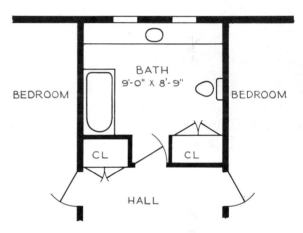

Fig. 17–22. Rearrange these fixtures.

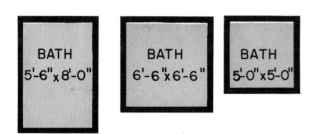

Fig. 17–19. Add fixtures to these plans.

Fig. 17–23. Rearrange this plan.

Fig. 17–20. Remodel this bath.

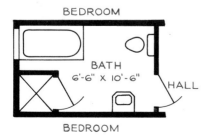

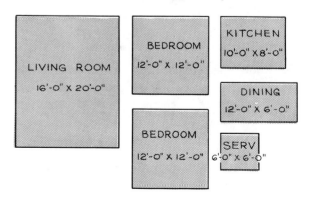

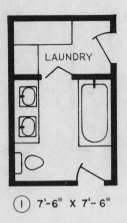

① 7'-6" X 7'-6"

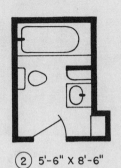

② 5'-6" X 8'-6"

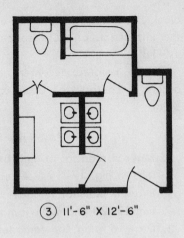

③ 11'-6" X 12'-6"

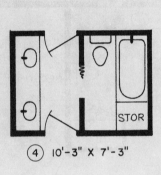

④ 10'-3" X 7'-3"

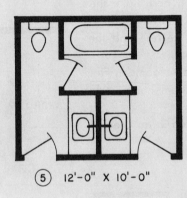

⑤ 12'-0" X 10'-0"

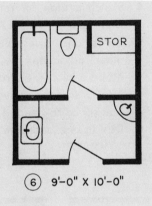

⑥ 9'-0" X 10'-0"

7. Design two bedrooms and a bath in an area 13' × 34'.

8. Design two bedrooms and a bath and a master-bedroom bath in an area of 350 square feet.

9. Redesign the floor plan shown in Fig. 24–9. Add two bedrooms and expand bath facilities to accommodate these rooms. Use Fig. 17–24 as a guide.

10. Know these architectural terms: *water closet, lavatory, fixture, open bath, sunken tub, shower stall, neo-angle tub, square tub, rectangular tub.*

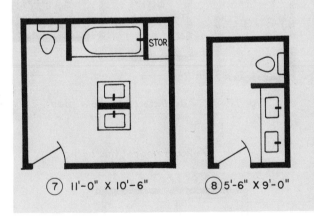

⑦ 11'-0" X 10'-6"

⑧ 5'-6" X 9'-0"

Fig. 17–24. Typical bath layouts.

PART II

Basic Architectural Plans

The general design of a structure is interpreted through several basic architectural plans. These include floor plans, elevations, and pictorial drawings. *Floor plans* show the arrangement of the internal parts of the design. *Elevations* graphically describe the exterior design. *Pictorial drawings* are prepared to show how the structure will appear when complete. In Part II you will learn how to prepare these basic architectural drawings.

Rendering by George A. Parenti for the Masonite Corporation

SECTION FOUR. DRAFTING TECHNIQUES

Most of the drafting skills and techniques used in architectural work are similar to those you have learned in mechanical drawing courses. However, there are some drafting procedures that are somewhat different. These involve the use of line techniques, various templates, lettering practices, timesaving devices, and dimensioning practices. The differences are primarily due to the large size of most architectural drawings and to the great speed with which architectural plans must be prepared. For these reasons architectural drawings contain many abbreviated techniques.

Unit 18. Architectural Line Weights

Architects use various line weights to emphasize or deemphasize areas of a drawing. Architectural draftsmen also use different line weights. Architectural line weights are standardized in order to make possible the consistent interpretation of architectural drawings. Figure 18–1 shows some of the common types of lines and line weights used on architectural drawings. You should learn the name of the line, the number of the pencil used to make the line, and the technique used to draw the line.

▶ Alphabet of Lines

Hard pencils, as shown in Fig. 18–2, are used for architectural layout work. Medium pencils are used for most final lines, and soft pencils are used

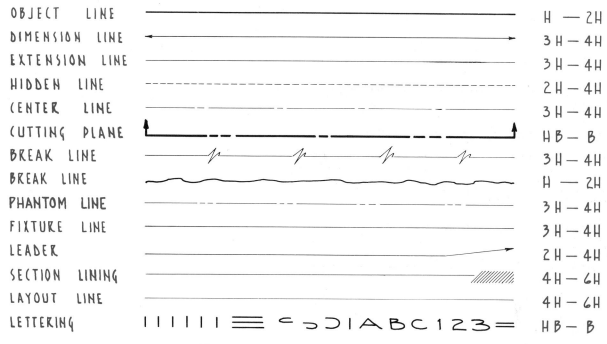

OBJECT LINE	H — 2H
DIMENSION LINE	3H — 4H
EXTENSION LINE	3H — 4H
HIDDEN LINE	2H — 4H
CENTER LINE	3H — 4H
CUTTING PLANE	HB — B
BREAK LINE	3H — 4H
BREAK LINE	H — 2H
PHANTOM LINE	3H — 4H
FIXTURE LINE	3H — 4H
LEADER	2H — 4H
SECTION LINING	4H — 6H
LAYOUT LINE	4H — 6H
LETTERING	HB — B

Fig. 18–1. Architectural line weights.

for lettering, cutting-plane lines, and shading pictorial drawings. Figure 18–2 shows a comparison of the various types of pencils and the lines they produce.

Floor-plan lines. Figure 18–3 shows some of the common lines used on architectural floor plans.

Object, or *visible, lines* are used to show the main outline of the building, including exterior walls, interior partitions, porches, patios, driveways, and walls. These lines should be the outstanding lines on the drawing.

Dimension lines are thin unbroken lines upon which building dimensions are placed.

Fig. 18–2. Pencils used for architectural drawing.

HARD   MEDIUM   SOFT

9H 8H 7H 6H 5H 4H 3H 2H H F HB B 2B 3B 4B 5B 6B 7B

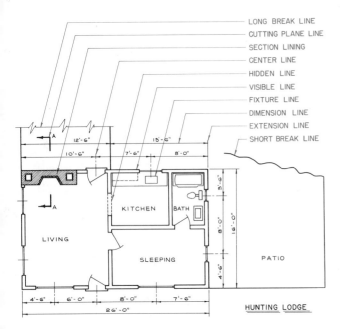

Fig. 18-3. Types of lines used on floor plans.

Extension lines extend from the building to permit dimensioning. They are drawn very lightly to eliminate confusion with the building outlines.

Hidden lines are used to show areas which are not visible on the surface but which exist behind the plane of projection. Hidden lines are also used in floor plans to show objects *above* the floor section, such as wall cabinets, arches, and beams.

Center lines denote the center of symmetrical objects such as exterior doors and windows. These lines are usually necessary for dimensioning purposes.

Cutting-plane lines are very heavy lines used to denote an area to be sectioned. The cutting-plane line often does not extend completely through the area to be sectioned, because it would interfere with other lines on the drawing. In this case, the only part of the line drawn is the extreme end of the line.

Break lines are used when an area cannot or should not be drawn entirely. A ruled line with free-hand breaks is used for long, straight breaks. A wavy, uneven freehand line is used for smaller, irregular breaks.

Phantom lines are used to indicate alternate positions of moving parts, adjacent positions of related parts, and for repeated detail.

Fixture lines outline the shape of kitchen, laundry, and bathroom fixtures, or built-in furniture. These lines are light to eliminate confusion with object lines.

Leaders are used to connect a note or dimension to part of the building. They are drawn lightly and sometimes are curved to eliminate confusion with other lines.

Section lines are used to draw the section lining in sectional drawings. A different material symbol is used for each building material. The section lining is drawn lightly enough to recede from the object lines.

Elevation lines. Figure 18-4 shows the application of the lines used on architectural elevation drawings. The technique and weight of each of the lines are exactly the same as those for the lines used on floor plans except that they are drawn on a vertical plane.

▶ **Paper**

Since the type of paper on which the line is drawn will greatly affect the line weight, different pencils may be necessary. Weather conditions, such as temperature and, to a greater degree, humidity, also greatly affect the line quality. In summer or during periods of high humidity, harder pencils must be employed.

Fig. 18-4. Types of lines used on elevation drawings.

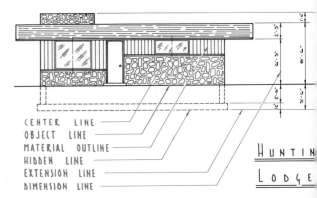

Problems

1. Identify the types of lines indicated by the letters in Fig. 18–5.

2. List the grade of pencil you would use to draw each of the lines shown in Figs. 18–3 and 18–4.

3. Practice drawing each of the lines shown in Fig. 18–1, using your T square and triangle.

4. Draw an object line, a dimension line, and a cutting-plane line on several different surfaces, such as tracing paper, tracing cloth, vellum, bond paper, and illustration board. Compare the results.

5. Define these terms: *line weights, alphabet of lines, hard lead, soft lead, object lines, dimension lines, extension lines, hidden lines, center lines, cutting-plane lines, break lines, phantom lines, fixture lines, leaders, section lines, elevation lines.*

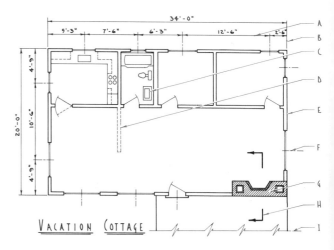

Fig. 18–5. Identify the types of lines.

Unit 19. The Architect's Scale

The architect's scale is the trademark of the architect, just as the stethoscope is the universal trademark of the physician.

▶ Reduced Scale

The architect's scale is used to reduce the size of a structure so that it can be drawn on paper of standard size; or it is used to enlarge a detail that may be too small to interpret or to dimension accurately (Fig. 19–1).

Divisions. Architect's scales are either open-divided or fully divided. In *fully divided scales* each main unit on the scale is fully subdivided throughout the scale. On o*pen-divided scales,* only the main units of the scale are graduated, with a fully subdivided extra unit at each end, as shown in Fig. 19–2. The main function of an architect's scale is to enable the architect, designer, and draftsman to think in relation to the actual size of the struc-

Fig. 19–1. An architect using an architect's scale.

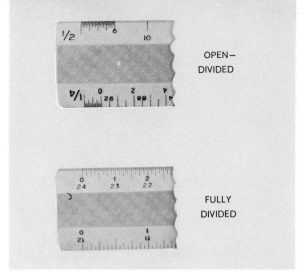

OPEN—DIVIDED

FULLY DIVIDED

Fredrick Post Company

Fig. 19–2. Types of graduation.

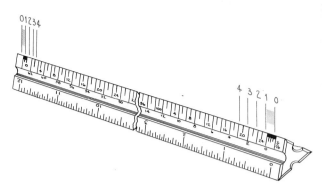

Fig. 19–5. The scale that reads from right to left is twice as large as the scale that reads from left to right.

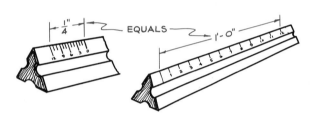

Fig. 19–3. ¼″ may represent 1′-0″ on a drawing.

ture and to convert these measurements into smaller values for illustration purposes. For example, when a drawing is prepared to a reduced scale in which 1′ (12″) is actually drawn ¼″ long, the architect does not think of this ¼″ line as representing ¼″

but as actually being 1′ long on the reduced scale, as shown in Fig. 19–3.

Types. Architect's scales are of either the bevel or the triangular type, as shown in Fig. 19–4. You will notice that the triangular scale has six sides which will accommodate a full scale of 12″ graduated into 16 parts to an inch, and ten other scales (two on each face), which include ratios of 3/32, 1/8, 3/16, 1/4, 3/8, 1/2, 3/4, 1, 1-1/2, and 3. Two scales are located on each face. One scale reads from left to right. The other scale, which is twice as large, reads from right to left. For example, the ¼″ scale and, half of this, the ⅛″ scale are placed on the same face. Similarly, the ¾″ scale and the ⅜″ scale are placed on the same face but are read from different directions. Be sure

Fig. 19–4. Types of architect's scales.

Fredrick Post Company

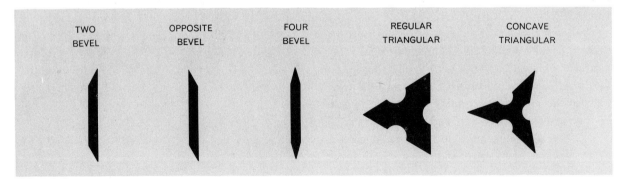

TWO BEVEL | OPPOSITE BEVEL | FOUR BEVEL | REGULAR TRIANGULAR | CONCAVE TRIANGULAR

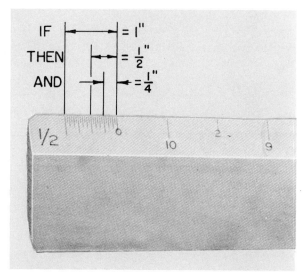

Fredrick Post Company

Fig. 19-6. If ½'' equals 1'', then ¼'' equals ½'', and ⅛'' equals ¼''.

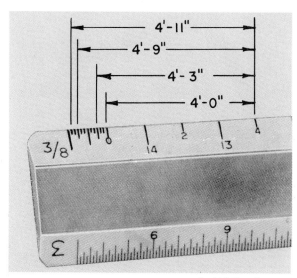

Fredrick Post Company

Fig. 19-8. Subdivisions at the end of an open-divided scale are used for inch measurement.

you are reading in the correct direction. Otherwise your measurement could be wrong, since the second row of numbers read from the opposite side at half scale, or twice the scale, as the case may be, as seen in Fig. 19-5.

The architect's scale can be used to make the divisions of the scale equal 1' or 1''. For example,

Fig. 19-7. If ½'' equals 1'-0'', then ¼'' equals 6'', and ⅛'' equals 3''.

Fredrick Post Company

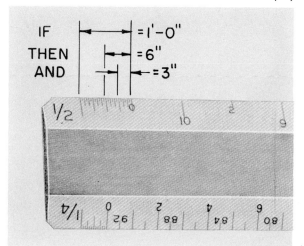

in the ½'' scale shown in Fig. 19-6, this ½'' represents 1'', and the same scale in Fig. 19-7 is shown representing 1'. Therefore ½'' can equal 1'' or 1'.

Since buildings are large, most major architectural drawings use a scale which relates the parts of an inch to a foot. Architectural details such as cabinet construction and joints often use the parts of an inch to represent 1''. In either case, on open-divided scales, which are almost universally used, the divided section at the end of the scale is not a part of the numerical scale. When measuring with the scale, start with the zero line, not with the fully divided section. Always start with the number of feet you wish to measure and then add the additional inches in the subdivided area. For example, in Fig. 19-8 the distance of 4'-11'' is derived by measuring from the line 4 to 0, then 11'' past 0, since each of the lines in the subdivided parts equals 1''. On smaller scales these lines may equal only 2'', but on larger scales they may equal ½''. Figure 19-9 shows a further application of this use of the architect's scale. You will notice that the dimensioned distance of 8'-0'' extends from the 8 to the 0 on the scale, and the 6'' wall is shown

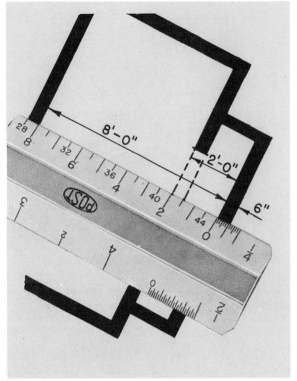

Fredrick Post Company

Fig. 19-9. Subdivisions of the architect's scale can be used to indicate overall dimensions and sub-dimensions.

as one-half of the subdivided foot on the end. Likewise you can read the distance of 2'-0'' on the ¼'' scale shown in this illustration.

Scale selection. The selection of the proper scale is sometimes difficult. If the structure to be drawn is extremely large, a small scale must be used. Smaller structures can be drawn on a larger scale, since they will not take up as much space on the drawing sheet. Most floor plans, elevations, and foundation plans of residences are drawn to ¼'' scale, whereas construction details pertaining to these drawings are often drawn to ½'', ¾'', or even 1'' = 1'. Remember that, as the scale changes, not only does the length of each line increase or decrease but the width of the various wall thicknesses and areas also increases or decreases. The actual appearance of a typical corner wall

drawn to ¹⁄₁₆'' = 1'-0'', ⅛'' = 1'-0'', ¼'' = 1'-0'', and ½'' = 1'-0'' is shown in Fig. 19-10. You can readily see that the wall drawn to the scale of ¹⁄₁₆'' = 1'-0'' is small and that much detail would be impossible. The ½'' = 1'-0'' wall would probably cover too large an area on the drawing if the building were very large. Therefore, the ¼'' and ⅛'' scales are the most popular for this type of work.

Use of scale. The architect's scale is only as accurate as its user and as the sharpness of his pencil. In using the scale, do not accumulate distances; that is, always lay out overall dimensions first—the width and the length. These will be correct and their position cannot change if you are slightly off in measuring any of the subdivisions that make up the overall dimension. Furthermore, if your overall dimensions are correct, you will find it easier to check your subdimensions, since if one is off, another will also be incorrect (Fig. 19-11).

Figure 19-12 shows the comparative distances used to measure 1'-9'' as it appears on various

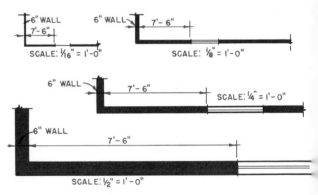

Fig. 19-10. Comparison of a similar wall drawn in several different scales.

Fig. 19-11. Establish overall dimensions first.

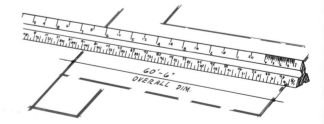

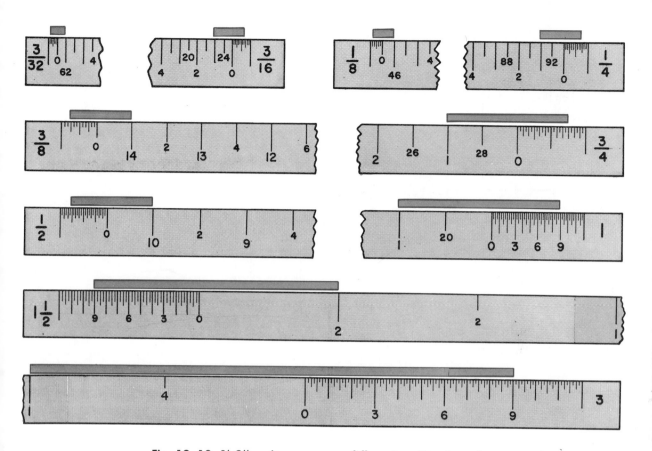

Fig. 19–12. 1'-9'' as it appears on different architect's scales.

Fig. 19–13. 5'-6'' shown on several architect's scales.

5'-6" on the 1"=1'-0" scale

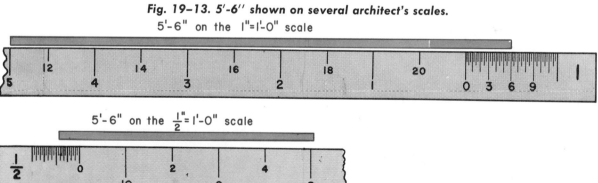

5'-6" on the $\frac{1}{2}$"= 1'-0" scale

5'-6" on the $\frac{1}{8}$"=1'-0" scale   5'-6" on the $\frac{1}{4}$"= 1'-0" scale

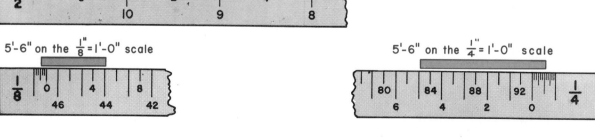

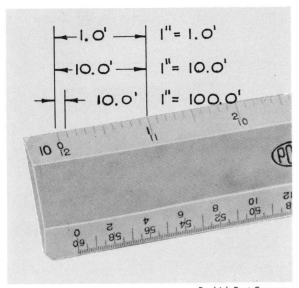

Fredrick Post Company

Fig. 19-14. The decimal scale.

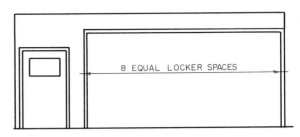

ELEVATION OF SOUTH WALL

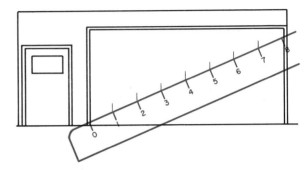

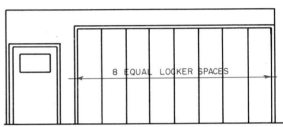

Fig. 19-16. Dividing an area into an equal number of parts.

architect's scales. All these scales represent 1'-9" as a reduced size. This same comparison would exist if we related the scales to 1" rather than 1'. In this case, a distance of 1¾" would correspond to 1'-9" on the foot representation. In this case the ³⁄₃₂", ³⁄₁₆", ⅛", ¼", ⅜", ½", and ¾" scales represent a distance smaller than 1¾", and the 1½" and 3" scales represent a distance 1½ and 3 times as large as the full scale. Figure 19-13

Fig. 19-15. A decimal scale of 30'-0" equal to 1".

Fredrick Post Company

shows the same comparison, using a distance of 5'-6" on the foot-equivalent scale. If an inch-equivalent scale were used, the distance shown would be 5½" in each case.

Decimal scale. In plot plans, surveys, and many landscape plans a decimal scale is used because various surveyors' and topographic maps are prepared on the basis of the metric system. A decimal scale divided into tenths can represent 1' = 1", 10' = 1', or 100' = 1', as shown in Fig. 19-14. Since large tracts of land are drawn on surveys and plot plan drawings, relationships of 20', 30', 40', 50', or 60' = 1" are quite common. Figure 19-15 shows a scale of 30' = 1".

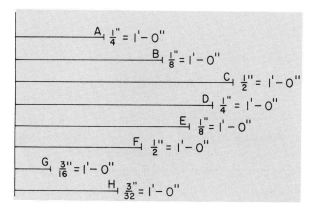

Fig. 19–17. *Measure these distances.*

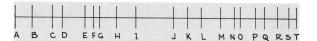

Fig. 19–18. *Measure the distances between the letters.*

▶ Full Architect's Scale

The full architect's scale is useful in dividing any area into an equal number of parts. The following are the steps involved:

1. Scale the distance available, as shown in Fig. 19–16.

2. Place the zero point of the architect's scale on one side of the area.

3. Align the other side with any even number digit that will divide into the number of areas needed.

4. Draw lines dividing this area.

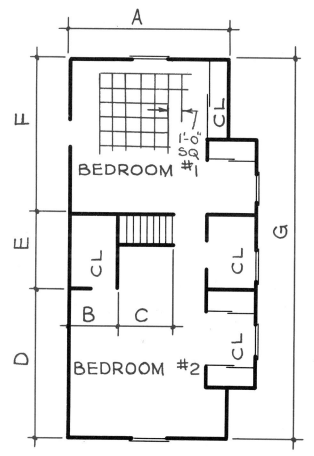

Fig. 19–19. *List the sizes of each room shown in this plan.*

Problems

1. Measure the distances indicated on the horizontal lines, using the scale indicated in Fig. 19–17.

2. Measure the distances between the following letters in Fig. 19–18, using the ¼″ = 1'-0″ scale: AB, AL, DE, EJ, KO, ST, FT, CK, EP.

3. Measure the same distances shown in Problem 2, using the ⅛″ = 1″ scale.

4. Answer the following questions concerning the plans shown in Fig. 19–19:

   a. What is the overall length of the building?

   b. What are the dimensions of Bedroom 1, including the closets?

   c. What is the length of the stairwell opening?

   d. What are the dimensions of Bedroom 2?

   e. Determine the length of dimensions A through G.

5. What scale has been used in the drawings in Fig. 1–8, page 15; Fig. 3–7, page 31; and Fig. 5–7, page 38?

6. Define these terms: *open-divided, fully divided, architect's scale, decimal scale, triangular scale, reduced scale, division, inch-equivalent scale, foot-equivalent scale, full scale.*

Unit 20. Drafting Instruments

A course in mechanical drawing usually precedes a course in architectural drawing. Therefore only the procedures, practices, and techniques which specifically relate to the use of instruments for architectural drafting are presented in this unit.

▶ T Square

The T square is used primarily as a guide for drawing horizontal lines and for guiding the triangle when drawing vertical and inclined lines. The T square is also the most useful instrument for drawing extremely long lines that deviate from the horizontal plane. Common T-square lengths for use in architectural drafting are 18″, 24″, 30″, 36″, and 42″.

T squares must be held tightly against the edge of the drawing board, and triangles must be held firmly against the T square to ensure accurate horizontal and vertical lines. Since only one end of the T square is held against the drawing board, considerable sag occurs when extremely long T squares are not held securely.

Horizontal lines. Horizontal lines are always drawn with the aid of some instrument such as the T square, parallel slide, or drafting machine. In drawing horizontal lines with the T square, the head of the T square is held firmly against the left working edge of the drawing board (if you are right-handed). This procedure keeps the blade in a horizontal position to draw horizontal lines from left to right. Figure 20–1 shows the T square placed on the drawing board in the correct manner for drawing floor plans and elevations. Figure 20–2 shows the correct method of drawing horizontal lines by the use of the T square.

Vertical lines. Triangles are used with the T square for drawing vertical or inclined lines. The 8″, 45° × 90° triangle and the 10″, 30° × 60° triangle are preferred for architectural work. Figure 20–2 shows the correct method of drawing vertical lines by the use of the T square and triangle.

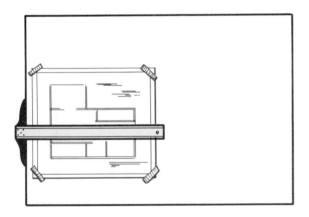

Fig. 20–1. A T square placed on a drawing board.

Fig. 20–2. Method of drawing horizontal and vertical lines with a T square.

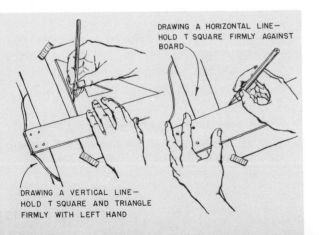

DRAWING A HORIZONTAL LINE—HOLD T SQUARE FIRMLY AGAINST BOARD

DRAWING A VERTICAL LINE—HOLD T SQUARE AND TRIANGLE FIRMLY WITH LEFT HAND

▶ Parallel Slide

The parallel slide performs the same function as the T square. It is used as a guide for drawing horizontal lines and as a base for aligning triangles in drawing vertical lines.

Extremely long lines are common in many architectural drawings such as floor plans and elevations. Since most of these lines should be drawn continuously, the parallel slide is used extensively by architectural draftsmen.

The parallel slide is anchored at both sides of the drawing board, as shown in Fig. 20–3. This

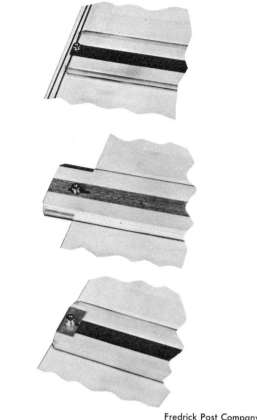

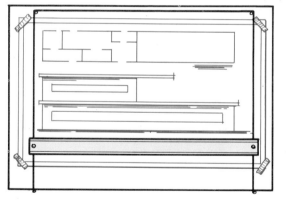

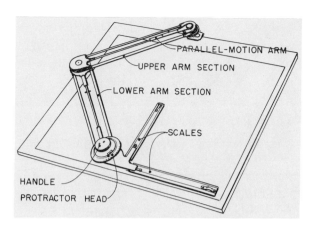

Fig. 20-4. A drafting machine.

Fig. 20-3. Use of the parallel slide.

attachment eliminates the possibility of sag at one end, which is a common objection to the use of the T square.

In using the parallel slide the drawing board can be tilted to a very acute angle without causing the slide to fall to the bottom of the board. If the parallel slide is adjusted correctly, it will stay in the exact position in which it is placed.

▶ Drafting Machine

Use of the drafting machine eliminates the need for the architect's scale, triangle, T square, or parallel slide. A drafting machine consists of a head to which two scales are attached (Fig. 20–4). These scales (arms) of the drafting machine are graduated like other architect's scales and are available in aluminum and plastic. The two scales are attached to the head of the drafting machine perpendicular to each other. The horizontal scale performs the function of a T square or parallel slide in drawing horizontal lines. The vertical scale performs the function of a triangle in drawing vertical lines.

The head of the drafting machine can be rotated so that either of the scales can be used to draw lines at any angle. When the indexing thumbpiece, as shown in Fig. 20–5, is depressed and then released, the protractor head of the drafting machine will lock into position every 15°. Figure 20–6 shows the intervals at which the scales will index from a horizontal line. If the indexing thumbpiece remains depressed, the protractor head can be aligned to any degree. The protractor brake wing nut is used to lock the head in position. If accuracy in minutes is desired, the *vernier scale* (Fig. 20–7) is used to set the protractor head at the desired angle. In this case, the vernier clamp is used to lock the head in the exact position when the desired setting is achieved.

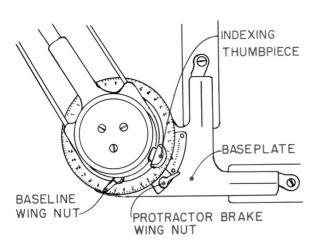

Fig. 20-5. Location of the indexing thumbpiece.

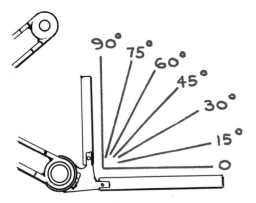

Fig. 20-6. Angles at which the scales will stop.

Fig. 20-7. Use of the vernier scale.

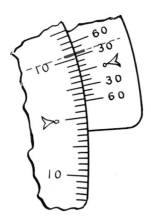

Fig. 20-8. A drafting machine mounted on a vertical slide.

The drafting machine is used to the greatest advantage in architectural work for the preparation of architectural detail drawings. It is sometimes unsatisfactory for large floor plans and elevations which require long horizontal or vertical lines. However, a drafting machine mounted on a vertical slide, as shown in Fig. 20-8, is very effective for large drawings that do not require continuous long lines.

For every position of the head of the drafting machine there are two possible positions of the elbow. If some position of the lower arm covers the vernier scales, shifting the elbow to the position shown in Fig. 20-9 will avoid this difficulty.

▶ **Flexible Rule**

Many architectural drawings contain irregular lines which must be repeated. Flexible rules, such as

Fig. 20-9. Alternative positions of the arms.

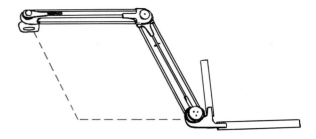

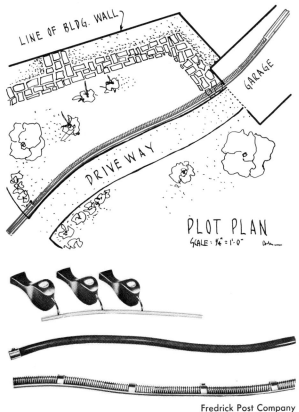

PLOT PLAN

SCALE: ¼" = 1'-0"

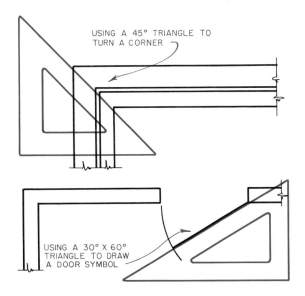

Fig. 20–11. Use of triangles.

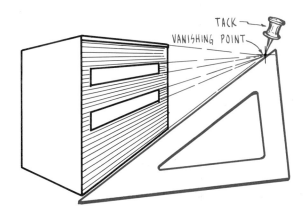

Fredrick Post Company

Fig. 20–10. Use of the flexible rule.

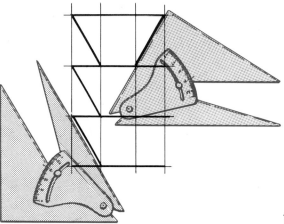

Fig. 20–12. Projecting lines to a vanishing point.

Fig. 20–13. Uses of the adjustable triangle.

those shown in Fig. 20–10, are used to repeat irregular curves that have no true radius or series of radii.

Triangles are used to draw vertical and inclined lines. The 45° triangle is frequently used to draw miter lines that are used to turn angles of buildings, as shown in Fig. 20–11. Triangles are used also to draw various symbols. Figure 20–11 shows the use of the 30° × 60° triangle in drawing a door symbol.

Triangles (and inverted T squares) are often used to project perspective lines from vanishing points, as shown in Fig. 20–12. The adjustable triangle is used to draw angles that cannot be laid out by combining the 45° and 30° × 60° triangles. Figure 20–13 shows the application of the adjustable triangle to architectural work.

125

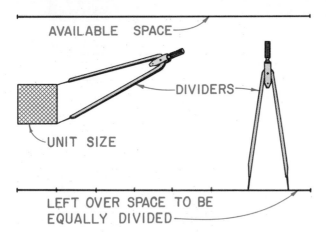

Fig. 20–14. The use of dividers in dividing areas.

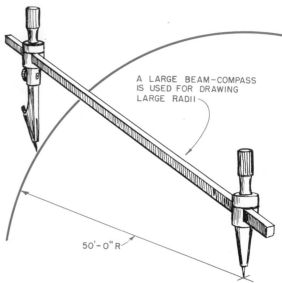

Fig. 20–16. The use of a large beam-compass.

► Dividers

Dividing an area into an equal number of parts is a common task performed by architectural draftsmen. In addition to the architect's scale (see Unit 19), the dividers are used for this purpose. To divide an area equally, first adjust the dividers

Fig. 20–15. The use of dividers to enlarge an area.

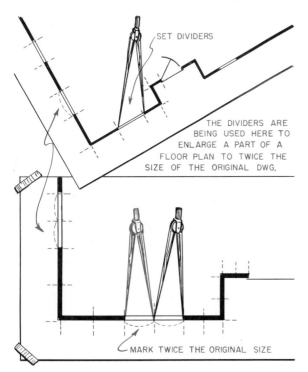

until they appear to represent the desired division of the area. Then place one point at the end of the area and step off the distance with the dividers. If the divisions turn out to be too short, increase the opening on the dividers by trial and error until the line is equally divided. If the divisions are too long, decrease the setting. Figure 20–14 shows the use of dividers in dividing an area into an equal number of parts.

Dividers are also used frequently to transfer dimensions and to enlarge or reduce the size of a drawing. Figure 20–15 shows the use of dividers to enlarge a floor plan. This work is done by setting the dividers to the distances on the plan and then doubling the size and stepping off the distance on the new plan.

► Compass

A compass is used on architectural drawings to draw circles, arcs, radii, and parts of many symbols. Small circles are drawn with a bow pencil compass by setting the bow to the desired radius, holding the stem between the thumb and forefinger, and rotating the compass with a clockwise forward motion and forward inclination.

Large circles on architectural drawings, such as those used to show the radius of driveways, walks, patios, and stage outlines, are drawn with a large beam-compass, as shown in Fig. 20–16.

Problems

1. Using a T square and triangle, parallel slide and triangle, or drafting machine, draw the floor plan shown in Fig. 25–1.

2. Using drafting instruments and architect's scale, draw the elevation shown in Fig. 30–1 to the scale 1/4" = 1'-0".

3. Identify the following terms: *T square, 45° triangle, 60° triangle, vertical lines, horizontal lines, parallel slide, drafting machine, flexible rule, dividers, compass.*

4. Use a flexible rule to layout the driveway shown in Fig. 24–9. Use a scale of 1/8" = 1'-0".

Unit 21. Timesavers

Architectural drawings must frequently be prepared quickly because construction often begins immediately upon completion of the working drawings. Under these conditions, speed in the preparation of drawings is of utmost importance. For this reason many timesaving devices are employed by architectural draftsmen. The purpose of these timesaving devices is to eliminate unnecessary time on the drawing board without sacrificing the quality of the drawing.

▶ Architectural Templates

Templates are pieces of paper, cardboard, metal, or plastic. Openings in the template are shaped to represent the outline of various symbols and fixtures. A symbol or fixture is traced on the drawing by following the outline with a pencil. This procedure eliminates the repetitious task of measuring and laying out the symbol each time it is to be used on the drawing.

General-purpose templates. Templates such as the one shown in Fig. 21–1 have openings that represent many different types of symbols and fixtures. This template is positioned to be used to outline a door symbol. Many other types of general-purpose templates are shown in Fig. 21–2.

Special-purpose templates. Many architectural templates, such as those shown in Fig. 21–3, are used to draw only one type of symbol. Special templates are available for doors, windows, landscape features, electrical symbols, plumbing symbols, furniture, structural steel, outlines, lettering, circle and ellipse guides. Figure 21–4 shows how a special landscape template is used to draw landscape symbols on a drawing. When symbols con-

Fig. 21–2. General-purpose architectural templates.

Timely Products Company

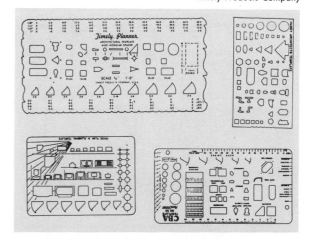

Fig. 21–1. Floor-plan symbols.

Timely Products Company

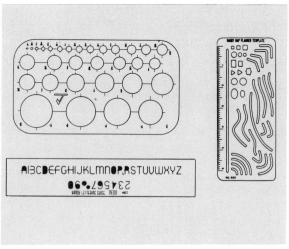

Rapidograph, Inc.

Fig. 21-3. Special-purpose templates.

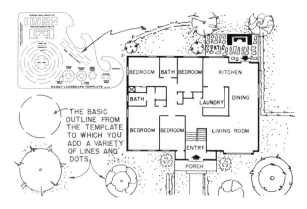

Fig. 21-4. Use of a landscape template.

Fig. 21-5A. Step One in using a window template.

Timely Products Company.

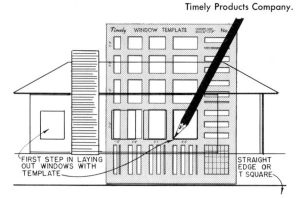

tain many intersecting lines, templates often provide only the basic outline. The detailing is completed by freehand methods. The landscape symbols shown in Fig. 21-4 are completed in this manner.

Each part of the symbol is drawn by using a different opening in the template. For example, in using the template shown in Fig. 21-5A, the center part of the template is employed to outline the window. The horizontal lines are then added, by using the openings at the right of the template, as shown in Fig. 21-5B. The vertical lines are added by using the opening at the bottom of the template.

When the major axis of a symbol is to be aligned with the lines of the drawing, it is necessary to use a T square, drafting machine, or parallel slide as a guide. This alignment is made by resting one true edge of the template against the blade of the T square, parallel slide, or drafting machine. This procedure is also necessary to ensure the alignment of symbols that are repeated in an aligned pattern.

Fig. 21-5B. Additional steps in using window templates.

Timely Products Company

▶ Overlays

An overlay is any sheet that is placed over the original drawing. The information placed on the overlay becomes part of the interpretation of the original drawing.

Temporary overlays. Most overlays are made by drawing on transparent material such as acetate, tracing cloth, or vellum. Overlays are used in the design process to add to or change features of the original drawing without marking the drawing.

Overlays are also used to add to a drawing features which would normally complicate the original drawing. Lines that would become hidden and many other details can be made clear by preparing this information on an overlay. Figure 21–6 shows the use of an acetate overlay in locating a building on a lot. The building can be moved to any position on the overlay until the final location is established. It can then be added to the original drawing.

Permanent overlays. Overlays which adhere to the surface of the drawing, such as the overlay shown in Fig. 21–7, save much drawing-board time. Attaching a preprinted symbol or fixture by this method is considerably faster than drawing it, even if a template is used.

Fig. 21–6. The use of an acetate overlay.

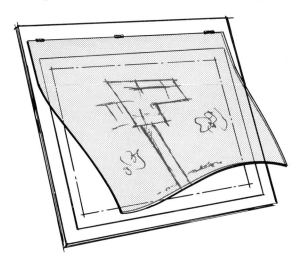

Chart-Pak, Inc.

Fig. 21–7. A permanent overlay.

In addition to fixture and symbol overlays, continuous material symbols are often used on architectural drawings. Figure 21–8 shows the use of a section-lining overlay on architectural drawings. These overlays are self-adhering and can be cut to any desired size or shape.

▶ Underlays

Underlays are drawings or parts of drawings which are placed under the original drawing and traced on the original.

Symbol underlays. Many symbols and features of buildings are drawn more than once. The same style of door or window or the same type of tree or shrubbery may be drawn many times by the architectural draftsman in the course of a day. It is a considerable waste of time to measure and lay out these features each time they are to be

Fig. 21–8. A section-lining overlay.

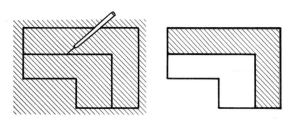

129

Fig. 21-9. Common architectural underlays.

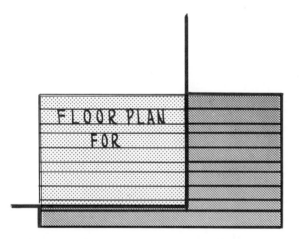

Fig. 21-10. Lettering guideline underlay.

guideline on the drawing can be considerably lighter, so that the draftsman does not need to erase heavy guidelines. The spacing of other lines, such as crosshatching and brick-symbol lines, is also prepared on underlays.

Drawing paper preprinted with title blocks is a considerable time saver (Fig. 21-11). However, when printed title blocks are not available, the title-block underlay is often used to save valuable layout time and to ensure the correct spacing of lettering.

Use of underlays. Underlays are master drawings. To be effective, they must be prepared to the correct scale and carefully aligned. The underlay is first positioned under the drawing and aligned with light guidelines (Fig. 21-12), then traced on the drawing. The underlay can now be

Fig. 21-11. Title-block underlay.

Fig. 21-12. Positioning of underlay.

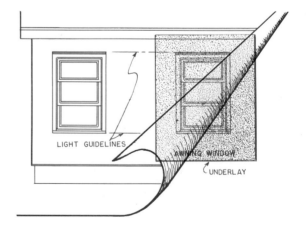

drawn. Therefore, many draftsmen prepare a series of underlays of the features repeated most often on their drawings. Figure 21-9 shows several underlays commonly used on architectural drawings. Underlays are commonly prepared for doors, windows, fireplaces, trees, walls, and stairs.

Lettering underlays. Lettering guidelines, as shown in Fig. 21-10, are frequently prepared on underlays. When the guidelines are placed under the drawing, the draftsman may trace the line from the original drawing, thus eliminating the measurement of each line. If the underlay remains under the drawing while it is being lettered, the

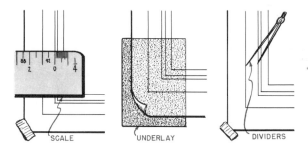

Fig. 21-13. The scale, underlay, or dividers may be used to lay out wall thicknesses.

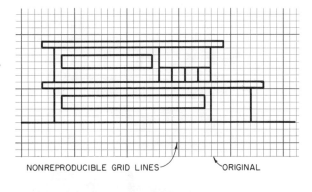

NONREPRODUCIBLE GRID LINES — — ORIGINAL

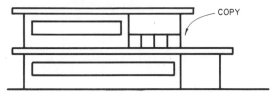

— COPY

Fig. 21-14. Nonreproducible grid paper.

removed or moved to a new location to trace the symbol or feature again if necessary. Architects use master underlays many times.

Underlays do not necessarily replace the use of instruments or scales in original design work. They are most effective when symbols are continually repeated. Figure 21-13 shows a comparison of the use of the scale, dividers, and underlay in laying out wall thicknesses. The use of the underlay in this case is only possible after the original wall dimensions have been established by the use of the scale.

▶ Grids

Grid sheets are used under the tracing paper as underlays and are removed after the drawing is finished, or the drawing is prepared on nonreproducible grid paper. Nonreproducible grid paper does not reproduce when the original drawing is copied through photographic processes. Figure 21-14 shows an original drawing complete with nonreproducible grid lines, and the print from this drawing without grid lines.

Squared paper. Squared (graph) paper is available in graduations of 4, 8, 16, and 32 squares per inch. Squared paper is also available in decimal-divided increments of 10, 20, and 30 or more squares per inch. Decimal-divided squared paper is used for the layout of survey and plot plans.

Pictorial grids. Grids prepared on isometric angles and preplotted to perspective vanishing points are used for pictorial illustrations. *Perspec-*

tive and *isometric* grid charts are available with many angles of projection (Fig. 21-15).

Perspective grids can be obtained with the vanishing point placed at various intervals from

Fig. 21-15. The use of a Cassel Perspective Indicator.

Graphic Indicator Co.

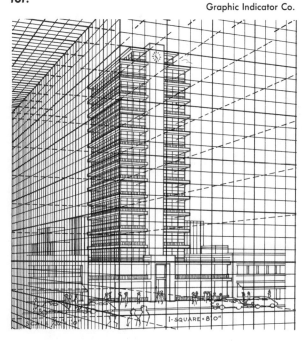

131

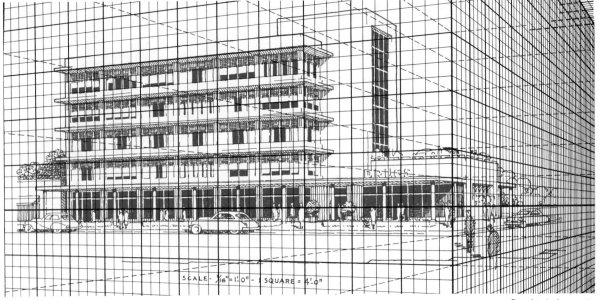

SCALE - ⅟₁₆" = 1'-0" - 1 SQUARE = 4'-0"

Fig. 21-16. A drawing may be projected in many locations.

Fig. 21-17. Architectural symbol tape.

the station point, and with the horizon placed in various locations, as shown in Fig. 21-16.

▶ Tape

Many types of manufactured tape can be substituted for lines and symbols on architectural drawings.

Pressure-sensitive tape. Tape with printed symbols and special lines is used to produce lines and symbols that otherwise would be difficult and time-consuming to construct. Figure 21-17 shows some of the various symbols and lines available in this type of tape. A special roll-on applicator enables the draftsman to draw curves by using tape, as shown in Fig. 21-18. This method is used

Fig. 21-18. Rolling on pressure-sensitive tape.

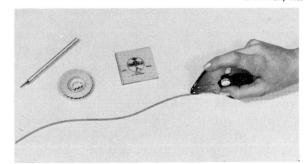

Fig. 21–19. Pressure-sensitive tape on map overlay.

Chart-Pak, Inc.

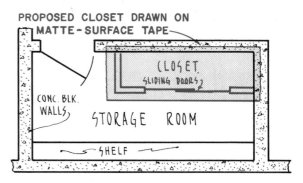

Fig. 21–21. A trial layout prepared on a matte-surface tape.

extensively on overlays (Fig. 21–19). Figure 21–20 shows other applications of this type of tape.

Matte-surface tape. Temporary changes can be added to a drawing by drawing the symbol, note, or change on translucent matte-surface tape. If the drawing is changed, the tape can be removed and a new symbol added, or the symbol can be made permanent. The proposed closet wall in Fig. 21–21 was prepared on transparent tape. If the arrangement is unsatisfactory, the tape can be removed without mutilating the drawing.

Masking tape. Masking tape has other time-saving uses besides its use to attach the drawing to the drawing board. Strips of masking tape help ensure the equal length of lines when the draftsman is ruling many close lines. Strips of tape are placed on the drawing to mask the areas not to be lined. The lines are then drawn on the paper and extended on the tape. When the tape is removed, the ends of the lines are even and sharp, as shown in Fig. 21–22. This procedure eliminates starting and stopping the pencil stroke with each line.

Since masking tape will pull out some graphite, a piece of paper can be placed on drawings to perform the masking function for large areas. If a small area is to remain unlined, sometimes it is easier to line through the surface and erase the small area with an erasing shield, as shown in Fig. 21–23.

Fig. 21–20. Reverse uses of pressure-sensitive tape.

Fig. 21–22. Method of masking out areas.

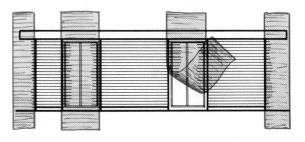

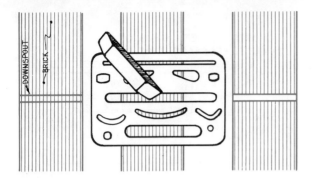

Fig. 21-23. The use of the erasing shield to remove symbol lines.

▶ Abbreviations

A stenographer uses shorthand to speed and condense her work. Architects also use shorthand. Architects' shorthand consists of symbols and abbreviations. When a symbol does not describe an object completely, a word or phrase must be used. Words and phrases occupy much space on a drawing; therefore abbreviations must be used to minimize this space. Following is a list of the abbreviations most commonly used on architectural plans.

Access panel	AP
Asphalt tile	AT
Bath tub	BT
Beam	BM
Bedroom	BR
Boundary	BDY
Brick	BRK
Building	BLDG
Center line	CL
Cut stone	CS
Down spout	DS
Drawing	DWG
Grade line	GL
Floor	FL
Footing	FTG
Foundation	FDN
Hose bibb	HB
Linear feet	LIN FT
Lavatory	LAV
Plaster	PL
Scale	SC

Problems

1. Prepare an underlay for a fireplace.

2. Prepare a title-strip underlay with the following information: your name, school or company, drawing number, teacher or supervisor, title of drawing series, title of specific drawing.

3. Prepare a lettering-guide underlay for $\frac{1}{8}''$, $\frac{1}{4}''$, and $\frac{3}{16}''$ letters.

4. Identify the following abbreviations: CL, FTG, HB, FL.

5. Redraw and add fixtures to the bathroom layout shown in Fig. 17–24.

6. Redraw and add fixtures to the kitchen shown in Fig. 25–18, using a template.

7. Add doors to the plan shown in Fig. 21–4, using a door template.

8. Add landscape features to the plan shown in Fig. 25–15, using a landscape-plan template.

9. Sketch a floor plan of your own home. Prepare an overlay to show how you would redesign the floor plan.

10. Prepare an underlay of trees and shrubbery, using Fig. 31–3 as a guide. Sketch Fig. 31–6, using the tree and shrubbery underlays to complete the landscape elevation.

11. On a plain sheet of paper prepare a floor-plan sketch of the room you are now in. When this is complete, prepare the same sketch on a piece of cross-section paper. Compare the results.

12. Use an overlay on a road map of your state. Plot a trip, using the overlay to mark your route.

13. Define the following terms: *template, general-purpose template, special-purpose template, overlay, temporary overlay, permanent overlay, underlay, lettering underlay, pictorial bridge, bridge, squared paper, graph paper, perspective, grid, modular grid, pressure-sensitive tape, matte-surface tape, masking tape, architectural abbreviations.*

Unit 22. Architectural Lettering

Architectural lettering differs greatly from other types of lettering used on engineering drawings because of the presentational nature of most architectural drawings. Architectural drawings not only must be correct and meaningful but must look attractive to the client.

▶ Purpose

Figure 22–1A shows a plan without any lettering. This plan does not communicate an adequate description of the size and function of the various components. All labels, notes, dimensions, and descriptions must be legibly lettered on architectural drawings if they are to function as an effective means of graphic communication.

Legible, well-formed letters and numerals do more for a drawing than merely aid in communication. Effective lettering helps give the drawing a finished and professional look. Poor lettering is the mark of an amateur. The plan shown in Fig. 22–1B is more easily interpreted and appears more professional because lettering was used.

▶ Styles

Because architectural designs are somewhat personalized, many lettering styles have been developed by various architects. Nevertheless, these personalized styles are all based on the American Standard Alphabet shown in Fig. 22–2.

Architectural styles seem to fall into two categories, the condensed style and the expanded style. The *condensed lettering style* is shown in Fig. 22–3. Condensed lettering is normally used

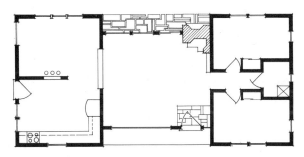

Fig. 22–1A. A plan without lettering.

Fig. 22–1B. The same plan with lettering added.

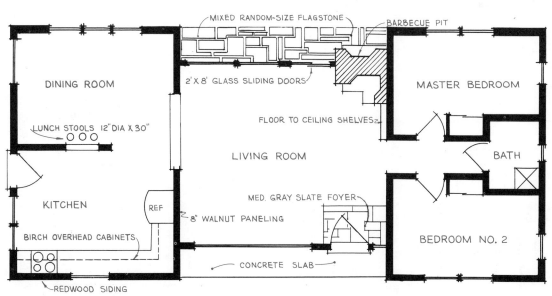

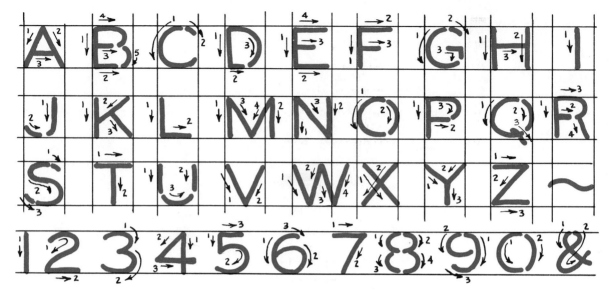

Fig. 22-2. The American Standard Alphabet.

to conserve horizontal space, as shown in Fig. 22-4.

The *expanded lettering style* shown in Fig. 22-5 is used primarily to conserve vertical space. The expanded lettering shown in Fig. 22-6 was used because a limited amount of vertical space existed, with little restriction on the amount of horizontal space.

▶ Rules for Architectural Lettering

Much practice is necessary to develop the skills and techniques necessary to letter effectively, correctly, and consistently. Although architectural lettering styles may differ greatly, nevertheless all professional draftsmen follow certain basic rules. If you follow these rules for lettering, you will develop accuracy, consistency, and speed in lettering your drawings.

1. Always use guidelines in lettering. Notice what a difference guidelines make in the lettering shown in Fig. 22-7.

Fig. 22-4. The use of condensed lettering.

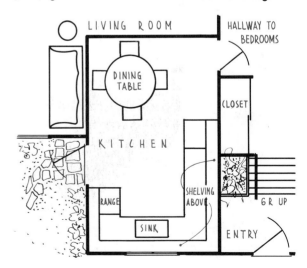

Fig. 22-3. A condensed alphabet.

CONDENSED:
A B C D E F G H I J K L M N
O P Q R S T U V W X Y Z
1 2 3 4 5 6 7 8 9 0

Fig. 22-5. An expanded alphabet.

Fig. 22-8. Always use a consistent style.

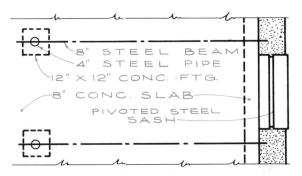

Fig. 22-6. Use of expanded lettering.

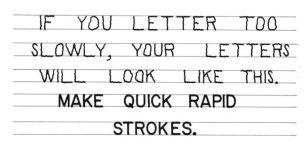

Fig. 22-9. Make each line quickly.

2. Choose one style of lettering and practice the formation of the letters of that style until you master it. Figure 22–8 compares the effect of using a consistent style with that of using an inconsistent style. Although each letter in the inconsistent style may be appropriate for the particular style, when the letters are combined, the effect is undesirable.

3. Make letters bold and distinctive. Avoid a delicate, fine touch.

4. Make each line quickly from the beginning to the end of the stroke. Do not attempt to draw letters as shown in Fig. 22–9.

Fig. 22-7. Always use guidelines.

USE GUIDELINES FOR GREATER

ACCURACY IN LETTERING.

LETTERING WITHOUT GUIDELINES

LOOKS LIKE THIS.

5. Practice with larger letters (about ¼'') and gradually reduce the size until you can letter effectively at ¹⁄₁₆''.

6. Practice spacing by lettering words and sentences, not alphabets. Figure 22–10 shows the effect of uniform and even spacing of letters.

7. Form the habit of lettering whenever possible—as you take notes, address envelopes, or write your name.

8. Practice only the capital alphabet. Lower-case letters are rarely used in architectural work.

9. Do not try to develop speed at first. Make each stroke quickly but take your time between letters and between strokes until you have mastered each letter, then gradually increase your speed. You will soon be able to letter almost as fast as you can write script.

Fig. 22-10. Uniform spacing is important.

UNIFORM SPACING
UNEVEN SPACING

Fig. 22-11. *Practice making horizontal and vertical lines.*

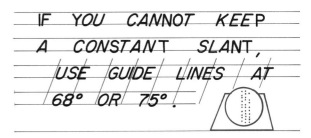

Fig. 22-12. *Maintain the same degree of slant if slant lettering is used.*

10. If your lettering has a tendency to slant in one direction or the other, practice making a series of vertical and horizontal lines, as shown in Fig. 22-11.

11. If slant lettering is desired, practice slanting the vertical strokes exactly $x°$. The problem with most slant lettering, as shown in Fig. 22-12, is that it is difficult to maintain the same degree of slant continually. The tendency is for more and more slant to creep into the style.

12. Letter the drawing last to avoid smudges and overlapping with other areas of the drawing.

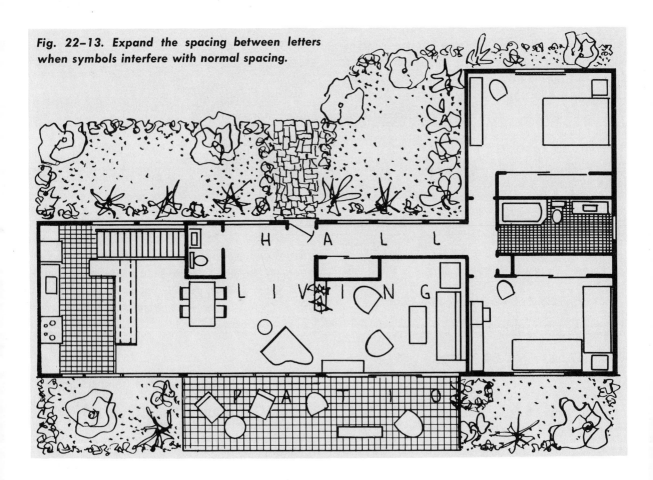

Fig. 22-13. *Expand the spacing between letters when symbols interfere with normal spacing.*

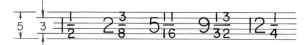

Fig. 22-14. Fraction proportions.

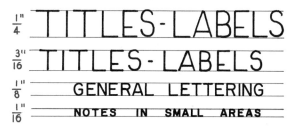

Fig. 22-15. Label sizes.

This procedure will enable you to space out your lettering and to avoid lettering through important details.

13. Use a soft pencil, preferably an HB. You may use even a softer pencil in practicing. A soft pencil will glide and is more easily controlled than a hard pencil. The latter will not glide, and you must exercise more control to exact the precise amount of pressure needed and to overcome the tendency of the pencil to follow the graining of the paper.

14. In large drawings that are completely filled with details and lines and where no large area for lettering occurs, such as maps and many floor plans, expand the spacing of the lettering to fit into the available area, as shown in Fig. 22-13.

15. Numerals used in architectural drawing should be adapted to the style, just as the alphabet is adapted. Notice the numerals in Figs. 22-3 and 22-5. Fractions also should be made consistent with the style. Fractions are $1\frac{2}{3}$ times the height of the whole number. The numerator and the denominator of a fraction are each $\frac{2}{3}$ of the height of the whole number, as shown in Fig. 22-14.

Notice also that in the expanded style, the fraction is slashed to conserve vertical space. The fraction takes the same amount of space as the whole number. (See Rule 5, Fig. 26-2.)

16. The size of the lettering should be related to the importance of the labeling (Fig. 22-15).

Problems

1. Letter your name and your complete address, using the expanded lettering style.
2. Letter your name and your complete address, using the condensed style.
3. Letter the preceding rules for lettering, using any style you choose.
4. Letter the name and address of three of your friends in $\frac{1}{4}''$ lettering, $\frac{3}{16}''$ lettering, and $\frac{1}{16}''$ lettering.
5. Letter the name of your town, county, and state.
6. Define the following terms: *American Standard Alphabet, condensed style, expanded style, consistent style, vertical strokes, horizontal strokes, lettering pencil, slant lettering.*

Fredrick Post Company

Fig. 22-16. Some common lettering templates.

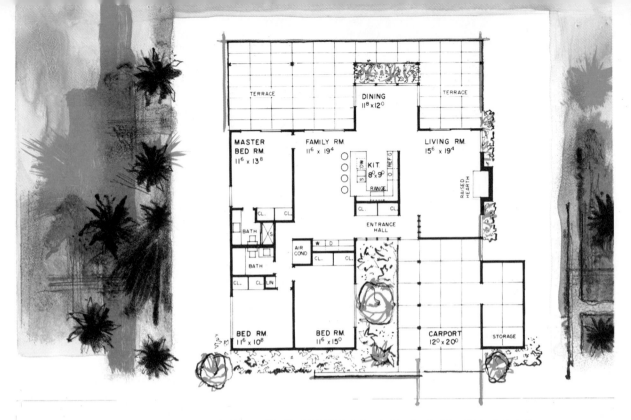

The floor plan with labeled rooms: TERRACE, DINING 11⁸ x 12⁰, TERRACE, MASTER BED RM 11⁶ x 13⁸, FAMILY RM 11⁶ x 19⁴, LIVING RM 15⁶ x 19⁴, KIT 8⁰ x 9⁰, RANGE, REF'G, DW, RAISED HEARTH, BATH, CL, S, AIR COND, W D, CL, ENTRANCE HALL, BATH, CL, CL, LIN, BED RM 11⁶ x 10⁸, BED RM 11⁶ x 15⁰, CARPORT 12⁰ x 20⁰, STORAGE

SECTION FIVE. DRAWING FLOOR PLANS

The most commonly used type of architectural drawing is the floor plan. The floor plan is a drawing of the outline and partitions of a building as you would see them if the building were cut horizontally about 4' above the floor line. The floor plan provides more specific information about the design of the building than any other plan. To design a floor plan that will be accurate and func-tional, the designer must determine what facilities will be included in the various areas of the building. He must combine the various areas into an integrated plan. Only then can he prepare a final floor plan which includes a description and sizes of all the materials and areas contained in his design. The floor plan is used as a base for the projection of other drawings.

Unit 23. Room Planning

Not long ago the outside of most homes was designed before the inside. A basic square, rec-tangle, or series of rectangles was established to a convenient overall size and then rooms were fitted into these forms.

Today the inside of most homes is designed before the outside, and the outside design is determined by the size and relationship of the in-side areas. This is known as designing "from the inside out."

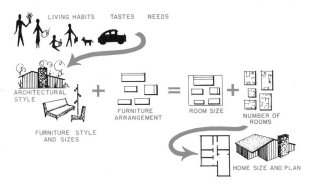

Fig. 23-1. The importance of room planning in arriving at the overall design.

▶ Basic Requirements

In designing from the inside out, the architect evolves the plan from basic room requirements. By learning about the living habits and tastes of the occupants, the architect determines what facilities are required for each room. In this way he can provide for the furniture, fixtures, and amount of space that will be appropriate for the activities.

▶ Sequence of Design

When designing from the inside out, the home planner first determines what furniture and fixtures are needed. Next he must determine the amount and size of furniture. The style selected will greatly affect the dimensions of the furniture.

After the furniture dimensions are established, furniture templates can be made and arranged in functional patterns. Room sizes can then be established by drawing a perimeter around the furniture placements.

When the room sizes are determined, rooms can be combined into areas, and areas into the total floor plan. Finally the outside is designed by projecting the elevations from the floor plan. Figure 23-1 shows the importance of room planning in the overall sequence of planning a home.

▶ Furniture

Furniture styles vary greatly in size and proportion. Sizes of furniture therefore cannot be decided on until the style is chosen. The furniture style should be consistent with the style of architecture (Fig. 23-2).

Fig. 23-2. Furniture style should be consistent with the architectural style.

Selection. Furniture should be selected according to the needs of the occupants (Fig. 23-3). A piano should be provided for someone interested in music. Considerable bookcase space must be provided for the avid reader. The artist, drafts-

Fig. 23-3. Living needs determine the amount of furniture.

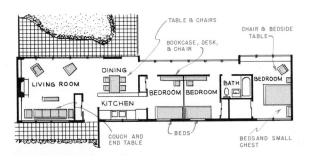

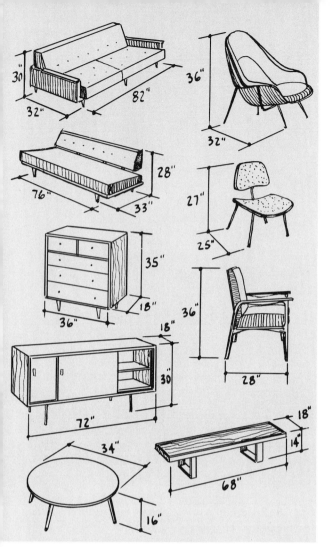

Fig. 23-4. Typical dimensions of furniture.

of each piece of furniture can also be added to the list, as shown below.

Living Room

1 couch 34″ × 100″
2 armchairs 30″ × 36″
1 chaise 28″ × 60″
1 TV 26″ × 24″
1 hi-fi 24″ × 56″
1 bookcase 15″ × 48″
1 floor lamp 6″ × 14″
1 coffee table 18″ × 52″
2 end tables 14″ × 30″
1 baby grand piano 60″ × 80″

Dining Room

1 dining table 44″ × 72″
2 armchairs 28″ × 36″
4 chairs 26″ × 36″
1 china closet 18″ × 42″
1 buffet 26″ × 56″

Similar lists should be prepared for the kitchen, bedrooms, nursery, bath, and all other rooms where furniture is required. Figure 23-4 shows some typical furniture dimensions which can be included with the furniture lists.

Fig. 23-5. Templates represent the width and length of each piece of furniture.

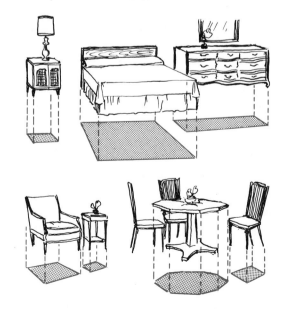

man, or engineer may require drafting equipment in the den or study. A good starting point in room planning is to list the uses to be made of each room. Then make a list of furniture needed for each of these activities. For example: I want to *watch television*. Therefore, I need a *television set* and a *lounge chair*. I want to *read*. Therefore, I need a *lounge chair*, a *reading lamp*, and a *bookcase*. I want to *listen to records*. Therefore, I need a *stereo* or a *hi-fi*.

From these requirements a rather comprehensive list of needed furniture can be compiled. When the exact style is determined, the width and length

Designed by Simon Krieks, Sr.; Cabinets by Stylecraft Interiors, Inc.; Inserts by Paul Hultberg; Photo by Louis Reens

Fig. 23-6. Allow floor space for wall furniture, even though it does not touch the floor.

Furniture templates. Arranging and rearranging furniture in a room is heavy work. It is much easier to arrange furniture by the use of templates (Fig. 23–5). *Furniture templates* are thin pieces of paper, cardboard, plastic, or metal which represent the width and length of a piece of furniture. They are used to determine exactly how much floor space each piece of furniture will occupy. One template is made for each piece of furniture on the furniture list.

Templates are always prepared to the scale that will be used in the final drawing of the house. The scale most frequently used on floor plans is ¼″ = 1'-0″. Scales of ³⁄₁₆″ = 1'-0″ and ⅛″ = 1'-0″ are also sometimes used.

Wall-hung furniture (Fig. 23–6), or any projection from furniture, even though it does not touch the floor, should be included in the template dimension because the floor space under this furniture is not usable for any other purpose.

Templates show only the width and length of furniture and the floor space covered (Fig. 23–7).

▶ **Room Arrangements**

Furniture templates are placed in the arrangement that will best fit the living pattern anticipated for the room. Space must be allowed for free flow

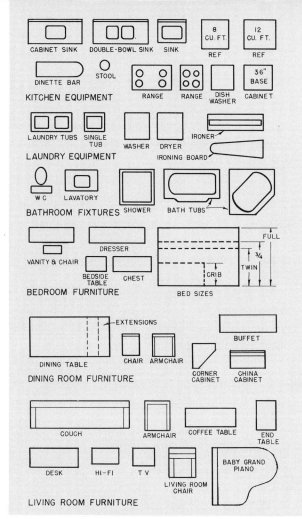

Scale ⅛″ = 1'-0″

Fig. 23–7. Typical furniture templates.

of traffic and for opening and closing doors, drawers, and windows. Figure 23–8 shows furniture templates placed in several different arrangements before the room dimensions are established.

Fig. 23–8. Room dimensions should be determined by arrangement and number of pieces of furniture.

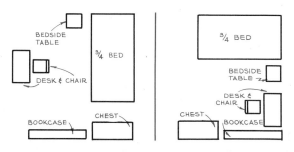

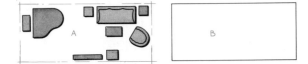

Fig. 23-9. A shows the correct method of determining room dimensions. B shows an incorrect method.

Determining room dimensions. After a suitable furniture arrangement has been established, the room dimensions can be determined by drawing an outline around the furniture, as shown in Fig. 23-9.

Room templates are made by cutting around the outline of the room. Figure 23-10 shows some typical room templates constructed by cutting around furniture template arrangements.

Common room sizes. Determining what room sizes are desirable is only one aspect of room planning. Since the cost of the home is largely determined by the size and number of rooms, room sizes must be adjusted to conform to the acceptable price range. Figure 23-11 shows sizes for each room in large, medium, and small dwellings. These dimensions represent only average widths and lengths. Even in large homes where perhaps no

Fig. 23-10. Typical placement of furniture templates.

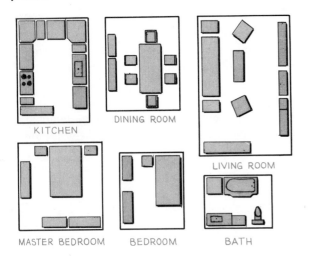

KITCHEN

DINING ROOM

LIVING ROOM

MASTER BEDROOM

BEDROOM

BATH

Size (SQ FT)	LR	DR	Kitchen	Bedrooms	Bath
Small	200	155	110	140	40
Average	250	175	135	170	70
Large	300	195	165	190	100

Fig. 23-11. Room sizes for large, medium, and small homes.

financial restriction exists, room sizes are limited by the size of building materials. Furthermore, a room can become too large to be functional for the purpose intended.

Checking methods. It is sometimes difficult to visualize the exact amount of real space that will be occupied by furniture or that should be allowed for traffic through a given room. One device used to give the layman a point of reference is to make a template of a human figure, as shown in Fig. 23-12. With this template you can vicariously move through the room to check the appropriate-

Fig. 23-12. Comparative size of rooms with the size of its inhabitants.

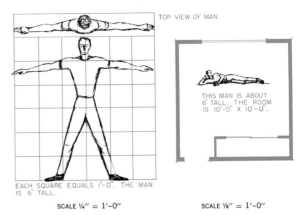

TOP VIEW OF MAN

THIS MAN IS ABOUT 6' TALL. THE ROOM IS 10'-0" X 10'-0".

EACH SQUARE EQUALS 1'-0". THE MAN IS 6' TALL.

SCALE ¼" = 1'-0"

SCALE ⅛" = 1'-0"

ness of furniture placement and the adequacy of traffic allowances.

The experienced architect and home-planner does not always go through the procedure of cutting out furniture templates and arranging them into patterns to arrive at room sizes. He can determine room sizes because he knows exactly how much space is required for various articles of furniture and for the surrounding areas. But he uses templates frequently to recheck his designs. Until you are completely familiar with furniture dimensions and the sizes of building materials, the use of the procedures outlined here is recommended.

Problems

1. Rearrange the following steps in room planning in their proper order:
   a. Make list of furniture needed.
   b. Choose furniture style.
   c. Choose home style.
   d. Determine living habits.
   e. Make furniture templates.
   f. Determine room dimensions.
   g. Arrange furniture templates.
   h. Determine sizes of furniture.
2. Choose a style of furniture suitable for use in your home. Visit a furniture store and sketch examples of furniture suitable for a modern, a colonial, and a period-style house.
3. Define your living needs and activities. List each piece of furniture needed for each room in order to fulfill these needs. Example:

Living Habit	Furniture Needed
Watching TV	TV set
Playing ping-pong	Ping-pong table
Writing	Desk, chair

4. Make a list of furniture you would need for a home you might design. This list should include the number of pieces and size (width and length) of each piece of furniture.
5. Make a furniture template ($\frac{1}{4}'' = 1'\text{-}0''$) for each piece of furniture you would include in a home of your design.
6. Place the furniture templates you have made in suitable arrangements for the living room, dining room, kitchen, bedrooms, and baths. Determine room sizes by drawing an outline around these template arrangements.
7. Measure the furniture in the living room of your home. Make a list of this furniture. Give the number of pieces and the size of each.
8. Make furniture templates for each piece of furniture in the living room of your home.
9. Rearrange the furniture in the living room of your home by using templates of that furniture.
10. Arrange the following furniture suitably for a large, average, and small living room: a couch, two armchairs, a television set, hi-fi, two end tables, two end-table lamps, two floor lamps, one coffee table, one bookcase.
11. Start a scrapbook of furniture styles by selecting examples from current magazines.
12. Define the following terms: *furniture template, furniture dimensions, room dimensions, furniture style.*

Unit 24. Floor-plan Design

The architect and designer develops and records his ideas through preliminary sketches which are later transformed into final working drawings. His ideas are directly translated into sketches that may approximate the final design. He knows through experience how large each room or area must be made to perform its particular function. He can mentally manipulate the relationships of areas and record his design ideas through the use of sketches. This skill is attained after much experience.

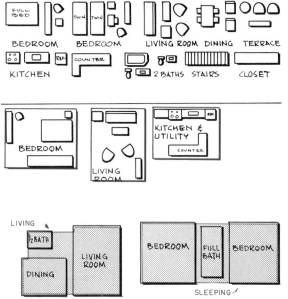

Fig. 24-1. Preliminary rough sketches of floor plans are prepared from template layouts of the living, service, and sleeping areas.

▶ Learning Design Procedures

Until you have gained considerable experience and skill in designing floor plans, you may have difficulty in creating floor plans by the exact methods professionals use. In the beginning you should rely on more tangible methods of designing.

The information in this unit outlines the procedures you should use in developing floor-plan designs. These procedures represent real activities which relate to the mental activities of a professional designer. Figure 24-1 shows the sequence of these design activities in developing a floor plan. You will notice that the sequence includes the development of room templates through the

use of furniture templates, as described in Unit 23. These room templates become the building blocks used in floor-plan designing. The room templates are arranged, rearranged, and moved into various patterns until the most desirable plan is achieved. Think of these room templates as pieces of a jigsaw puzzle which are manipulated to produce the final picture. Figure 24-2 shows a typical set of room templates prepared for use in floor-plan design.

▶ Planning with Room Templates

A residence or any other building is not a series of separate rooms, but a combination of several activity areas. In the design of floor plans, room templates are first divided into area classifications, as shown in Fig. 24-3. The templates are then arranged in the most desirable plan for each area (Fig. 24-4). Next the area arrangements are combined in one plan (Fig. 24-5). The position of each room is then sketched and revised to achieve more unity.

As you combine these areas, you will need to rearrange and readjust the position of individual rooms. At this time you should consider the traffic

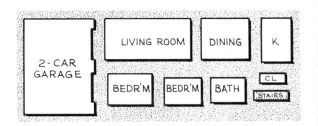

Fig. 24-2. Room templates prepared for floor-plan design use.

Fig. 24-3. Room templates divided into areas.

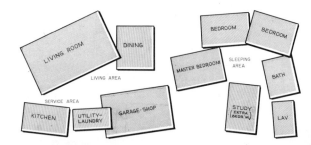

pattern, compass direction, street location, and relationship to landscape features. Space must be allowed for stairways and halls. Figure 24–6 shows some common allowances for stairwells and halls on the floor plan. Unless closets have been incorporated in the room template, adequate space must also be provided for such storage spaces.

Rooms and facilities such as recreation room, laundry, workshop, and heating equipment are sometimes placed in the basement. When such use is made of the basement, the designer must be sure that the floor plan he develops provides sufficient space on the lower level for these facilities. In two-story dwellings, the sleeping area is usually placed on the level above the ground floor. Templates should also be developed for rooms on this level, but they must be adjusted to conform to the sizes established for the primary level.

▶ Floor-plan Sketching

Preparing a layout for a room template is only a preliminary step in designing the floor plan. The template layout shows only the desirable size, proportion, and relationship of each room to the entire plan.

Preliminary sketching. Template layouts such as the one shown in Fig. 24–5 usually contain many irregularities and awkward corners because room dimensions were established before the

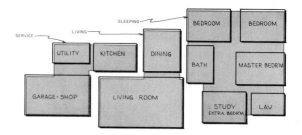

Fig. 24–4. Templates arranged into areas.

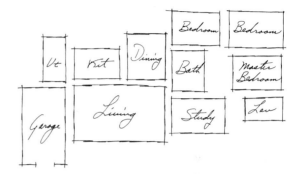

Fig. 24–5. Area templates combined into one plan.

overall plan was completed. These offsets and indentations can be smoothed out by increasing the dimensions of some rooms and changing slightly the arrangement of others. These alterations are usually made by sketching the template layout, as shown in Fig. 24–7A. At this time such features as fireplaces, closets, and divider walls can be added where appropriate.

Fig. 24–6. Space must be allowed for halls and stairways.

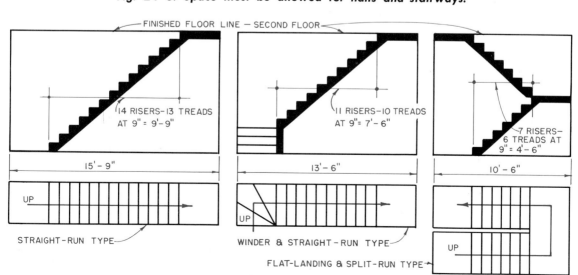

Think of this first floor-plan sketch as only the beginning. Many sketches are usually necessary before the designer achieves an acceptable floor plan. In successive sketches such as the one shown in Fig. 24–7B, the design should be refined further. Costly and unattractive offsets and indentations can be eliminated. Modular sizes can be established that will facilitate the maximum use of standard building materials and furnishings. The exact positions and sizes of doors, windows, closets, and halls can be determined.

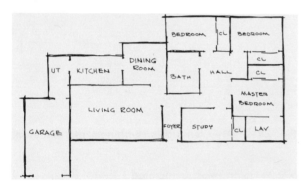

Fig. 24–7A. A preliminary sketch.

Fig. 24–7B. A refined sketch.

Fig. 24–7C. A final sketch.

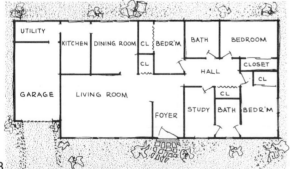

Fig. 24–8. Many different plans are possible within the same amount of space.

Through resketching, continued refinement of the design is pursued until a satisfactory sketch, as shown in Fig. 24–7C, is reached. Except for very minor changes, it is always better to make a series of sketches than to erase and change the original sketch. Many designers use tracing paper to trace the acceptable parts of the design, and resolve the poor features on the new sheet. This procedure also provides the designer with a record of the total design process. Early sketches sometimes contain solutions to problems that develop later in the final design.

Plan variations. Many variations and arrangements of rooms are possible within the same amount of space. Figure 24–8 shows some methods of rearranging and redistributing space to overcome poor design features.

Fig. 24–9. A final sketch prepared on cross-section paper.

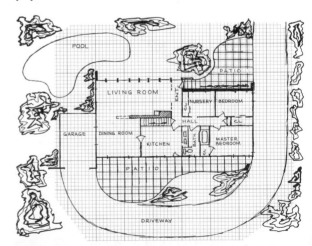

Final sketching. Single-line sketches such as those shown in Fig. 24–7 are satisfactory for basic planning purposes. However, they are not adequate for establishing final sizes. A final sketch (Fig. 24–9) should be prepared on cross-section paper to provide a more adequate description of wall thicknesses and to include property features. This sketch should include the exact position of doors, windows, and partitions. It should also include the location of shrubbery, trees, patios, walks, driveways, courts, pools, and gardens. Only after a final sketch is completed can the designer proceed with the preparation of the final floor-plan working drawings.

▶ **Open Planning**

When the rooms of a plan are divided by solid partitions, doors, or arches, the plan is known as a *closed plan.* A closed plan is shown in Fig. 24–10A. If, however, the partitions between the rooms of an area are eliminated, such as the partitions between the entrance, living room, and activities room in Fig. 24–10B, the plan is known as an *open plan.*

The open plan is used most extensively and advantageously in the living area. Here the walls that separate the entrance foyer, living room, dining room, activities room, and recreation room

Fig. 24–11. An open plan.

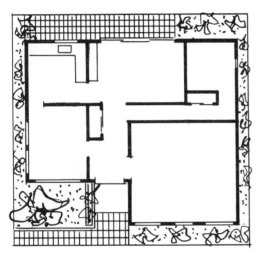

Fig. 24–10A. A closed plan.

Fig. 24–10B. An open plan.

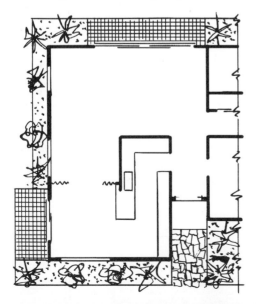

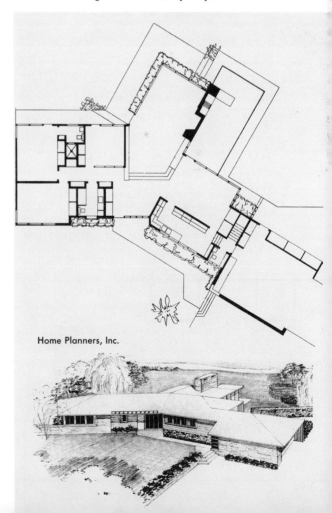

Home Planners, Inc.

can be removed or partially eliminated (Fig. 24–11). These open areas are created to provide a sense of spaciousness, to aid lighting efficiency, and to increase the circulation of air through the areas.

Obviously not all the areas of a residence lend themselves well to open-planning techniques. For example, a closed plan is almost always used in the sleeping area.

The floor plan for an open plan is developed in the same manner as for the closed plan. However, in the open plan the partitions are often replaced by dividers or by variations in level to set apart the various functions.

▶ Expandable Plans

Owing to limitations of time or of money, it is sometimes desirable to construct a house over a long period of time. When the period is thus prolonged, the construction should be phased into several steps. The basic part of the house can be constructed first. Then additional rooms (usually bedrooms) can be added in future years as the need develops.

When future expansion of the plan is anticipated, the complete floor plan should be drawn

Fig. 24–12. An expandable plan.

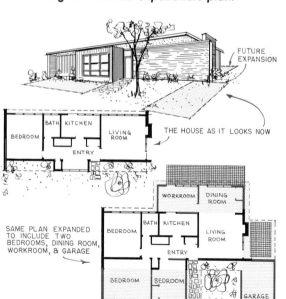

THE HOUSE AS IT LOOKS NOW

SAME PLAN EXPANDED TO INCLUDE TWO BEDROOMS, DINING ROOM, WORKROOM, & GARAGE

Fig. 24–13. Arrange these templates into a suitable floor plan.

before the initial construction begins, even though the entire plan may not be complete at that time. If only part of the building is planned and built, and a later addition is made, the addition will invariably look tacked-on. This appearance can be avoided by designing the floor plan for expansion, as shown in Fig. 24–12.

Problems

1. Prepare room templates and use them to make a functional arrangement for the living area, service area, and sleeping area of a house.

2. Arrange templates for a sleeping area, service area, and living area in a total composite plan.

3. Make a floor-plan sketch of the arrangement you completed in Problem 2. Have your instructor criticize this sketch, and revise it according to his recommendations.

4. After you have completed a preliminary line sketch, prepare a final sketch complete with wall thicknesses, overall dimensions, driveways, walks, and shrubbery. Use Fig. 24–9 as a guide.

5. Arrange the templates found in Fig. 24–13 in a floor-plan arrangement. Make a sketch of this arrangement and revise the sketch until you arrive at a suitable plan.

6. Make room templates of each room in your own home. Rearrange these templates according to a remodeling plan. Make a sketch of this plan.

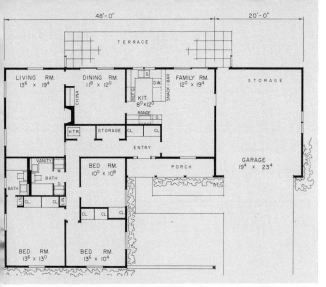

Home Planners, Inc.

Fig. 24–14. Convert this closed plan to an open plan.

7. Convert the floor plan shown in Fig. 24–14 to an open plan. Sketch your solution.

8. Resketch the plan shown in Fig. 24–15 adding a dining room, utility room, entrance foyer, patio, and swimming pool.

9. Combine the area arrangements shown in Fig. 24–16 in a total plan. Sketch your solution.

10. Define the following terms: *room template, floor-plan sketching, sketch, template layout, final sketching, open planning, closed plan, expandable plan.*

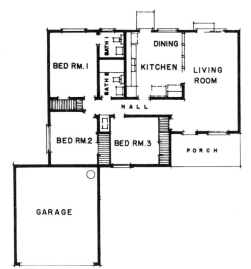

Signature Homes

Fig. 24–15. Add a dining room, utility room, entrance foyer, patio, and swimming pool to this plan.

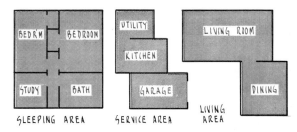

Fig. 24–16. Combine these areas into a workable plan.

Unit 25. Complete Floor Plan

A floor plan is a drawing of the outline and partitions of a building as you would see them if the building were cut (sectioned) horizontally about 4′ above the floor line, as shown in Fig. 25–1. There are many types of floor plans, ranging from very simple sketches to completely dimensioned and detailed floor-plan working drawings.[1]

▶ **Types of Floor Plans**

Figure 25–2 shows some of the various types of floor plans. The single-line drawing (Fig. 25–2A), the abbreviated plan (Fig. 25–2B), and the pictorial floor plan (Fig. 25–2C) are commonly pre-

[1] Specialized floor plan symbols are shown in the section pertaining to each specialized plan. See Section Thirteen for electrical symbols, Section Fourteen for heating symbols, Section Fifteen for plumbing symbols, Section Seven for location-plan symbols, and Section Six for elevation symbols.

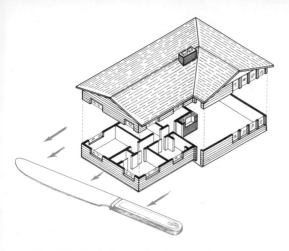

Fig. 25–1. A floor plan is a section cut through the building 4' above the floor line.

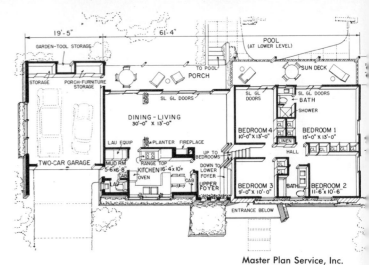

Master Plan Service, Inc.

Fig. 25–2C. A pictorial floor plan.

pared for interpretation by the layman. Bird's-eye views such as the one shown in Fig. 25–2D are often prepared to convey a sense of depth to the viewer. Pictorial plans such as the type shown in Fig. 25–2E are often prepared to show the relationship among various areas of the lot.

These plans are satisfactory for general use. However, a completely dimensioned floor plan is necessary to show the degree of detail suitable for construction purposes.

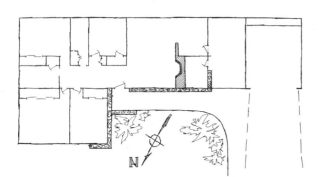

Fig. 25–2A. A single-line floor plan.

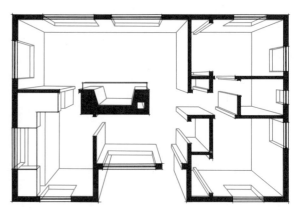

Fig. 25–2D. A bird's-eye view floor plan.

Fig. 25–2B. An abbreviated floor plan.

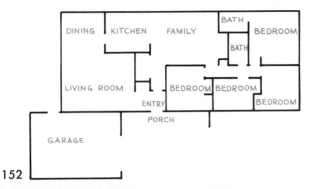

Fig. 25–2E. A flat pictorial floor plan.

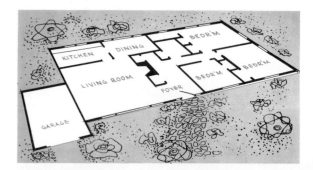

Floor-plan sketches such as those shown in Fig. 25-2 are sufficient for rough layout and preliminary design purposes, but are not accurate or complete enough to be used as working drawings. An accurate floor plan, complete with dimensions and material symbols, must be prepared. When a plan of this type is developed, the contractor can interpret the desires of the designer without consultation. The prime function of a working-drawing floor plan is to communicate information to the contractor. A complete floor plan eliminates many misunderstandings between the designer and the builder. If an incomplete floor plan is prepared, the builder must use his own judgment to fill in the omitted details. When he does so, the function of the designer is transferred to the builder.

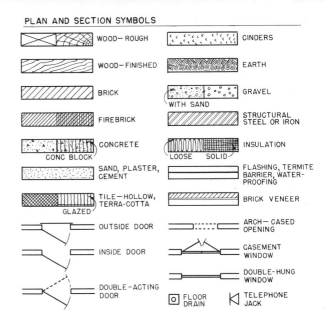

PLAN AND SECTION SYMBOLS

WOOD— ROUGH

WOOD—FINISHED

BRICK

FIREBRICK

CONCRETE
CONC BLOCK

SAND, PLASTER, CEMENT

TILE—HOLLOW, TERRA-COTTA
GLAZED

OUTSIDE DOOR

INSIDE DOOR

DOUBLE—ACTING DOOR

CINDERS

EARTH

GRAVEL
WITH SAND

STRUCTURAL STEEL OR IRON

INSULATION
LOOSE   SOLID

FLASHING, TERMITE BARRIER, WATER-PROOFING

BRICK VENEER

ARCH— CASED OPENING

CASEMENT WINDOW

DOUBLE-HUNG WINDOW

FLOOR DRAIN

TELEPHONE JACK

Fig. 25-3. Typical floor-plan symbols.

▶ Floor-plan Symbols

Architects substitute symbols for materials and fixtures, just as stenographers substitute shorthand for words. It is obviously more convenient and timely to draw a symbol of a material than to repeat a description every time that material is used. It would be impossible to describe all construction materials used on floor plans, such as fixtures, doors, windows, stairs, and partitions, without the use of symbols. Figure 25–3 shows some common floor-plan symbols, and Fig. 25–4 shows the application of these symbols to a floor plan.

Although architectural symbols are standardized, some variations of symbols are used in different parts of the country; Fig. 25–5 shows several methods architects use for drawing the outside walls of frame buildings.

Learning and remembering floor-plan symbols will be easier if you associate each symbol with the actual material or facility it represents. For example, as you learn the telephone-jack symbol, you should associate this symbol with the actual appearance of the telephone jack, as shown in Fig. 25–6.

Floor-plan symbols often represent the exact appearance of the floor-plan section as viewed from above, but sometimes this representation is not possible. Many floor-plan symbols are too intricate to be drawn to the scale $1/4'' = 1'-0''$ or $1/8'' = 1'-0''$. Therefore, many details are eliminated on the floor-plan symbols. Figure 25–7 shows the construction method and the symbol used to depict the various materials on the floor plan. Figure 25–7 also shows details of walls for which only the outlines are shown on the accompanying floor plan.

▶ Steps in Drawing Floor Plans

For maximum speed, accuracy, and clarity, the following steps, as illustrated in Fig. 25–8, should be observed in laying out and drawing floor plans:

1. Block in the overall dimensions of the house and add the thickness of the outside walls with a very hard pencil (6H).

2. Lay out the position of interior partitions with a 6H pencil.

3. Locate the position of doors and windows by center line and by their widths.

4. Darken the object lines with a 2H pencil.

5. Add door and window symbols with a 2H pencil.

6. Add symbols for stairwells.

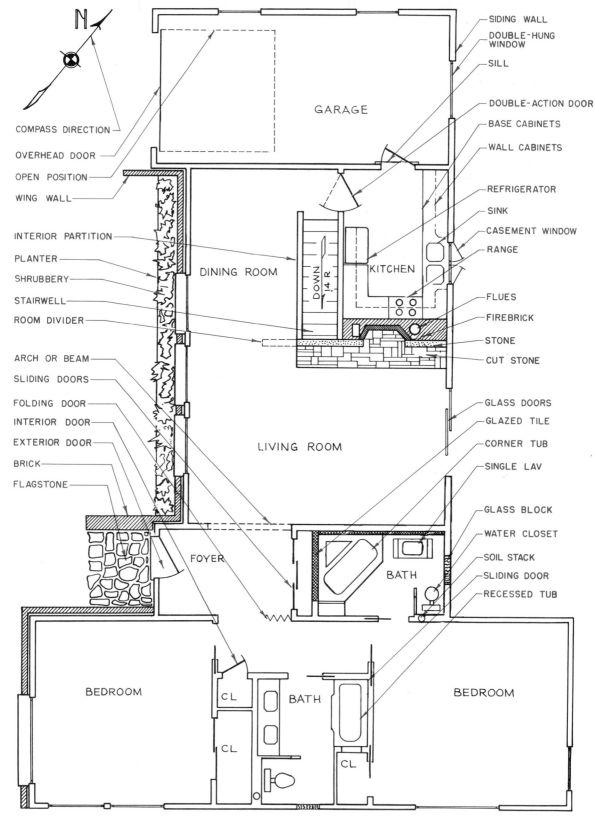

N

COMPASS DIRECTION
OVERHEAD DOOR
OPEN POSITION
WING WALL

INTERIOR PARTITION
PLANTER
SHRUBBERY
STAIRWELL
ROOM DIVIDER

ARCH OR BEAM
SLIDING DOORS
FOLDING DOOR
INTERIOR DOOR
EXTERIOR DOOR
BRICK
FLAGSTONE

GARAGE

DINING ROOM

DOWN 14 R

KITCHEN

LIVING ROOM

FOYER

BATH

BEDROOM

CL

CL

BATH

CL

BEDROOM

SIDING WALL
DOUBLE-HUNG WINDOW
SILL
DOUBLE-ACTION DOOR
BASE CABINETS
WALL CABINETS
REFRIGERATOR
SINK
CASEMENT WINDOW
RANGE
FLUES
FIREBRICK
STONE
CUT STONE

GLASS DOORS
GLAZED TILE
CORNER TUB
SINGLE LAV
GLASS BLOCK
WATER CLOSET
SOIL STACK
SLIDING DOOR
RECESSED TUB

Fig. 25-4. The application of floor-plan symbols.

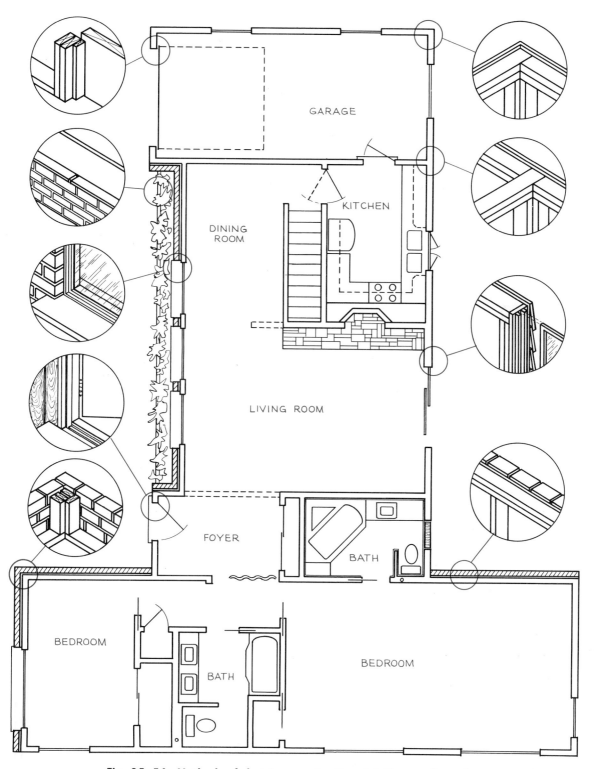

GARAGE

KITCHEN

DINING
ROOM

LIVING ROOM

FOYER

BATH

BEDROOM

BATH

BEDROOM

Fig. 25-5A. Methods of showing construction details on a floor plan.

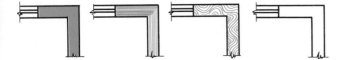

Fig. 25-5B. Methods of showing wall construction on a floor plan.

Western Electric Company

Fig. 25-6. A solid triangle is used to denote a telephone jack.

7. Erase extraneous layout lines if they are too heavy. If they are extremely light, they can remain.

8. Draw the outlines of kitchen and bathroom fixtures.

9. Add the symbols and sections for any masonry work, such as fireplaces and planters.

10. Dimension the drawing (see Unit 26).

11. Erase lettering and dimensioning guidelines.

▶ Second-floor Plan

Bilevel, two-story, one-and-one-half-story, and split-level homes require a separate floor plan for the second, third, and all additional levels. This floor plan is prepared on tracing paper placed directly over the first-floor plan to ensure alignment of walls and bearing partitions. When the

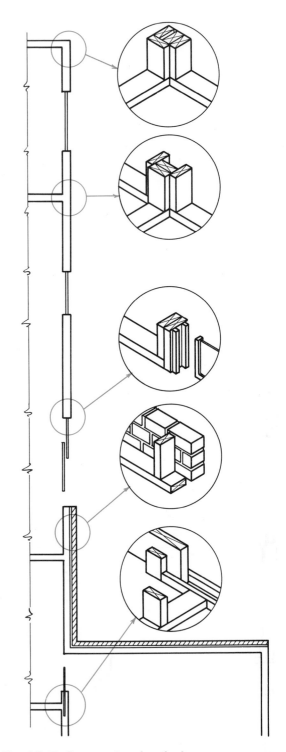

Fig. 25-7. Construction details that are represented by floor-plan symbols.

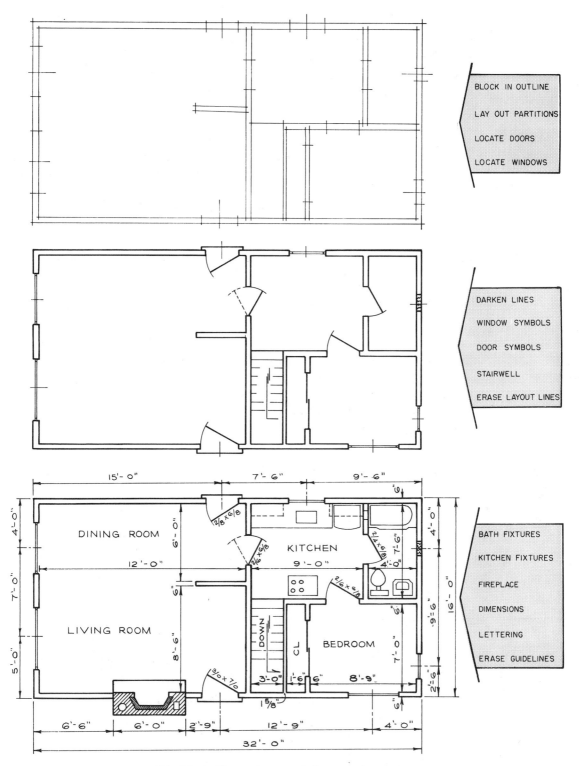

BLOCK IN OUTLINE
LAY OUT PARTITIONS
LOCATE DOORS
LOCATE WINDOWS

DARKEN LINES
WINDOW SYMBOLS
DOOR SYMBOLS
STAIRWELL
ERASE LAYOUT LINES

BATH FIXTURES
KITCHEN FIXTURES
FIREPLACE
DIMENSIONS
LETTERING
ERASE GUIDELINES

DINING ROOM

KITCHEN

LIVING ROOM

DOWN

CL

BEDROOM

15'-0"   7'-6"   9'-6"

4'-0"   6'-0"

12'-0"   9'-0"

7'-0"   6'

8'-6"   7'-0"

2/8 X 6/8

2/6 X 6/8

2/4 X 6/8

2/6 X 6/8

3/0 X 7/0

3'-0"   1'-6"   6"   8'-9"

1 5/8"

6'-6"   6'-0"   2'-9"   12'-9"   4'-0"

5'-0"

4'-0"   7'-6"   4'-0"   9'-6"   2'-6"   16'-0"

32'-0"

Fig. 25–8. The sequence of drawing floor plans.

157

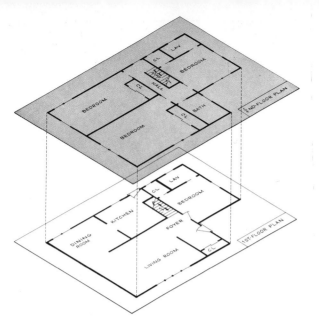

Fig. 25–9. Projection of the second-floor plan.

major outline has been traced, the first-floor plan is removed. Figure 25–9 shows the method of projecting a second-floor plan from the first-floor plan. Alignment of features such as stairwell openings, outside walls, plumbing walls, and chimneys is critical in preparing the second floor plan. Figure 25–10A shows a typical second-floor plan of a one-and-one-half-story house with the roof line broken. This drawing, in addition to revealing the second-floor plan, shows the outline of the roof. In this plan, dotted lines are used to show the outline of the building under the roof.

Figure 25–10B shows a second-floor plan of a two-story house. In this plan there is no break since the first-floor plan is the same size as the second-floor plan. This plan is usually prepared by tracing over the first-floor outline.

Fig. 25–10A. A one-and-one-half story second-floor plan.

SHED DORMER

PLUMBING WALL

ROOF

OVERHANG

GABLE END

CHIMNEY AT 2ND FLOOR

ROOF BREAK LINE

HOUSE OUTLINE

ROOF OUTLINE

GABLE OVER ENTRANCE

CL BATH CL

HALL

BEDROOM

DOWN CL CL

BEDROOM

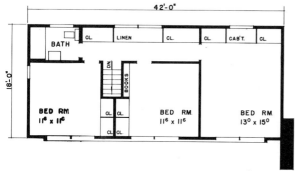

Fig. 25-10B. A full second-floor plan.

Home Planners, Inc.

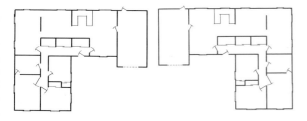

Fig. 25-11. A reversed plan.

▶ Alternative Plans

A technique frequently used to alter or adapt the appearance of the house and the location of various rooms is the practice of reversing a floor plan. Figure 25-11 shows a floor plan with its reversed counterpart. This reversal is accomplished by turning the floor plan upside down and tracing the mirror image of the floor plan to provide either a right-hand or a left-hand plan.

Fig. 25-12. Complete a floor plan of this sketch.

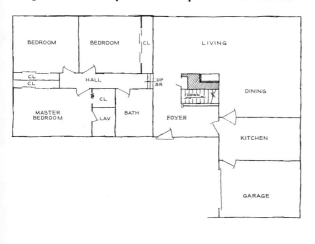

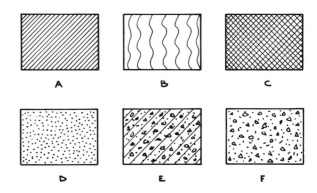

Fig. 25-13. Identify these symbols.

Problems

1. Draw a complete floor plan, using a sketch of your own design as a guide. Use the scale ¼″ = 1′-0″.

2. Draw a complete floor plan from the sketch shown in Fig. 25-12. Use the scale ¼″ = 1′-0″.

3. Measure the rooms in your home. Draw a complete floor plan of your home. Use the scale ¼″ = 1′-0″ or ⅛″ = 1′-0″.

4. After making a floor-plan sketch of your home, revise this sketch to show how you would propose to remodel your home. Then make a complete floor-plan drawing of the remodeled design. Use the scale ¼″ = 1′-0″ or ⅛″ = 1′-0″.

5. Draw the second-floor plan of your own home. Use the scale ¼″ = 1′-0″.

6. Identify the symbols shown in Fig. 25-13.

7. Draw a complete floor plan, using the sketch shown in Fig. 25-14 as a guide. Make any

Fig. 25-14. Draw a complete floor plan of this cabin.

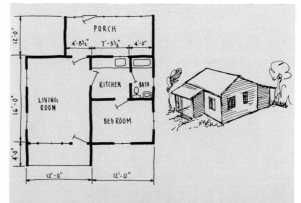

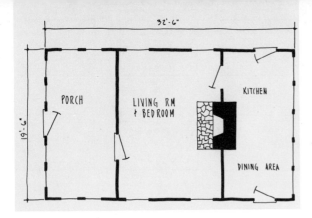

Fig. 25–15. Draw a complete floor plan using this layout as a guide.

alterations necessary to adapt the cabin to your own needs, as a hunting cabin or sea-side lodge, for example.

8. Draw a complete floor plan, using the sketch shown in Fig. 25–15 as a guide.

9. Draw a complete floor plan from the abbreviated plan shown in Fig. 25–16.

10. Project and draw the second-floor plan from the first-floor plan shown in Fig. 25–17. Use the elevation as a reference in your projection.

Fig. 25–16. Draw a complete floor plan of this abbreviated plan.

Home Planners, Inc.

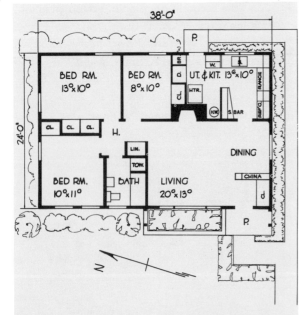

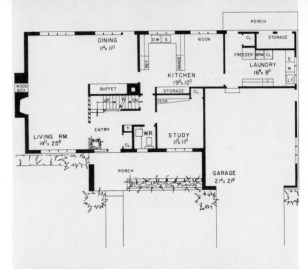

Home Planners, Inc.

Fig. 25–17. Draw a second-floor plan for this house.

11. Draw a complete floor plan, using the sizes and basic plan shown in Fig. 25–18 as a guide. Use the scale $\frac{1}{4}'' = 1'\text{-}0''$. A basic elevation outline has been provided without doors or windows.

Fig. 25–18. Draw a complete floor plan of this single-line floor plan.

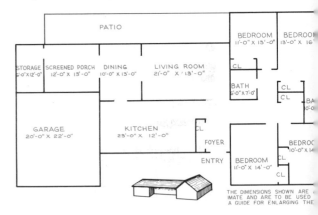

12. Identify the symbols shown in Fig. 25–19.
13. Define these terms: *floor plan, single-line floor plan, pictorial floor plan, bird's-eye view, floor-plan symbols, second-floor plan, alternative plan, plumbing wall, right-hand plan, left-hand plan.*

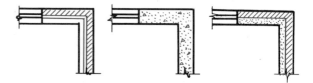

Fig. 25–19. Identify these symbols.

Unit 26. Floor-plan Dimensioning

In colonial times, simple cabins could be built without architectural plans and without established dimensions. The outline of the house and the position of each room could be determined experimentally by pacing off approximate distances. The owner could then erect his own dwelling, using existing materials and adjusting sizes and dimensions as he proceeded. As he worked, the owner acted in the capacity of an architect, designer, contractor, carpenter, and materials manufacturer.

Today building materials are so varied, construction methods are so complex, and design requirements so demanding that a completely dimensioned drawing is necessary to ensure the completion of any building exactly as designed.

▶ **Size Description**

Dimensions show the builder the width and length of the building; they show the location of doors and windows and the position of stairs, fireplaces, and planters. Just as symbols and notes show exactly what materials are to be used in the building, dimensions show what sizes the materials are to have and exactly where they are to be located.

Dimensioning architectural drawings differs from dimensioning mechanical drawings in many ways and for many reasons. Because a building which may be 50′ or 100′ long must be drawn on a sheet that is only several feet long, a very small scale (¼″ = 1′-0″ or ⅛″ = 1′-0″) must be used. The use of such a small scale means that many

dimensions must be crowded into a very small area. Therefore, only major dimensions such as the overall width and length of the building and of separate rooms, closets, halls, and wall thicknesses are shown on the floor plan. Dimensions too small to show directly on the floor plan are described either by means of notes on the floor plan or by separate, enlarged details. Enlarged details are sometimes merely enlargements of of some portion of the floor plan, or an allied section indexed to the floor plan. Separate details are usually necessary to interpret adequately the dimensioning of fireplaces, planters, built-in cabinets, door and window details, stair-framing details, or any unusual construction methods.

Complete dimensions. The number of dimensions included on a floor plan depends largely on how much freedom of interpretation the architect wants to give to the builder. If complete dimensions are shown on the plan, a builder cannot deviate greatly from the original design. However, if only a few dimensions are shown, then the builder or contractor must himself determine many of the sizes of areas, fixtures, and details. When you rely on the discretion of a builder to provide his own interpretation or formulation of dimensions, you place the builder in the position of a designer. A good builder is not expected to be a good designer. Neither is he expected to be a mind reader. Supplying adequate dimensions will eliminate these possibilities.

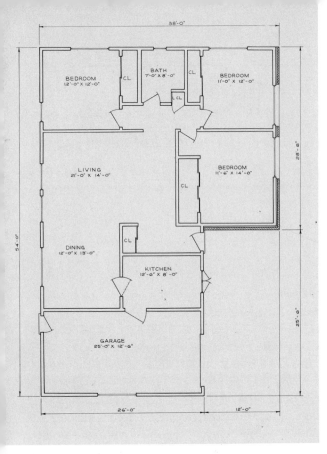

Fig. 26-1. A floor plan with a minimum of dimensioning.

Limited dimensions. A floor plan with only limited dimensions is shown in Fig. 26-1. This type of dimensioning, which shows only the overall building dimensions and the width and length of each room, is sufficient to summarize the relative sizes of the building and its rooms for the prospective owner. These dimensions are not sufficient for building purposes.

A floor plan must be completely dimensioned (Fig. 26-2) to ensure that the house will be constructed precisely as designed. These dimensions convey the exact wishes of the architect and owner to the builder, and little tolerance is allowed the contractor in interpreting the size and position of the various features of this plan—the exact size of each room, closet, partition, door, or window is given.

▶ Rules for Dimensioning

Many construction mistakes result from errors in architectural drawings. Most errors in architectural drawing result from mistakes in dimensioning. Dimensioning errors are therefore costly in time, efficiency, and money. Familiarization with the following rules for dimensioning floor plans will eliminate much confusion and error. These rules are illustrated by the numbered arrows in Fig. 26-2.

1. Architectural dimension lines are unbroken lines with dimensions placed above the line.

2. Foot and/or inch marks are used on all architectural dimensions.

3. Dimensions over 1' are expressed in feet and inches.

4. Dimensions less than 1' are shown in inches only.

5. Fractional dimensions are often slashed to conserve vertical space.

6. Dimensions should be placed to read from the right or from the bottom of the drawing.

7. Overall building dimensions are placed outside the other dimensions.

8. Line and arrowhead weights for architectural dimensioning are the same as those used in dimensioning mechanical drawings.

9. Room sizes may be shown by stating width and length.

10. When the area to be dimensioned is too small for the numerals, they are placed outside the extension lines.

11. Rooms are sometimes dimensioned from center lines of partitions; however, rule 13 is preferred.

12. Window and door sizes may be shown directly on the door or window symbol or may be indexed to a door or window schedule.

13. Rooms are dimensioned from wall to wall, exclusive of wall thickness.

14. Curved leaders are often used to eliminate confusion with other dimension lines.

15. When areas are too small for arrowheads, dots may be used to indicate dimension limits.

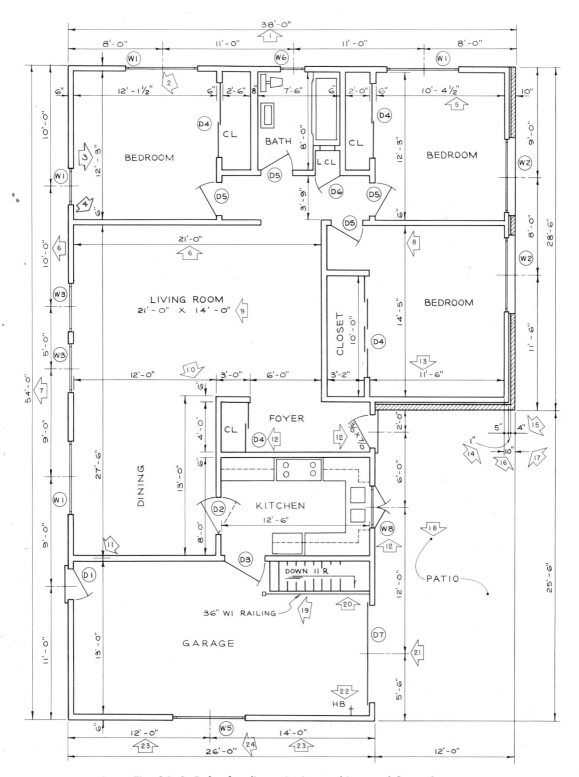

Fig. 26–2. Rules for dimensioning architectural floor plans.

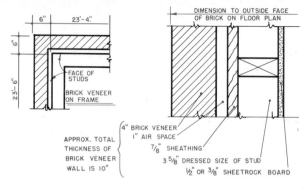

Fig. 26-3. Brick or stone dimensions must be added to the framing dimensions.

Labels in figure:
- DIMENSION TO OUTSIDE FACE OF BRICK ON FLOOR PLAN
- FACE OF STUDS
- BRICK VENEER ON FRAME
- APPROX. TOTAL THICKNESS OF BRICK VENEER WALL IS 10"
- 4" BRICK VENEER
- 1" AIR SPACE
- 7/8" SHEATHING
- 3 5/8" DRESSED SIZE OF STUD
- 1/2" OR 3/8" SHEETROCK BOARD
- 6" 23'-4" 23'-6"

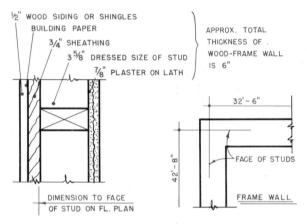

Fig. 26-4. When only framing dimensions are desired, the dimensions should read only to the face of the stud.

Labels in figure:
- 1/2" WOOD SIDING OR SHINGLES
- BUILDING PAPER
- 3/4" SHEATHING
- 3 5/8" DRESSED SIZE OF STUD
- 7/8" PLASTER ON LATH
- APPROX. TOTAL THICKNESS OF WOOD-FRAME WALL IS 6"
- DIMENSION TO FACE OF STUD ON FL. PLAN
- 32'-6"
- 42'-8"
- FACE OF STUDS
- FRAME WALL

16. The dimensions of brick or stone veneer must be added to the framing dimension (Fig. 26-3).

17. When the space is small, arrowheads may be placed outside the extension lines.

Fig. 26-5. Methods of dimensioning various wall and partition thicknesses.

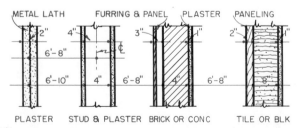

Labels in figure:
- METAL LATH   FURRING & PANEL   PLASTER   PANELING
- 2" 4" 3" 1" 2" 1"
- 6'-8" ℄
- 6'-10" 4" 6'-8" 4" 6'-8" 8"
- PLASTER   STUD & PLASTER   BRICK OR CONC   TILE OR BLK

18. A dot with a leader refers to the large area noted.

19. Dimensions that cannot be seen on the floor plan or those too small to place on the object are placed on leaders for easier reading.

20. In dimensioning stairs, the number of risers is placed on a line with an arrow indicating the direction (down or up).

21. Windows, doors, pilasters, beams, and areaways are dimensioned to their center lines.

22. Use abbreviations when symbols do not show clearly what is intended.

23. Subdimensions must add up to overall dimensions ($14'-0'' + 12'-0'' = 26'-0''$).

24. Architectural dimensions always refer to the actual size of the building regardless of the scale of the drawing. The building in Fig. 26-2 is 38'-0'' wide.

25. When framing dimensions are desirable, rooms are dimensioned by distances between studs in the partitions (Fig. 26-4).

26. Since building materials vary somewhat in size, first establish the thickness of each component of the wall and partition, such as furring thickness, panel thickness, plaster thickness, stud thickness, brick and tile thicknesses. Add these thicknesses together to establish the total wall thickness. Common thicknesses of wall and partition materials are shown in Fig. 26-5.

All other rules of floor-plan dimensioning adhere to the *American Standard Drafting Manual*.

Fig. 26-6. The modular grid.

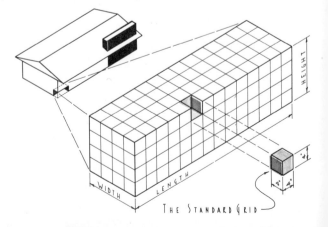

Labels in figure:
- HEIGHT
- WIDTH
- LENGTH
- THE STANDARD GRID

▶ Modular Construction

Buildings to be erected with modular components must be designed within modular limits. In dimensioning by the modular system, building dimensions are expressed in standard sizes. This procedure ensures the proper fitting of the various components. Planning rooms to accommodate standard materials also saves considerable labor, time, and material. The modular system of coordinated drawings is based on a standard grid placed on the width, length, and height of a building, as shown in Fig. 26–6.

In modular designing, an effort is made to establish all building dimensions (width, length, and height) to fall on some 4″ module, if the building material can be selected to conform to this module. As new building materials are developed, their sizes are established to conform to modular sizes. However, many building materials do not conform to the 4″ grid, and therefore the dimensioning procedure must be adjusted accordingly. Dimensions that align with the 4″ module are known as *grid dimensions*. Dimensions that do not align with the 4″ module are known as *non-grid dimensions*. Figure 26–7 shows the two methods of indicating grid dimensions and non-grid dimensions. Grid dimensions are shown by conventional arrowheads, and non-grid dimensions are shown by dots instead of arrowheads on the dimension lines.

In many detail drawings it is possible to eliminate the placement of some dimensions by placing the grid lines directly on the drawing, as shown in the detail given in Fig. 26–8. When the 4″ grid lines coincide exactly with the material lines, no dimensions are needed, since each line represents 4″ and any building material that is an increment of 4″ is reflected by placement on this grid. Other

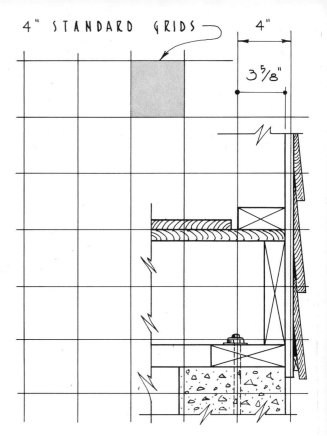

Fig. 26–8. Modular dimensions as applied to detail drawings.

dimensions that do not coincide, such as the 3⅝″ stud dimension shown in Fig. 26–8, must be dimensioned by conventional methods.

Problems

1. Dimension a floor plan that you have completed for a previous assignment.
2. Sketch or draw and dimension the floor plan shown in Fig. 26–9. Use the scale ¼″ = 1'-0″.

Fig. 26–9. Dimension this floor plan.

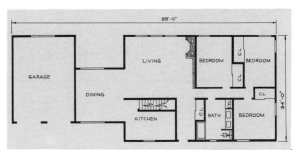

Fig. 26–7. Modular dimensioning methods.

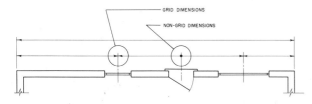

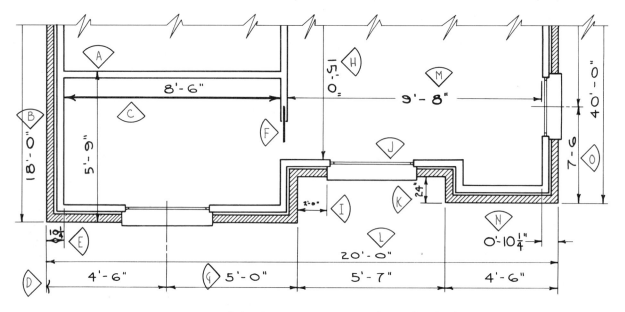

Fig. 26–10. Find the dimensioning errors shown by the letters.

Fig. 26–11. Draw a floor plan of this house complete with dimensions.

Home Planners, Inc.

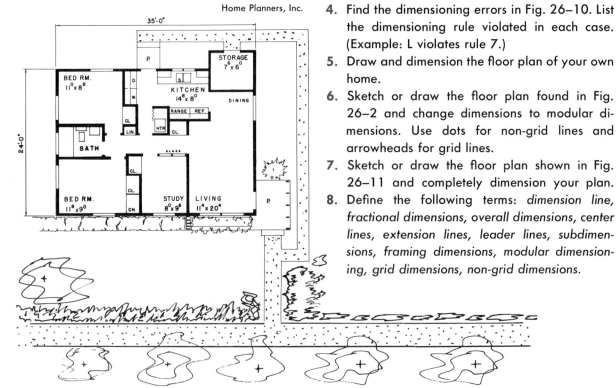

3. Dimension the floor plan shown in Fig. 26–9 by the modular method.

4. Find the dimensioning errors in Fig. 26–10. List the dimensioning rule violated in each case. (Example: L violates rule 7.)

5. Draw and dimension the floor plan of your own home.

6. Sketch or draw the floor plan found in Fig. 26–2 and change dimensions to modular dimensions. Use dots for non-grid lines and arrowheads for grid lines.

7. Sketch or draw the floor plan shown in Fig. 26–11 and completely dimension your plan.

8. Define the following terms: *dimension line, fractional dimensions, overall dimensions, center lines, extension lines, leader lines, subdimensions, framing dimensions, modular dimensioning, grid dimensions, non-grid dimensions.*

SECTION SIX. ELEVATION DRAWINGS

The main features of the interior of a building are shown on the floor plan. The main features of the outside of a building are shown on elevation drawings. *Elevation drawings* are orthographic drawings of the exterior of a building. Elevation drawings are prepared to show the design, materials, dimensions, and final appearance of the exterior of a building.

Unit 27. Elevation Design

Designing the elevation of a structure is only one part of the total design process. However, this is the part of the building that most people see, and it is the part they use to judge the entire structure.

▶ Relationship with the Floor Plan
Since a structure is designed from the inside out, the design of the floor plan normally precedes the design of the elevation. The complete design process requires a continual relationship between the elevation and the floor plan through the entire process.

Much flexibility is possible in the design of elevations, even in those designed from the same floor plan. Figure 27–1 shows the development of two different elevations from the same basic floor plan. When the location of doors, windows, and chimneys has been established on the floor plan, the development of an attractive and functional elevation for the structure still depends on the factors of roof style, overhang, grade-line position, and relationship of windows, doors, and chimneys to the building line. Figure 27–1 clearly shows that choosing a desirable elevation design

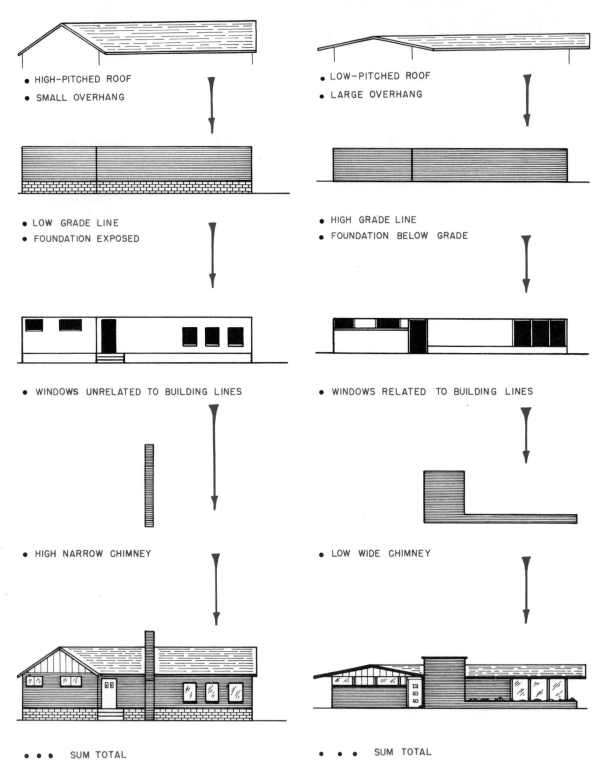

- HIGH-PITCHED ROOF
- SMALL OVERHANG

- LOW-PITCHED ROOF
- LARGE OVERHANG

- LOW GRADE LINE
- FOUNDATION EXPOSED

- HIGH GRADE LINE
- FOUNDATION BELOW GRADE

- WINDOWS UNRELATED TO BUILDING LINES

- WINDOWS RELATED TO BUILDING LINES

- HIGH NARROW CHIMNEY

- LOW WIDE CHIMNEY

- • • SUM TOTAL

- • • SUM TOTAL

Fig. 27–1. Many factors affect the total appearance of the elevation.

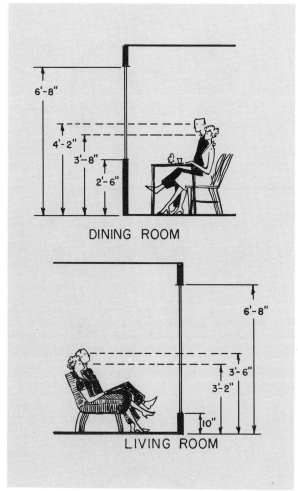

DINING ROOM

6'-8"
4'-2"
3'-8"
2'-6"

6'-8"
3'-6"
3'-2"
10"

LIVING ROOM

Small Homes Council

Fig. 27–2. Vertical distances, such as the heights of windows and doors, can only be shown on an elevation drawing.

is not an automatic process which follows the floor-plan design, but a development which calls on the imagination.

The designer should keep in mind the fact that only horizontal distances can be established on the floor plan and that the vertical heights, such as heights of windows and doors, must be shown on the elevation. As these vertical heights are established, the appearance of the outside and the functioning of the heights as they affect the internal functioning of the house must be considered, as shown in Fig. 27–2.

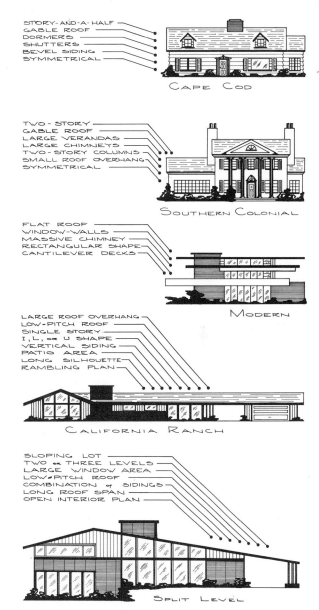

STORY-AND-A-HALF
GABLE ROOF
DORMERS
SHUTTERS
BEVEL SIDING
SYMMETRICAL

CAPE COD

TWO-STORY
GABLE ROOF
LARGE VERANDAS
LARGE CHIMNEYS
TWO-STORY COLUMNS
SMALL ROOF OVERHANG
SYMMETRICAL

SOUTHERN COLONIAL

FLAT ROOF
WINDOW-WALLS
MASSIVE CHIMNEY
RECTANGULAR SHAPE
CANTILEVER DECKS

MODERN

LARGE ROOF OVERHANG
LOW-PITCH ROOF
SINGLE STORY
I, L, or U SHAPE
VERTICAL SIDING
PATIO AREA
LONG SILHOUETTE
RAMBLING PLAN

CALIFORNIA RANCH

SLOPING LOT
TWO or THREE LEVELS
LARGE WINDOW AREA
LOW-PITCH ROOF
COMBINATION of SIDINGS
LONG ROOF SPAN
OPEN INTERIOR PLAN

SPLIT LEVEL

Fig. 27–3. The style of architecture will greatly determine the exterior appearance of the building.

▶ Fundamental Shapes

The style of architecture will greatly determine the basic type of structure and the appearance of the elevation (Fig. 27–3).

Basic types. Within basic styles of architecture there is considerable flexibility in the type of structure.

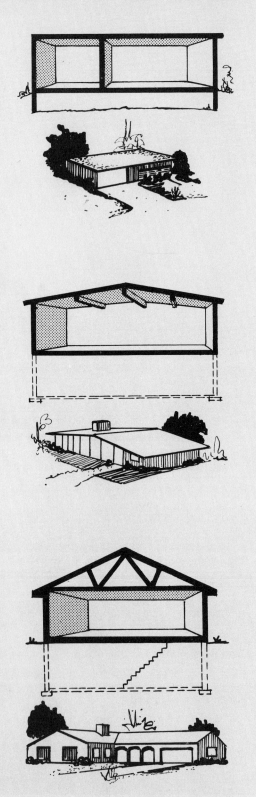

Fig. 27-4. Types of one-story structures.

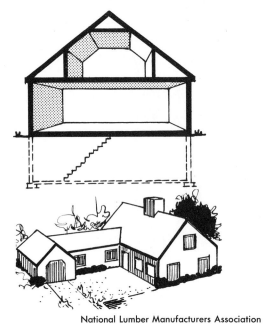

National Lumber Manufacturers Association
Fig. 27-5. A one-and-one-half-story home.

Fig. 27-6. A two-story house.
National Lumber Manufacturers Association

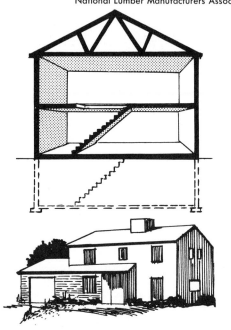

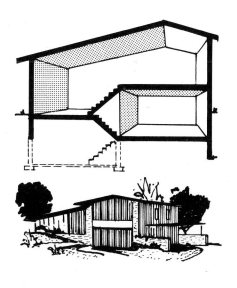

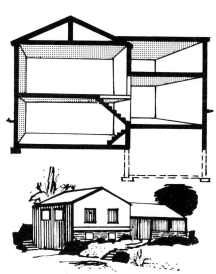

National Lumber Manufacturers Association

Fig. 27–7. A split-level home.

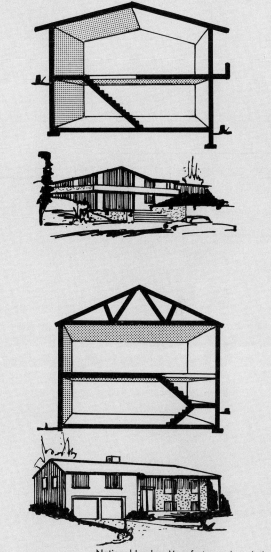

National Lumber Manufacturers Association

Fig. 27–8. The bilevel house.

Fig. 27–9. Basic types of roofs.

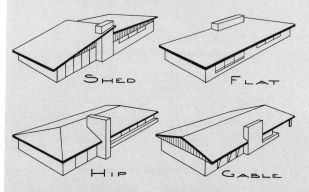

The basic types of structures include the one-story (Fig. 27–4), the one-and-one-half-story (Fig. 27–5), the two-story (Fig. 27–6), the split-level (Fig. 27–7), and the bilevel types (Fig. 27–8).

Roof styles. Nothing affects the silhouette of a house more than the roof line. The most common types of roofs are the gable roof, hip roof, flat roof, and shed roof (Fig. 27–9). Changing the roof style of a structure greatly affects the appear-

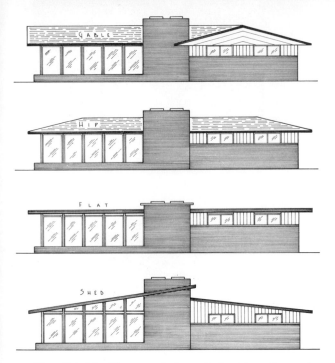

Fig. 27-10. The type of roof greatly affects the appearance of the elevation.

Sol Vista Homes; Robert Barnett, architect

Fig. 27-11. A house with a gable roof.

Fig. 27-12. A high-pitch gable roof.

ance of the elevation even when all other factors remain constant, as shown in Fig. 27-10.

Gable roofs, as shown in Fig. 27-11, are used extensively on Cape Cod and ranch-type homes. The pitch (angle) of a gable roof varies from the high-pitch roofs found on chalet-type buildings (see Fig. 27-12) to the low-pitch roofs found on most ranch-type homes. Figure 27-13 shows the relationship between the actual appearance of a gable roof and the appearance of a gable roof on an elevation drawing.

Fig. 27-13. The appearance of a gable roof on an elevation drawing.

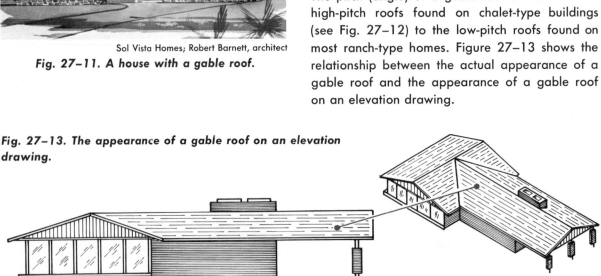

Fig. 27–14. A house with a hip roof.

Fig. 27–15. The appearance of a hip roof on an elevation drawing.

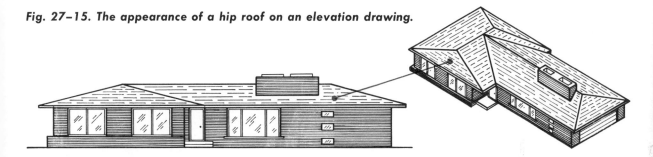

Hip roofs are used when roof-line protection is desired around the entire perimeter of the building. Notice how the hip-roof overhang shades the windows of the house in Fig. 27–14. For this reason hip roofs are very popular in warm climates. Figure 27–15 shows the method of drawing hip roofs on elevation drawings. Hip roofs are commonly used on Regency and French Provincial homes.

Flat roofs are used to create a low silhouette on many modern homes (Fig. 27–16). Since no support is achieved by the leaning together of rafters, slightly heavier rafters are needed for flat roofs. Built-up asphalt construction is often used on flat roofs, and water may also be used as an insulator and solar heater. Figure 27–17 illustrates

Fig. 27–16. A home with a flat roof.

Fig. 27–17. The appearance of a flat roof on an elevation drawing.

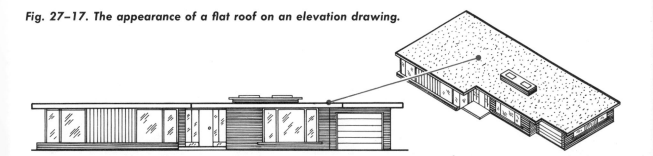

Fig. 27–18. A shed roof with celestial windows.

Fig. 27–21. A geodesic dome.

the method of drawing flat roofs on elevations.

Shed roofs are flat roofs that are higher at one end than at the other. They may be used effectively when two levels exist and where additional light is needed. The use of celestial windows between the two sheds (Fig. 27–18) can help to provide skylight-type illumination. The double shed is really very advantageous on hillside split-level structures. Figure 27–19 shows a method of illustrating shed roofs on elevations.

Miscellaneous roof types. In addition to the common roof types already mentioned, the *gambrel, mansard,* and *butterfly roofs* and the *geodesic dome* are gaining in popularity (Fig. 27–20). The geodesic dome may constitute the roof (Fig. 27–21) or may extend completely to the ground and be part of the side wall structure as well.

Fig. 27–22. Roof overhang is needed for protection from sun, rain, and snow.

Fig. 27–19. The appearance of a shed roof on an elevation drawing.

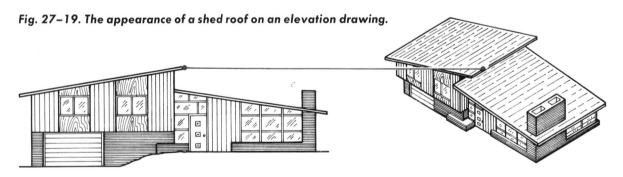

Fig. 27–20. Other types of roofs.

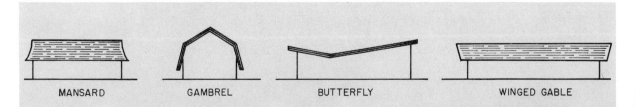

MANSARD GAMBREL BUTTERFLY WINGED GABLE

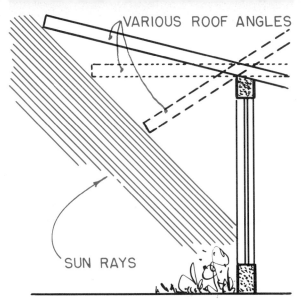

VARIOUS ROOF ANGLES

SUN RAYS

Fig. 27-23. The angle of the overhang determines its length.

Fig. 27-25A. The effect of a small overhang.

Fig. 27-25B. The advantage of a large overhang.

Overhang. Sufficient roof overhang should be provided to afford protection from the sun, rain, and snow (Fig. 27-22). The length and the angle of the overhang will greatly affect its appearance and its functioning in providing protection. Figure 27-23 shows that when the pitch is low, a larger overhang is needed to provide protection. However, with a high-pitch roof the overhang may be extended and block the view from the inside.

To provide protection and at the same time allow sufficient light to enter the windows, slatted

overhangs similar to those shown in Fig. 27-24 may be used.

Figure 27-25A shows the effect of a small overhang. Figure 27-25B shows the protection afforded by a large overhang. The overhang does not always need to be parallel to the sides of the house. Notice how the roof line in Fig. 27-26

Fig. 27-24. Slatted roof overhang.

Briar Hill Stone Company

Fig. 27-26. Additional protection can be achieved by changing the angle and overhang of the roof.

Allan J. Gelbin, architect

Fig. 27-27. A house with well-related lines and areas.

Home Planners, Inc.

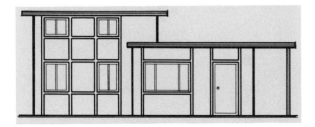

Fig. 27-28A. An elevation drawing showing related lines.

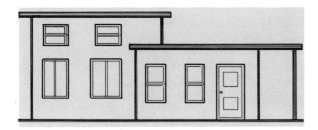

Fig. 27-28B. Unrelated elevation lines.

affords additional protection when the point of the overhang is extended from the outside wall.

This arrangement makes possible very large distances from wall to gutter.

▶ Form and Space

The total appearance of the elevation depends upon the relationship among the areas of the elevation such as surfaces, doors, windows, and chimneys. The balance of these areas, the emphasis placed on various components of the elevation, the texture, the light, the color, and the shadow patterns all affect greatly the general appearance of the elevation.

▶ Related Areas

The elevation should appear as one integral and functional facade rather than as a surface in which holes have been cut for windows and doors and to which structural components, such as chimneys, have been added without reference to the other areas of the elevation. Figure 27-27 shows a house with well-related lines and areas. Doors, windows, and chimney lines should constitute part of the general pattern of the elevation and should not exist in isolation. Figure 27-28A shows an elevation in which the windows and doors are related to the major lines of the elevation. Figure 27-28B shows the same elevation with unrelated doors and windows.

Windows. When the vertical lines of the windows are extended to the eave line from the ground line or planter line or some division line in the separation of materials, the vertical lines become related to the building. Horizontal lines of a window extending from one post to another, or from one vertical separation in the elevation to another, as between a post and a chimney, also help to relate the window to the major lines of the

Fig. 27-29. Effective relationship between roof, windows, siding, and chimney.

Home Planners, Inc.

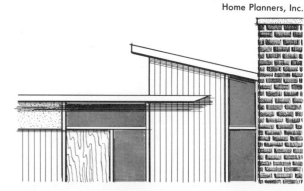

176

elevation. For example, the windows in Fig. 27–29 were related by being extended to fill the area between posts and between the door and eave line.

Doors. Doors can easily be related to the major lines of the house by extending the area above the door to the ridge line, or divider, and making the side panels consistent with the door size, as shown in Fig. 27–30. A comparison between Fig. 27–31A and Fig. 27–31B shows the effect of extending the door lines vertically and horizontally to integrate the door with the window line and the overall surface of the elevation.

▶ Shape

Although it is important to relate the lines of the elevation to each other, nevertheless, the overall shape of the elevation should reflect the basic shape of the building. Do not attempt to camouflage the shape of the elevation. An example of such camouflage is the old Western store (Fig. 27–32), whose builder tried to disguise the actual elevation by constructing a false front.

Patio walls, fences, or other structures may block the view of the elevation wall. If such blocking occurs, it is advisable to draw the elevation with the wall in position, to show how the elevation will appear when viewed from a distance (Fig. 27–33A). It is advisable also to draw the elevation as it will exist inside the wall (Fig. 27–33B).

Balance. The term *balance* refers to the symmetry of the elevation. An elevation is either *for-*

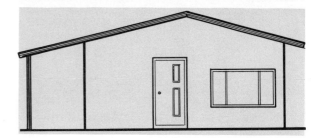

Fig. 27–31A. Unextended door and window lines.

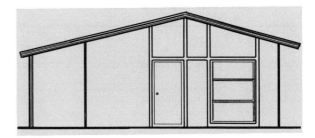

Fig. 27–31B. Door and window lines extended horizontally and vertically.

Fig. 27–32. Avoid elevation camouflage.

mally or *informally* balanced (Fig. 27–34). Formal balance is used extensively in colonial and period styles of architecture. Informal balance is more widely used in modern residential architecture. Informally balanced elevations are frequently used in modern designs such as ranch and split-level styles.

Emphasis. Elevation emphasis, or accent, can be achieved by several different devices. An area may be accented by mass, by color, or by material. Every elevation should have some point of emphasis. Compare the two elevations in Fig.

Fig. 27–30. A door unit related to the other lines of the elevation.

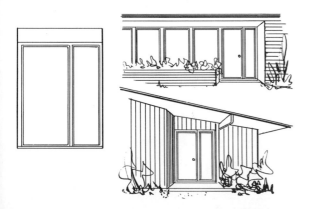

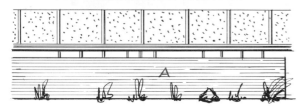

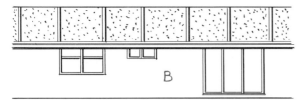

Fig. 27-33. It is sometimes necessary to draw an elevation with an obstructing feature (A) and without it (B).

27-35. They are the same except that in the first example the chimney has been accented to provide a focal point.

Light and color. An elevation that is composed of all light areas or all dark areas tends to be uninteresting and neutral. Some balancing of light, shade, and color is desirable in most elevations. This can be achieved through developing shadow patterns by depressing areas, by using overhang, by grating, and by color variation, as shown in Fig. 27-36.

Texture. An elevation contains many types of materials—glass, wood, masonry, ceramics—but these must be carefully and tastefully balanced to be effective. An elevation comprised of too few materials is ineffective and neutral. Likewise an elevation which uses too many materials, especially masonry, is equally objectionable.

In choosing the materials for the elevation, the designer should not mix horizontal and vertical

Fig. 27-34. A formally and an informally balanced elevation.

Fig. 27-35. Every elevation should have some point of emphasis.

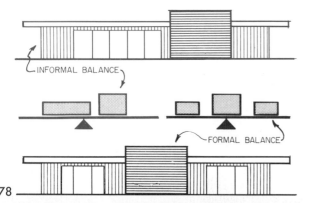

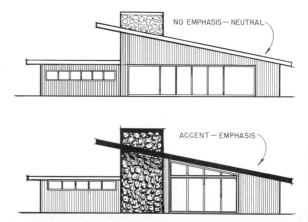

Fig. 27–36. Light, shade, and color should be balanced on every elevation.

Fig. 27–38. Emphasis placed on the horizontal eave line.

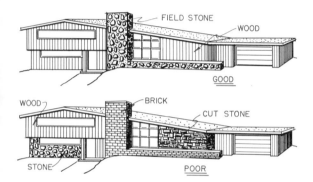

Fig. 27–37. The effect of combining too many materials.

siding or different types of masonry. If brick is the primary masonry used, brick should be used throughout. It should not be mixed with stone. Similarly, it is not desirable to mix several types of brick or several types of stone. Figure 27–37 shows the effect of mixing too many materials in an elevation.

▶ Lines

The lines of an elevation are the *ground line, eave line,* and *ridge line.* These are horizontal lines. One of these lines should be emphasized. In Fig. 27–38, the horizontal eave line has been accented by being extended from the center of the building over the carport. The lines of an elevation can help to create horizontal or vertical emphasis. If the ground line, ridge line, and eave line are accented, the emphasis will be placed on the horizontal, as shown in Fig. 27–39. If the emphasis is placed on vertical lines such as corner posts and columns, the emphasis will be vertical. Figure 27–40 shows a comparison between placing the emphasis on horizontal lines and placing the emphasis on vertical lines. In general, low buildings will usually appear longer and lower if the emphasis is placed on horizontal lines.

Lines should be consistent—that is, the lines of an elevation should appear to flow together as one

Fig. 27–39. Horizontal emphasis.

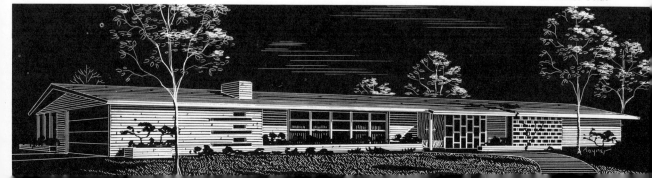

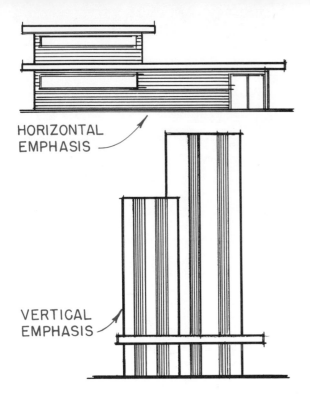

HORIZONTAL EMPHASIS

VERTICAL EMPHASIS

Fig. 27–40. Emphasis on vertical and on horizontal lines.

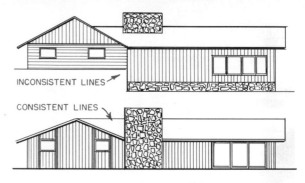

INCONSISTENT LINES

CONSISTENT LINES

Fig. 27–41. Consistent lines are essential for a good elevation design.

integrated line pattern. It is usually better to continue a line through an elevation for a long distance than to break the line and start it again. Figure 27–41 shows the difference between a building with consistent lines and a building with inconsistent lines. Rhythm can be developed by the use of lines, and lines can be repeated in various patterns. When a line is repeated, the basic consistency of the elevation is considerably

strengthened. Notice how the emphasis is placed on the horizontal lines in the house shown in Fig. 27–42, yet a certain rhythmic repetition is achieved by repeating the vertical post design in several areas of the structure.

Problems

1. Sketch an elevation of your own design. Trace the elevation, adding a flat roof, gable roof, shed roof, and butterfly roof. Choose the one you like best and the one that is most functional for your design.

2. Sketch the front elevation of your home. Vary the roof style, making it consistent with the major lines of the elevation. Redesign the elevation, relating the door and window lines to the major lines of the building.

Fig. 27–42. Emphasis is placed on horizontal lines on this house.

New Homes Guide

Fig. 27–43. *Resketch this elevation to eliminate the inconsistent use of materials.*

3. Too many materials are used in the building shown in Fig. 27–43. Sketch an elevation of this house and change the building materials to be consistent with the design.

4. Identify the roof types shown in Fig. 27–44.

5. Sketch the elevation shown in Fig. 27–45 with a hip roof, double-shed roof, and gable roof. Resketch this illustration, using different siding materials.

6. Identify the roof shown in Fig. 27–39.

7. Resketch the bottom elevation shown in Fig. 27–35. Place the emphasis on an area of the elevation other than the chimney.

8. Resketch the formally balanced elevation shown in Fig. 27–34. Convert this elevation to an informally balanced elevation.

9. Resketch the elevation shown in Fig. 27–19. Change the roof style and siding materials.

10. Resketch the elevation shown in Fig. 27–17, using a gable roof.

11. Sketch the elevation shown in Fig. 27–15, using a double-shed roof.

12. Define the following terms: *one-story house, one-and-one-half-story house, bilevel, split-level, hip roof, flat roof, gable roof, shed roof, high pitch, low pitch, celestial windows, gambrel roof, mansard roof, butterfly roof, overhang, related lines, unrelated lines, ridge lines, eave lines, ground lines, formal balance, informal balance, texture emphasis.*

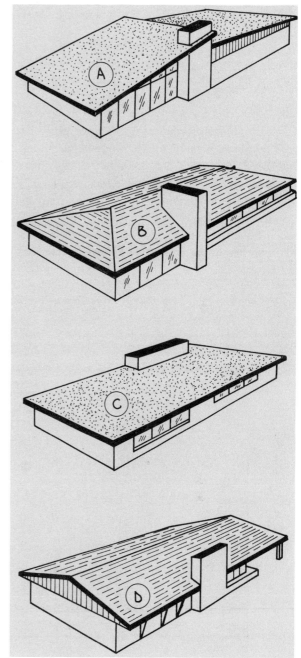

Fig. 27–44. *Identify these roof styles.*

Fig. 27–45. *Redesign this elevation with a different roof.*

Unit 28. Elevation Projection

Elevation drawings are projected from the floor plan of an architectural drawing just as the side views are projected from the front view of an orthographic drawing. Figure 28–1 shows how elevations are projected from the floor plan. The position of the chimney, doors, windows, overhang, and building corners are projected directly from the floor plan outward to the elevation plane. If you trace the projection of the chimney from the plan to each of the elevations shown in Fig. 28–1, you will see the relative position of the chimney as you view the house from four different directions.

▶ Elevation Planes

You may think of the elevation as a drawing placed on a vertical plane. Figure 28–2 shows how this vertical plane is related to the floor-plan projection.

Functional orientation. Floor elevations are normally projected from the floor plan. When these elevations are classified according to their function, they are called the front elevation, the rear elevation, the right elevation, and the left elevation. The front view of the house is known as the *front elevation*. The view projected from the rear of the house is known as the *rear elevation*. The view

Fig. 28–1. Projection of the basic elevations from the floor plan.

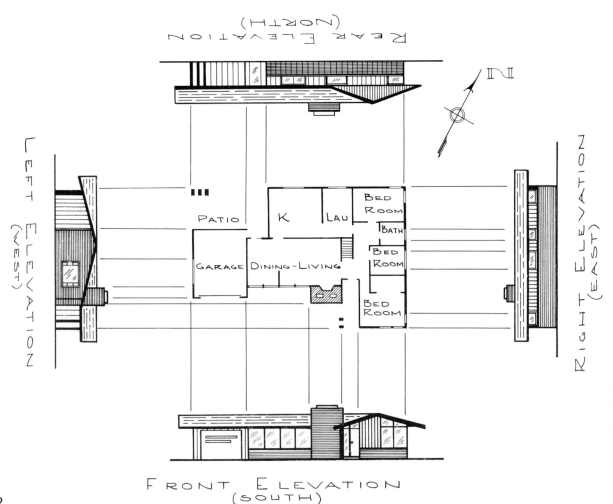

projected from the right side of the house is known as the *right elevation,* and the view projected from the left side of the house is known as the *left elevation.* When these elevations are all projected on the same drawing sheet, the rear elevation appears to be upside down and the right and left elevations appear to rest on their sides. Owing to the large size of most elevation drawings, and because of the desirability of drawing elevations as we normally see them, each elevation is usually drawn on a separate sheet. Even when they are drawn on the same sheet, they are drawn as we normally see them, with the ground line on the bottom and the roof on the top.

Compass orientation. Points of the compass, north, east, south, and west, are often used by architects to describe and label elevation drawings. This method is preferred when there is no so-called front or rear view to a structure. When this method is used, the north arrow on the floor plan is the key to the designation of the elevation title. For example, in Fig. 28–2A the rear elevation is facing north. Therefore the rear elevation could also be called the north elevation. Here the front elevation is also the south elevation, the left elevation is the west elevation.

Auxiliary elevations. When a floor plan has more than four sides, or sides that deviate from the normal 90° projection, an auxiliary elevation view is often necessary. To project an auxiliary elevation, follow the same rules for projecting orthographic auxiliaries. Project the auxiliary elevation perpendicular to the wall of the floor plan from which you are projecting, as shown in Fig. 28–2B. When an auxiliary elevation is drawn, it is usually prepared in addition to the standard elevations and does not replace them. It merely clarifies the foreshortened lines of the major elevations caused by the receding angles.

▶ **Steps in Projecting Elevations**

The major lines of an elevation are derived by projecting vertical lines from the floor plan and measuring the position of horizontal lines from the ground line.

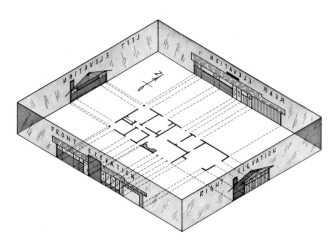

Fig. 28–2A. Elevation plane of projection.

Fig. 28–2B. Auxiliary elevation projection.

Home Planners, Inc.

183

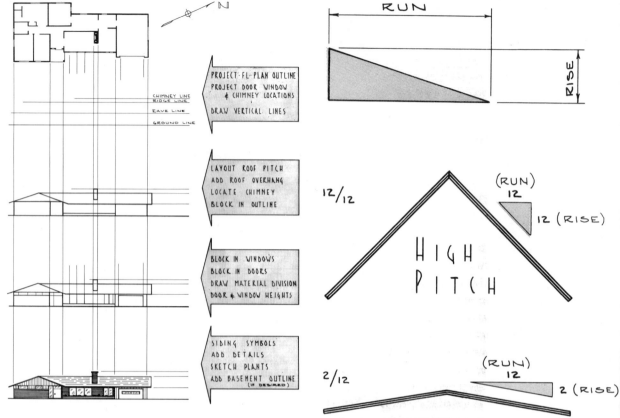

Fig. 28-3. The sequence of projecting elevations.

Fig. 28-4. A high-pitch and a low-pitch roof.

Vertical-line projection. Vertical lines representing the main lines of the building should first be projected as shown in Fig. 28–3. These lines show the overall length and width of the building. They also show the length of the major parts or offsets of the building.

Horizontal-line projection. Horizontal lines which represent the height of the eave line, ridge line, and chimney line above the ground line are projected to intersect with the vertical lines drawn from the floor plan, as shown in Fig. 28–3. The intersection of these lines provides the overall outline of the elevation.

Roof-line projection. The ridge line and eave line cannot be accurately located until the *roof pitch* (angle) is established. On a high-pitch roof there is a greater distance between the ridge line and the eave line than on a low-pitch roof. Figure 28–4 shows a high-pitch roof and a low-pitch roof.

Pitch is the angle of the roof and is described as the "rise over the run" (rise/run). *Run* is the horizontal distance covered by a roof. *Rise* is the vertical distance. The run is always expressed in units of 12. Therefore, the pitch shows the proportion of the rise to 12.

When the roof pitch is established, the rise and the run should be drawn to scale and the roof angle established by connecting the extremities of these lines, as shown in Fig. 28–5. Next, the roof angle can be extended and the overhang measured from the outside wall to the eave. When the center line of the house is established, the exact positions

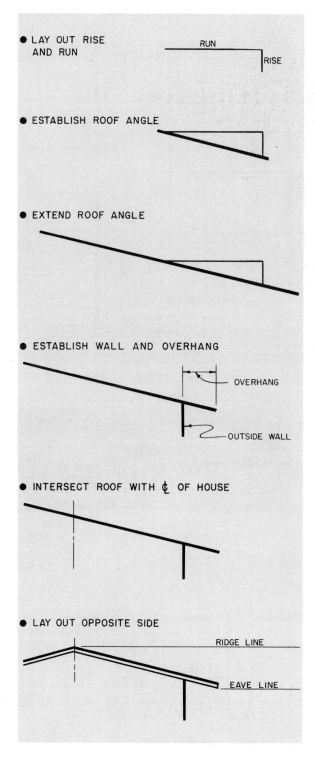

• LAY OUT RISE AND RUN

RUN

RISE

• ESTABLISH ROOF ANGLE

• EXTEND ROOF ANGLE

• ESTABLISH WALL AND OVERHANG

OVERHANG

OUTSIDE WALL

• INTERSECT ROOF WITH ¢ OF HOUSE

• LAY OUT OPPOSITE SIDE

RIDGE LINE

EAVE LINE

Fig. 28-5. The sequence of projecting roof outline.

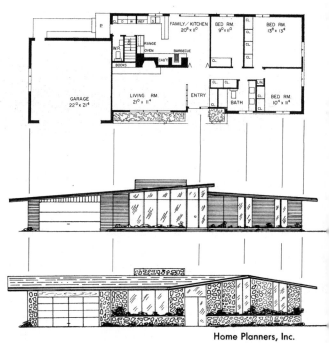

P CLO W REF S

FAMILY / KITCHEN
20⁰ x 11⁰

BED RM.
9⁰ x 11⁰

BED RM.
13⁸ x 13⁴

W.R.

RANGE

OVEN

BARBECUE

CL

CL

BOOKS

CAB'T

GARAGE
22⁰ x 21⁴

LIVING RM.
21⁰ x 11⁴

ENTRY

CL CL

CL LIN

CL

BATH

CL

BED RM.
10⁴ x 11⁴

CL

Home Planners, Inc.

Fig. 28-6. Two different elevation styles projected from one floor plan.

of the ridge line and eave line are established, and the eave line and ridge line are projected and blocked in as shown in Fig. 28–3.

Blocking in the outline. After the roof outline has been established, the major lines of the house are drawn. This drawing is made by following the outline developed from the intersection of horizontal and vertical lines, as shown in Fig. 28–3. The outlines of materials, doors, windows, chimney, and roof are drawn in their final line weight.

Adding elevation symbols. The next step is to add the elevation symbol for each material and feature on the elevation, as shown in Figs. 29–1 and 29–2.

▶ Flexibility

It is possible to project many different elevation styles from one floor plan. The pitch, size of overhang, position of the grade line, window position and style, chimney size and style, and the door

Signature Homes

Fig. 28–7. Sketch the south elevation of this plan.

style and position all can be manipulated to create different effects. Figure 28–6 shows two different elevations projected from the same floor plan. Here the change was accomplished primarily by varying the distances between the major lines of the elevation.

Problems

1. Project the front, rear, right, and left elevations of a floor plan of your own design.

2. Sketch the front elevation of your home.

3. Sketch or draw the south elevation of the floor plan shown in Fig. 28–7.

4. Project and sketch or draw the front elevation suggested in the pictorial drawing and floor plan in Fig. 28–8.

5. Sketch or draw all four elevations of the plan shown in Fig. 28–9.

6. Complete the elevation projection problem

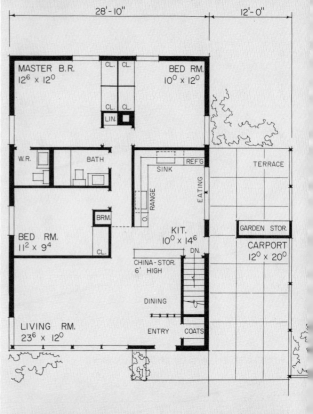

Home Planners, Inc.

Fig. 28–8. Draw the front elevation of this plan.

Fig. 28–9. Sketch or draw all four elevations of this plan.

Home Planners, Inc.

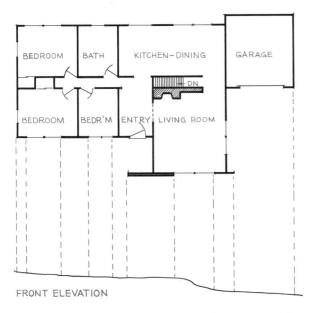

FRONT ELEVATION

Fig. 28–10. Complete the front elevation on the terrain as shown.

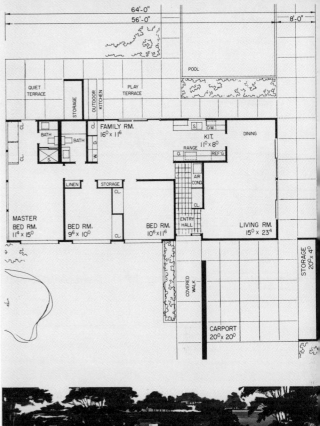

Home Planners, Inc.

Fig. 28–11. Sketch the front and left elevations of this house.

shown in Fig. 28–10 by drawing the elevation on the terrain as shown.

7. Sketch the front and left elevations of the house shown in Fig. 28–11.

8. Define the following terms: *front elevation, rear elevation, right elevation, left elevation, north elevation, east elevation, south elevation, west elevation, auxiliary elevations, pitch, rise, run, elevation symbols.*

Unit 29. Elevation Symbols

Symbols are needed to clarify and simplify elevation drawings. Symbols help to describe the basic features of the elevation. They show what building materials are used, and they describe the style and position of doors and windows. Symbols also help to make the elevation drawing look realistic. Some of the most common elevation symbols are

shown on the elevation drawing in Figs. 29–1 and 29–2.

▶ **Material Symbols**

Figure 29–3 shows the relationship between the actual construction and the symbol used to represent that construction. Most architectural symbols

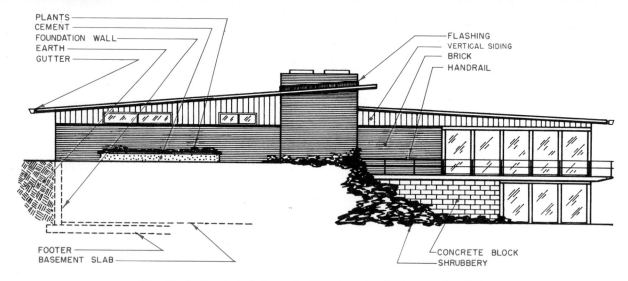

Fig. 29-1. Symbols help make the elevation look more realistic.

Fig. 29-2. Common elevation symbols.

Fig. 29-3. The relationship between symbols and actual construction.

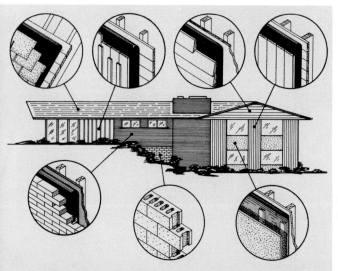

look very similar to the material they represent. However, in many cases the symbol does not show the exact appearance of the material. For example, the symbol for brick, as shown in Fig. 29-3, does not include all the lines shown in the pictorial drawing. Representing brick on the elevation drawing exactly as it appears is a long, laborious, and unnecessary process. Therefore, many elevation symbols are simplifications of the actual appearance of the material. The symbol often resembles the appearance of the material at a distance.

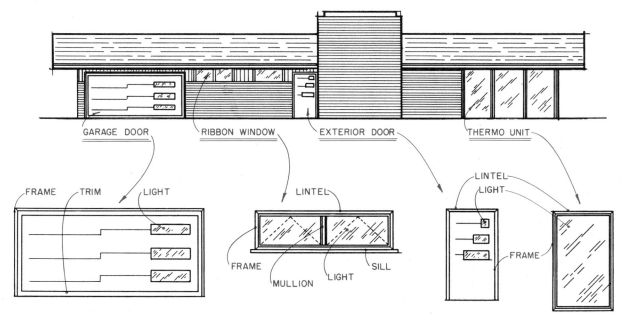

Fig. 29-4. Window symbols as they appear on elevation drawings.

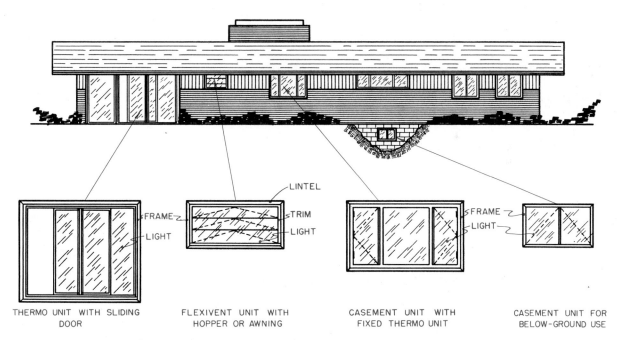

Fig. 29-5. Often it is not possible to show all details of windows on elevation drawings.

▶ Window Symbols

The position and style of windows greatly affect the appearance of the elevation. Windows are therefore drawn on the elevation with as much detail as the scale of the drawing permits. Parts of windows that should be shown on all elevation drawings include the sill, sash, mullions, and muntins (Fig. 29-4). Figure 29-5 shows the

Fig. 29-6. The placement of the hinge is shown by the dotted line.

method of illustrating casement-, awning-, and slider-type windows.

In addition to showing the parts of a window, it is also necessary to show the direction of hinge for casement- and awning-type windows on the elevation drawing. Figure 29-6 shows the method of indicating the direction of the hinge on elevation drawings. The direction of the hinge is shown by dotted lines. The point of the dotted line shows the part of the window to which the hinge is attached.

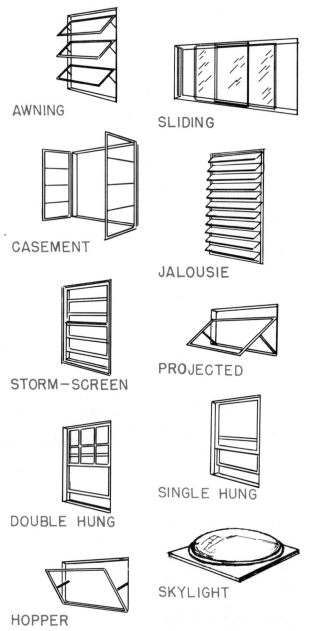

AWNING

SLIDING

CASEMENT

JALOUSIE

STORM—SCREEN

PROJECTED

DOUBLE HUNG

SINGLE HUNG

SKYLIGHT

HOPPER

Fig. 29-7. Common window styles.

Many different styles of windows are available, as shown in Fig. 29-7. Figure 29-8 shows the methods of illustrating some of these windows on elevation drawings.

Architects often use an alternative method of showing window styles on elevation drawings. In

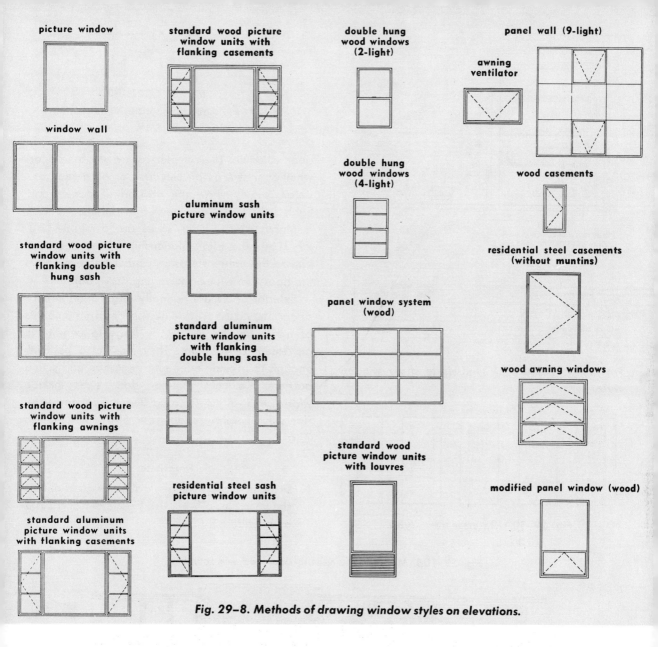

Fig. 29–8. Methods of drawing window styles on elevations.

this alternative method, the draftsman prepares a window-detail drawing, as shown in Fig. 29–9, to a rather large scale. He prepares a window drawing in different detail for each different style of window to be used. When the elevation is drawn, only the position of the window is shown. The style of window to be included in this opening is then shown by a letter or number indexed to the letter or number used for the large detail drawing. Sometimes the window symbol is abbreviated

and indexed in the same way to a more complete detail. Unit 51 contains further treatment of door and window schedules.

▶ **Door Symbols**

Doors are shown on elevation drawings by methods similar to those used for illustrating window style and position. They are either drawn completely if the scale permits, or they are shown in abbreviated form, or merely the outline is indexed to a

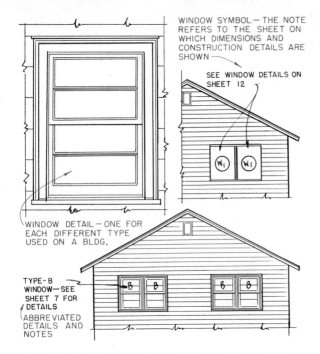

WINDOW SYMBOL — THE NOTE REFERS TO THE SHEET ON WHICH DIMENSIONS AND CONSTRUCTION DETAILS ARE SHOWN

SEE WINDOW DETAILS ON SHEET 12

WINDOW DETAIL — ONE FOR EACH DIFFERENT TYPE USED ON A BLDG.

TYPE-B WINDOW — SEE SHEET 7 FOR DETAILS

ABBREVIATED DETAILS AND NOTES

Fig. 29-9. The use of symbols to show window style.

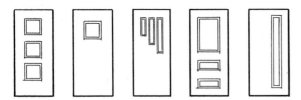

Fig. 29-10A. Exterior door styles.

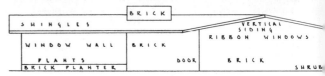

Fig. 29-11. Add symbols to this elevation.

door schedule. The complete drawing of the door, whether shown on an elevation or on a separate detail, should show the division of panels and lights, sill, jamb, and head-trim details.

Many exterior door styles are available (Fig. 29-10A). The total relationship of the door and trim to the entire elevation cannot be seen unless the door trim is also shown (Fig. 29-10B).

Exterior doors are normally larger than interior doors. They must provide access for larger amounts of traffic and be sufficiently large to permit the movement of furniture. They must also be thick enough to provide adequate insulation and sound barriers. Common exterior door sizes include widths of 2'-8", 3'-0", and 3'-6". Common exterior door heights range from 6'-8" or 7'-0" to 7'-6".

Problems

1. Draw and add symbols to the elevation outline shown in Fig. 29-11. Use Figs. 29-1 and 29-2 as a guide.

Fig. 29-10B. Methods of drawing door and window trim.

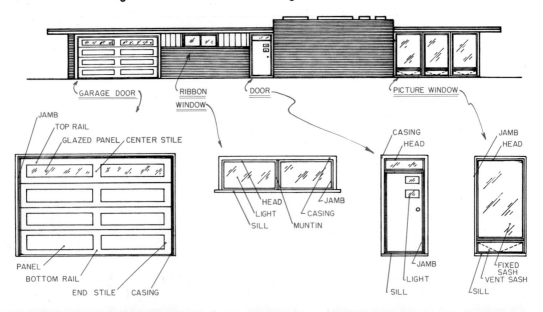

Fig. 29-12. Identify these elevation symbols.

2. Redesign the front elevation of your home. Change siding materials and door and window styles.

3. Add elevation symbols to an elevation of your own design.

4. Identify the elevation symbols shown in Fig. 29-12.

5. Draw the front elevation of the house shown in Fig. 29-13. Show approximate elevation symbols.

6. Redesign the front elevation of the house shown in Fig. 29-13, using brick or stone as the basic siding material.

7. Draw the front elevation of the house shown in Fig. 29-14. Use symbols for the siding materials shown in this picture.

8. Draw the front and right elevations of the home shown in Fig. 29-15. Use the existing siding materials or redesign the elevation, changing the materials as you wish.

Fig. 29-13. Draw the front elevation of this house, complete with symbols.

Signature Homes

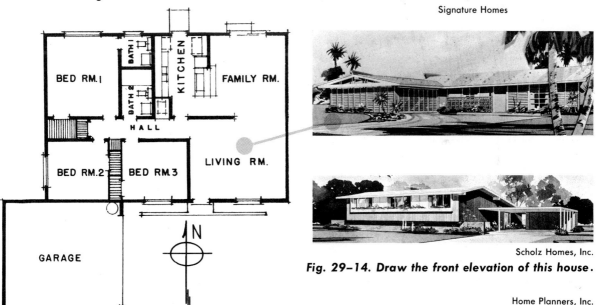

Scholz Homes, Inc.

Fig. 29-14. Draw the front elevation of this house.

Home Planners, Inc.

Fig. 29-15. Draw the right and front elevations of this home.

Unit 30. Elevation Dimensioning

Horizontal width and length dimensions are placed on floor plans. Vertical (height) dimensions are placed on elevation drawings.

Many dimensions on elevation drawings show the vertical distance from a datum line. The *datum line* is a horizontal plane that remains constant. Sea level is commonly used as the datum for many drawings, although any distance from sea level can be conveniently used.

Dimensions on elevation drawings show the height above the datum of the ground line. They also show the distance from the ground line to the floor, ceiling, and ridge and eave lines, and to the tops of chimneys, doors, and windows. Distances below the ground line are shown by dotted lines.

▶ Rules for Elevation Dimensioning

Elevation dimensions must conform to basic standards to ensure consistency of interpretation. The arrows on the elevation drawing in Fig. 30–1 show the application of the following rules for elevation dimensioning:

1. Vertical elevation dimensions should be read from the right of the drawing.

2. Levels to be dimensioned should be labeled with a note, term, or abbreviation.

3. Room heights are shown by dimensioning from the floor line to the ceiling line.

4. The depth of footers (footings) is dimensioned from the ground line.

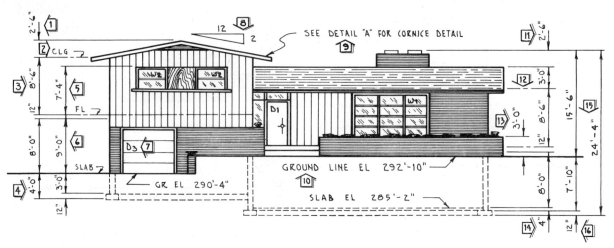

Fig. 30–1. Rules for elevation dimensioning.

Fig. 30–2. Add dimensions to this elevation.

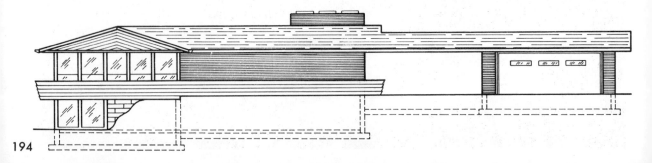

Fig. 30–3. Draw and dimension the front elevation of this house.

5. Heights of windows and doors are dimensioned from the floor line to the top of the windows or doors.

6. Elevation dimensions show only vertical distances. Horizontal distances are shown on the floor plan.

7. Windows and doors may be indexed to door or window schedule, or the style of the windows and doors may be shown on the elevation drawing.

8. The roof pitch is shown by indicating the rise over the run.

9. Dimensions for small, complex, or obscure areas should be indexed to a separate detail.

10. Ground-line elevations are expressed as heights above the datum.

11. Heights of chimneys above the ridge line are dimensioned.

12. Floor and ceiling lines are shown by center lines that function as extension lines.

13. Heights of planters and walls are dimensioned from the ground line.

14. Thicknesses of slabs are dimensioned.

15. Overall height dimensions are placed on the outside of subdimensions.

16. Thicknesses of footers (footings) are dimensioned.

Problems

1. Add the elevation dimensions to an elevation drawing of your own design.

2. Add dimensions to the elevation drawing shown in Fig. 30–2.

3. Dimension an elevation drawing of your home.

4. Draw an elevation of the home shown in Fig. 30–3. Completely dimension this elevation, following the rules for dimensioning outlined in this unit.

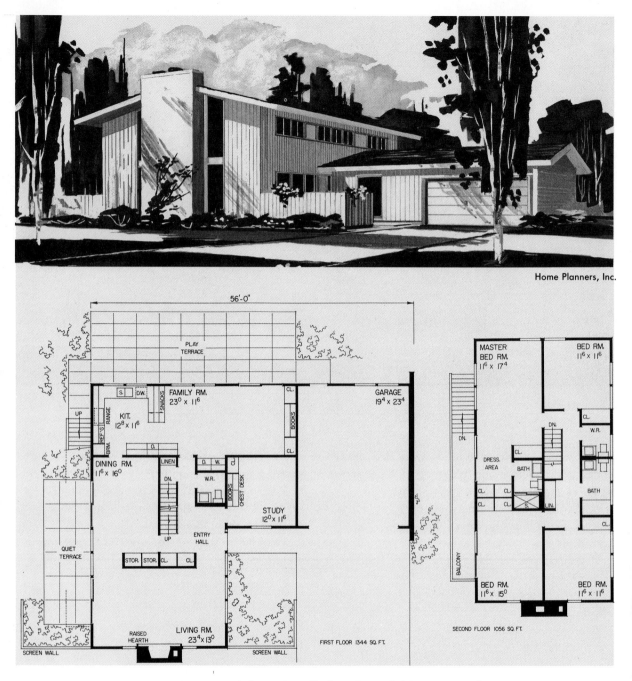

Fig. 30–4. Draw and dimension all elevations of this two-story home.

5. Draw four elevations of the home shown above.
6. Define these terms: *datum line, sea level, vertical dimensions, ground line, ceiling line, ridge line, eave line, chimney line, room height, door schedule, window schedule, slab thickness, footer thickness, overall dimensions, subdimensions.*

Unit 31. Landscape Rendering

Elevation drawings, although accurate in every detail, do not show exactly what the house will look like when it is complete and landscaped. The reason is that elevation drawings do not show the position of trees, shrubbery, and other landscape features that would be part of the total elevation design. Adding these landscape features to the elevation drawing creates a more realistic drawing of the house.

▶ Interpretive Drawing

Figure 31–1 shows some of the advantages of adding landscape features to an elevation drawing. The elevation shown in Fig. 31–1A, when dimensioned, would be adequate for construction purposes. However, the illustration shown in 31–1B more closely approximates the final appearance of the house.

Dimensions and hidden lines are omitted when landscape features are added to elevation drawings. Drawings of this type are prepared solely to interpret and predict the final appearance of the house. They are not used for construction purposes.

Fig. 31–1. Before and after landscape rendering.

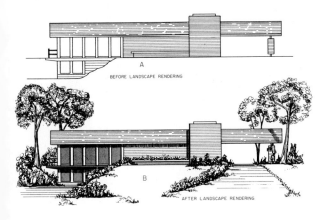

▶ Sequence

An elevation drawing is converted into a landscape elevation drawing in several basic steps, as shown in Fig. 31–2. After material symbols are added to the elevation, the positions of trees and shrubs are added. The elevation lines within the outlines of the trees and shrubs are erased, and details are added. Finally, shade lines are added to trees, windows, roof overhangs, chimneys, and other major projections of the house. The addition of landscape features should not hide the basic lines of the house. If many trees or shrubs are placed in front of the house, it is best to draw them in their winter state.

Fig. 31–2. Sequence of adding landscape features to an elevation.

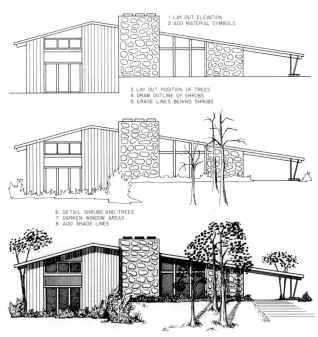

Fig. 31–3. Sketches for drawing trees and shrubbery on an elevation.

Figure 31–3 shows several methods of drawing trees and shrubs on elevation drawings. The draftsman should use the medium that best suits the elevation drawing to be rendered.

▶ Landscape Planning

The importance of effective landscape design is obvious when the property shown in Fig. 31–4 is compared with the property shown in Fig. 31–5.

Fig. 31–4. Landscaping affects the appearance of the elevation.

Julius Shulman Photo

Fig. 31–5. A house looks bare without landscaping.

Fig. 31–6. Add landscape features to this elevation.

Functional landscape planning not only enhances the appearance of the house but also provides shade from the sun and a baffle from the wind. When carefully planned, landscaping can provide area privacy and traffic control.

Problems

1. Add landscape features to the elevation shown in Fig. 31–6.

2. Add trees, shrubs, plants, and shadows to an elevation of your own design.

3. Add landscape features to an elevation drawing of your home. Improve the present landscape treatment.

4. Draw a front elevation of the house shown in Fig. 31–7. Add landscape features to this drawing.

5. Define these terms: *landscape rendering, interpretive drawings, shade lines.*

Fig. 31–7. Draw a front elevation of this house and add landscape features.

Scholz Homes, Inc.

SECTION SEVEN. PICTORIAL DRAWINGS

Pictorial drawings, isometric and perspective, are picture-like drawings. They show several sides of an object in one drawing. Isometric drawings are used extensively in mechanical engineering work. However, the perspective drawing is the more popular type of architectural pictorial drawing. Since the subject of most architectural pictorial drawings is much larger than that of most engineering drawings, perspective techniques are necessary to eliminate distortion of the object.

Unit 32. Exteriors

A *perspective drawing*, more than any other type of drawing, resembles a photograph of the exterior of a building (Fig. 32–1). This is true because the parts of the building that are furthest from your view appear to recede. For example, as you look down a railroad track, the tracks appear to come together and vanish at a point on the distant horizon.

On the perspective drawing, the receding lines of a building are purposely drawn closer together on one side or several sides of the building to create the illusion of depth. The point at which these lines intersect on a perspective drawing is known as the *vanishing point*. Just as railroad tracks would appear to come together at the horizon, the vanishing points in a perspective drawing are always placed on a horizon line. In preparing perspective drawings, the horizon line is the same as your line of sight. If the horizon line is placed through the building, the building will appear at

Libbey-Owens-Ford Glass Company

Fig. 32–1. A photograph that is similar to a perspective drawing.

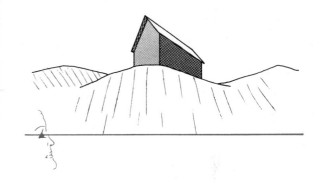

your eye level. If the horizon line is placed below the building, it will appear to be above your eye level. If the horizon line is placed above the building, it will appear to be below your line of sight (Fig. 32–2).

Perspective drawings do not reveal the true size and shape of the building but are used for interpretive purposes only. Perspective drawings are never used for working designs. To make the drawing appear more realistic, the actual length of the receding sides of the drawing are shortened. Figure 32–3 shows a perspective drawing with shortened sides and an *isometric drawing* which is prepared to the true dimensions of the building. The two sides of the isometric drawing appear distorted because we are accustomed to seeing areas decrease in depth from our point of vision.

▶ **One-point Perspective**

A one-point perspective is a drawing in which the front view is drawn to its true scale and all receding sides are projected to a single vanishing point located on the horizon. If the vanishing point is placed directly behind the object, as shown in Fig. 32–4, no sides would show unless they were drawn with dots (hidden lines). If the vanishing point is placed directly on the right or on the left

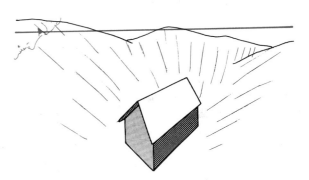

Fig. 32–2. The effect of horizon-line placement.

Fig. 32–3. The length of receding lines should be shortened on perspective drawings.

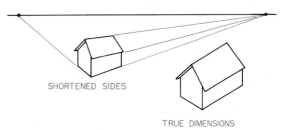

SHORTENED SIDES

TRUE DIMENSIONS

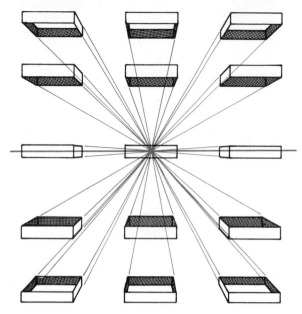

Fig. 32–4. A one-point perspective can show any three sides.

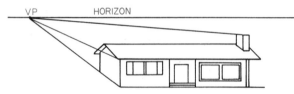

Fig. 32–5. Connect corners of the front view to the vanishing point.

of the object, with the horizon passing through the object, only one side will show. If the object is placed above the horizon line and vanishing point, the bottom of the object will show. If the object is placed below the horizon line and vanishing point, the top of the object will show.

Fig. 32–6. The use of two vanishing points on the horizon.

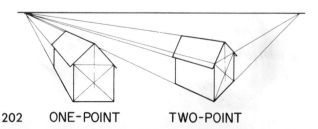

ONE-POINT   TWO-POINT

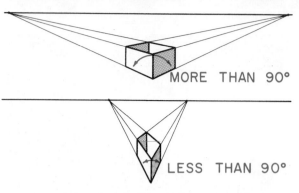

MORE THAN 90°

LESS THAN 90°

Fig. 32–7. The distance between vanishing points affects the angles of the object.

The one-point perspective is relatively simple to draw. The front view is drawn to the exact scale of the building. The corners of the front view are then projected to one vanishing point. Follow these steps in drawing or sketching a one-point perspective:

1. Draw the front view of the object (building). Draw the horizon line above, below, or through the building.

2. Mark the position of the vanishing point on the horizon line: to the left if you want to see the left side of the building; to the right if you want to see the right side of the building; to the rear if you want to see only the front.

3. Project all corners of the front view to the vanishing point, as shown in Fig. 32–5.

4. Estimate the depths of the receding sides and draw a vertical line parallel with the vertical lines of the front view to indicate the back corner of the building.

5. Make all object lines heavy, and eradicate the horizon line and projection lines leading to the vanishing point.

▶ Two-point Perspective

A two-point perspective is a drawing in which the receding sides are projected to two vanishing points, one on each end of the horizon line. In a two-point perspective, no sides are drawn exactly to scale. All sides recede to vanishing points. Therefore, the only true-length line on a two-point perspective is the corner of the building from which the sides are projected (Fig. 32–6).

Fig. 32–8. The effect of placing the right vanishing point closer to the building than the left vanishing point.

When the vanishing points are placed close together on the horizon line, considerable distortion results because of the acute receding angles (Fig. 32–7). When the vanishing points are placed further apart, the drawing looks more realistic. One vanishing point is often placed further from the building than the other vanishing point. This placement allows one side of the building to recede at a sharp angle, and the front of the building to recede less sharply. The vanishing points for the perspective drawing shown in Fig. 32–8 have been placed closer to the right of the building than to the left. Consequently, the receding angle on the right is great, and the receding angle from the front of the building is slight.

▶ **Vertical Placement**

The distance an object is placed above or below the horizon line also affects the amount of distortion in the drawing. Moving an object a greater distance vertically from the horizon line has the same effect as moving the vanishing points closer together. Objects placed close to the horizon line, either on it, above it, or below it, are less distorted than objects placed a great distance from the horizon (Fig. 32–9).

▶ **Sequence**

In drawing or sketching a simple two-point perspective, the steps outlined in Fig. 32–10 can be followed. However, in projecting a two-point perspective from an established floor plan, the steps in Fig. 32–11 should be followed. These steps are shown by the circled numbers in Fig. 32–11A, B, C, and D, as follows:

1. Draw a horizontal line across the entire width of the paper. This is the *picture plane* (Fig. 32–11).

2. Draw an outline of the *plan view* of the building. Place on the picture plane the corner of

Fig. 32–9. Less distortion occurs close to the horizon.

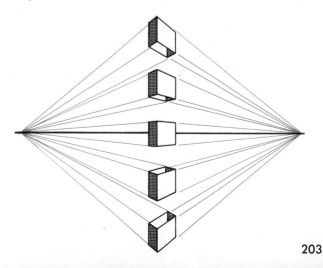

203

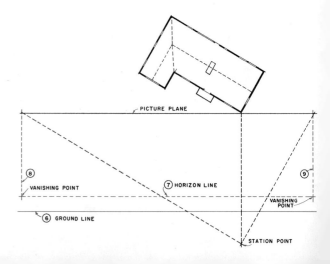

Fig. 32-10. Steps in preparing a two-point perspective.

the plan view you want to appear nearest the viewer. Rotate the plan view to the most desirable angle.

3. Draw a line perpendicular to the picture plane where the corner of the plane touches it.

4. Draw a line parallel to the front wall of the building to intersect the picture plane at a distance from the building approximating the position of a vanishing point.

5. From the point of intersection of lines 3 and 4, draw a line parallel to the side of the building nearest the picture plane, to the picture plane. The intersection of lines 3, 4, and 5 is known as the *station point,* which is the position from which the drawing is viewed. The finished perspective drawing should closely resemble what you would see if you viewed the completed structure from the station point (Fig. 32–11A).

6. Draw the ground line parallel to the picture plane (Fig. 32–11B).

7. Draw the horizon line 6' above the ground line.

8. Draw a vertical line from the intersection of the picture plane and line 4, to intersect the horizon line. The intersection of line 8 and the horizon line is vanishing point 1.

9. Draw a vertical line from the intersection of the picture plane and line 5 to intersect the horizon line. This intersection is vanishing point 2.

10. Draw the elevation on the ground line. If the perspective drawing is prepared on tracing paper, the elevation may be inserted under the paper and aligned with the ground line. Push map pins into the drawing board on vanishing point 1, vanishing point 2, and the station point (Fig. 32–11C).

Fig. 32–11A. Establish the picture plane and station point.

Fig. 32–11B. Locate vanishing points and ground-line.

11. With a large triangle or an inverted T square against the station point, draw a light layout line from the station point to each intersection and door and window opening on the plan view. Mark the points at which these lines intersect the picture plane.

12. Project the points on the picture plane vertically to the ground line. The line drawn from the point where the corner of the plane intersects the picture plane (line X) will be the only line that is true to scale. All lines projected to the vanishing point will originate from line X.

13. Project the vertical points from the elevation to line X (base line). These lines include the ridge line, eave line, tops of doors, tops of windows, bottoms of windows, porches, and planters. Connect these points of intersections to vanishing point 2 to derive the outline of the right side. Project these points to vanishing point 1 to derive the outline of the left (front) of the house.

14. Project the plane of any parts or extensions to the building to the picture plane and vertically to the ground line. Where this line (BV) intersects the ridge, eave, door, and window lines of the foundation, secondary base line points are established, from which the offset or extension may be projected (Fig. 32–11D).

15. Project points in the plan to intersect the picture plane. Connect these intersections to the ground line by a line drawn perpendicular to the ground line, as in step 11.

16. From the points of intersection between line BB and the elevation points, project layout lines to vanishing point 2. Where these layout lines intersect line AA, draw lines to vanishing point 1. Make the object lines heavy and eradicate the projection lines.

17. Draw the position of any vertical extension to the building, such as chimneys, by projecting an extended line to intersect the picture plane. Then project a vertical line to intersect the height of the chimney as projected from the elevation. These points of intersection are then connected with the vanishing points. Draw lines from the corners of the chimney to the station point. Mark the points at which these lines intersect the picture plane. From these points of intersection, project lines to intersect the vanishing-point lines.

▶ Three-point Perspective

Three-point perspective drawings are used to overcome the height distortion of tall buildings. In a one- or two-story building the vertical lines recede so slightly that for all practical purposes they are drawn vertically. However, the top or bottom of extremely tall buildings appears smaller than the area nearest the viewer. A third vanishing point, as shown in Fig. 32–12, may be used to provide the desired recession. The greater the vertical distance between the horizon and vanishing point 3,

Fig. 32–11C. Project and intersect similar floor-plan and elevation lines.

Fig. 32–11D. Project building extensions from the floor plan and elevation.

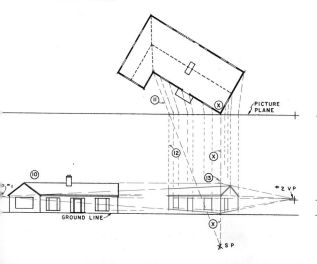

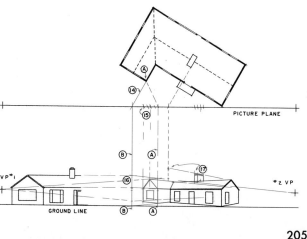

205

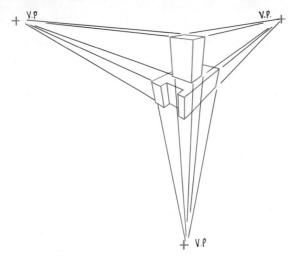

Fig. 32-12. The use of a third vanishing point.

the more closely the vertical lines approach a parallel state, and the less distortion. The closer vanishing point 3 is placed to the object, the more acute the angle and, therefore, the more distortion. If vanishing point 3 is placed so far below or above the horizon that the angles are hardly distinguishable, then the advantage of a three-point perspective is lost and a two-point perspective with parallel vertical lines would be desirable.

Problems

1. Project a two-point perspective drawing from the floor plan and elevation shown in Fig. 32-13.

2. Draw a two-point perspective of the house shown in Fig. 32-14. Use the scale ⅛″ = 1′-0″.

3. Trace the photograph shown in Fig. 32-15. Find the position of the vanishing point and the horizon.

4. Extend the vanishing-point lines shown in Fig. 32-16. Find the position of vanishing point 1, of vanishing point 2, and of the horizon.

5. Project a one- and two-point perspective drawing of the garage shown in Fig. 32-17.

6. Use the layout and floor plan shown in Fig. 32-18 to project a two-point perspective. Sketch a design of the elevation prior to projection.

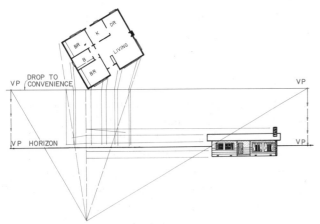

Fig. 32-13. Project a two-point perspective of this house.

Fig. 32-14. Draw a two-point perspective of this house.

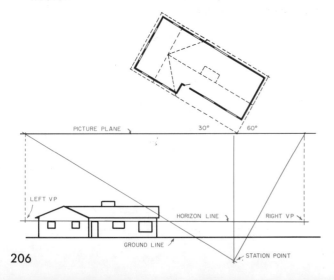

Fig. 32-15. Find the vanishing points.

Libbey-Owens-Ford Glass Company

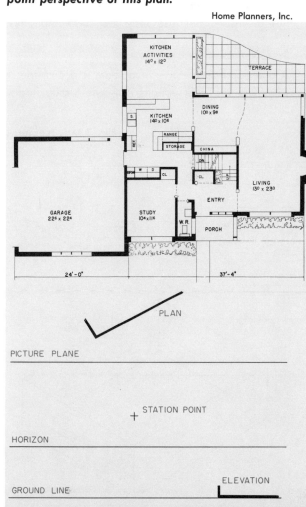

32–16. Find the position **~~of~~ the horizon and ~~va~~nishing points.**

Home Planners, Inc.

7. Draw a one-point and a two-point perspective of your own home.
8. Draw a two-point perspective of a building of your own design.
9. Sketch a three-point perspective of the tallest building in your community.
10. Identify these terms: *pictorial, one-point perspective, two-point perspective, three-point perspective, isometric, vanishing point, horizontal, vertical, parallel, horizon, station point, base line.*

Fig. 32–17. Draw a one- and two-point perspective of this garage.

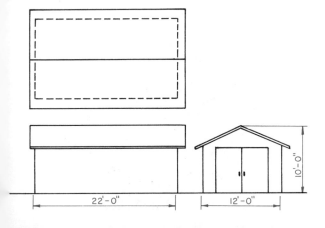

Fig. 32–18. Design an elevation and project a two-point perspective of this plan.

Home Planners, Inc.

Unit 33. Interiors

A pictorial drawing of the interior of a building may be an isometric drawing, a one-point perspective, or a two-point perspective. Pictorial drawings are prepared for the entire floor plan (pictorial floor plan). More commonly, however, pictorial drawings are prepared for a single room or living area.

▶ Isometric Drawings

Isometric drawings using constant angles of 30° from the horizontal are most effective for pictorial floor plans (Fig. 33–1). There are no receding lines on an isometric drawing. Isometric lines are always parallel and may therefore be prepared to an exact scale.

Isometric drawings of room interiors are usually not desirable, because they lack receding lines.

▶ One-point Perspective

A one-point perspective of a room is a drawing in which all the intersections between walls, floors,

Home Planners, Inc.

Fig. 33–2. A one-point interior perspective.

ceilings, and furniture may be projected to one vanishing point (Fig. 33–2). Drawing a one-point perspective of the interior of a room is similar to drawing the inside of a box with the front of the box removed. In a one-point interior perspective, walls perpendicular to the plane of projection, such as the back wall, are drawn to their proper scale and proportion. The vanishing point on the horizon line is then placed somewhere on this wall (actually behind this wall). The points of intersection where this wall intersects the ceiling and floor are then projected from the vanishing point to

Fig. 33–1. Isometric drawing of a floor plan.

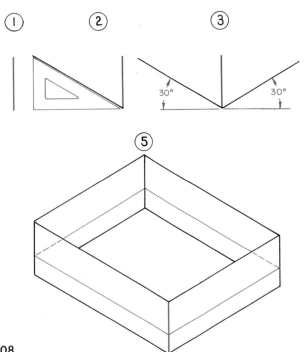

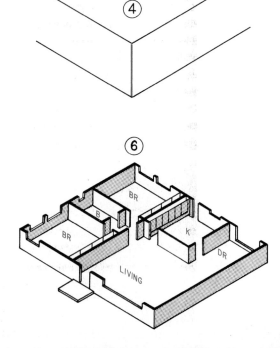

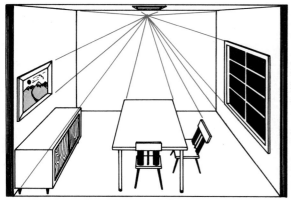

Fig. 33–3A. The effect of a high central vanishing point.

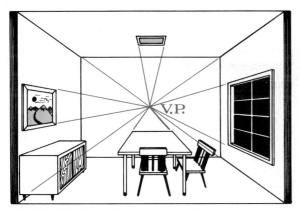

Fig. 33–3B. The effect of a centrally located vanishing point.

Fig. 33–3C. The effect of a low central vanishing point.

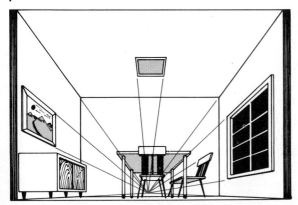

form the intersection between the side walls and the ceiling and the side walls and the floor.

Vertical placement. If the vanishing point is placed high, very little of the ceiling will show in the projection, but much of the floor area will be revealed (Fig. 33–3A). If the vanishing point is placed near the center of the back wall, an equal amount of ceiling and floor will show (Fig. 33–3B). If the vanishing point is placed low on the wall, much of the ceiling but very little of the floor will

Fig. 33–4. The effect of the horizontal placement of the vanishing point.

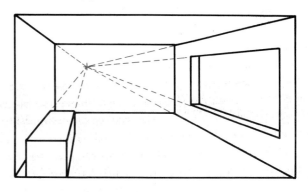

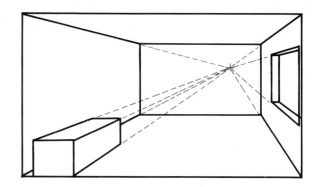

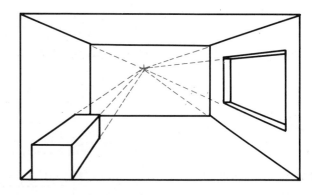

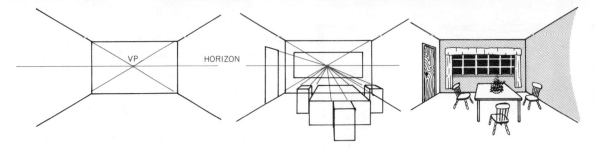

Fig. 33–5. Always "block-in" furniture and people.

be shown (Fig. 33–3C). Since the horizon line and the vanishing point are at your eye level, you can see that the position of the vanishing point in Fig. 33–3 affects the angle from which you view the object.

Horizontal placement. Moving the vanishing point from right to left on the back wall has a similar effect on the side walls. If the vanishing point is placed to the left of the wall, more of the right wall will be revealed. Conversely, if the vanishing point is placed near the left side, more of the right wall will be revealed in the projection. If the vanishing point is placed in the center, an equal amount of right wall and left wall will be shown (Fig. 33–4).

When projecting wall offsets and furniture, always *block-in* the overall size of the item to form a perspective view, as shown in Fig. 33–5. The details of furniture or closets or even of persons can then be completed within this blocked-in cube or series of cubes.

▶ **Two-point Perspective**

Two-point perspectives are normally prepared to show the final design and decor of two walls of a room. The base line on an interior two-point perspective is similar to the base line on an exterior two-point perspective. The base line in the drawing shown in Fig. 33–6 is the corner of

Fig. 33–6. A two-point interior perspective.

Home Planners, Inc.

HORIZON

V P

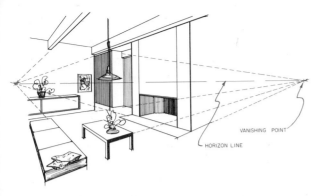

Fig. 33–7. Each object in a room is projected to the vanishing point.

Fig. 33–3. The sequence used in drawing two-point interior perspectives.

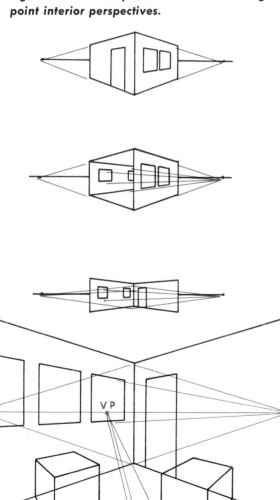

VP   VP

Home Planners, Inc.

Fig. 33–9. Find the vanishing points.

the fireplace. Two rooms or an L room can then be shown projected to each vanishing point.

Once the walls are projected to the vanishing points in the two-point perspective, each object in the room can also be projected to the vanishing point as in external two-point perspectives. Projecting the coffee table shown in Fig. 33–7 to the vanishing point is the same as projecting a flat-roof house or building.

The sequence of steps in drawing two-point interior perspectives is shown in Fig. 33–8.

Problems

1. Trace the drawing shown in Fig. 33–9. With a colored pencil, project the ceiling and floor lines to find the vanishing points and the horizon line.

2. Trace the perspective shown in Fig. 33–10. Find the position of the vanishing points. Extend the drawing to include the left wall of the living area.

Fig. 33–10. Expand this drawing.

Home Planners, Inc.

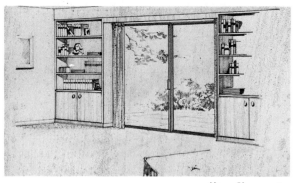

Home Planners, Inc.

Fig. 33–11. Draw the remainder of the left wall.

3. Extend the left wall in the room shown in Fig. 33–11. Draw a chair and sofa on this wall.
4. Prepare a one-point interior perspective of your own room.
5. Prepare a one-point perspective of a room of your own design.
6. Draw a one-point interior perspective of a classroom. Prepare one drawing to show much of the ceiling and left wall. Prepare another drawing to show much of the floor and right wall.
7. Define these terms: *isometric, interior perspective.*

Unit 34. Rendering

To *render* a pictorial drawing is to make the drawing appear more realistic. This may be done through the media of pencil, pen and ink, water colors, pastels, and air brush. Drawings are rendered by adding realistic texture to the materials and establishing shade and shadow patterns.

▶ Media

Soft pencils are one of the most effective media for rendering architectural drawings because tones can be greatly varied by the weight of the line and the smudge blending that can be accomplished by rubbing a finger over penciled areas.

Pen-and-ink renderings of architectural drawings vary greatly. Strokes must be placed further apart to create light effects, and closer together to produce darker effects (Fig. 34–1).

▶ Shade

When you *shade* an object, you make light the part of the object exposed to the sun and make dark the part of the object not exposed to the sun. Notice the

Fig. 34–1. Three types of renderings.
General Motors Corporation; Signature Homes

Home Planners, Inc.

Fig. 34-2. A shaded drawing.

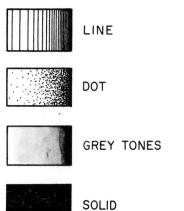

LINE

DOT

GREY TONES

SOLID

Fig. 34-3. Methods of shading.

shaded areas on the left portion of the wall shown in Fig. 34-2. The right wall of this house has been rendered extremely light to show that it is exposed to sunlight. When objects with sharp corners are exposed to strong sunlight, one area may be extremely light and the other side of the object extremely dark. However, when objects and buildings have areas that are round (cylindrical), so that their parts move gradually from dark to light areas, a gradual shading from extremely dark to extremely light must be made. Figure 34-3 shows several methods of shading with lines, dots, or grey areas.

▶ Shadow

In order to determine what areas of the building will be drawn darker to indicate shadowing, the angle of the sun in the illustration must be established. When the angle of the sun is established (Fig. 34-4), all shading should be consistent with the direction and angle of the shadow. On buildings that are drawn considerably below the horizon line, shadow patterns will often reveal more than the actual outline can reveal. Notice how the shadow pattern of the roof on the house shown in Fig. 34-5 reveals the slotted area over the entrance. Areas are shaded to show the shape of the entire house, the roof overhang, trees, fences, walls, and shrubbery. Notice the realism achieved in the house shown in Fig. 34-6 by providing projection of tree shadows and roof-overhang shadows on the house. Adding shadows helps show the building as it is usually viewed.

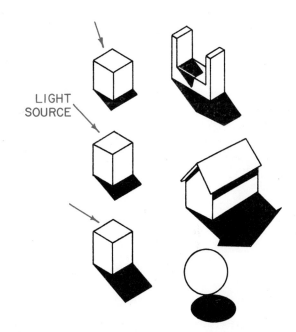

LIGHT SOURCE

Fig. 34-4. Shade the area opposite the light source.

Fig. 34-5. Shadows reveal hidden outlines.

Southern California Gas Company

Fig. 34–6. Shadows are needed to add realism.

Fig. 34–7. Methods of illustrating texture.

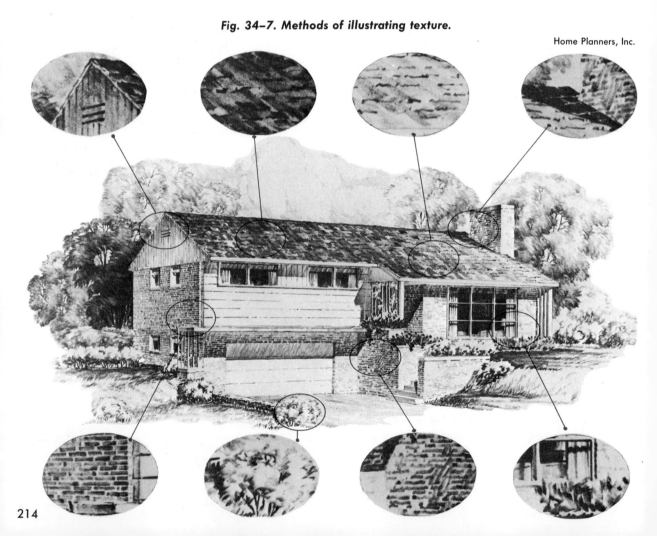

▶ Texture

Giving *texture* to an architectural drawing means making building materials appear as rough or as smooth as they actually are. Smooth surfaces are no problem since they are very reflective and hence are very light. Only a few reflection lines are usually necessary to illustrate smoothness of surfaces such as aluminum, glass and painted surfaces. On rough surfaces the thickness or roughness of the material can often be shown by shading. Figure 34–7 shows some of the techniques that can be used to illustrate the texture of shingles, brick, siding, and foliage.

▶ Sequence

In preparing pictorial renderings, proceed in the following sequence, as shown in Fig. 34–8:

1. Block-in with single lines the projection of the perspective (Fig. 34–8A).

2. Sketch the outline of building materials in preparation for rendering (Fig. 34–8B). This work can be done with a soft pencil, a ruling pen, or a crow-quill pen. Establish a semi-angle and sketch shadows and shading. Darken windows, door areas, and under roof overhangs.

3. Add texture to the building materials. For example, show the position of each brick with a chisel-point pencil. Leave the mortar space white and lighten the pressure for the areas that are in direct sunlight (Fig. 34–8C).

4. Complete the rendering by emphasizing light and dark areas and establishing more visible contrasts of light and dark shadow patterns (Fig. 34–8D).

▶ Abbreviated Rendering

Often it is necessary or desirable to render only one part of a building. In such cases, the other attached parts may be only outlined and the rendering gradually diminished, instead of making an abrupt stop. The rendering shown in Fig. 34–9 was prepared only to show the porch of the house. However, the relationship to the remainder of the house is important and is therefore shown in outline.

Fig. 34–8A. Blocking in the basic outline.

Fig. 34–8B. Value sketch in preparation for rendering.

Fig. 34–8C. Texture added to building materials.

Fig. 34–8D. The completed rendering.

Fig. 34-9. A partial rendering.

Problems

1. Render a perspective drawing of your own house.
2. Render a perspective drawing of a house of your own design.
3. Render a perspective sketch of your school. Choose your own medium: pencil, pen and ink, water colors, pastels, or air brush.
4. Complete the perspective shown in Fig. 34-10 and completely render the drawing in pencil.
5. Render the perspective drawing shown in Fig. 34-11.

Fig. 34-11. Render this drawing.

6. Identify these terms: *render, texture, shade, shadow, chisel point, crow-quill.*

Fig. 34-10. Complete this rendering.

216

PART III

Technical Plans

Basic architectural plans, such as floor plans, elevations, and pictorial drawings, are adequate for describing the general design of a structure. However, to ensure that the building will be completed as specified, a more complete and detailed description of the construction features of the design must be prepared. Technical architectural plans are prepared for this purpose. These include location plans, sectional drawings, foundation plans, framing plans, specifications, building codes, electrical plans, air-conditioning plans, plumbing diagrams, and modular-construction plans. In Part III you will learn the basic practices and procedures in preparing technical architecural plans.

SECTION EIGHT. LOCATION PLANS

Location plans are necessary to give the builder essential information about the property. They are of three types: the plot, the landscape, and the survey. The *plot plan* shows the location of all structures on the property. The *landscape plan* shows how the various features of the landscape will be used in the overall design. The *survey plan* shows the geographical features of the property.

Unit 35. Plot Plans

Plot plans are used to show the location and size of all buildings on the lot. Overall building dimensions and lot dimensions are shown on plot plans. The position and size of walks, drives, patios, and courts are also shown. Compass orientation of the lot is given, and contour lines are sometimes shown. Figure 35–1 shows the key figures and the symbols commonly used on plot plans.

▶ Guides for Drawing Plot Plans

The numbered arrows in Fig. 35–2 illustrate the following guides for drawing plot plans:

1. Draw only the outline of the house. Cross-hatching is optional.
2. Draw the outlines of other buildings on the lot.

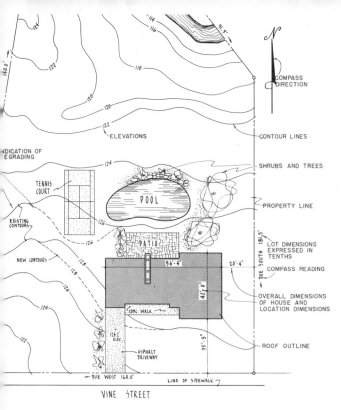

Fig. 35–1. Plot-plan symbols.

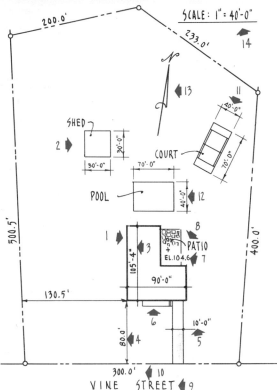

Fig. 35–2. Guides for drawing plot plans.

3. Show overall building dimensions. Figure 35–3 shows dimensional standards recommended for plot plans.

4. Locate each building by dimensioning from the property line to the building (Fig. 35–3). The property line shows the legal limits of the lot on all sides.

5. Show the position and size of driveways.

6. Show the location and size of walks.

7. Indicate grade elevation of key surfaces such as patios, driveways, and courts.

8. Outline and show the appropriate symbol for the surface material used on patios and terraces.

9. Label streets adjacent to the outline.

10. Place overall lot dimensions either on extension lines outside the property line, or directly on the property line.

11. Show the size and location of courts.

12. Show the size and location of pools, ponds, or other bodies of water.

13. Indicate the compass orientation of the lot by the use of a north arrow.

14. Use a decimal scale such as $\frac{1}{10}'' = 1'\text{-}0''$, or $\frac{1}{20}'' = 1'\text{-}0''$ for preparing the plot plan.

▶ Alternative Features

Although plot plans should be prepared according to the standards shown in Fig. 35–2, many optional features also may be included in plot plans. For example, sometimes the interior partitions of the residence are given to show a correspondence between the outside living areas and those inside. Some architects prefer to include only the outline of the building on the plot plan, while others favor crosshatching or shading the buildings.

The position of entrances to buildings are sometimes noted on plot plans, as shown in Fig. 35–4. This device provides an interpretation of the access to the house from the outside, without requiring a detailed plan of the inside.

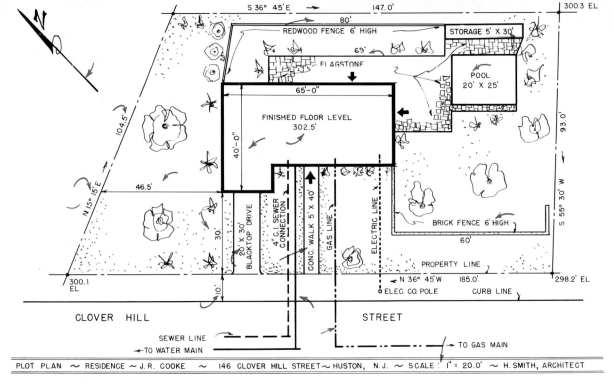

Fig. 35-3. Plot-plan dimensions.

Contour lines are another optional feature on plot plans. On lots that deviate greatly in contour, contour lines are sometimes almost mandatory.

The plot plan is also often used to show the outline of the roof, as in Fig. 35–5. When this outline is shown, the drawing gives the effect of looking down on the top of the lot.

▶ **Variation in Plan**

There are more ways than one to place buildings on a lot. Sometimes alternative plot plans are developed to determine the best overall arrangement, as shown in Fig. 35–6. Variations are also possible in developing almost any detail of a plot plan.

Fig. 35-4. Entrance symbols.

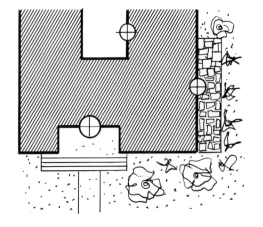

Fig. 35-5. The roof outline is often shown on plot plans.

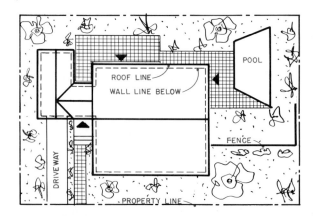

220

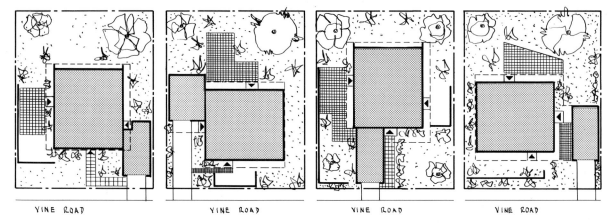

YINE ROAD   YINE ROAD   VINE ROAD   VINE ROAD

Fig. 35–6. Alternative plot plans.

Problems

1. Draw a plot plan of your own home.
2. From a survey plan you have developed, complete a plot plan showing the position of a residence.
3. Place the outline of a residence on the plot plan shown in Fig. 35–7. Include a two-car garage, swimming pool, and tennis court on this plan. Remember to take full advantage of existing landscape features.
4. Draw a plot plan for the house shown in Fig. 35–8. Make the lot 100' × 125'.
5. Define these terms: *plot plan, lot, compass orientation, contour lines, property line, grade elevation.*

Fig. 35–7. Locate a residence on this lot.

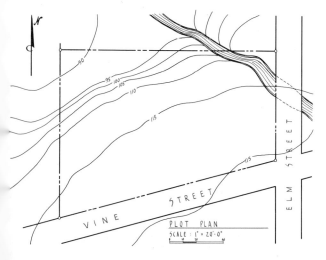

VINE STREET

ELM STREET

PLOT PLAN
SCALE : 1" = 20'-0"

Fig. 35–8. Draw a plot plan for this home.

36'-5"

STORAGE

CARPORT
12⁰ x 20⁰

KITCHEN
8⁰ x 16⁰

RANGE

S   W-D   REF   CL.

STORAGE   HTR. RM.

SNACK
BAR

BED RM.
8⁶ x 12⁰

CL.

BATH

CL.

24'-0"

LIVING RM.
13⁶ x 24⁰

BED RM.
10⁰ x 12⁰

BALCONY

221

Unit 36. Landscape Plans

The primary function of the landscape plan is to show the types and location of vegetation for the lot. It may also show the contour of the land and the position of buildings. Such features are often necessary to make the placement of the vegetation meaningful.

Symbols are used on landscape plans to show the position of trees, shrubbery, flowers, vegetable gardens, hedgerows, and lawns. Figure 36–2 shows some common symbols used on landscape plans.

A landscape architect or gardening contractor designs and prepares the landscape plan. He does so in cooperation with the designing architect. The landscape architect specifies the type and location of all trees, shrubs, flowers, hedge, and ground cover. He often proposes changes in the existing contour of the land to enhance the appearance and function of the site.

▶ **Guides for Preparing Landscape Plans**

The following guides in preparing landscape plans are illustrated by the numbered arrows shown in Fig. 36–1:

1. The elevation of all trees is noted to show the datum level.

2. Vegetable gardens are shown by outlining the planting furrows.

3. Orchards are shown by outlining each tree in the pattern.

Fig. 36–1. Guides for preparing landscape plans.

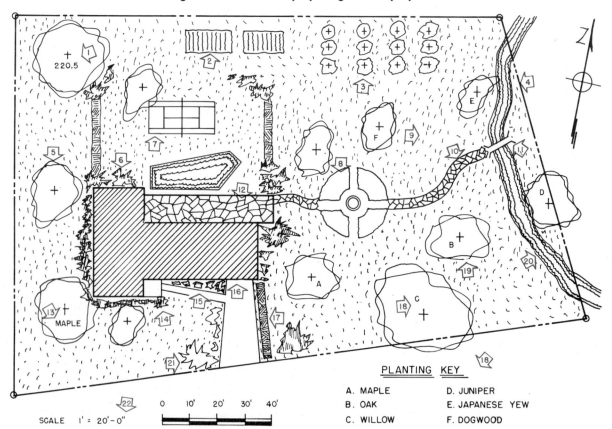

SCALE 1' = 20'-0"

0   10'   20'   30'   40'

PLANTING KEY

A. MAPLE   D. JUNIPER
B. OAK   E. JAPANESE YEW
C. WILLOW   F. DOGWOOD

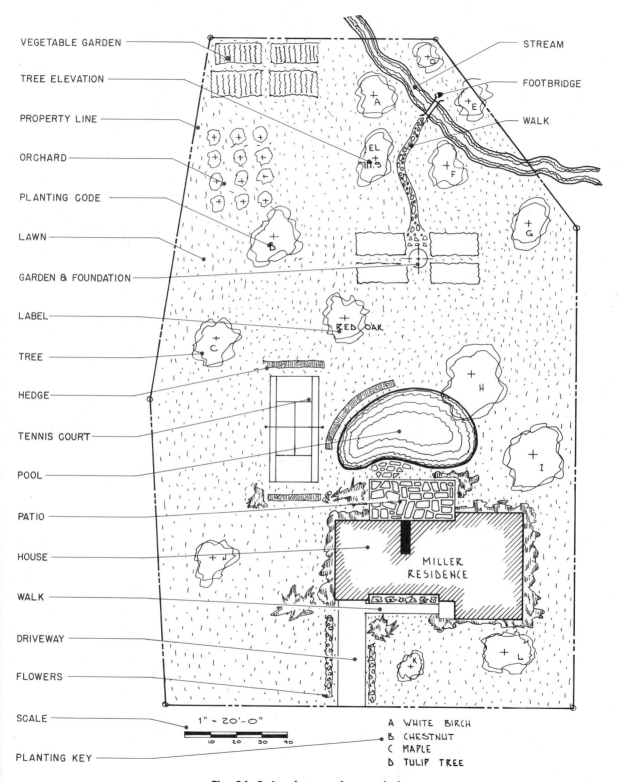

VEGETABLE GARDEN

TREE ELEVATION

PROPERTY LINE

ORCHARD

PLANTING CODE

LAWN

GARDEN & FOUNDATION

LABEL

TREE

HEDGE

TENNIS COURT

POOL

PATIO

HOUSE

WALK

DRIVEWAY

FLOWERS

SCALE

PLANTING KEY

STREAM

FOOTBRIDGE

WALK

EL 117.5

RED OAK

MILLER RESIDENCE

1" = 20'-0"

10   20   30   40

A WHITE BIRCH
B CHESTNUT
C MAPLE
D TULIP TREE

Fig. 36–2. Landscape-plan symbols.

223

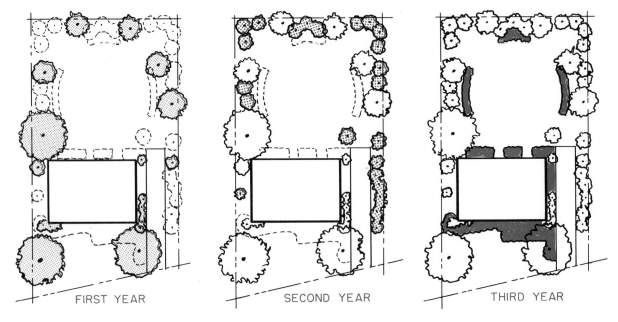

Fig. 36–3. Phased landscape plan.

4. The property line is shown to define the limits of the lot.

5. Trees are located to provide shade and windbreaks and to balance the decor of the site.

6. Shrubbery is used to provide privacy, define boundaries, outline walks, conceal foundation walls, and balance irregular contours.

7. The outline and subdivisions of courts are shown.

8. Flower gardens are shown by their outline.

9. Lawns are shown by small, sparsely placed vertical lines.

10. The outlines of all walks and planned paths are shown.

11. Conventional map symbols are used for small bridges.

12. The outline and surface covering of all patios and terraces are indicated.

13. The name of each tree and shrub is labeled on the symbol.

14. All landscaping should enhance the function and appearance of the site.

15. Flowers should be located to provide maximum beauty and ease of maintenance.

16. The house is outlined, crosshatched, or shaded. In some cases, the outline of the floor plan is shown in abbreviated form. This helps to show the relationship of the outside to the inside living areas.

17. Hedge is used as a screening device to provide privacy, to divide an area, to control traffic, or to serve as a windbreak.

18. Each tree or shrub is indexed to a planting schedule, if there are too many to be labeled on the drawing, as suggested in rule 13.

19. A tree is shown by drawing an outline of the area covered by its branches. This symbol varies from a perfect circle to irregular lines representing the appearance of branches. A plus sign ($+$) indicates the location of the trunk.

20. Water is indicated by irregular parallel lines.

21. Shrubbery in front of the house should be low in order not to interfere with traffic or with window location.

22. An engineer's scale is used to prepare landscape plans. This is because surveyors use this measure.

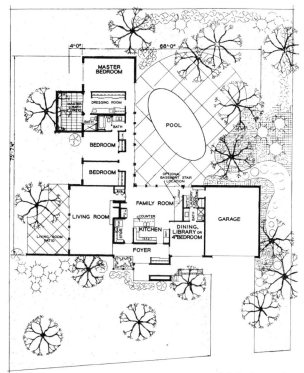

Scholz Homes, Inc.

Fig. 36-4. An interpretive landscape plan without detail dimensions.

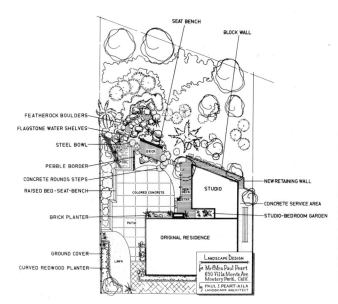

Fig. 36-5A. A landscape plan with all materials labeled.

Paul Peart, landscape architect

Fig. 36-5B. Picture of the area shown in Fig. 36-5A.

▶ Phasing

The complete landscaping of a lot may be prolonged through several years. This procedure is sometimes followed because of a lack of time to accomplish all the planting necessary, or for financial reasons. Figure 36-3 shows a landscape plan divided into three different phases for completion. When a landscape plan is phased, the total plan is drawn and then different shades or colors are used to designate the items that will be planted in the first year, in the second year, and in the third year. A plan can be phased over many years or several months, depending on the schedule for completion of the landscaping.

▶ Variations

Many landscape plans, such as the one shown in Fig. 36-4, are strictly interpretive and contain few or no dimensions. The plan shown in Fig.

36-5 contains no dimensions. The position of the view shown in Fig. 36-5B is indicated by the arrow in Fig. 36-5A.

▶ Combination Plans

Often the lot or estate is too large to be shown accurately on a standard landscape plan. A scale such as 1″ = 20′-0″ may not show the entire

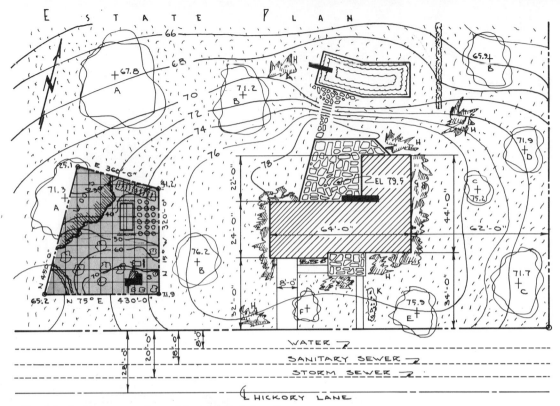

Fig. 36-6. An estate plan with a partial detail.

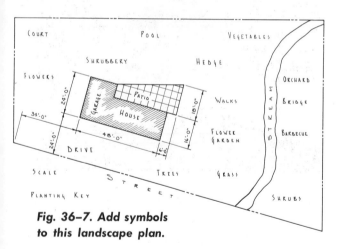

Fig. 36-7. Add symbols to this landscape plan.

estate; or a scale must be used that is so small that the features cannot be readily identified, labeled, and dimensioned. One solution to such a problem is to prepare a total plan of the large estate to a large scale. This is indexed to a drawing of the immediate area around the house. Figure 36-6

Fig. 36-8. Place this house on a 100' x 200' lot.

Home Planners, Inc.

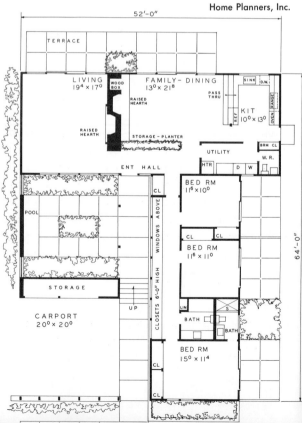

226

shows the total estate plan with the insert showing the lower right-hand corner of the estate developed in more detail.

It is sometimes desirable or necessary to combine all the features of the survey, plot plan, and landscape plan in one plan. In such a combination, all the symbol dimensions are incorporated in one location plan, as shown in Fig. 36–6. This includes contour lines and the exact position of vegetation and buildings.

Problems

1. Add landscape features to your own plot plan.
2. Draw the symbols listed in Fig. 36–7.
3. Place the house shown in Fig. 36–8 on a 100' × 200' lot. Prepare a landscape drawing of the lot according to your own taste.
4. Define these terms: *landscape plan, landscape symbol, landscape architect, gardening contractor, datum level, orchards, tree-location symbol, map symbols, botanical names.*

Unit 37. Survey Plans

A *survey* is a drawing showing the exact size, shape, and levels of a lot. When prepared by a licensed surveyor, the survey can be used as a legal document. It is filed with the deed to the property. The lot survey includes the length of each boundary, tree locations, corner elevations, contour of the land, and position of streams, rivers, roads or streets, and utility lines. It also lists the name of the owner of the lot and of the owner or title of adjacent lots.

A survey drawing must be accurate and must communicate a complete description of the features of the lot. Symbols are used extensively to describe the features of the terrain. Figure 37–1 shows the survey symbols most frequently used. Some symbols depict the appearance of a feature. Most survey symbols are *schematic* representations of some feature.

▶ **Guides for Drawing Surveys**

The numbered arrows in Fig. 37–2 correspond to the following guides for preparing survey drawings:

1. Record the elevation above the datum of the lot at each corner.

2. Represent the size and location of streams and rivers by wavy lines (blue lines on geographical surveys).

3. Use a cross to show the position of existing trees. The elevation of existing tree positions at the base of the trunk is shown.

Fig. 37–1. Survey-plan symbols.

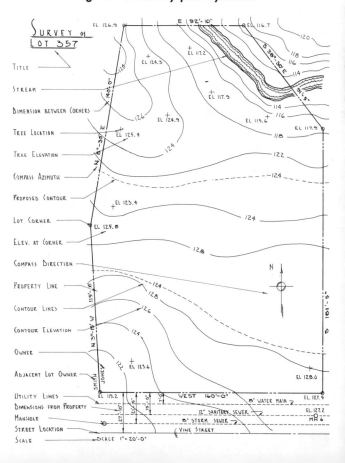

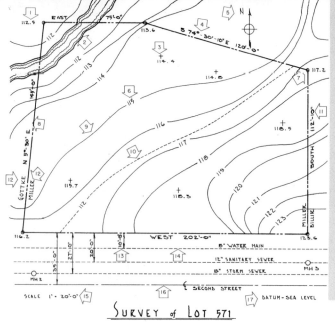

Fig. 37-2. Guides for preparing survey plans.

Fig. 37-3. An engineer's scale.

4. Indicate the compass direction of each property line by degrees, minutes, and seconds (see Fig. 37-4).

5. Use a north arrow to show compass direction.

6. Break contour lines to insert the height of contour above the datum (see Fig. 37-11 and Fig. 37-12).

7. Show lot corners by small circles.

8. Draw the property line by using a repeated short line with two dots.

9. Show elevations above the datum or sea level by contour lines (brown lines on geographical survey maps—see Fig. 37-13).

10. Show any proposed change in grade line by dotted contour lines.

11. Show plot dimensions by indicating the distance between corners (dots) and the property line.

12. Give the names of owners of adjacent lots outside the property line. Place these names outside the property line. The name of the owner of the property is shown inside the property line.

13. Dimension the distance from the property line to all utility lines.

14. Show the position of utility lines by dotted lines. Utility lines are labeled according to their function.

15. Draw surveys with an engineer's scale (decimal scale, Fig. 37-3). Common scales for surveys are $1/10'' = 1'-0''$ and $1/20'' = 1'-0''$.

16. Show existing streets and roads either by center lines or by curb or surface outlines.

17. Indicate the datum level used as reference for the survey.

▶ Lot Layout

The size and shape of lots can be determined by several different methods. However, the methods of dimensioning lots are the same.

Lot dimensions. The exact shape of the lot is shown by the property line. The property line is dimensioned by its length and angle. The angle of each property line from north is known as an *azimuth.* Figure 37-4 shows how the azimuth of each line is determined with a compass or protractor. In Fig. 37-4, **N** indicates that the bearing of the property line reads from north; 65° means that the property is 65° from north; **E** means that the line is between north and east. Hence, **N65°E** means "65° from north heading east."

The angle of the property line is established by intersecting the property line with the center of the compass when the compass needle is aligned with north. The degree of the angle of this prop-

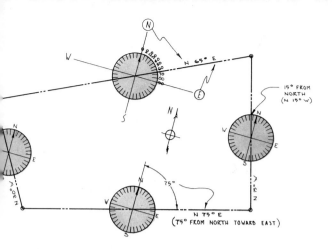

Fig. 37–4. Azimuth projection.

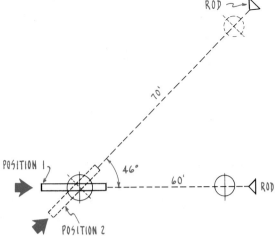

Fig. 37–6. A line can be projected to a rod at any visible distance.

erty line is then read on the circumference of the compass, as shown in Fig. 37–5.

Transit method. Surveyors use a transit to establish the angle (azimuth) of each property line. The *transit* is a telescope which can be set at any desired angle. Once an angle is set, the line may be projected to a rod at any visible distance, as shown in Fig. 37–6. A second line can then be projected by rotating the transit to the desired angle between the property lines. The rotation and projection are shown in position 2, Fig. 37–6.

In measuring the length of each property line, surveyors use a steel tape or chain (Fig. 37–7). Figure 37–8 shows the sequence of using the transit and chain to establish the angle and the length of each property line. Step 1 shows the projection of a line 50' long. Step 2 shows the rotation of an angle 45° from this line. Step 3 shows a line projected 35° from the other end of the first line at a distance of 25'. Step 4 shows the projection to intersect the line established in Step 2.

Fig. 37–5. Property-line angles are read on the circumference of the compass.

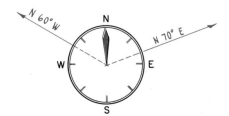

Heights of various parts of the line are established by sighting through a level from a known to an unknown distance. Figure 37–9 shows how a level is used to measure a distance from the known to an unknown distance. In Fig. 37–9A, position A is ½' higher than position B. Figure

Fig. 37–7. Steel tape used by surveyors to measure the length of property lines.

Fig. 37–8. The sequence of establishing the angle and length of each property line.

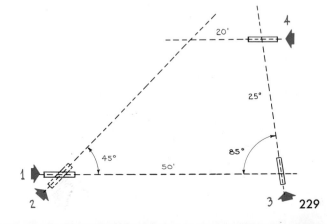

229

Fig. 37–9A. Establishing height with a level.

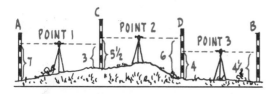

Fig. 37–9B. Projecting several elevations from one point.

Fig. 37–9C. View of a rod through a level.

37–9B shows how several elevations can be projected from one known point. For example, if position A is a known value above the datum, a level line can be projected to position C. By measuring any distance up on point C, a level line can be established between C and D, and likewise between D and B. Figure 37–9C shows what the

surveyor sees as he looks through the level and determines the elevation on a rod.

To establish levels with the transit, the surveyor sets up the instrument so that all points can be seen through the telescope. The reading from the rod on the cross hairs is recorded. The rod is then moved to the second position to be established. The rod is raised or lowered until the original reading is located. The bottom of the rod is then on the same level with the original point.

To obtain the difference in elevation between two points, such as points A and B in Fig. 37–9A, sight on a rod held over point A. Note the reading where the horizontal cross hairs of the telescope cut the graduation on the rod. Then with the rod held at point B, rotate the telescope in a horizontal plane. Again sight on the rod. Note where the horizontal cross hairs cut the graduation on the rod (Fig. 37–9C). The difference between reading A (6′) and reading B (6½′) will give the difference in elevation between the two points. The ground at point B is ½′ lower than at point A.

When for any reason, such as irregularities in the ground or large differences in elevation, the two points whose difference in elevation is to be found cannot be determined from a single point, intermediate points must be used, as shown in Fig. 37–9C.

Plane-table method. The plane-table method is an alternative method of plot layout. This method is less accurate than the transit method since it relies on the naked eye and not on a graduated telescope. Furthermore, this method is generally used to draw a lot that has been established rather than to lay out a lot.

The *plane table* is a drawing board mounted on a tripod. The plane table is placed on a starting point, as shown in step 1, Fig. 37–10. The first line is established by sighting from corner A to corner B. The distance from corner A to corner B is then measured and drawn to scale on the plane table. Next the line AE is drawn by sighting from the starting point A to corner E.

In step 2, the plane table is moved over corner B, with line AB in the same position. Line BC is

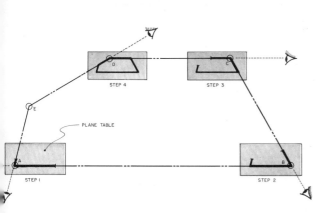

Fig. 37-10. The plane-table method of property-line layout.

Fig. 37-12. Projection of a profile from contour lines.

then established by sighting from corner B to corner C and measuring this distance. Step 3 establishes line CD by moving the plane table to corner C and sighting to corner D. Step 4 completes the layout by sighting from corner D back to corner E.

Contour lines show the various heights of the lot above an established plane known as the *datum*. Sea level is the universal datum line, although many municipalities have established datum points to aid surveyors. The datum is always zero.

Contour lines result from an imaginary cut made through the terrain at regular intervals. Figure 37-11 shows how this cut forms contour lines. The *contour interval*, or the vertical distance between contour lines, can be any convenient distance. It is usually an increment of 5. Contour intervals of 5′, 10′, 15′, and 20′ are common on large surveys. The use of smaller contour intervals provides a more accurate description of the slope

and shape of the terrain than does the use of larger intervals.

Land on any part of a contour line has the same altitude, or height, above the datum. Contour lines are therefore always continuous. The area intersected by contour lines may be so vast that the lines may go off the drawing. However, if a larger geographical area were drawn, the lines would ultimately meet and close. Figure 37-12 shows how contours are projected from a profile through a hill. Contour lines that are very close together indicate a very steep slope. Contour lines that are far apart indicate a more gradual slope.

▶ **Geographical Surveys**

Geographical survey maps are similar to surveys except that they cover extremely large areas. The entire world is divided into geographical survey regions. However, not all these regions have been surveyed. When large areas are to be covered,

Fig. 37-11. Contour lines result from imaginary cuts made through the terrain.

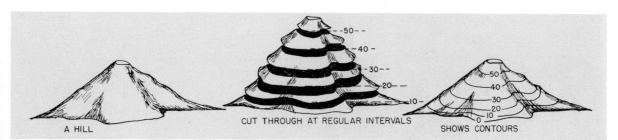

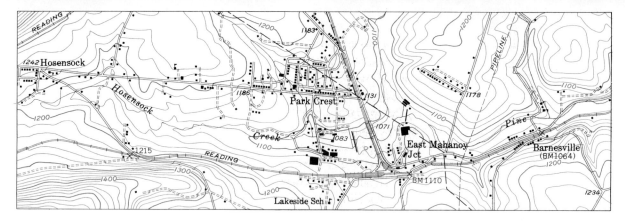

Fig. 37-13A. Segment of a geographical survey map.

a small scale is used. When smaller areas are to be covered, a larger scale, such as 1 to 25,000, can be used. Figure 37–13A shows a typical portion of a geographical survey map. Geographical survey maps show the general contour of the area, natural features of the terrain such as rivers and streams, and man-made features such as roads, railroads, houses, and streets.

Figure 37–13B shows an aerial photograph of the same area shown in the survey map in Fig. 37–13A. Figure 37–15 shows the official symbols used on geographical survey maps.

Problems

1. Make a survey of a lot in your neighborhood using the plane-table method.
2. Use a compass to find the azimuth of streets that surround your home.
3. Select a lot in your community suitable for a home site and prepare a survey of this property.
4. Find what the established datum for your community is.
5. Determine the azimuth of each property line shown in Fig. 37–14. Use a protractor or compass.
6. What is the contour angle used in Fig. 37–14?
7. Find identical features in the geographical survey map shown in Fig. 37–13A and those shown in Fig. 37–13B, the aerial photograph.
8. Draw a survey of the ideal property on which you would like to build a home.
9. Identify the following terms: *survey, contour lines, lot cornice, dotted contour lines, utility lines, azimuth bearing, transit, angle, surveyor, plane table, contour interval, geographical surveys.*

Fig. 37-13B. An aerial photograph of the same area shown in Fig. 37-13A.

Fig. 37-14. Determine the azimuth of each property line.

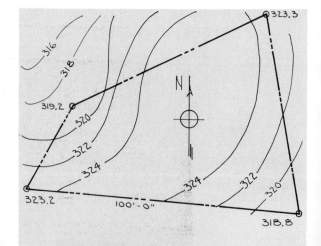

TOPOGRAPHIC MAP SYMBOLS

VARIATIONS WILL BE FOUND ON OLDER MAPS

Hard surface, heavy duty road, four or more lanes	
Hard surface, heavy duty road, two or three lanes	
Hard surface, medium duty road, four or more lanes	
Hard surface, medium duty road, two or three lanes	
Improved light duty road	
Unimproved dirt road—Trail	
Dual highway, dividing strip 25 feet or less	
Dual highway, dividing strip exceeding 25 feet	
Road under construction	

Railroad: single track—multiple track	
Railroads in juxtaposition	
Narrow gage: single track—multiple track	
Railroad in street—Carline	
Bridge: road—railroad	
Drawbridge: road—railroad	
Footbridge	
Tunnel: road—railroad	
Overpass—Underpass	
Important small masonry or earth dam	
Dam with lock	
Dam with road	
Canal with lock	

Buildings (dwelling, place of employment, etc.)	
School—Church—Cemeteries	Cem
Buildings (barn, warehouse, etc.)	
Power transmission line	
Telephone line, pipeline, etc. (labeled as to type)	
Wells other than water (labeled as to type)	o Oil o Gas
Tanks; oil, water, etc. (labeled as to type)	• ● ⊘ Water
Located or landmark object—Windmill	o ⊻
Open pit, mine, or quarry—Prospect	⚒ x
Shaft—Tunnel entrance	▫ Y

Horizontal and vertical control station:

tablet, spirit level elevation	BM △ 3899
other recoverable mark, spirit level elevation	△ 3938
Horizontal control station: tablet, vertical angle elevation	VABM △2914
any recoverable mark, vertical angle or checked elevation	△5675
Vertical control station: tablet, spirit level elevation	BM ✕945
other recoverable mark, spirit level elevation	✕ 890
Checked spot elevation	✕ 5923
Unchecked spot elevation—Water elevation	✕ 5657 870

Boundary: national	
state	
county, parish, municipio	
civil township, precinct, town, barrio	
incorporated city, village, town, hamlet	
reservation, national or state	
small park, cemetery, airport, etc.	
land grant	
Township or range line, U.S. land survey	
Township or range line, approximate location	
Section line, U.S. land survey	
Section line, approximate location	
Township line, not U.S. land survey	
Section line, not U.S. land survey	
Section corner: found—indicated	+
Boundary monument: land grant—other	▫ ▫
U.S. mineral or location monument	▲

Index contour	Intermediate contour	
Supplementary contour	Depression contours	
Fill	Cut	
Levee	Levee with road	
Mine dump	Wash	
Tailings	Tailings pond	
Strip mine	Distorted or broken surface	
Sand area	Gravel beach	

Perennial streams	Intermittent streams	
Elevated aqueduct	Aqueduct tunnel	
Water well—Spring	Disappearing stream	
Small rapids	Small falls	
Large rapids	Large falls	
Intermittent lake	Dry lake	
Foreshore flat	Rock or coral reef	
Sounding—Depth curve	Piling or dolphin	
Exposed wreck	Sunken wreck	
Rock, bare or awash—dangerous to navigation	*	⋇

Marsh (swamp)	Submerged marsh	
Wooded marsh	Mangrove	

Fig. 37–15. Symbols used on geographical survey maps.

SECTION NINE. SECTIONAL DRAWINGS

Sectional drawings reveal the internal construction of an object. Architectural sectional drawings are prepared for the entire structure (full sections), or are prepared for specific parts of the building (detail sections). The size and complexity of the part usually determines the type of section.

Unit 38. Full Sections

Architects frequently prepare drawings which show a building cut in half. Their purpose is to show how the building is constructed. These drawings are known as *longitudinal* or *transverse sections*. *Longitudinal* means "lengthwise." A longitudinal section is a section showing a lengthwise cut through the house. *Transverse* means "across." A transverse section is a section showing a cut across the building.

Transverse and longitudinal sections have the same outlines as the elevation drawings of the building. Figure 38–1 is a section cut perpendicular to the short axis of the building. Figure 38–2 is a section cut parallel to the major axis of the building.

▶ The Cutting Plane

The cutting plane is an imaginary plane which passes through the building. The position of the cutting plane is shown by the cutting-plane line. The cutting-plane line is a long heavy line with two dashes. Figure 38–3 shows a cutting-plane line and the cutting plane it represents. The cutting-plane line is placed in the part to be sectioned, and the arrows at its extremes show the direction from which the section is supposed to be viewed. For example, in Fig. 38–4, section BB would be viewed from the right; section AA would be viewed from the left.

The cutting-plane line often interferes with many dimensions, notes, and details. An alternative

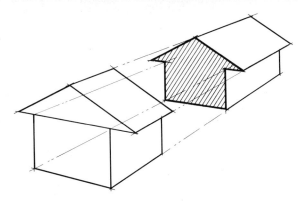

Fig. 38–1. A transverse section through the minor axis of the building.

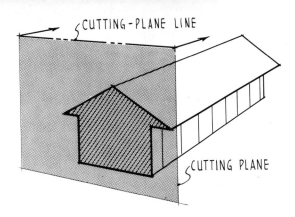

Fig. 38–3. The cutting plane and cutting-plane line.

method of drawing cutting-plane lines is used to overcome this interference. The alternative method is shown in Fig. 38–5. Notice that only the extremes of the cutting-plane line are used. The cutting-plane line is then assumed to be in a straight line between these extremes.

When a cutting-plane line must be offset to show a different area, the corners are illustrated as shown in Fig. 38–6. The *offset cutting plane* is often used to show different wall sections on one sectional drawing.

▶ Symbols

Section-lining symbols represent the way building materials look when they are cut through. A floor-plan drawing is actually a horizontal section. Many of the symbols used in floor plans also

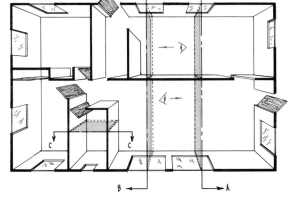

Fig. 38–4. Arrows on the cutting-plane line determine the position from which these sections are viewed.

Fig. 38–5. The alternative method of drawing cutting-plane lines.

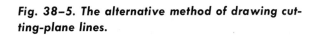

Fig. 38–2. A longitudinal section through the major axis of the building.

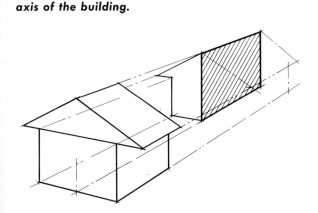

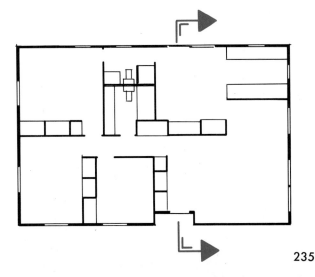

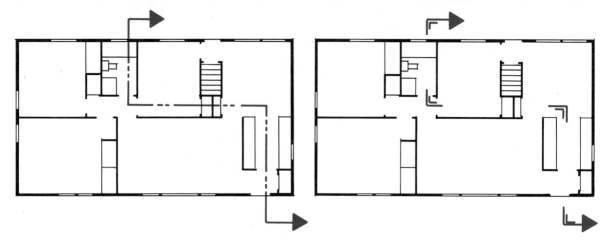

Fig. 38–6. The use of an offset cutting-plane line.

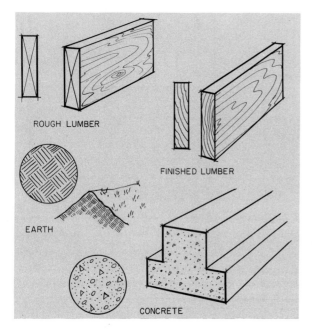

ROUGH LUMBER

FINISHED LUMBER

EARTH

CONCRETE

Fig. 38–7. Some common sectional symbols.

apply to longitudinal sections. However, there are some materials that are only found in longitudinal sections. The symbols for these materials are shown in Fig. 38–7. Even though an attempt is made to have section-lining symbols look like the material they represent, many are purely symbolic in order to conserve time on the drawing board.

A building material is only sectioned when the cutting-plane line passes through the material. However, the outline of all other materials visible behind the plane of projection must also be drawn in the proper position and scale.

Figure 38–8 shows the various building materials as they appear in a transverse section across the gable end of a residence. Figure 38–9 shows the same building materials as they appear when the cutting-plane line is placed parallel with the beam and a ridge of the house.

Fig. 38–8. A section of a house perpendicular to the roof ridge.

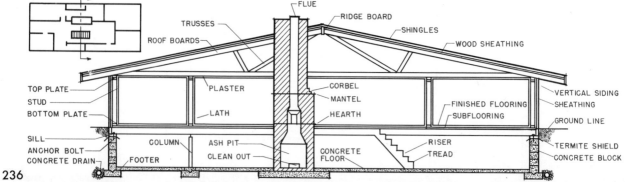

FLUE

TRUSSES

ROOF BOARDS

RIDGE BOARD

SHINGLES

WOOD SHEATHING

TOP PLATE

STUD

BOTTOM PLATE

PLASTER

LATH

CORBEL

MANTEL

HEARTH

FINISHED FLOORING

SUBFLOORING

VERTICAL SIDING

SHEATHING

GROUND LINE

SILL

ANCHOR BOLT

CONCRETE DRAIN

COLUMN

FOOTER

ASH PIT

CLEAN OUT

CONCRETE FLOOR

RISER

TREAD

TERMITE SHIELD

CONCRETE BLOCK

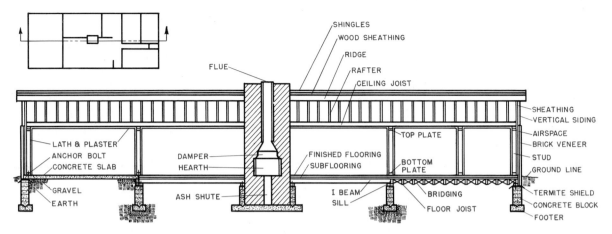

Fig. 38-9. A section through a house parallel with the roof ridge.

Because longitudinal sections show the construction method used in the entire building, they must be drawn to a relatively small scale. The use of this small scale often makes the drawing and interpretation of minute details extremely difficult or impossible. Removed sections of details such as the cornice, sill, and footer are sometimes used to eliminate this problem (Fig. 38–10).

▶ **Steps in Drawing Longitudinal Sections**

In drawing the longitudinal section, the architect actually constructs the framework of a house on paper. Figure 38–11 shows the progressive steps in the layout and drawing of a gable-end section:

1. Lightly draw the floor line approximately at the middle of the drawing sheet.

2. Measure the thickness of the subfloor and of the joist and draw lines representing these under the floor line.

3. From the floor line measure up and draw the ceiling line.

4. Measure down from the floor line to establish the top of the basement slab and footer line, and draw in the thickness of the footer.

5. Draw two vertical lines representing the thickness of the foundation and the footer.

6. Construct the sill detail and show the alignment of the stud and top plate.

7. Measure the overhang from the stud line and draw the roof pitch by projecting from the top plate on the angle which represents the rise over the run.

8. Establish the ridge point by measuring the distance from the outside wall horizontally to the center of the structure.

9. Add details and symbols representing siding and interior finish.

Fig. 38-10. Three common sectional details are the cornice, sill, and footer details.

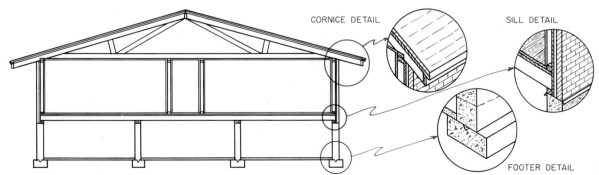

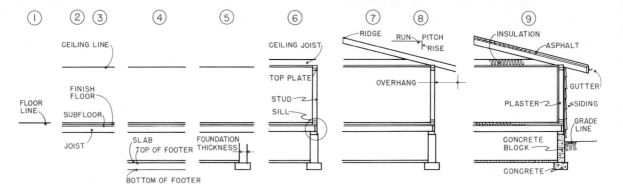

Fig. 38-11. Sequence of projecting an elevation section.

▶ Sectional Dimensioning

Since longitudinal sections expose the size and shape of building materials and components not revealed on floor plans and elevations, the longitudinal section is an excellent place on which to locate many detail dimensions. Longitudinal-section dimensions primarily show specific elevations, distances, and the exact size of building materials.

Figure 38-12 shows some of the more important dimensions that can be placed on longitudinal sections. The rules for dimensioning elevation drawings apply also to longitudinal elevation sections (see Unit 30).

▶ Multilevel Sections

Longitudinal sections are especially effective and necessary for showing the various methods of constructing multilevel buildings, since footers, grade lines, slabs, and floor lines vary greatly. Figure

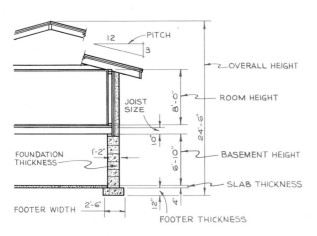

Fig. 38-12. Methods of dimensioning elevation sections.

Fig. 38-13. A section through a split-level home.

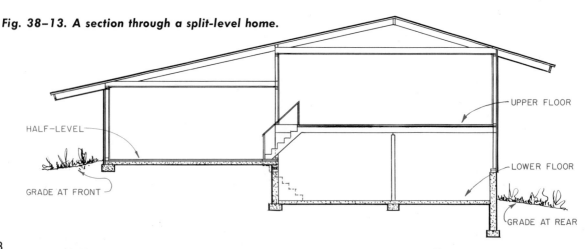

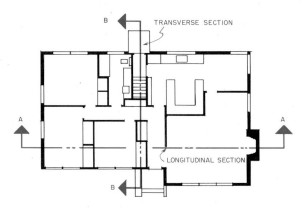

Fig. 38–14. Draw the dimension sections AA and BB.

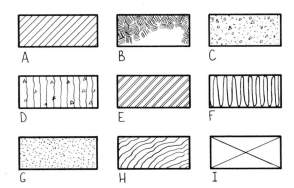

Fig. 38–15. Identify these materials.

38–13 shows a section of a split-level home. It is difficult to show the relationship of the various levels and the construction of each without using this type of section.

Problems

1. Draw a longitudinal section of a house you have designed.
2. Draw a longitudinal section of your home.
3. Draw a longitudinal section of your school building.
4. Draw and dimension a longitudinal section AA of the plan indicated in Fig. 38–14.
5. Draw section BB, Fig. 38–14.
6. Identify the symbols found in Fig. 38–15.
7. Define these terms: *longitudinal section, whole section, cutting plane, offset cutting plane, section lining, transverse section.*

Unit 39. Detail Sections

Because longitudinal sections are usually drawn to a small scale ($\frac{1}{8}'' = 1'-0''$ or $\frac{1}{4}'' = 1'-0''$), many parts are difficult to interpret and dimension. In order to reveal the exact position and size of many small members, the draftsman needs an enlarged section.

▶ Vertical Wall Sections

One method of showing sections larger than is possible in the longitudinal section is through the use of *break lines* to reduce vertical distances on exterior walls. Using break lines allows the draftsman to draw the area larger than is possible when the entire length is included in the drawing. Break lines are placed where the material does not change over a long distance. Figure 39–1 shows the difference between a brick-veneer wall drawn completely to a small scale and the same wall enlarged by the use of break lines. Figure 39–2

Fig. 39–1. Sections can be drawn larger when break lines are used.

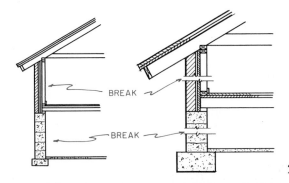

239

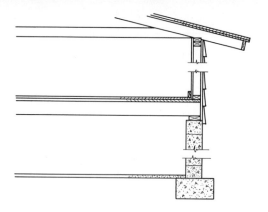

Fig. 39-2. The use of break lines on a frame-wall section.

shows the use of break lines to enlarge a frame-wall section.

When a very large section is needed for interpretation or dimensioning purposes, it is sometimes impossible to draw the entire wall section even with the use of break lines. In this case a *removed section* is prepared. Removed sections are frequently drawn for the ridge, cornice, sill, footer, and beam areas as shown in Fig. 39-3.

Cornice sections. Figure 39-4 shows several typical cornice sections and the pictorial interpretation of each. Cornice sections are used to show the relationship between the outside wall, top plate, and rafter construction. Some cornice sections show gutter details.

Fig. 39-3. Removed sections are often drawn of the ridge, cornice, sill, footer, and beam areas.

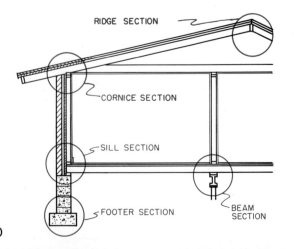

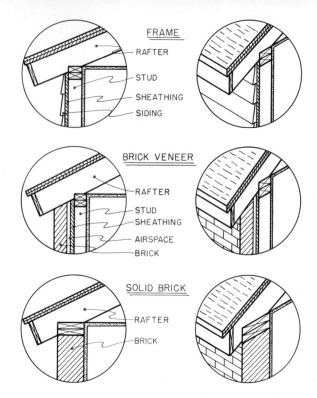

Fig. 39-4. Compare the pictorial section with the orthographic section.

Fig. 39-5. A comparison of sill sections and the sill construction they represent.

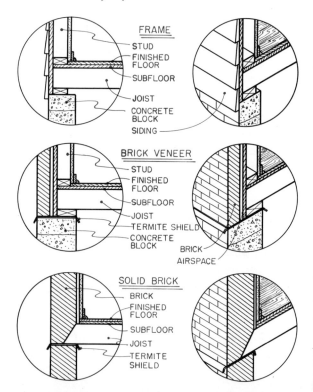

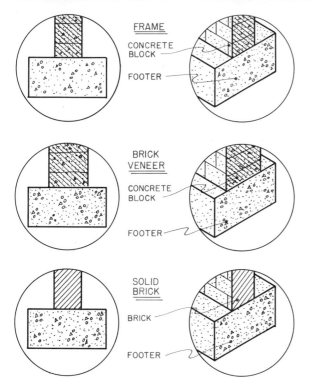

Fig. 39–6. Footer sections.

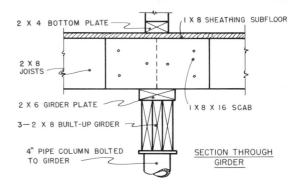

2 X 4 BOTTOM PLATE

1 X 8 SHEATHING SUBFLOOR

2 X 8 JOISTS

2 X 6 GIRDER PLATE

3 — 2 X 8 BUILT-UP GIRDER

4" PIPE COLUMN BOLTED TO GIRDER

1 X 8 X 16 SCAB

SECTION THROUGH GIRDER

Fig. 39–8. Section through a built-up wood girder.

Sill sections. Sill sections, as shown in Fig. 39–5, explain graphically how the foundation supports and intersects with the floor system and the outside wall.

Footer sections. A footer section is needed to show the width and length of the footer, the type of material used, and the position of the foundation wall on the footer. Figure 39–6 shows several footer details and the pictorial interpretation of each type.

Beam details. Beam details are necessary to show how the joists are supported by beams and how the beams support columns or foundation walls. As in all other sections, the position of the cutting-plane line is extremely important. Figure 39–7 shows two possible positions of the cutting plane. If the cutting-plane line is placed parallel to the beam, you see a cross section of the joist, as shown in A. If the cutting-plane line is placed perpendicular to the beam, you see a cross section of the beam, as shown in B. Figure 39–8 shows a similar section through a built-up wood girder.

Sometimes it is desirable or necessary to show the relationship between the beam detail and a detail of the sill area. This relationship is especially needed when a room is sunken or elevated. In Fig. 39–9 the beam and sill areas on one sectional

Fig. 39–7. Beam sections can be drawn from two angles.

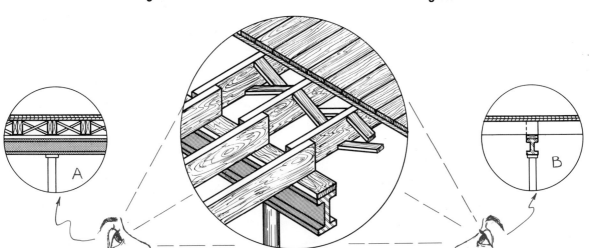

A

B

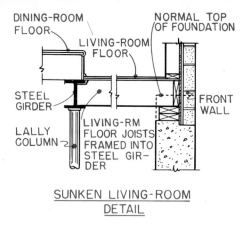

SUNKEN LIVING-ROOM
DETAIL

Fig. 39-9. The beam section and sill section can be shown on the same drawing by use of break lines.

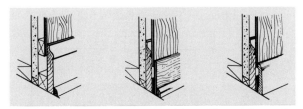

United States Plywood Corporation

Fig. 39-10. Pictorial sections through the base of an interior partition.

drawing are shown by breaking the area between the sill and the beam.

Interior-wall sections. To illustrate further the methods of constructing inside partitions, sections are often drawn of interior walls at the base and at the ceiling. *Base sections* (Fig. 39-10) show how the wall-finishing materials are attached to the studs and how the intersection between the floor and wall is constructed. The section at the ceiling, as shown in Fig. 39-11, is drawn to show the intersection between the ceiling and the wall and to show how the finishing materials of the wall and ceiling are related.

Fig. 39-11. Pictorial section at the intersection of interior wall and ceiling.

United States Plywood Corporation

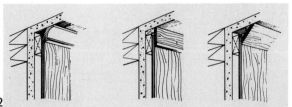

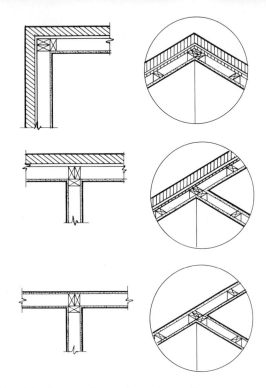

Fig. 39-12. Horizontal sections through exterior-wall intersections.

▶ **Horizontal-Wall Sections**

Horizontal wall sections are drawn of interior and exterior walls.

Exterior walls. A floor plan is a horizontal section. However, many details are omitted from the floor plan because of the small scale used. Very few construction details are necessary to interpret adequately the floor plan. If the floor plan is drawn exactly as a true horizontal section, it will appear similar to the sections shown in Fig. 39-12. When more information is needed to describe the exact construction of the outside corners and the intersections between interior partitions and outside walls, horizontal sections of the type shown in Fig. 39-12 are prepared.

Interior-wall sections. Typical sections are often drawn of interior-wall intersections. Unusual wall-construction methods are always sectioned. For example, a horizontal section is needed to show the inside corner construction of a paneled wall (Fig. 39-13). An outside corner section of

Fig. 39–13. Section of an inside panel-wall corner.

Fig. 39–14. Section of an outside panel-wall corner.

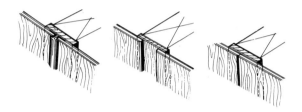

Fig. 39–15. Panel-joint details.

the same type of paneling construction is shown in Fig. 39–14. Horizontal sections are also used extensively to show how paneled joints and other building joints are constructed (Fig. 39–15).

Horizontal sections are also very effective in illustrating the various methods of attaching building materials together. For example, the sections shown in Fig. 39–16 illustrate the various methods for attaching furring and paneling to interior walls.

▶ Window Sections

Because much of the actual construction of most windows is hidden, a section is necessary for the correct interpretation of most window-construction methods. Figure 39–17 shows the areas of windows that are commonly sectioned. These include sections of the head, jamb, and sill construction.

Vertical sections. Sill sections and head sections are vertical sections and are sometimes prepared on the same sectional drawing. Preparing sill and

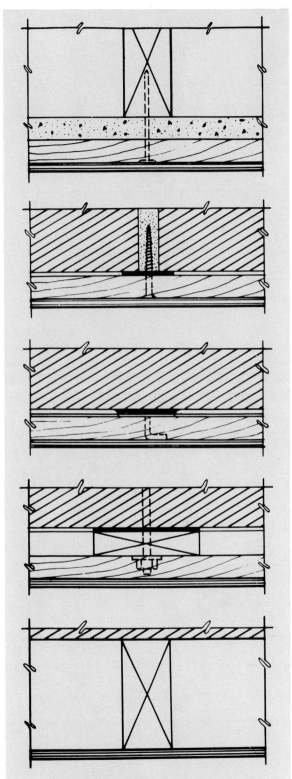

Fig. 39–16. Sections show methods of attaching paneling.

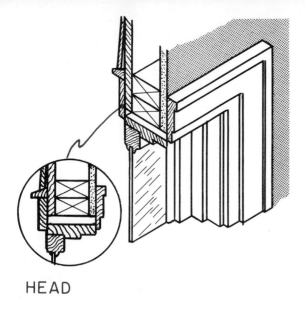

HEAD

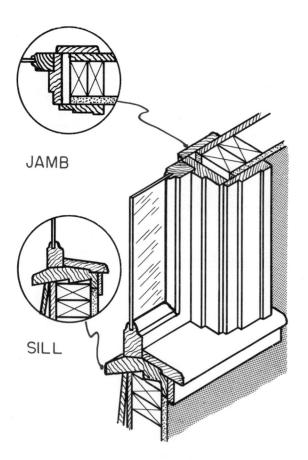

JAMB

SILL

Fig. 39–17. Window head, jamb, and sill section.

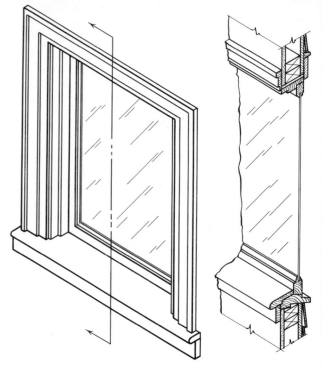

Fig. 39–18. Head and sill sections are in the same plane.

head sections on the same drawing is possible only when a small scale is used. If a larger scale is needed, the sill and head must be drawn independently, or a break line must be used. Figure 39–18 shows the relationship between the cutting-plane line and the sill and head sections. The circled areas in Fig. 39–19 show the areas that are removed when a separate head and sill section is prepared.

Fig. 39–19. Projection of the head and sill section.

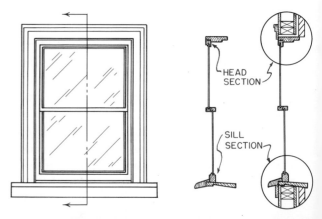

HEAD
SECTION

SILL
SECTION

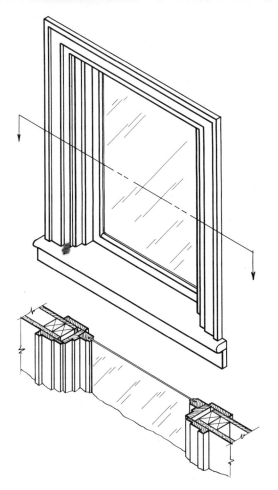

Fig. 39–20. The right and left jamb are in the same plane.

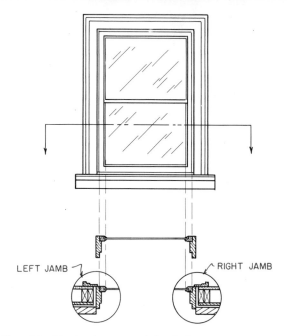

LEFT JAMB

RIGHT JAMB

Fig. 39–21. Projection of the left- and right-jamb section.

ship between a commercially manufactured window and the framing methods necessary for correct fitting is shown in Fig. 39–22. Notice that this section shows the head, sill, and jamb construction in one pictorial view.

Fig. 39–22. A pictorial section showing sill, jamb, and head details.

Ceco Steel Products Corporation

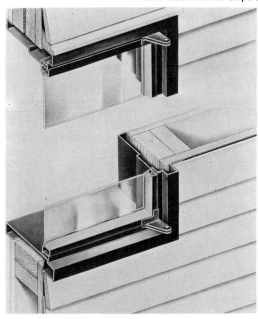

Horizontal sections. When a cutting plane line is extended horizontally across the entire window, the resulting sections are known as *jamb sections.* Figure 39–20 shows the derivation of the jamb section from a horizontal cutting plane line. Figure 39–21 shows the method of projecting the jamb details from the window elevation drawing. Since the construction of both jambs is usually the same, the right jamb drawing is the reverse of the left. Only one jamb detail is normally drawn. The builder therefore interprets the right jamb or left jamb as the reverse of the other.

Commercial details. Many window manufacturers utilize pictorial sectioning techniques to show the correct installation of windows. The relation-

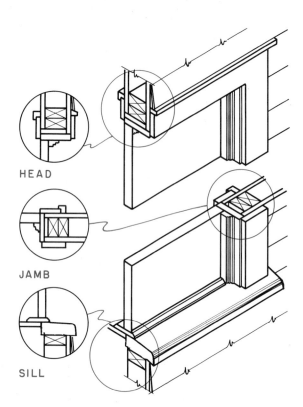

Fig. 39–23. Head, jamb, and sill details can be removed or drawn pictorially.

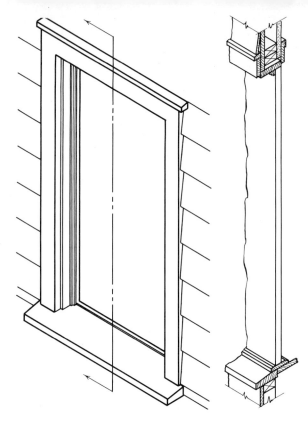

Fig. 39–24. The head and sill sections of a door in the same plane.

▶ Door Sections

A horizontal section of all doors is shown on a floor plan. However, this section is almost completely symbolic and lacks sufficient detail. An enlarged jamb, head, and sill section, as shown in Fig. 39–23, is necessary to describe completely the door-construction methods used. When a cutting-plane line is extended vertically through the sill and head, a section similar to the one shown in Fig. 39–24 is revealed. However, these sections are often too small to show the desired degree of detail necessary for construction. A removed section, as shown in Fig. 39–25, is drawn to show the enlarged head and sill sections. A break line is often used to reduce the distance between the head and sill sections.

Since doors are normally not as wide as they are high, an adequate jamb detail can be projected, as shown in Fig. 39–26, without the use of break lines or removed sections. Figure 39–27 shows the method of projecting the left and right jamb sections from the door elevation drawing. Occasionally architectural draftsmen prepare sectional drawings of the rough framing details of the door head, sill, and jamb, exclusive of the door and door frame assembly. In such drawings, the draftsman draws the framing section with the door frame and door removed, as shown in Fig. 39–28. Usually, however, door sections are prepared with the framing trim and door in their proper locations.

Drawings of garage doors and industrial-type doors are usually prepared with sections of the brackets and apparatus necessary to house the door assembly, as shown in Fig. 39–29. This is done even when stock equipment is used.

Rarely is the architectural draftsman called upon to prepare sectional drawings of internal

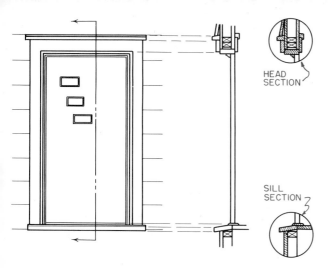

Fig. 39–25. Projection of the head and sill sections of a door frame.

Fig. 39–26. Right and left door-jamb details are in the same plane.

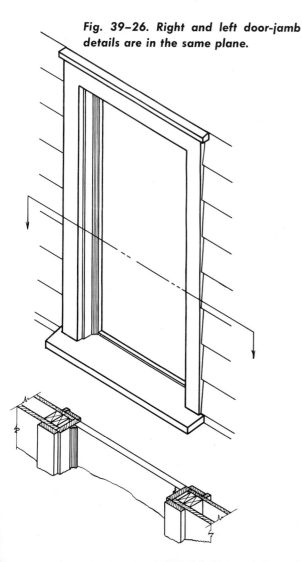

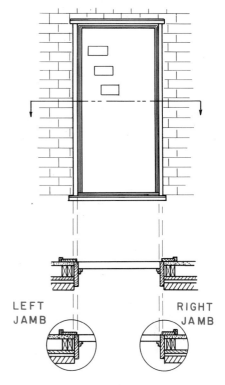

LEFT JAMB   RIGHT JAMB

Fig. 39–27. The projection of the left and right door-jamb section.

Fig. 39–28. The relationship between the door, door-frame assembly, and wall frame.

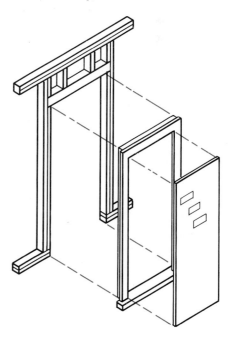

247

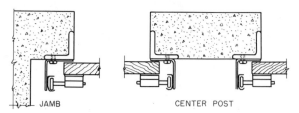

JAMB CENTER POST

Fig. 39-29. Special brackets and devices often require detailed sectional drawing.

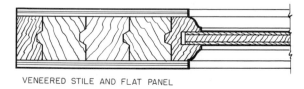

VENEERED STILE AND FLAT PANEL

Fig. 39-30. Interior-door construction is shown by a sectional drawing.

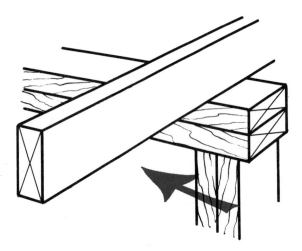

Fig. 39-31. Draw a section through the beam as shown by the arrow.

door construction details. Most doors are purchased from manufacturers' stock.

Occasionally doors are supplied by the manufacturer specifically for a building. Only when a special door is to be manufactured is a sectional drawing of the internal door construction detail prepared, as shown in Fig. 39-30.

Problems

1. Draw a large cornice, sill, and footer section from the circled sections shown in Fig. 39-3.

2. Draw a section through the girder, as shown in Fig. 39-8, revolving the cutting plane line 90°.

3. Draw a head, jamb, and sill section of the window shown in Fig. 39-22.

4. Draw a sill, cornice, and footer section of a house you have designed.

5. Draw a section through the beam as indicated by the arrow in Fig. 39-31.

6. Draw a sill, cornice, and footer section of your home.

7. Prepare an interior-wall section at the ceiling and at the floor line to accompany the section shown in Fig. 38-8.

8. Draw a sill, cornice, and footer detail of the section shown in Fig. 38-8.

9. Draw a detail section of the area where the column, beam, and interior partition intersect in Fig. 38-8.

10. Draw a sill and footer detail of the section shown in Fig. 38-9.

11. Draw a detail section of the intersection of the inside foundation-support wall, I beam, and interior partition, as shown in Fig. 38-9.

12. Prepare an orthographic section from the pictorial sections of the cornice, sill, and footer shown in Fig. 38-10.

13. Identify these terms: *break line, removed section, interior-wall sections, vertical wall sections, horizontal wall sections, jamb sections, head sections, sill sections.*

Special Products, Visking Company;
Division of Union Carbide Corporation

SECTION TEN. FOUNDATION PLANS

The methods and materials used in constructing foundations vary greatly in different parts of the country and are continually changing. The basic principles of foundation construction are the same, regardless of the application.

Every structure needs a foundation. The function of a foundation is to provide a level and uniformly distributed support for the structure. The foundation must be strong enough to support and distribute the load of the structure, and sufficiently level to prevent the walls from cracking and the doors and windows from sticking. The foundation also helps to prevent cold air and dampness from entering the house. The foundation waterproofs the basement and forms the supporting walls of the basement.

Unit 40. Foundation Members

The structural members of the foundation vary according to the design and size of the foundation.

▶ Footing

The footing, or footer (Fig. 40–1), distributes the weight of the house over a large area. Concrete is commonly used for footers because it can be poured to maintain a firm contact with the supporting soil. Concrete is also effective because it can withstand heavy weights and is a relatively decay-proof material. Steel reinforcement is sometimes added to the concrete footer to keep the concrete from cracking and to provide additional support (Fig. 40–2). The footer must be laid on solid ground to support the weight of the building effectively and evenly. In cold climates the footer must be placed below the frost line.

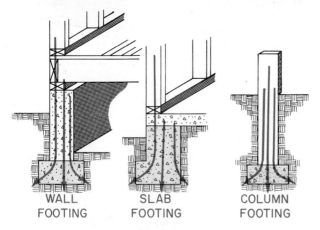

Fig. 40-1. Footers distribute the weight of the building over a wide area.

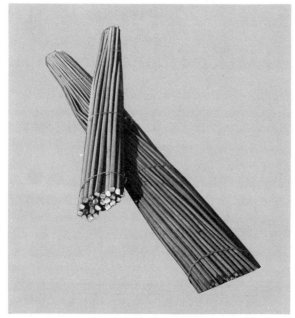

Fig. 40-2. Steel reinforcing rods add strength to the footer.

Fig. 40-3. Foundation walls are constructed of concrete, stone, brick, or concrete block.

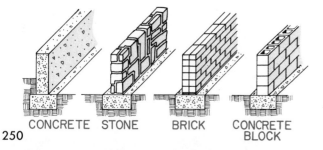

CONCRETE   STONE   BRICK   CONCRETE BLOCK

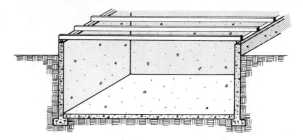

Fig. 40-4. A foundation wall can also be a basement wall.

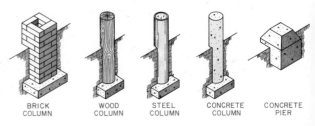

BRICK COLUMN   WOOD COLUMN   STEEL COLUMN   CONCRETE COLUMN   CONCRETE PIER

Fig. 40-5. Piers and columns are made of concrete, brick, steel, or wood.

▶ Foundation Walls

The function of the foundation wall is to support the load of the building above the ground line and to transmit the weight of the house to the footing. Foundation walls are normally made of concrete, stone, brick, or concrete block (Fig. 40-3). When a complete excavation is made for a basement, foundation walls also provide the walls of the basement (Fig. 40-4).

▶ Piers and Columns

Piers and columns are vertical members, usually made of concrete, brick, steel, or wood, which are used to support the floor systems (Fig. 40-5). Piers or columns may be used as the sole support of the structure; or they may be used in conjunction with the foundation wall and provide only the intermediate support between girders or beams.

▶ Anchor Bolts

Anchor bolts are embedded in the top of the foundation walls or piers (Fig. 40-6). The exposed part of the bolt is threaded so that the first wood member (the sill) can be bolted onto the top of the

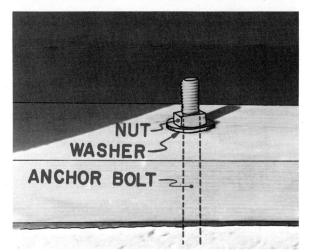

Fig. 40–6. Anchor bolts hold the sill to the foundation.

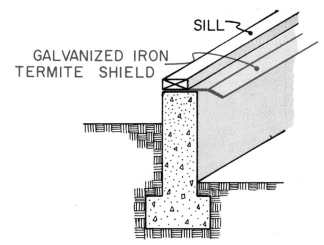

Fig. 40–8. Placement of a termite shield between the foundation and the sill protects the wood from termites.

foundation wall. Anchor bolts for residential use are ½" in diameter and 10" long. They are spaced at approximately 6' intervals, starting 1' from each corner.

▶ Sills

Sills are wood members that are fastened with anchor bolts to the foundation wall (Fig. 40–7). Sills provide the base for attaching the exterior walls to the foundation.

A galvanized iron sheet is often placed under the sill to check termites (Fig. 40–8), since the sill is normally the lowest wood member used in the construction. Building laws specify the distance required from the bottom of the sill to the grade line inside and outside the foundation.

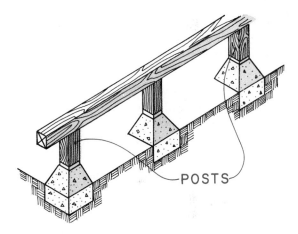

Fig. 40–9. Posts transmit the weight of girders and beams to the footings.

Fig. 40–7. The sill is the point of contact between the foundation and the framework of the building.

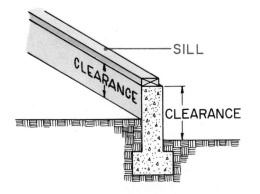

▶ Posts

Posts are wood members that support the weight of girders or beams and transmit the weight to the footings (Fig. 40–9).

▶ Cripples

Cripples are used to raise the floor level without the use of a higher foundation wall (Fig. 40–10). Since the load of the structure must be transmitted through the cripples, these are usually heavy members, often four-by-fours (4×4's) and spaced at close intervals.

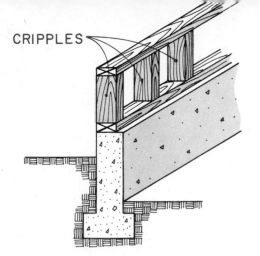

CRIPPLES

Fig. 40–10. Cripples raise the height of a floor without raising the foundation height.

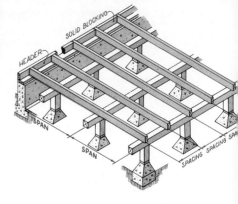

TYPICAL JOIST SPANS		
JOIST SIZE	JOIST SPAC.	JOIST SPAN
2×6	12"	10'-0"
	16"	9'-0"
	24"	7'-6"
2×8	12"	13'-0"
	16"	12'-0"
	24"	10'-6"
2×10	12"	16'-0"
	16"	15'-0"
	24"	12'-0"
2×12	12"	20'-0"
	16"	18'-0"
	24"	15'-0"
2×14	12"	23'-0"
	16"	21'-0"
	24"	17'-0"

Fig. 40–12. Joists support the floor and rest on girders.

▶ Girders

Girders are major horizontal support members upon which the floor system is laid. They are supported by posts and piers and are secured to the foundation wall as shown in Fig. 40–11. Girder sizes are closely regulated by building codes. The allowable span of the girder depends on the size of the girder. A decrease in the size of a girder means that the span must be decreased by adding additional column supports under the girder. Built-up wood girders for residential construction are normally made from 2 × 8's or 2 × 10's spiked together.

▶ Steel Beams

Steel beams perform the same function as wood girders. However, steel beams can span larger areas than can wood girders of an equivalent size.

▶ Joists

Joists are the part of the floor system that is placed on the girders. Joists span either from girder to girder or from girder to the foundation wall. The ends of the joists butt against a header or extend to the end of the sill, with blocking placed between them as shown in Fig. 40–12.

Problems

1. Draw a slab foundation plan to the scale ½" = 1'-0" for the floor plan shown in Fig. 1–2.
2. Draw a T-foundation plan for Fig. 40–13, using the scale ¼" = 1'-0".
3. Draw a slab foundation for Fig. 40–13, using the scale ¼" = 1'-0".
4. Know these architectural terms: *foundation, structural members, footing, concrete, foundation wall, pier, column, anchor, sill, post, cripple, girder, span, spacing, joists.*

Fig. 40–11. Girders are major horizontal support members.

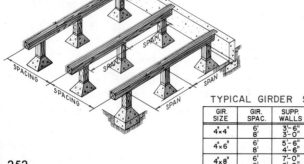

TYPICAL GIRDER SPANS			
GIR. SIZE	GIR. SPAC.	SUPP. WALLS	NO WALL SUPP.
4"×4"	6'	3'-6"	4'-6"
	8'	3'-0"	3'-6"
4"×6"	6'	5'-6"	6'-6"
	8'	4'-6"	5'-6"
4"×8"	6'	7'-0"	8'-6"
	8'	6'-0"	7'-6"

Fig. 40–13. Draw a T foundation for this plan.

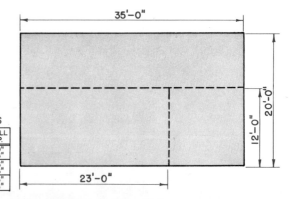

Unit 41. Foundation Types

The type of foundation the architect selects for a structure depends on the nature of the soil, the size and weight of the structure, the climate, building laws, and the relationship of the floor to the grade line (Fig. 41–1). Foundations are divided into three basic types: the T foundation, the slab foundation, and the pier and column foundation (Fig. 41–2).

▶ T Foundations

The T foundation consists of a trench footer upon which is placed a concrete wall or a concrete-block wall. The combination of the footer and the wall forms an inverted T. The T foundation is popular in structures with basements or when the bottom of the first floor must be accessible (Fig. 41–3).

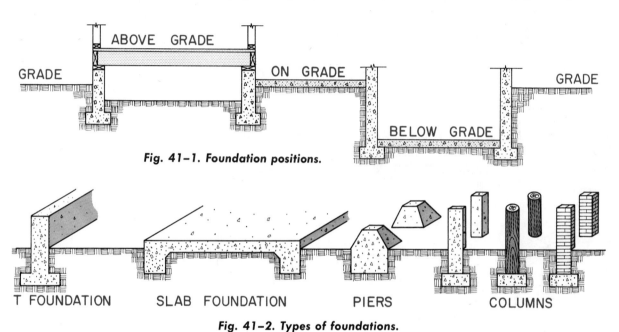

Fig. 41–1. Foundation positions.

Fig. 41–2. Types of foundations.

Fig. 41–3. Elements of a T foundation.

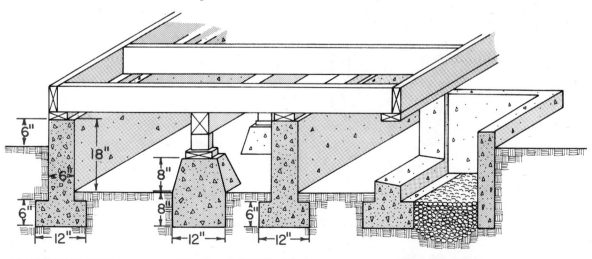

EXTERIOR WALL   PIER   INTERIOR WALL   ACCESS AREA

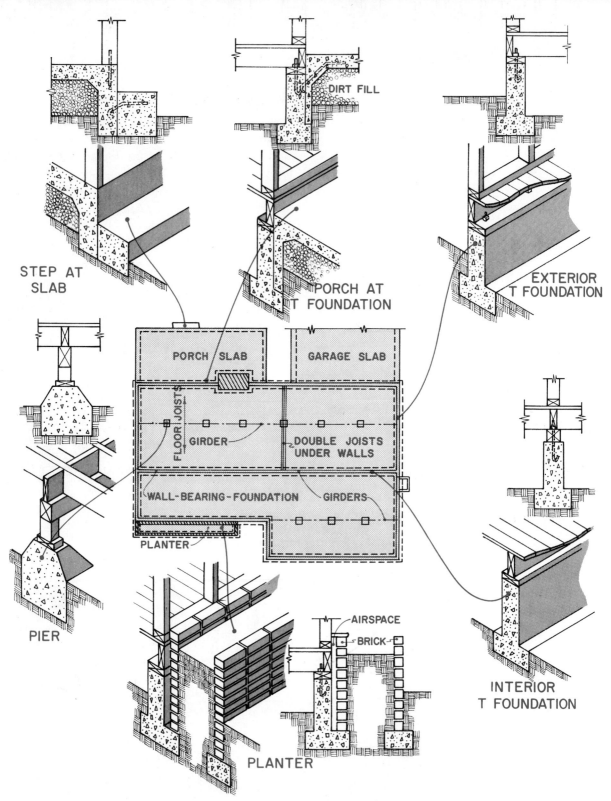

STEP AT
SLAB

PORCH AT
T FOUNDATION

DIRT FILL

EXTERIOR
T FOUNDATION

PORCH SLAB

GARAGE SLAB

FLOOR JOISTS

GIRDER

DOUBLE JOISTS
UNDER WALLS

WALL-BEARING-FOUNDATION

GIRDERS

PLANTER

PIER

PLANTER

AIRSPACE

BRICK

INTERIOR
T FOUNDATION

Fig. 41-4. Methods of drawing T-foundation details.

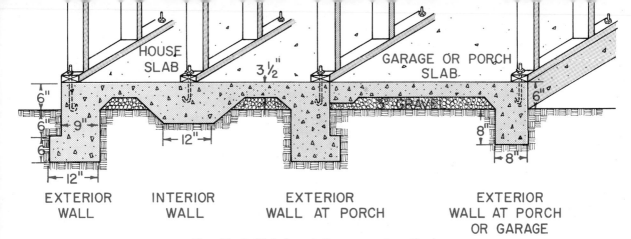

HOUSE SLAB

GARAGE OR PORCH SLAB

$3\frac{1}{2}$"

6"

6"

9"

12"

GRAVEL

6"

8"

8"

EXTERIOR
WALL

INTERIOR
WALL

EXTERIOR
WALL AT PORCH

EXTERIOR
WALL AT PORCH
OR GARAGE

Fig. 41–5. Slab-foundation support methods.

Fig. 41–6. Slab-foundation details.

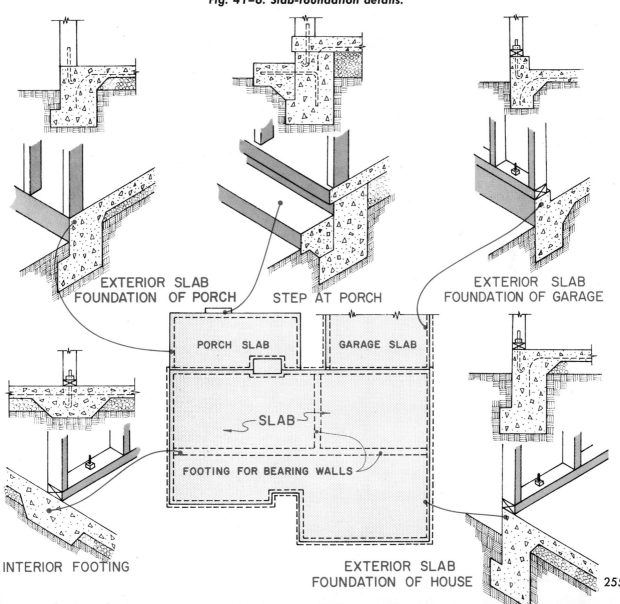

EXTERIOR SLAB
FOUNDATION OF PORCH

STEP AT PORCH

EXTERIOR SLAB
FOUNDATION OF GARAGE

PORCH SLAB

GARAGE SLAB

SLAB

FOOTING FOR BEARING WALLS

INTERIOR FOOTING

EXTERIOR SLAB
FOUNDATION OF HOUSE

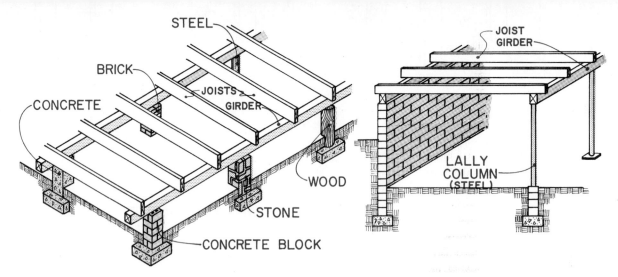

Fig. 41-7. Pier and column construction.

(Fig. 41-3). The details of construction relating to the T foundation and the methods of representing this construction on the foundation plan are shown in Fig. 41-4.

Fig. 41-8. Sketch a T-foundation, slab-foundation, and pier-foundation detail for this plan.

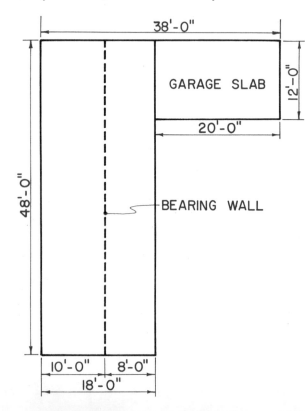

Slab Foundations

A slab foundation is a poured solid slab of concrete. The slab is poured directly on the ground, with footers placed where extra support is needed (Fig. 41-5). A slab foundation requires considerably less labor to construct than do most other foundation types. Details of the slab foundation and methods of drawing slab foundations are shown in Fig. 41-6.

Pier and Column Foundations

The pier and column foundation consists of individual footers upon which columns are placed. Fewer materials and less labor are needed for the pier and column foundation (Fig. 41-7). The main objection to using pier and column foundations for most residence work is that a basement is not possible when this type of construction is used.

Problems

1. Sketch Fig. 41-8, using the scale ¼″ = 1'-0″ for a T foundation.
2. Sketch Fig. 41-8, using the scale ¼″ = 1'-0″ for a slab foundation.
3. Sketch Fig. 41-8, using the scale ¼″ = 1'-0″ for a pier foundation.
4. Know these architectural terms: *contractor, grade, slab, T foundation, column, frost depth.*

Unit 42. Foundation Construction Methods

The designer must be familiar with all methods of foundation construction in order to design the most practical and economical foundation (Fig. 42–1). When the designer has chosen the most appropriate type of foundation for the type of soil, climate, and structure to be supported, he must prepare working drawings that will facilitate the layout, excavation, and construction of the foundation.

▶ Layout

The size and shape of the foundation are normally laid out with a transit and measuring tape. String is then used with batter boards to indicate the exact position of the excavation line, footer line, and foundation wall line, as shown in Fig. 42–2. The angle of the corners can be set with a transit, as described in Unit 37, or square corners can be laid out by the 8–6–10 unit method of obtaining a right angle, as shown in Fig. 42–3.

▶ Excavations

Foundation plans should clearly show what parts of the foundation are to be completely excavated, partly excavated for crawl space, or unexcavated. The depth of the excavation should be shown also on the elevation drawings. If a basement is planned, the entire excavation for the basement is dug before the footers are poured. If there is to be no basement, a trench excavation is made.

Fig. 42–1. Conditions of the terrain determine the type of foundation used.

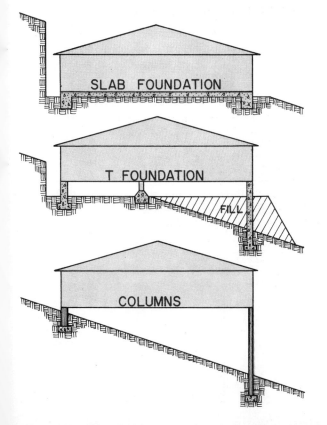

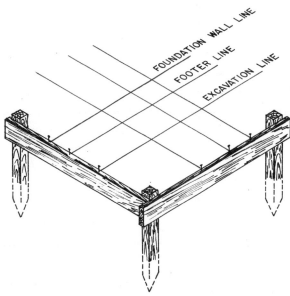

Fig. 42–2. Batter-board layout method.

Fig. 42–3. Establishing right angles by the 8-6-10 unit method.

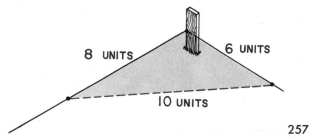

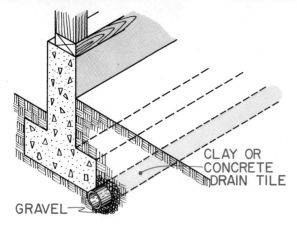

Fig. 42–4. A poured T foundation.

Fig. 42–7. A reinforced slab foundation.

▶ T Foundations

The T foundation is prepared by pouring the footer in an excavated trench, leveling the top of the footer, and erecting a concrete block or masonry wall on top of the footer. If concrete foundation walls are to be used, building forms are erected

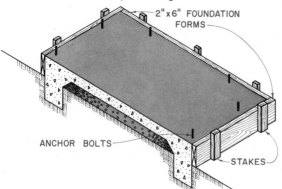

Fig. 42–5. Slab-form construction.

Fig. 42–6. Leveling the slab.

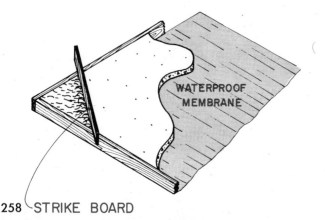

258 STRIKE BOARD

on top of the footer. Concrete is poured into these forms (Fig. 42–4). After the concrete dries, the wood is removed and may be reused for other forms. When a poured foundation wall is to be used, the concrete mix is sand, gravel, water, and cement. After the forms are filled, the concrete is leveled with a strike board, so that they have a rough, nonslip surface.

▶ Slab Foundations

The excavation for a slab foundation is made for the footings only. Two-by-fours are used to construct the forms for the slab, as shown in Fig. 42–5. The entire foundation is then poured and the top of the slab leveled with a strike board (Fig. 42–6). Slab foundations and basement floors in T foundations should be waterproofed by waterproof membrane placed between the slab and the ground. Slabs are often reinforced with steel wire

Fig. 42–8. Determine the size of excavation and the amount of concrete needed for this foundation.

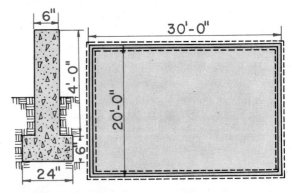

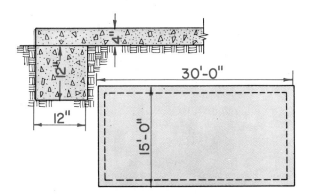

Fig. 42–9. *Determine the size of the excavation and the amount of concrete needed for this foundation.*

mesh placed inside the slab before pouring, as shown in Fig. 42–7.

Types and sizes and mixtures of materials for foundations are rigidly controlled by most building codes. It is imperative for the designer to check the building code of the area in which he is designing.

Problems

1. In Fig. 42–8, how many cubic feet of dirt must be excavated? How many cubic yards? How many cubic feet of concrete must be poured for the footing? How many cubic yards for the slab?

2. In Fig. 42–9, how many cubic yards of dirt must be excavated for the footings? How many cubic yards of concrete will be used?

3. What is the concrete mix for foundations in your community? Check your building code.

4. List several different types of foundations and materials used in your community.

5. Know these architectural terms: *excavations, foundation forms, steel wire mesh, strike board, waterproof membrane.*

Unit 43. Fireplaces

Provision must be made in the foundation plans to support the weight of the fireplace and chimney (Fig. 43–1). A solid reinforced concrete footer is used in most residences. This footer is 12″ thick and extends 12″ past the perimeter of the chimney.

▶ **Fireplace**

The main part of the fireplace is the *firebox.* The firebox reflects heat and draws smoke up the chimney. Included in the firebox are the sides, back, smoke chamber, flue, throat, and damper (Fig. 43–2). Most fireboxes are constructed in a factory. The mason places the firebox in the proper location in the chimney construction and lines it with fire brick.

Masonry used in fireplaces and chimneys is usually of brick, stone, or concrete; and firebrick

Fig. 43–1. *The size and place of the fireplace and chimney determine the type of foundation needed to support its weight.*

Home Planners, Inc.

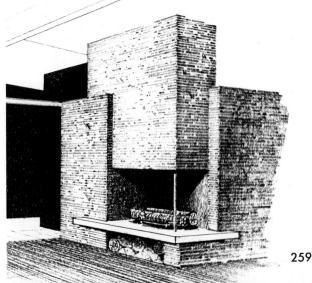

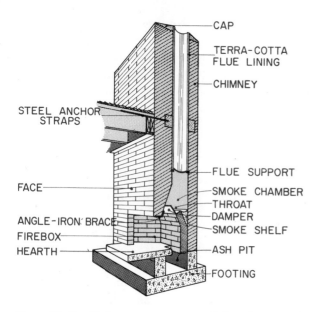

Fig. 43-2. *Major components of fireplace and chimney structure.*

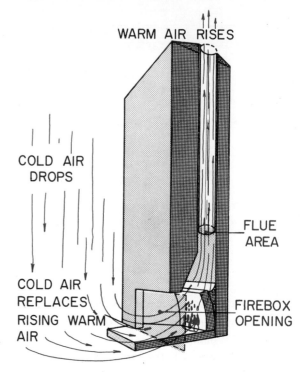

Fig. 43-4. *The functioning of a fireplace flue.*

Fig. 43-3. *A sectional drawing of a fireplace and chimney.*

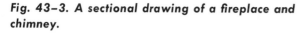

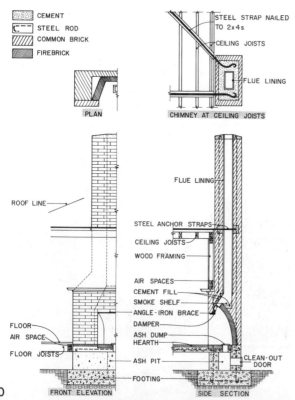

is used to line the firebox. The hearth also should be constructed of fire-resistant material such as brick, tile, marble, or stone.

The best method of drawing the construction details of a fireplace is to prepare a sectional drawing, as shown in Fig. 43-3. This gives the position of the firebox and the size of materials used in the footer, hearth, face, flue, and cap of the chimney. It also shows the relationship of the chimney to the floor and ceiling lines of the structure.

▶ Chimney

A chimney extends from the footer through the roof of the house. The footer should be of sufficient size to support the entire weight of the chimney. The chimney extends above the roof line to provide a better draft for drawing the smoke and to eliminate the possibility of sparks igniting the roof.

The height of the chimney above the roof line varies somewhat, according to local building codes. In most areas the distance is two feet.

The chimney is secured to ceiling and floor joists by iron straps imbedded in the brickwork. Floor joists and ceiling joists around the chimney and fireplace and hearth should have sufficient clearance to protect them from the heat. Most building codes specify this distance.

The designer must also indicate the type and size of flues to be inserted in the chimney. One flue is necessary for each fireplace or furnace leading into the chimney. The flue from the fireplace or from the furnace in the basement extends directly to the top of the chimney, completely bypassing the first-floor fireplaces. The first-floor fireplace flues completely bypass the second-floor fireplace flues. Bypassing takes place with any higher floors. Each flue must be at least one-tenth the opening of the fireplace to accommodate the rise of warm air, as shown in Fig. 43–4.

▶ **Prefabricated Fireplaces**

Metal fireplaces constructed of heavy-gage steel are available in a variety of shapes (Fig. 43–5). They are relatively light woodburning stoves and therefore need no concrete foundation. A stovepipe leading into the chimney provides the exhaust flue (Fig. 43–6). Since metal emits more heat than masonry does, the metal fireplace is much more efficient, especially if centrally located. These fireplaces can be mounted on the walls, on legs, or built into the chimney. Nevertheless a fire-resistant material such as concrete, brick, stone, or tile must be used beneath and around these fireplaces (Fig. 43–7).

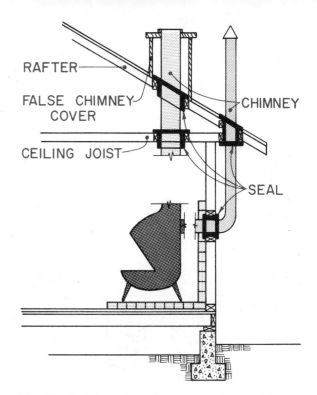

Fig. 43–6. Adequate exhaust must be provided for prefabricated fireplace.

Problems

1. Redraw the fireplace in Fig. 43–1, using the scale ½" = 1'-0".
2. Redesign the front of the fireplace in Fig. 43–1.
3. Compare the price of a masonry fireplace to that of a prefabricated iron fireplace.
4. Know these architectural terms: *firebox, chimney, smoke chamber, flue, throat, damper, draft, draw, ceiling joist, firebrick, prefabricated fireplace, chimney sections.*

Fig. 43–5. A prefabricated metal fireplace.

Copper & Brass Research Association

Fig. 43–7. Fire-resistant material must be used around the fireplace area.

Olson-Spencer & Associates; Southern California Edison Company

261

Bethlehem Steel Company

SECTION ELEVEN. FRAMING PLANS

Most of the basic engineering principles upon which modern framing methods are based have been known for centuries. However, it has not been until recent years that the development of materials and construction methods has allowed the utilization of these principles. Today's architect can choose among many basic materials in the design of the basic structural framework of a building. New and improved methods of erecting structural steel, new developments in laminating and processing preformed wood structural members, developments and refinements in the use of concrete and masonry, products such as pre-stressed concrete slabs, and continual progress in standardization in the design of structural components—all these provide the architect with the flexibility to design the most appropriate structural system for a building at the lowest possible cost and with the smallest waste of materials and time.

Unit 44. Types of Framing

New construction materials and new methods of using conventional materials provide the architect with much flexibility in framing design.

Stronger buildings can now be erected with lighter and fewer materials.

▶ Principles of Framing

Regardless of the materials used and the methods employed, the physical principles upon which structural design is based remain constant. In most structures the roof is supported by the wall framework and interior partitions or columns. Each exterior wall and bearing partition is supported by the *foundation*, which, in turn, is supported by a *footing*. The footing distributes this load over a wide area of load-bearing soil and thus ties the entire structural system to the ground (Fig. 44-1).

Early framing methods. In earlier centuries, people did not have strong, light framing materials such as structural steel, aluminum, or sized and seasoned lumber. Therefore, extremely heavy material such as stone was used to support the great weight of a building. Foundations were large and footers enormous, to support and spread the heavy load. Walls were frequently constructed larger at the base than at the top, and a very elaborate system of column support was developed, as shown in the Doric order in Fig. 44-2.

Current framing methods. Today most buildings are constructed with a basic skeleton framework. A structural tie, such as *sheathing* or *diagonal bracing*, is covered with protective siding. The structural system is somewhat related to the structure of most vertebrates. The framework functions like the skeleton in providing the basic rigid frame. The structural tie, whether it be sheathing on a wooden structure or cross-bracing on a steel framework, acts like the muscles in holding the framework in the desired position. The protective covering, which is similar to the skin, provides the necessary protection from the weather (Fig. 44-3).

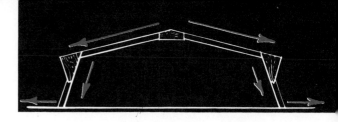

Fig. 44-1. Major lines of support.

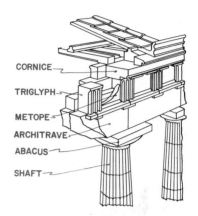

CORNICE

TRIGLYPH

METOPE

ARCHITRAVE

ABACUS

SHAFT

Fig. 44-2. The column support of the Doric order of architecture.

Fig. 44-3. The skeleton of a building is similar to the skeleton of a person.

FRAMEWORK

CHIMNEY OPENING — RIDGE BOARD — RAFTERS — STUDS — GARAGE–DOOR OPENING

STRUCTURAL TIES

PLYWOOD SHEATHING — WINDOW OPENINGS

BRICK — ROOFING — SIDING — DOORS & WINDOWS — PROTECTIVE COVERING

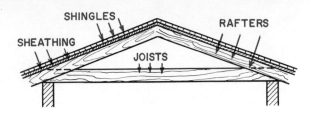

Fig. 44-4. Dead loads.

Fig. 44-5. Live loads.

Fig. 44-6. Live loads acting upon a roof.

Fig. 44-7. The framework of a building is designed to overcome tension, compression, shear, and torsion.

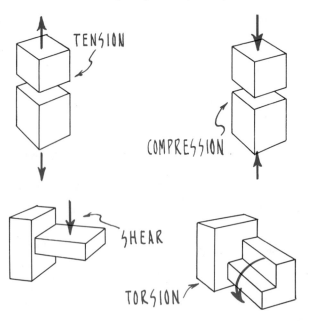

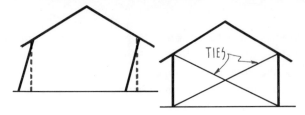

Fig. 44-8. The stability of a structure is determined by its design.

▶ **Loads**

Loads that must be supported by the structure are divided into two types, live loads and dead loads.

Dead loads. Dead loads are those loads caused by the weight of the construction materials. The dead loads of the roof (Fig. 44-4) must be supported by the walls or bearing partitions. The dead loads of the walls must be supported by the foundation. Every piece of lumber, plywood, glass, and sheetmetal, and every nail and brick adds to the total dead load of the structure.

Live loads. Live loads are those loads that may vary from structure to structure. Live loads of a floor include furniture and people, as shown in Fig. 44-5. Live loads of a roof include such variables as wind, snow, and even rain when the roof is flat (Fig. 44-6). As you learn more about the construction of roofs, floors, and walls in the succeeding units you will learn how to design these structurally so that they will withstand normal live and dead loads.

▶ **Strength of Materials**

The stability of the building depends on the strength of the material used and the connection of members to overcome *tension, compression, shear,* and *torsion* (Fig. 44-7). The strength of the building material is irrelevant if the building is not structurally stable. Likewise, the building will be inadequate if the building materials are weak, regardless of the stability of the design (Fig. 44-8).

The strength of building material is significant only when related to the structure. Most lumber and even steel are relatively flexible until tied into the structure. Grasp a piece of paper between your thumb and forefinger, as shown in Fig. 44-9.

Fig. 44–9. The strength of a material is related to its shape.

The other end of the paper will drop. If you fold this same piece of paper, you will be able to support it from one end easily. This principle is applied to the use of structural members in building design.

Figure 44–10 shows that turning a member on its side will reduce the *vertical deflection* significantly but that *horizontal deflection* will be unaffected. Combining the horizontal and vertical components of the member (to make a channel) reduces both the vertical and horizontal deflection. Combining two horizontal members with one vertical member (as in an I beam) provides even more stability.

It would seem that the design of structures is a relatively simple matter. The materials must be strong enough and the structure rigid enough. But it is not that simple. Care must be taken not to overdesign the structure. A beam that is one size too large will not support the structure any better than will a member of the right size. Overdesigning (except for allowing safety margins) a few items of this kind can cost thousands of dollars on a large job. For example, the member used to support the loads in Fig. 44–11A is considerably overdesigned. The support used in Fig. 44–11B is satisfactory. The support used in Fig. 44–11C is inadequately designed. Achieving the perfect balance, as shown in Fig. 44–11B, is the goal of every structural designer.

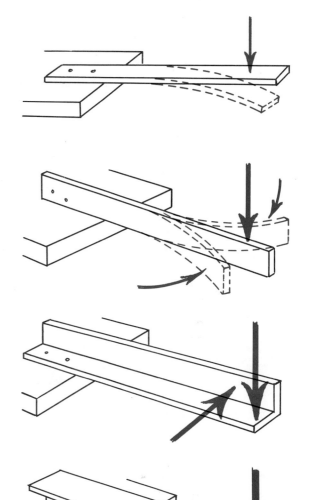

Fig. 44–10. Deflections can be eliminated by combining members.

Fig. 44–11. Structural stability depends on the support and the spacing of support members.

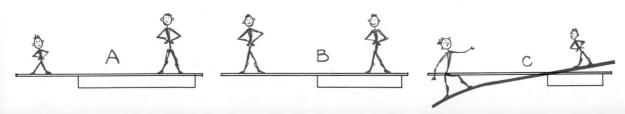

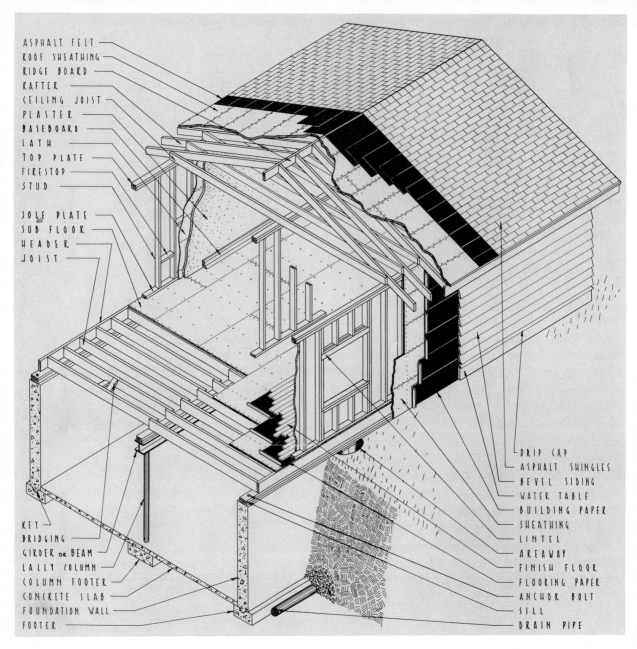

ASPHALT FELT
ROOF SHEATHING
RIDGE BOARD
RAFTER
CEILING JOIST
PLASTER
BASEBOARD
LATH
TOP PLATE
FIRESTOP
STUD

SOLE PLATE
SUB FLOOR
HEADER
JOIST

KEY
BRIDGING
GIRDER or BEAM
LALLY COLUMN
COLUMN FOOTER
CONCRETE SLAB
FOUNDATION WALL
FOOTER

DRIP CAP
ASPHALT SHINGLES
BEVEL SIDING
WATER TABLE
BUILDING PAPER
SHEATHING
LINTEL
AREAWAY
FINISH FLOOR
FLOORING PAPER
ANCHOR BOLT
SILL
DRAIN PIPE

Fig. 44–12. Residential skeleton framing.

▶ Wood Framing

Early pioneers in this country used wood as the basic construction material in building log cabins. Wood was used in its raw form to make the entire solid wall.

Conventional framing. With the passing of the log cabin from the American scene, the *skeleton-frame* type of wood construction was developed.

This was made possible through the development of machinery capable of mass-producing sized and seasoned lumber that could be used interchangeably for framing purposes. However, limits on the size of lumber that could be processed effectively on the job led to the use of relatively small structural members placed at close intervals. Figure 44–12 shows the anatomy of a house constructed by this method. The framing methods shown herein have been in use practically from the end of the log-cabin period to the present day.

Post and beam construction. The use of post and beam construction methods has been increased by the popularity of the indoor–outdoor living area. The practicality of manufacturing large heat-resistant windows and window walls (Fig. 44–13) and the accessibility of larger wood members have popularized the post and beam method of construction. This method is based on the use of larger members spaced at greater intervals. This spacing accommodates large windows and sliding doors that unite the indoors and outdoors in a single living space.

Figure 44–14 shows a comparison of the post and beam method of construction and the conventional method. Figure 44–15 shows some of the basic details of post and beam construction. The preparation of the various framing plans using both the post and beam and the conventional wood-framing method will be presented in succeeding units.

▶ **Steel Framing**

Steel framing is similar in principle to post and beam framing. Figure 44–16 shows a comparison between the use of posts, beams, and planks in

Libbey-Owens-Ford Glass Company

Fig. 44-13. Application of the post and beam methods.

Fig. 44-14. Post and beam construction compared to conventional construction.

Fig. 44-15. Basic details of post and beam construction.

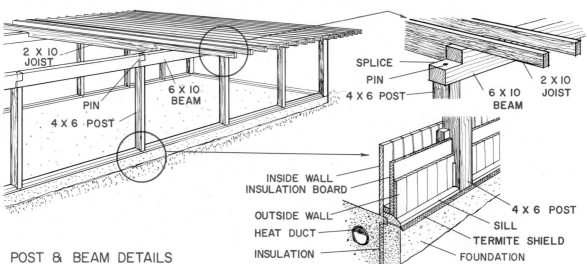

POST & BEAM DETAILS

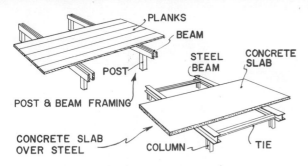

Fig. 44–16. Comparison of post and beam construction with steel and concrete slab construction.

Bethlehem Steel Company; American Iron and Steel Institute

Fig. 44–17. Steel framing permits the use of large spans.

post and beam construction and the use of columns, beams, and slabs in steel construction.

Steel columns perform the same function as wooden posts in providing the vertical support. Steel beams, like wood girders, support the floor or roof system. Steel framing, however, can support and span longer distances because of the rigidity of structural steel members. For this reason, steel framing is used to erect extremely high multiple-story buildings. In fact, the greatest utili-

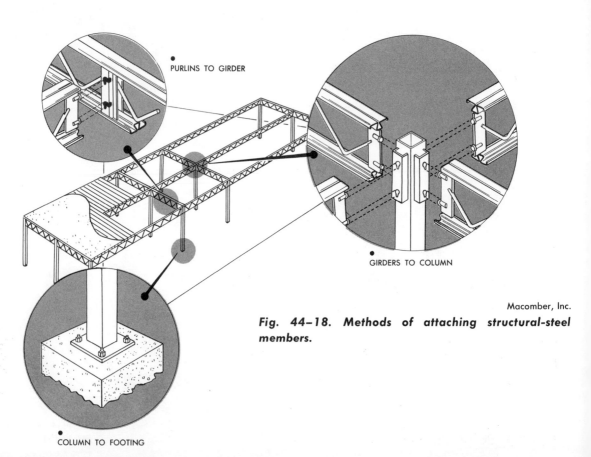

PURLINS TO GIRDER

GIRDERS TO COLUMN

COLUMN TO FOOTING

Macomber, Inc.

Fig. 44–18. Methods of attaching structural-steel members.

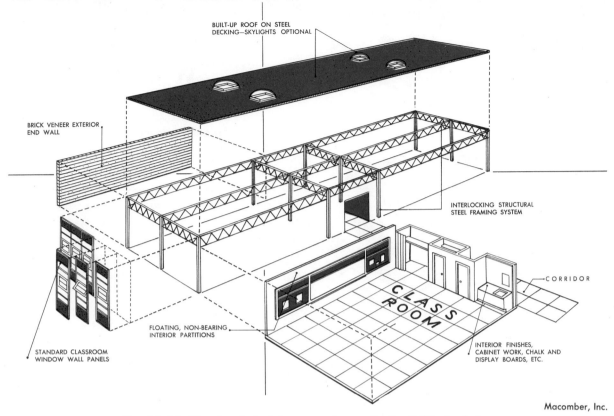

BUILT-UP ROOF ON STEEL
DECKING—SKYLIGHTS OPTIONAL

BRICK VENEER EXTERIOR
END WALL

INTERLOCKING STRUCTURAL
STEEL FRAMING SYSTEM

CORRIDOR

FLOATING, NON-BEARING
INTERIOR PARTITIONS

STANDARD CLASSROOM
WINDOW WALL PANELS

INTERIOR FINISHES,
CABINET WORK, CHALK AND
DISPLAY BOARDS, ETC.

CLASS ROOM

Macomber, Inc.

Fig. 44–19. Structural-steel framework permits flexibility in design.

zation of structural-steel framing has been for large commercial and industrial buildings such as schools, churches, office buildings.

Steel has also gained popularity as a framing material for smaller structures. Large cantilever decks, as shown in Fig. 44–17, are possible because of the long distances that can be spanned by steel beams.

Because of the rigid attachment of steel members to each other and to footers and walls, a minimum of crossbracing is needed (Fig. 44–18). Structural-steel framework can be designed to span long distances without intervening support. Longer spans create large unobstructed areas by eliminating the need for columns or bearing partitions. These large clear-span areas provide the designer with considerable flexibility in the design and location of interior partitions. Figure 44–19 shows some of the flexibilities in the interior design and

in the placement of the exterior-wall treatment in steel construction.

Structural-steel members are available in a variety of shapes and sizes. Figure 44–20 shows some of the standardized shapes used in architectural work.

▶ Prefabrication

From the time of the construction of the Pyramids, men have been building with prefabricated component parts. The word *fabricate* simply means "to put together." The combination of *pre* and *fabricate* indicates that the parts of the structure are put together prior to erection, at a place permitting more controlled and more desirable conditions than are possible at a building site.

Beginnings. In its simplest form, prefabrication dates back to the time when primitive man cut and trimmed wood and tanned skins before he built

NAME	SYMBOL	SECTION	PICTORIAL
SQUARE BAR	⌗	■	
ROUND BAR	φ	●	
PLATE	℞	▬	
ANGLE	∠	L	
CHANNEL	⊔	L	
BULB ANGLE	BULB∠	L	
WIDE FLANGE	WF	I	
I-BEAM	I	I	
TEE	T	T	
ZEE	Z	⌐	
LALLY COLUMN	◎	O	

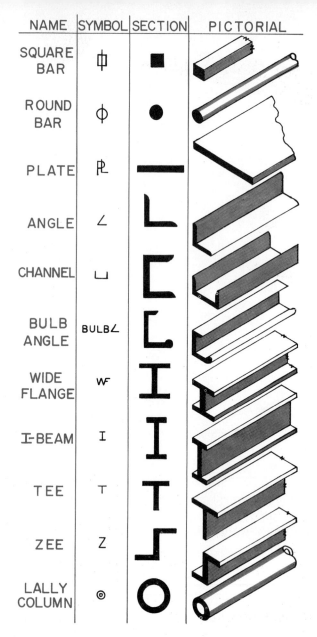

Fig. 44-20. Standard structural-steel shapes.

Fig. 44–21. An early application of the principle of prefabrication.

more popular for precut houses. Its use was a modified do-it-yourself approach to home building. A few companies then ventured into prefabrication of a more complete house package including ceiling panels, wall panels, and floor panels, complete with plumbing and electrical work installed in the walls. At the same time, conventional builders were accepting prefabrication to a great extent. They recognized, for example, that a better and less expensive window sash could be produced in a plant than could be handmade on the job site. As builders became more aware of the time, labor, and materials that could be saved by prefabrication, they began to use preassembled cabinets, prefitted doors, prefinished sink tops, prefinished floors, and other prefabricated parts.

Prefabrication today. Today, the most successful companies producing factory-made homes rely on constructing building panels, exterior panels, partitions, and floor systems by conventional framing methods. They simply apply the techniques of mass production to their production methods. The goal is to minimize custom-job work without sacrificing the quality of the construction.

The National Association of Home Builders has sponsored the design and construction of an experimental house to determine to what extent factory-finished materials can be applied through-

Fig. 44–22. Prefabrication techniques were used in the Civil War.

a shelter (Fig. 44–21). Hannibal carried prefabricated huts across the Alps in his war with the Romans. Portable buildings were used by the Army in the 1800s for barracks and small field hospitals. The Union Army used these structures for its troops during the Civil War (Fig. 44–22).

Throughout the twentieth century—in fact, almost until World War II—prefabrication became

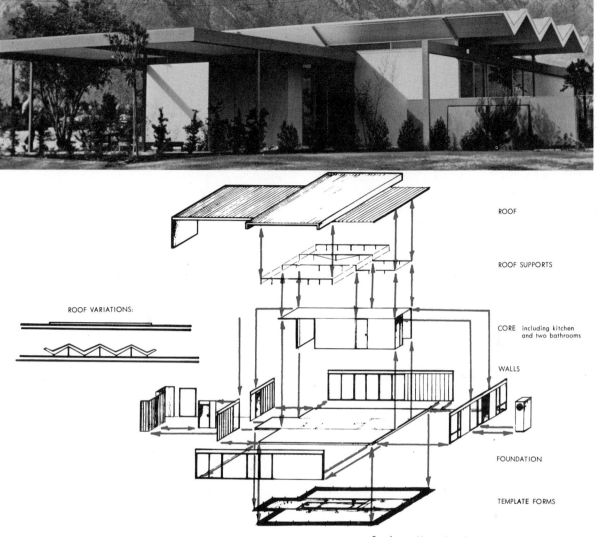

ROOF

ROOF SUPPORTS

ROOF VARIATIONS:

CORE including kitchen and two bathrooms

WALLS

FOUNDATION

TEMPLATE FORMS

Steelways Magazine; American Iron and Steel Institute

Fig. 44–23. Maximum utilization of factory components.

out the house. Figure 44–23 shows some of the basic components of this design, which include the following:

1. A precut steel post and beam foundation system

2. Combination sheathing and siding finished with polyvinyl fluoride film

3. Vinyl-finished interior wallboard

4. Combination subflooring completely finished at the factory

5. Reinforced plastic shower stalls and roofing boards coated with Hypalon that fasten to rafters by a concealed nailing system.

Research and development in all phases of our technology will contribute to the increased use of factory-produced and factory-finished materials for architectural purposes.

Problems

Identify the following architectural terms: *span, framework, skeleton frame, structural tile, sheathing, live load, dead load, tension, compression, shear, torsion, deflection, equilibrium, conventional wood framing, post and beam framing, column, beam, post, plank, cantileverage, bearing partition, non-bearing partition.*

Unit 45. Floor-framing Plans

Platform-floor systems are those systems that are suspended from foundation walls and/or beams.

▶ Types of Platform-floor Systems

Platform-floor systems are divided into three types: the conventional floor-framing systems, plank and beam floor systems, and panelized floor systems. These types are shown in Fig. 45–1.

Conventional systems. The conventionally framed platform system provides a most flexible method of floor framing for a wide variety of design conditions. Floor joists are spaced at 16″ intervals and are supported by the side walls of the foundation or by beams.

Plank and beam systems. The plank and beam (post and beam) method of floor framing utilizes individual framing members that are much larger and less numerous than conventional framing members. Because of the size and rigidity of the members the necessity for bridging for stability is eliminated.

Panelized systems. Panelized floor systems are composed of preassembled sandwich panels of a variety of skin and core materials. Core-panel systems are used for long clear spans over base-

ment construction and for shorter spans in nonbasement houses.

Other experimental methods of core-component design and construction are continually being developed and refined to reduce the on-site construction costs. Research in engineering and wood technology is continually extending the use of components for support systems.

▶ Design

The design of the floor system depends on the load, type of material, size of the members, spacing of

Fig. 45–2. The design of the floor system depends on many factors.

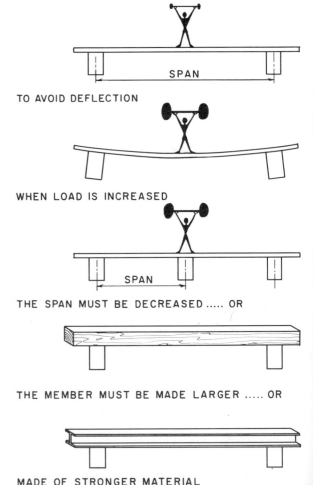

TO AVOID DEFLECTION

WHEN LOAD IS INCREASED

THE SPAN MUST BE DECREASED ..... OR

THE MEMBER MUST BE MADE LARGER ..... OR

MADE OF STRONGER MATERIAL

Fig. 45–1. Types of platform-floor systems.

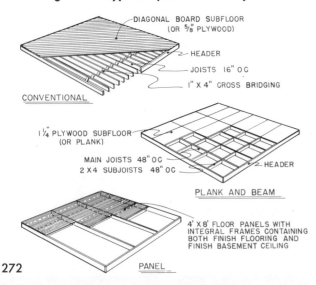

DIAGONAL BOARD SUBFLOOR (OR ⅝″ PLYWOOD)

HEADER

JOISTS 16″ OC

1″ X 4″ CROSS BRIDGING

CONVENTIONAL

1¼″ PLYWOOD SUBFLOOR (OR PLANK)

MAIN JOISTS 48″ OC
2 X 4 SUBJOISTS 48″ OC

HEADER

PLANK AND BEAM

4′ X 8′ FLOOR PANELS WITH INTEGRAL FRAMES CONTAINING BOTH FINISH FLOORING AND FINISH BASEMENT CEILING

PANEL

Live load—pounds per square foot	Spacing	2 inches wide by depth of—					3 inches wide by depth of—				
		6	8	10	12	14	6	8	10	12	14
10.........	12	12- 9	16- 9	21- 1	24- 0	—	14- 7	19- 3	24- 0	—	—
	16	11- 8	15- 4	19- 4	23- 4	24- 0	13- 6	17- 9	22- 2	24- 0	—
	24	10- 3	14- 6	17- 3	20- 7	24- 0	11-11	15- 9	19-10	23- 9	24- 0
20.........	12	11- 6	15- 3	19- 2	23- 0	24- 0	13- 3	17- 6	21- 9	24- 0	—
	16	10- 5	13-11	17- 6	21- 1	24- 0	12- 0	16- 1	20- 2	24- 0	—
	24	9- 2	12- 3	15- 6	18- 7	21- 9	10- 6	14- 2	17-10	21- 6	24- 0
30.........	12	10- 8	14- 0	17- 9	21- 4	24- 9	12- 4	16- 4	20- 5	24- 5	—
	16	9- 9	12-11	16- 3	19- 6	22- 9	11- 4	14-11	18- 9	22- 7	26- 4
	24	8- 6	11- 4	14- 4	17- 3	20- 2	10- 0	13- 2	16- 8	19-11	23- 4
40.........	12	10- 0	13- 3	16- 8	20- 1	23- 5	11- 8	15- 4	19- 3	23- 1	26-11
	16	9- 1	12- 1	15- 3	18- 5	21- 5	10- 8	14- 0	17- 8	21- 3	24-10
	24	7-10	10- 4	13- 1	15- 9	18- 5	9- 4	12- 4	15- 7	18- 9	22- 1
50.........	12	9- 6	12- 7	15-10	19- 1	22- 4	11- 0	14- 7	18- 4	22- 0	25- 8
	16	8- 7	11- 6	14- 7	17- 6	20- 5	10- 0	13- 4	16-10	20- 3	23- 8
	24	7- 3	9- 6	12- 1	14- 7	17- 0	8-10	11- 9	14-10	17-10	20-10
60.........	12	9- 0	12- 0	15- 2	18- 3	21- 4	10- 6	14- 0	17- 7	21- 1	24- 7
	16	8- 1	10-10	13- 8	16- 6	19- 3	9- 7	12-10	16- 1	19- 4	22- 7
	24	6- 8	8-11	11- 3	13- 7	15-11	8- 5	11- 3	14- 1	17- 0	20- 0
70.........	12	8- 7	11- 6	14- 6	17- 6	20- 6	10- 1	13- 5	16-11	20- 5	23- 9
	16	7- 8	10- 2	12-10	15- 6	18- 3	9- 3	12- 3	15- 5	18- 7	21-10
	24	6- 5	8- 5	10- 7	12- 9	15- 0	8- 0	10- 7	13- 4	16- 1	18-10

Fig. 45–3. Maximum spans for joists.

the support members, and distance between the major support members (span). Figure 45–2 shows that as the load is increased, the span must be decreased to compensate for the increase, or the member must be made larger or of a stronger material. The design of floor systems, therefore, demands very careful calculation in determining the live and dead loads acting on the floor; in selecting the most appropriate material for posts, beams or girders, and blocking; in determining the exact size of the posts, beams, and deck materials and joists; and in establishing the exact spacing between posts, girders, and joists.

The parts of a floor system that must be selected on the basis of loads, material, size, and spacing include the deck, joist, girders or beams, and posts or columns.

▶ Deck

The deck of a floor system is composed of a subfloor and a finished floor. A *subfloor* is a floor usually made of dressed sheathing lumber or plywood, which is laid over the floor joist and over which the finished floor is laid. The functions of the subfloor are as follows:

1. It increases the strength of the floor and provides a surface for the laying of a thin finished floor.

2. It helps to stiffen the position of the floor joist.

3. It serves as a working surface during construction.

4. It helps to deaden sound.

5. It prevents dust from rising through the floor.

6. It helps to insulate.

The *finished floor* provides a wearing surface over the subfloor, or over the joist if there is no subfloor. Hardwood, such as oak, maple, beach, and birch, is used for finished floors. Tile is often used as a finished floor. It may be laid directly on the subflooring.

▶ Joists

To determine the type of joists, the load, spacing, and strength of the joists must be considered.

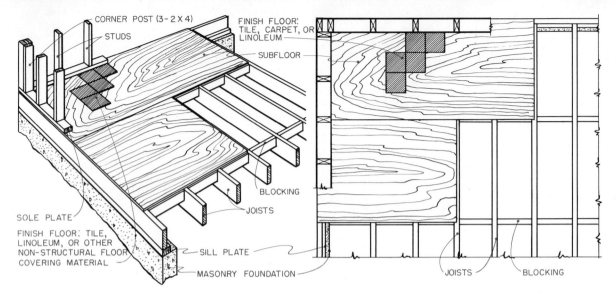

Fig. 45–4A. Floor-framing plan with blocking shown.

Loads. Only live loads bear directly on the decking and joists. Therefore, the total live loads for the room having the heaviest furniture and the heaviest traffic should be used to compute the total load for the entire floor. To find the live load in pounds per square foot, divide the total loads in the room by the number of square feet supporting the load.

Spacing. When the live load is determined, the size and spacing of joists can be established by referring to Fig. 45–3. This table is based on #1 Southern white pine with a fiber stress of 1,200 pounds per square inch and a modulus of elasticity (ratio of stress and strain) of 1,600,000 pounds per square inch. For other materials, such as redwood or Douglas fir lumber, with different fiber stresses and different moduli of elasticity, a different chart should be used. For example, if the live loads are approximately 40 pounds per square foot and 16″ spaces are desired between joists, you can see that a 2 × 8 is good for a spacing of only 12′-1″. For a span larger than 12′-1″, a 2 × 10 joist is necessary.

Size. You can see, therefore, that as the size, spacing, and load vary, the spans must vary accordingly. Or if the span is changed, the dimen-

sions of the spacing of the joist must change accordingly. Figure 45–4A indicates the method of drawing part of the floor-framing plan which shows the size and position of joists and the blocking between joists. In this particular detail, the relative position of the subfloor, finished floor, sill, and exterior walls is also shown. In Fig. 45–4B there is an alternative floor system showing the relationship between the joists of the floor and the finished floor and sill.

In some systems the floor system may appear to have no joists, as shown in Fig. 45–5. However, in this system the girder and blocking perform the function of the joist. The girders rest directly on posts, and the subflooring rests directly on the girders, which are spaced more closely than most girders which support joists.

▶ **Headers**

Whenever it is necessary to cut regular joists to provide an opening for a stair-well or a hearth, it is necessary to provide auxiliary joists called *headers*. Headers are placed at right angles to the regular joists, to carry the ends of joists that are cut. A header cannot be of greater depth than any other joist; hence, headers are usually doubled

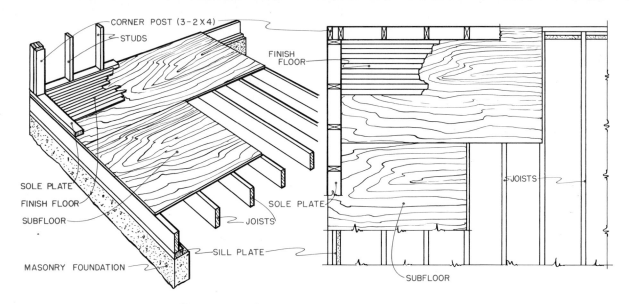

Fig. 45–4B. Floor-framing plan without blocking.

(placed side by side) to compensate for the additional load. Figure 45–6 shows the use of the double header as compensation for the joists that are cut to provide space for the fireplace.

Additional support is also needed under bearing partitions. Figure 45–7 shows the use of double joists under partitions. The method of drawing the double joists both on the floor-framing plan and on the floor-framing elevation drawing is also shown.

▶ **Girders and Beams**

All the weight of the floor system, including the live loads and the dead loads, are transmitted

Fig. 45–5. Method of drawing floor-framing systems without joists.

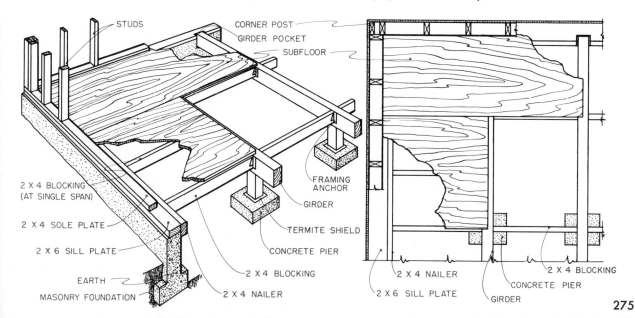

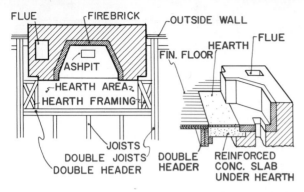

Fig. 45-6. *Double headers are used around the fireplaces.*

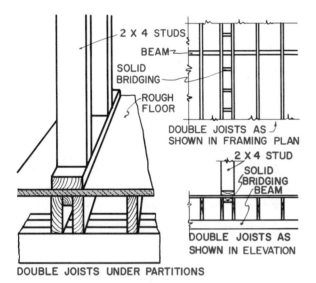

Fig. 45-7. *Double joists are used under partitions.*

Fig. 45-8. *The area supported by a girder.*

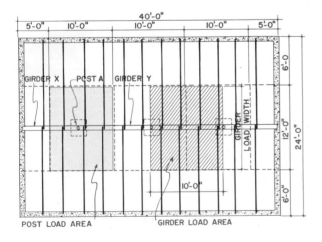

to bearing partitions. These loads are then transmitted either to the foundation wall or to horizontal supports known as *girders* or *beams*. To determine the exact spacing, size, and type of beam to support the structure, follow these steps:

1. Determine the total load acting on the entire floor system in pounds per square foot. Divide the total live and dead loads by the number of square feet of floor space. For example, if the combined load for the floor system shown in Fig. 45-8 is 48,000 pounds, then there are 50 pounds per square foot of load acting on the floor (48,000 pounds divided by 960 square feet equals 50 pounds per square foot).

2. Lay out the proposed position of all columns and beams. It will also help to sketch the position of the joists to be sure that the joist spans are correct, as shown in Fig. 45-8.

3. Determine the number of square feet supported by the girder (girder load area). The *girder load area* is determined by multiplying the length of a girder from column to column by the girder load width. The *girder load width* is the distance extending on both sides of the center line of the girder, halfway to the nearest support, as shown in Fig. 45-8. The remaining distance from a girder load area to the outside wall is supported by the outside wall.

4. To find the load supported by the girder load area, multiply the girder load area by the load per square foot. For example, the girder load in Fig. 45-8 is 6,000 pounds (120 square feet × 50 pounds per square foot).

5. Select the most suitable material to carry the load at the span desired. Built-up wood girders are equivalent to steel I beams in many respects. However, I beams will span a greater length without intervening support.

6. Select the exact size and classification of the beam or girder. Use the chart shown in Fig. 45-9 to select the most appropriate wood girder. For example, to support 6,000 pounds over a 10' span, either an 8 × 8 solid girder or a 6 × 10 built-up girder would suffice. The girder should be strong enough to support the load, but any

Girder size	Safe load in lbs. for spans from 6 to 10 feet.				
	6 ft.	7 ft.	8 ft.	9 ft.	10 ft.
6 x 8 solid	8,306	7,118	6,220	5,539	4,583
6 x 8 built-up	7,359	6,306	5,511	4,908	4,062
6 x 10 solid	11,357	10,804	9,980	8,887	7,997
6 x 10 built-up	10,068	9,576	8,844	7,878	7,086
8 x 8 solid	11,326	9,706	8,482	7,553	6,250
8 x 8 built-up	9,812	8,408	7,348	6,544	5,416
8 x 10 solid	15,487	14,732	13,608	12,116	10,902
8 x 10 built-up	13,424	12,768	11,792	10,504	9,448

Fig. 45–9. Safe loads for wood girders.

size larger is a waste of materials. The only alternative to increasing the size of the girder is to decrease the size of the span.

▶ **Steel Beams**

The method for ascertaining the size of steel beams is the same as for determining the size of wood beams. As wood beams vary in width for a given depth, steel beams vary in weight, depth, and thickness of webs and flanges; and classifications vary accordingly. The chart shown in Fig. 45–10 shows the relationship of the span, the load, the depth, and the weight of standard I beams and channels. A steel beam may be selected by referring to the desirable span and load and then choosing the most appropriate size (depth and weight) for the I beam. For example, a 5″ × 12.25-pound I beam will support 6.5 pounds per square foot.

▶ **Columns**

When girders or beams do not completely span the distance between foundation walls, wood posts, steel-pipe columns, masonry columns, or steel-beam columns must be used for intervening support. To determine the most appropriate size and classification of posts or columns to support the girders or beams, follow these steps:

1. Determine the total load in pounds per square foot for the entire floor area by multiplying the total load by the number of square feet of floor space.

2. Determine the spacing of posts necessary to support the ends of each girder. Great distances between posts should be avoided because great weight would concentrate on one footing. Long spans also require extremely large girders. For example, it is possible to span a distance of 30′, but to do so, a 15″ I beam would be needed. The extreme weight and cost of this beam would be prohibitive. On the other hand if only a 6′ span were used, the close spacing might greatly restrict the flexibility of the internal design. As a rule, use the shortest span that will not interfere with the design function of the area.

3. Find the number of square feet supported by each post. A post will carry the load on a girder to the midpoint of the span on both sides. For example, post A in Fig. 45–8 carries half the load of girder X and girder Y in the direction of the joist. The post also carries half the load to the nearest support wall on either side of the post. The number of square feet supported by post A in Fig. 45–8 is therefore 120 square feet (10′ × 12′).

4. Find the load supported by the post support area. Multiply the number of square feet by the load per square foot (120 × 50).

5. Determine the height of a post. The height of the post is related to the span of a beam. The 4 × 4 post shown in Fig. 45–11 may be more

Span in feet	4 inches deep by—				5 inches deep by—			6 inches deep by—			7 inches deep by—		
	7.7	8.5	9.5	10.5	10.0	12.25	14.75	12.5	14.75	17.25	15.3	17.5	20.0
4......	9.0	9.5	10.1	10.7	14.5	16.2	18.0	21.8	23.8	26.0	31.0	33.4	36.0
5......	7.2	7.6	8.0	8.5	11.6	13.0	14.4	17.4	19.0	20.8	24.8	26.7	28.7
6......	6.0	6.3	6.7	7.1	9.7	10.8	12.0	14.5	15.9	17.3	20.7	22.2	24.0
7......	5.1	5.4	5.7	6.1	8.3	9.3	10.3	12.5	13.6	14.9	17.7	19.1	20.5
8......	4.5	4.7	5.0	5.3	7.3	8.1	9.0	10.9	11.9	13.0	15.5	16.7	18.0
9......	4.0	4.2	4.5	4.7	6.5	7.2	8.0	9.7	10.6	11.6	13.8	14.8	16.0
10.....	3.6	3.8	4.0	4.3	5.8	6.5	7.2	8.7	9.5	10.4	12.4	13.3	14.4
11.....	—	—	—	—	5.3	5.9	6.5	7.9	8.7	9.5	11.3	12.1	13.1
12.....	—	—	—	—	—	—	—	7.3	7.9	8.7	10.3	11.1	12.0
13.....	—	—	—	—	—	—	—	6.7	7.3	8.0	9.5	10.3	11.1
14.....	—	—	—	—	—	—	—	6.2	6.8	7.4	8.9	9.5	10.3
15.....	—	—	—	—	—	—	—	—	—	—	8.3	8.9	9.6
16.....	—	—	—	—	—	—	—	—	—	—	7.7	8.3	9.0
17.....	—	—	—	—	—	—	—	—	—	—	—	—	—
18.....	—	—	—	—	—	—	—	—	—	—	—	—	—
19.....	—	—	—	—	—	—	—	—	—	—	—	—	—
20.....	—	—	—	—	—	—	—	—	—	—	—	—	—

Span in feet	8 inches deep by—				9 inches deep by—				10 inches deep by—			
	18.4	20.5	23.0	25.5	21.8	25.0	30.0	35.0	25.4	30.0	35.0	40.0
4......	42.7	45.2	48.2	51.1	56.6	60.9	67.6	74.2	73.3	80.1	87.5	94.8
5......	34.1	36.1	38.5	40.9	45.3	48.7	54.1	59.4	58.6	64.1	70.0	75.8
6......	28.5	30.1	32.1	34.1	37.7	40.6	45.1	49.5	48.8	53.4	58.3	63.2
7......	24.4	25.8	27.5	29.2	32.3	34.8	38.6	42.4	41.9	45.8	50.0	59.2
8......	21.3	22.6	24.1	25.5	28.3	30.5	33.8	37.1	36.6	40.1	43.7	47.4
9......	19.0	20.1	21.4	22.7	25.2	27.1	30.0	33.0	32.6	35.6	38.9	42.1
10.....	17.1	18.1	19.3	20.4	22.6	24.4	27.0	29.7	29.3	32.0	35.0	37.9
11.....	15.5	16.4	17.5	18.6	20.6	22.2	24.6	27.0	26.6	29.1	31.8	34.5
12.....	14.2	15.1	16.1	17.0	18.9	20.3	22.5	24.7	24.4	26.7	29.2	31.6
13.....	13.1	13.9	14.8	15.7	17.4	18.7	20.8	22.8	22.5	24.6	26.9	29.2
14.....	12.2	12.9	13.8	14.6	16.2	17.4	19.3	21.2	20.9	22.9	25.0	27.1
15.....	11.4	12.0	12.8	13.6	15.1	16.2	18.0	19.8	19.5	21.4	23.3	25.3
16.....	10.7	11.3	12.0	12.8	14.2	15.2	16.9	18.6	18.3	20.0	21.9	23.7
17.....	10.0	10.6	11.3	12.0	13.3	14.3	15.9	17.3	17.2	18.8	20.6	22.3
18.....	9.5	10.0	10.7	11.4	12.6	13.3	15.0	16.5	16.3	17.8	19.4	21.1
19.....	9.0	9.5	10.1	10.8	11.9	12.8	14.2	15.6	15.4	16.9	18.4	20.0
20.....	8.5	9.0	9.6	10.2	11.3	12.2	13.5	14.8	14.7	16.0	17.5	19.0

Fig. 45–10. Safe loads for I beams, showing number of pounds per square foot a beam will support at a given span.

than adequate to support a given weight if the height of the post is 6'. However, this same 4 × 4 post may be totally inadequate to support the same weight when the length is increased to 20'.

6. Determine the type of column needed to support the load at the anticipated height.

7. Select the thickness and width of the post needed to support the load at the given height.

Use Fig. 45–12 for lumber posts. Use Fig. 45–13 for I-beam columns. Use Fig. 45–14 to determine the correct diameter of steel-pipe column supports.

▶ Plans

The more complete the architectural plan is, the better the chances are that the building will be constructed exactly as designed. If a floor-framing plan is not prepared to accompany the basic architectural plans, then the framing of the floor system is left entirely to the desires of the builder. Some architectural plans do not include a floor-framing plan. Only the direction of joists and the possible location of beams or girders are shown on the floor plan. Figure 45–15A shows a plan of this type on a floor plan. In Fig. 45–15, B and C show other methods of drawing floor-framing plans. All are related to the basic floor plan shown in Fig. 45–15A.

The most complete and most acceptable method of drawing floor-framing plans is shown in Fig. 45–15B. Each structural member is represented by a double line which shows its exact thickness.

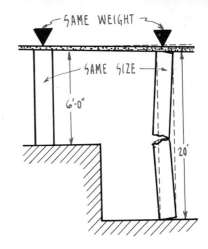

Fig. 45–11. *A heavier post is needed to support the same load when the height is increased.*

The more abbreviated plan shown in Fig. 45–15C is a short-cut method of drawing floor-framing plans. A single line is used to designate each member. Chimney and stair openings are shown by diagonals. Only the outline of the foundation and post locations is shown. The abbreviated floor-framing plan given in Fig. 45–15D

Fig. 45–12. *Maximum loads for lumber posts.*

Nominal size, inches	3 by 4	4 by 4	4 by 6	6 by 6	6 by 8	8 by 8
Actual size, inches	2⅝ by 3⅝	3⅝ by 3⅝	3⅝ by 5⅝	5½ by 5½	5½ by 7½	7½ by 7½
Area in square inches	9.51	13.14	20.39	30.25	41.25	56.25
Height of column:						
4 feet	8,720	12,920	19,850	30,250	41,250	56,250
5 feet	7,430	12,400	19,200	30,050	41,000	56,250
6 feet	5,630	11,600	17,950	29,500	40,260	56,250
6 feet 6 inches	4,750	10,880	16,850	29,300	39,950	56,000
7 feet	4,130	10,040	15,550	29,000	39,600	55,650
7 feet 6 inches	—	9,300	14,400	28,800	39,000	55,300
8 feet	—	8,350	12,950	28,150	38,300	55,000
9 feet	—	6,500	10,100	26,850	36,600	54,340
10 feet	—	—	—	24,670	33,600	53,400
11 feet	—	—	—	22,280	30,380	52,100
12 feet	—	—	—	19,630	26,800	50,400
13 feet	—	—	—	16,920	23,070	47,850
14 feet	—	—	—	14,360	19,580	44,700

Depth in inches	10	9	8	7	6	5	4	3
Weight per pound per foot	25.4	21.8	18.4	15.3	12.5	10.0	7.7	5.7
Effective length:								
							33.3	24.6
3 feet	110.7	94.8	80.1	66.5	54.2	43.1	33.0	23.5
4 feet	110.7	94.8	80.1	65.9	52.1	39.7	29.1	20.3
5 feet	109.5	91.2	74.9	60.0	46.9	35.1	25.3	17.2
6 feet	101.7	83.9	68.3	54.1	41.8	30.7	21.8	14.6
7 feet	93.8	76.7	61.8	48.5	37.0	26.8	18.7	12.3
8 feet	86.0	69.7	55.7	43.3	32.7	23.4	16.1	10.5
9 feet	78.7	63.2	50.1	38.6	28.9	20.4	13.9	—
10 feet	71.8	57.2	45.0	34.5	25.5	17.9	—	—
11 feet	65.5	51.8	40.5	30.8	22.6	—	—	—
12 feet	59.7	47.0	36.5	27.6	20.2	—	—	—
13 feet	54.5	42.6	33.0	24.7	—	—	—	—
14 feet	49.8	38.7	29.8	—	—	—	—	—
Area in square inches	7.38	6.32	5.34	4.43	3.61	2.87	2.21	1.64

Fig. 45–13. Safe loads for I-beam columns.

uses a technique similar to the one used in floor plans to show the entire area where uniformly distributed joists are placed. The direction of joists is shown by an arrow. The size and spacing of joists are shown by notes placed on the arrow. This type of framing plan is usually accompanied by numerous detail drawings such as the one shown in Fig. 45–4.

Fig. 45–14. Safe loads for steel-pipe columns.

Nominal size, inches	6	5	4½	4	3½	3	2½	2	1½
External diameter, inches	6.625	5.563	5.000	4.500	4.000	3.500	2.875	2.375	1.900
Thickness, inches	.280	.258	.247	.237	.226	.216	.203	.154	.145
Effective length:									
5 feet	72.5	55.9	48.0	41.2	34.8	29.0	21.6	12.2	7.5
6 feet	72.5	55.9	48.0	41.2	34.8	28.6	19.4	10.6	6.0
7 feet	72.5	55.9	48.0	41.2	34.1	26.3	17.3	9.0	5.0
8 feet	72.5	55.9	48.0	40.1	31.7	24.0	15.1	7.4	4.2
9 feet	72.5	55.9	46.4	37.6	29.3	21.7	12.9	6.6	3.5
10 feet	72.5	54.2	43.8	35.1	26.9	19.4	11.4	5.8	2.7
11 feet	72.5	51.5	41.2	32.6	24.5	17.1	10.3	5.0	—
12 feet	70.2	48.7	38.5	30.0	22.1	15.2	9.2	4.1	—
13 feet	67.3	46.0	35.9	27.5	19.7	14.0	8.1	3.3	—
14 feet	64.3	43.2	33.3	25.0	18.0	12.9	7.0	—	—
Area in square inches	5.58	4.30	3.69	3.17	2.68	2.23	1.70	1.08	0.80
Weight per pound per foot	18.97	14.62	12.54	10.79	9.11	7.58	5.79	3.65	2.72

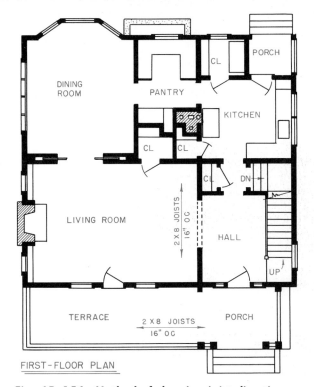

FIRST-FLOOR PLAN

Fig. 45–15A. Method of showing joist direction on floor plan.

Fig. 45–15B. Floor-framing plan showing material thicknesses.

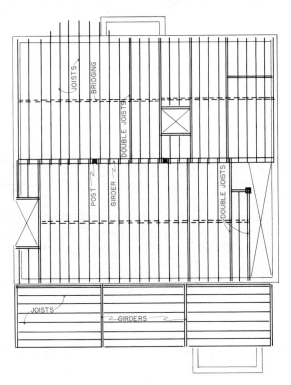

Fig. 45–15C. Simplified method of drawing floor-framing plans.

Fig. 45–15D. Abbreviated method of drawing floor-framing plans.

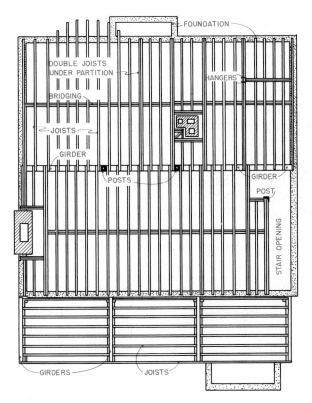

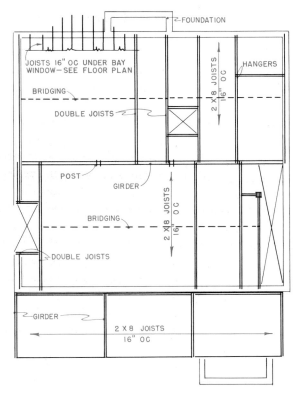

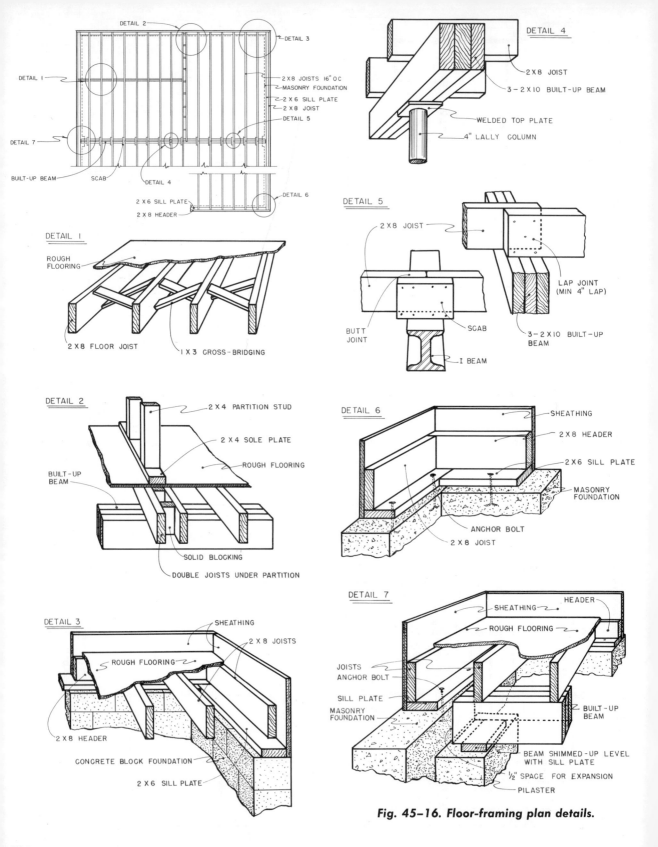

Fig. 45–16. Floor-framing plan details.

▶ Details

Although many floor-framing plans are completely interpretable for the experienced builder, others may require that the detail of some segment of the plan be prepared separately to explain more clearly the construction methods recommended. The detail is drawn to eliminate the possibility of error in interpretation or to explain more thoroughly some unique condition of the plan. Details may be merely enlargements of what is already on the floor-framing plan. They may be prepared for dimensioning purposes, or they may show a view from a different angle to reveal the underside or elevation view for better interpretation.

Figure 45–16 shows a floor-framing plan and several details that have been removed for clarity. Detail 1 shows the position of cross-bridging. Detail 2 shows the relationship of the built-up beam, the double joist under the partition, and the solid bridging. Detail 3 shows the sill construction in relation to the floor joist and rough flooring, and to the foundation. Detail 4 shows the method of supporting the built-up beam by the *lally* (steel) *column* and the joist position on the beam. Detail 5 shows several alternative methods of supporting the joist over a built-up beam or an I beam; thus the builder is given an option. Detail 6 shows the attachment of the typical box sill to the masonry foundation. Detail 7 shows the method of supporting the built-up beam with a pilaster, and the tie-in with the box sill and joist.

Depending on the size, material, and relative floor heights, there are many methods of attaching joists to girders or beams. The representation of these intersections on floor-framing plans is sometimes misinterpreted because the lines of the floor plan do not reflect differences in heights; the lines show only that they pass over other members. Figure 45–17 shows the method of illustrating these intersections on the floor-framing plan. A pictorial detail is often drawn to reinforce the interpretation of the floor-framing plan.

Fig. 45–17. Methods of drawing intersections.

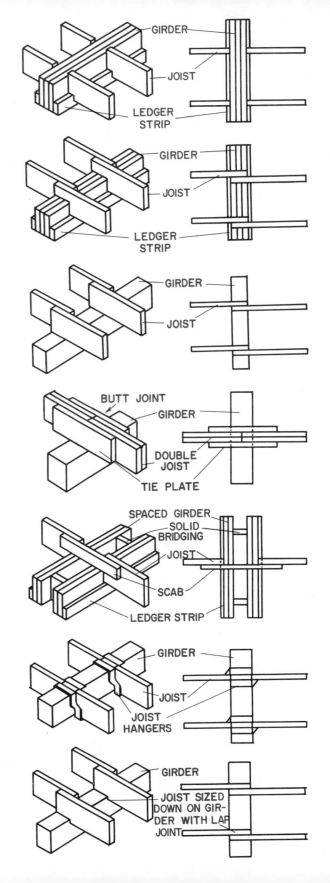

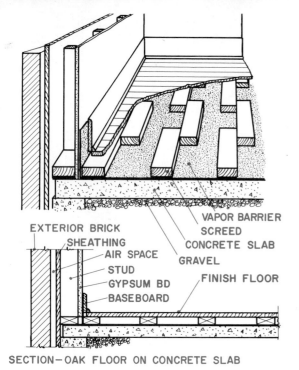

Fig. 45–18. *An elevation section showing floor-framing construction.*

SECTION—OAK FLOOR ON CONCRETE SLAB

EXTERIOR BRICK
SHEATHING
AIR SPACE
STUD
GYPSUM BD
BASEBOARD

VAPOR BARRIER
SCREED
CONCRETE SLAB
GRAVEL
FINISH FLOOR

Fig. 45–19. *Splices that resist compression, tension, and bending.*

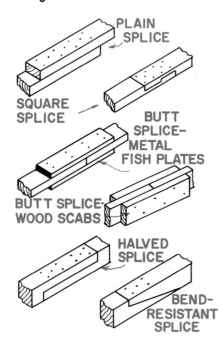

PLAIN SPLICE
SQUARE SPLICE
BUTT SPLICE-METAL FISH PLATES
BUTT SPLICE-WOOD SCABS
HALVED SPLICE
BEND-RESISTANT SPLICE

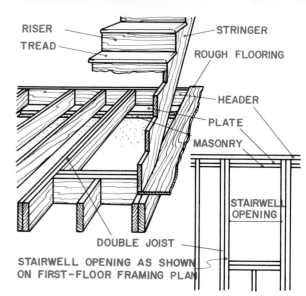

RISER
TREAD
STRINGER
ROUGH FLOORING
HEADER
PLATE
MASONRY
STAIRWELL OPENING
DOUBLE JOIST

STAIRWELL OPENING AS SHOWN ON FIRST-FLOOR FRAMING PLAN

Fig. 45–20. *Methods of drawing a stairwell opening.*

In addition to pictorial drawings, elevation sections are also used extensively to aid in the interpretation of floor-framing plans. An elevation section reveals a relationship of the construction members exactly 90° from the projection of the plan. The construction of the floor systems given in Fig. 45–18 is better shown by elevation drawings than by floor-framing plans.

Recommended methods of splicing lumber when necessary, so that spliced members will be as strong as single members, should also be detailed to eliminate building failures. The splices shown in Fig. 45–19 will resist compression, tension, and bending.

▶ **Stair-well Framing**

The stair-well opening as drawn on the floor-framing plan shows the relative position of the double joists and headers. Frequently more information is needed concerning the relationship of the other parts of the stair assembly to the stair-well opening shown in Fig. 45–20. Information concerning the size and position of the various parts of the stair assembly is shown in Fig. 45–21. Such information is often shown in a separate detail.

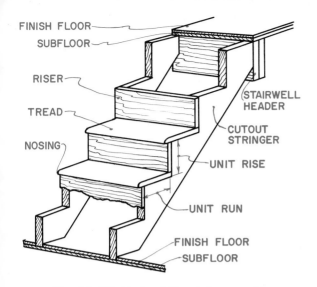

Fig. 45-21. Parts of the stair assembly.

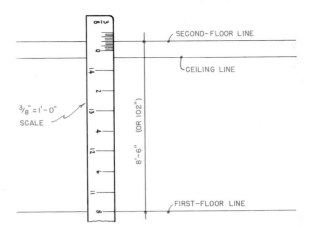

Fig. 45-22A. Lay out the distance from the first-floor level to the second-floor level.

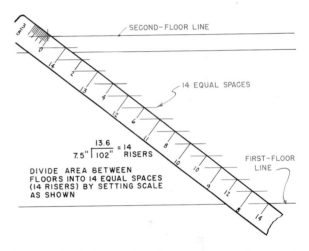

Fig. 45-22B. Determine the number of risers and extend the riser lines.

Fig. 45-22C. Lay out total run.

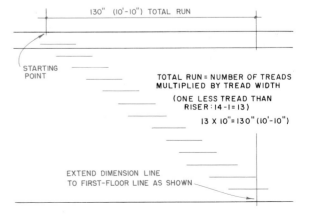

Since the stair-well opening must be precisely shown on the floor-framing plan, a complete design of the stair system should precede the preparation of the floor-framing plan. The steps outlined in Fig. 45–22 show the sequences necessary for determining the exact dimensions of the entire stair structure.

1. Lay out the distance from the first-floor level to the second-floor level exactly to scale (Fig. 45–22A). Convert this distance to inches and add the position of the ceiling line.

2. Determine the most desirable riser heights (7½" is normal). Divide the number of inches between floor levels by the desired riser height to find the number of risers needed (Fig. 45–22B). Divide the area between the floors into spaces equaling the number of risers needed. This work can be done by inclining the scale.

3. Extend the riser-division lines lightly for an inch.

4. Determine the total length of the run (Fig. 45–22C). Lay out this distance from a starting point near the top riser line and measure the total run horizontally. Extend this line vertically to the first-floor line. The total run is the number of treads multiplied by the width of each tread. There is always one less tread than riser.

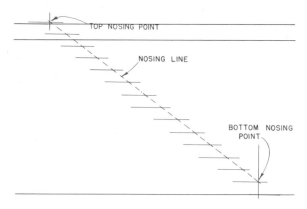

Fig. 45-22D. *Locate nosing points and draw nosing line.*

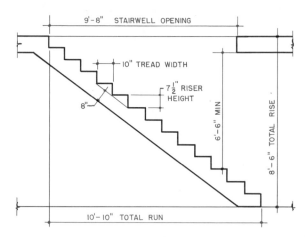

Fig. 45-22G. *Erase guidelines and add dimensions.*

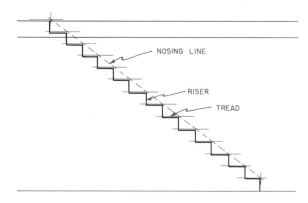

Fig. 45-22E. *Draw riser lines and tread lines.*

Fig. 45-22F. *Establish headroom clearance, stair-well opening, and soffit line.*

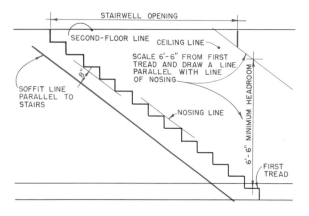

5. Locate the top and bottom nosing points (Fig. 45-22D). Mark the intersection between the starting point of the total run and the intersection between the end of the total run and the first riser line.

6. Draw the nosing line by connecting the bottom nosing point with the top nosing point.

7. Draw riser lines intersecting the nosing points and the light riser lines (Fig. 45-22E).

8. Make the tread lines and the riser lines heavy.

9. Draw the soffit line the same as the thickness of the stringer. Establish headroom clearances. Draw a parallel line 6'-6" above the nosing line (Fig. 45-22F). Establish the stair-well opening by cutting the joists where the headroom clearance line intersects the bottom of the joist.

10. Show the outline of the carriage or stringer assembly.

11. Erase all layout lines and make all object lines heavier (Fig. 45-22G).

12. Add dimensions to describe the length of the stair-well opening, the size of the tread widths, the riser height, the minimum headroom, the total rise, and the total run.

When the basic information pertaining to the overall dimensions and relationships of the stair assembly is established, a complete sectional drawing showing thicknesses and floor-framing tie-ins

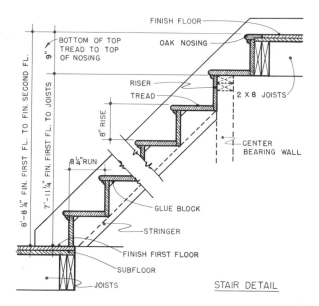

Fig. 45–23. Sectional drawing of a stair assembly.

Macomber, Inc.

Fig. 45–24. Steel floor framing.

can be prepared, as shown in Fig. 45–23. In this sectional drawing, the headers and the position of the bearing walls are shown.

▶ Steel

Floor-framing plans for steel construction are prepared like other floor-framing plans. The exact positions of columns, beams, and purlins are dimensioned and the classification of each member indicated on the plan (Fig. 45–24). Details should accompany steel-framing drawings to indicate the method of attaching steel members to each other (Fig. 45–25). Details also should show the method of attaching members to various other construction materials, such as masonry walls (Fig. 45–26).

Problems

1. Identify the floor-framing terms illustrated in Fig. 45–27.
2. Determine the size of joists for the floor-framing plan shown in Fig. 45–28. Base your calculations on a combined load of 80 pounds per square foot.

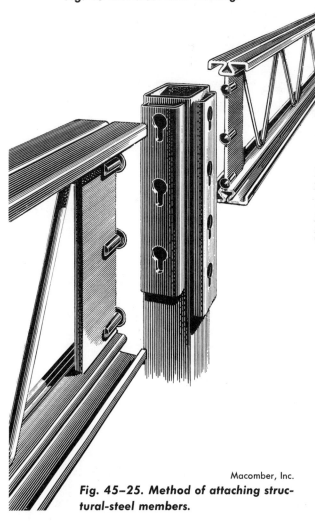

Macomber, Inc.

Fig. 45–25. Method of attaching structural-steel members.

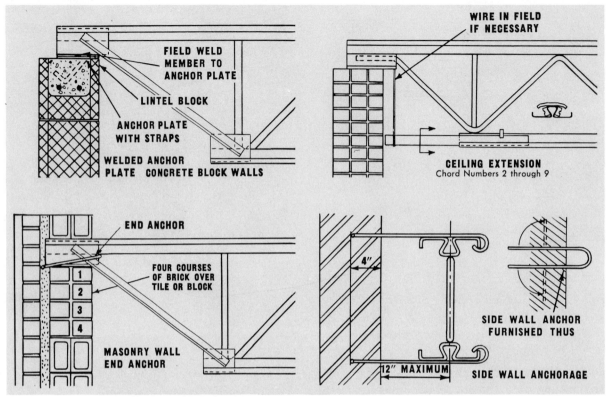

FIELD WELD MEMBER TO ANCHOR PLATE

LINTEL BLOCK

ANCHOR PLATE WITH STRAPS

WELDED ANCHOR PLATE CONCRETE BLOCK WALLS

WIRE IN FIELD IF NECESSARY

CEILING EXTENSION
Chord Numbers 2 through 9

END ANCHOR

FOUR COURSES OF BRICK OVER TILE OR BLOCK

MASONRY WALL END ANCHOR

4"

12" MAXIMUM

SIDE WALL ANCHOR FURNISHED THUS

SIDE WALL ANCHORAGE

Macomber, Inc.

Fig. 45–26. Methods of attaching structural steel to masonry walls.

Fig. 45–27. Identify these floor-framing members.

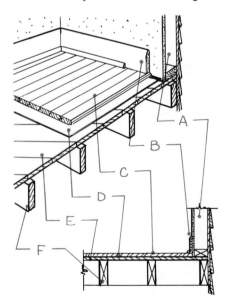

A
B
C
D
E
F

3. Determine the size of the wood girder needed to support 80 pounds per square foot in the plan shown in Fig. 45–28. What size of steel beam would be needed to carry the same load?

4. What size of column would be needed to support an 80-pound-per-square-foot load in Fig. 45–28?

5. Eliminate one of the columns in Fig. 45–28 and readjust the load between two columns. What size of columns and beams will you need to support this system?

6. Design and draw a floor-framing plan for a house of your own. List the size and spacing of all materials.

7. Draw a floor-framing plan of the house in which you now live.

8. Sketch an abbreviated floor-framing plan for the floor plan shown in Fig. 6–1.

9. Define the following architectural terms: *panel framing, deflection, load, spacing, modulus of elasticity, fiber stress, maximum span, blocking, bridging, girder pocket, girder, built-up girder, pier, post, column, beam, header, double header, double joists, girder-load area, post-load area, lally column, I beam, channel, joist hanger, scab, ledger strip, butt joint, square splice, butt splice, halved splice, bent splice, stair-well opening, tread, riser, nosing, unit run, unit rise, stringer, top nosing point, bottom nosing point, nosing line.*

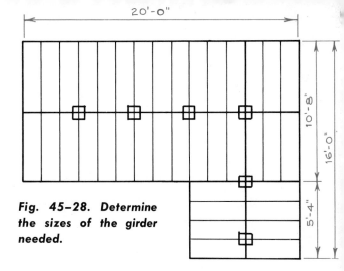

Fig. 45–28. Determine the sizes of the girder needed.

Unit 46. Exterior-wall Framing Plans

Exterior-wall construction for most residential buildings is of either a conventional or a post and beam type. The typical method of erecting walls for most conventional buildings follows the braced-frame system and has changed little since its introduction in this country. Prefabrication methods have led to variations in the erection of exterior panels, ranging from the panelization of only the basic framing panel to the completely panelized exterior, including plumbing and electrical work, doors, and windows, as shown in Fig. 46–1.

Regardless of the method of construction or fabrication, the preparation of exterior-panel drawings is relatively the same, whether they are prepared for factory use or for field use.

▶ Framing Elevations

An exterior-wall framing panel, such as the one which is shown being erected in Fig. 46–2, is best constructed by using a framing *elevation drawing* as a guide. The wall-framing elevation drawing is the same as the north, south, east, or west elevation of the building, with all the building materials removed except the basic framing. Figure 46–3 shows a wall-framing elevation compared with a pictorial drawing of the same wall. Notice that the framing elevation is an orthographic projection and does not reveal a second dimension or angle of projection. Figure 46–4 shows some of the basic framing members included in framing elevations.

Fig. 46–1. Methods of wall paneling.

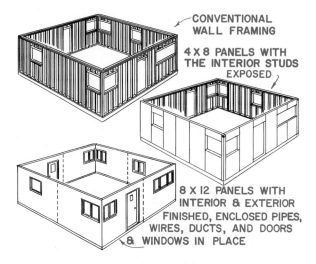

CONVENTIONAL WALL FRAMING

4 X 8 PANELS WITH THE INTERIOR STUDS EXPOSED

8 X 12 PANELS WITH INTERIOR & EXTERIOR FINISHED, ENCLOSED PIPES, WIRES, DUCTS, AND DOORS & WINDOWS IN PLACE

Fig. 46–2. Erection of an exterior wall panel.

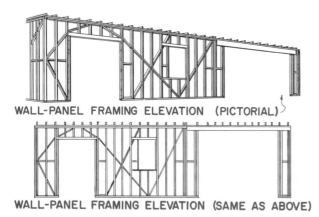

WALL-PANEL FRAMING ELEVATION (PICTORIAL)

WALL-PANEL FRAMING ELEVATION (SAME AS ABOVE)

Fig. 46–3. Wall-framing elevation.

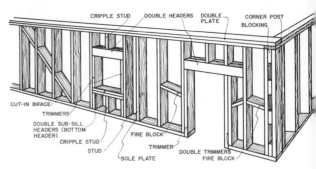

Fig. 46–4. Basic framing members shown in the framing elevations.

The framing elevation is projected from the floor plan and elevation, as shown in Fig. 46–5. Since floor-plan wall thicknesses normally include the thickness of siding materials, care should be taken to project the outside of the framing line to the framing drawing and not the outside of the siding line. In projecting door and window openings, the framing opening as outlined on the manufacturing specifications or on the door–window schedule should be rechecked when the final openings for doors and windows are projected both from the floor plan and from the elevation.

If aligned correctly, the elevation will supply all the projection points for the horizontal framing

Fig. 46–5. Projection of an exterior-framing elevation from the floor plan and elevation drawing.

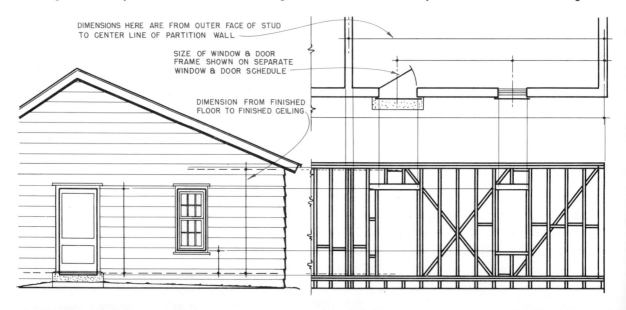

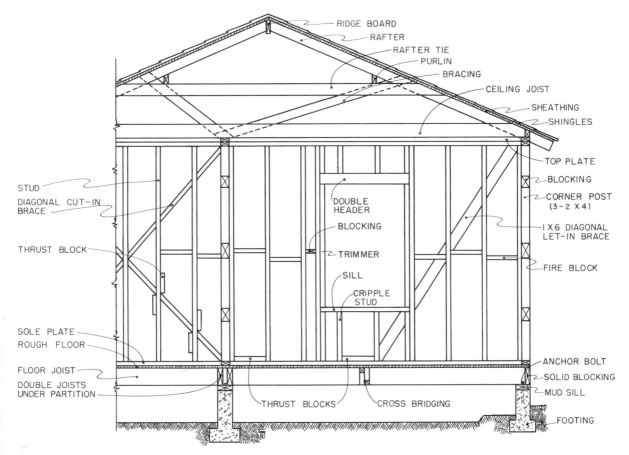

Fig. 46–6. A framing elevation incorporated in a complete section of the building.

members, and the floor plan will provide all the points of projection for the location of vertical members.

▶ Complete Sections

Another method of illustrating the framing methods used in wall construction is shown in Fig. 46–6. In this drawing, the elevation-framing information is incorporated in a complete sectional drawing of the entire structure. The advantage of this type of drawing is that it shows the relationship of the elevation-panel framing to the foundation-floor system and roof construction. Since this is a sectional drawing, blocking, joists, or any other member that is intersected by the cutting-plane line is shown by diagonals.

▶ Bracing

One of the problems in preparing and interpreting framing-elevation drawings is to determine whether bracing is placed on the inside of the wall, on the outside of the wall, or between the studs. Figure 46–7A shows the methods of illustrating *let-in* braces that are notched on the outside of the wall so that the outer face of the brace is flush with the stud. Figure 46–7B shows the method of illustrating *cut-in* braces that are nailed between the studs; and Fig. 46–7C shows the methods of illustrating diagonal braces that are on the inside faces of the studs.

Similar difficulties often occur in interpreting the true position of headers, cripple studs, plates, and trimmers. Figure 46–8 shows the method of

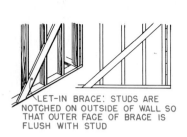

LET-IN BRACE: STUDS ARE NOTCHED ON OUTSIDE OF WALL SO THAT OUTER FACE OF BRACE IS FLUSH WITH STUD

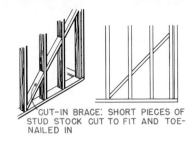

CUT-IN BRACE: SHORT PIECES OF STUD STOCK CUT TO FIT AND TOE-NAILED IN

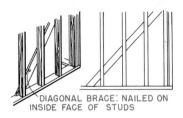

DIAGONAL BRACE: NAILED ON INSIDE FACE OF STUDS

Fig. 46-7. Methods of illustrating braces.

illustrating the position of these members on the framing-elevation drawing to eliminate confusion and simplify interpretation.

▶ **Panel Elevations**

Panel elevations show the attachment of sheathing to the framing. It is often desirable or necessary to show the relationship between the *panel layout* and the *framing layout* of an elevation when the panel drawing and the framing drawing are combined in one drawing. The diagonals which indicate the position of the panels are drawn with dotted lines, as shown in Fig. 46-9. When only the panel layouts are shown, the outline of the panels and diagonals are drawn solid, as shown in Fig. 46-9. Usually, however, in this case, a separate framing plan must also be prepared and correlated with the panel elevation.

Fig. 46-8. Methods of illustrating the positions of headers and cripples.

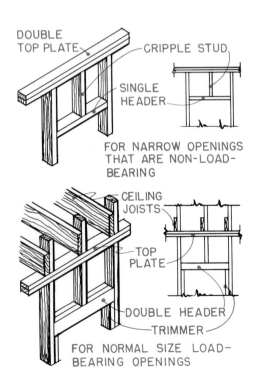

DOUBLE TOP PLATE — CRIPPLE STUD

SINGLE HEADER

FOR NARROW OPENINGS THAT ARE NON-LOAD-BEARING

CEILING JOISTS

TOP PLATE

DOUBLE HEADER

TRIMMER

FOR NORMAL SIZE LOAD-BEARING OPENINGS

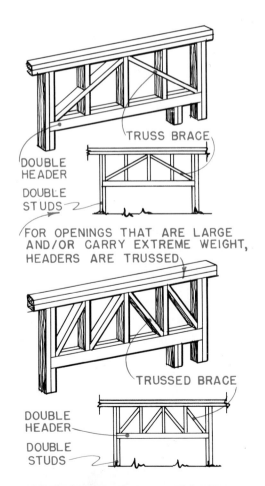

TRUSS BRACE

DOUBLE HEADER

DOUBLE STUDS

FOR OPENINGS THAT ARE LARGE AND/OR CARRY EXTREME WEIGHT, HEADERS ARE TRUSSED

TRUSSED BRACE

DOUBLE HEADER

DOUBLE STUDS

▶ Dimensions

The method of dimensioning panel and framing-elevation drawings is shown in Fig. 46–10. Overall widths, heights, and spacing of studs should be given. Control dimensions for the heights of horizontal members and *rough openings* (framing openings) for windows should also be included. If the spacing of studs does not automatically provide the rough opening necessary for the window, the rough-opening width of the window should also be dimensioned.

▶ Details

Not all the information needed to frame an exterior wall can be shown on the elevation drawing. One of the most effective means of showing information at right angles to the elevation drawing is by removed sections.

Rendering by George A. Parenti for Masonite Corporation

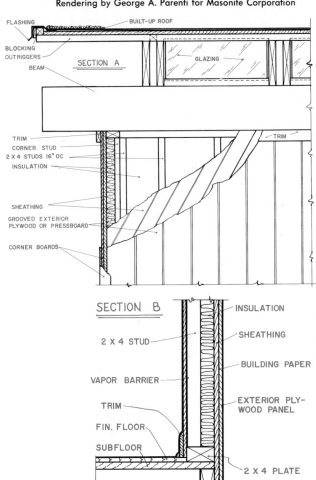

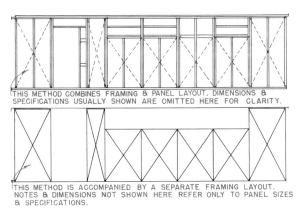

Fig. 46–9. Diagonal lines are used to show the position of panels.

Fig. 46–10. Methods of dimensioning panel and framing elevations.

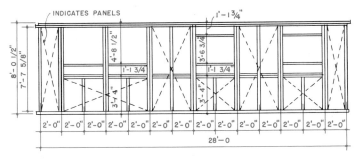

Fig. 46–11. Removed sections may be indexed to a floor plan, an elevation or pictorial drawings.

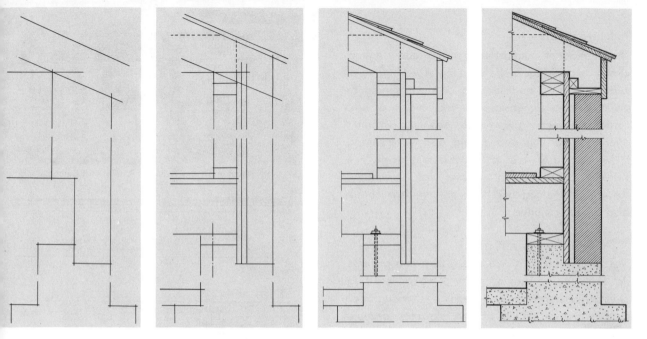

Fig. 46–12. The sequence of laying out a typical external wall section.

▶ Removed Sections

Removed sections may be indexed to the floor plan or elevation, as indicated in Section Nine. They may be removed sections from a pictorial drawing, as shown in Fig. 46–11. In this example, Section A describes the framing method employed on the wall and roof intersections, using break lines to expose the framing. Section B shows a wall section at the sill, revealing the intersection between the foundation-floor system and the exterior wall. These sections also show the inside wall treatment, insulation, sheathing, and exterior siding. Removed sections are effective in showing enlarged details.

▶ Sectional Breaks

A larger scale is used on wall sections if the use of break lines is employed. Figure 46–12 shows the sequence of steps used to lay out and draw a typical external wall section.

1. Determine the width of the walls, foundation, and footer.

2. Lay out the angle of the roof and point of intersection of the roof and top plate. Lay out the width of the joist and sill.

3. Block in the position of roof rafters, top plates, sole plate, and roof floor lines.

4. Draw vertical lines to indicate the width of stud, insulation, air space, and brick.

Fig. 46–13. Horizontal section showing corner-post construction.

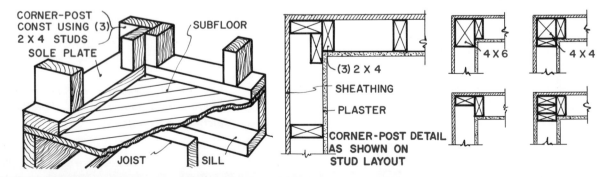

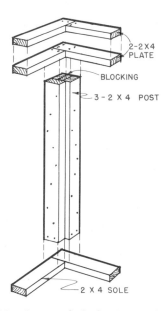

Fig. 46–14. An exploded view of corner-post construction.

Norman F. Carver, designer

Fig. 46–15. The relationship between siding materials and framing materials is important.

5. Add details of the outlines of roof boards and shingles. Show outlines of roof boards and shingles. Show outline of cornice construction.

6. Draw horizontal lines representing break lines. Add section-lining symbols.

▶ Pictorial Detail

A pictorial detail or horizontal section of a wall is often used to clarify the relationship of framing members. This method is especially helpful in describing the layout of corner posts, as shown in Fig. 46–13. The horizontal section is more accurate in showing exact size and position of studs, but the pictorial drawing is more effective in showing the total relationship among sole plate, corner-post studs, and box-sill construction.

▶ Exploded Views

Exploded views are most effective in showing internal construction that is hidden when the total assembly is drawn in its completed form. Figure 46–14 shows an exploded view of a corner-post construction, which reveals the position of the corner post on the sole. It shows also the construc-

tion and position of the top plate on the corner post. This method of detailing is also extensively used in cabinet work.

▶ Siding Details

New siding materials are constantly being developed and new applications found for existing materials. Growing emphasis on the use of siding-panel components designed to modular limits increases the necessity for carefully describing the relationship between the basic framing and exterior-wall coverings (Fig. 46–15).

One method of showing the relationship between the basic framing and siding materials is the *breakaway pictorial drawing*, as shown in Fig. 46–16. This is the type of drawing that can most effectively be interpreted by the layman. However, it is most difficult to dimension for construction purposes. A more effective method of showing the exact position of siding materials is the *vertical or horizontal section*. Figure 46–17 shows the *sectional method* of representing a typical brick veneer wall. Compare the plan section and the elevation section with the related pictorial drawing. Follow

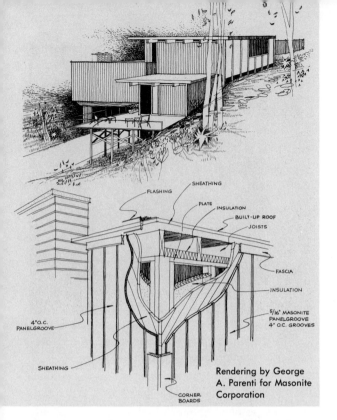

Rendering by George
A. Parenti for Masonite
Corporation

Fig. 46–16. The use of a breakaway pictorial section to show construction details.

Fig. 46–17. Construction details can be shown on a plan section or an elevation section.

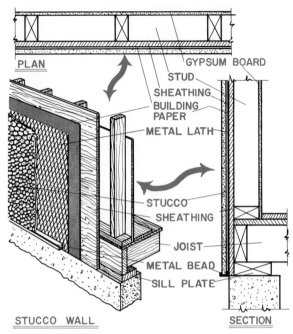

STUCCO WALL

SECTION

Fig. 46–18. The relationship between a plan and an elevation section of a stucco wall.

Fig. 46–19. The relationship between a plan and an elevation section of a board and batten wall.

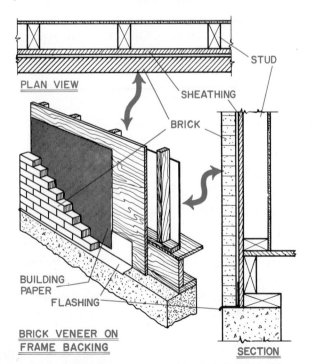

BRICK VENEER ON
FRAME BACKING

SECTION

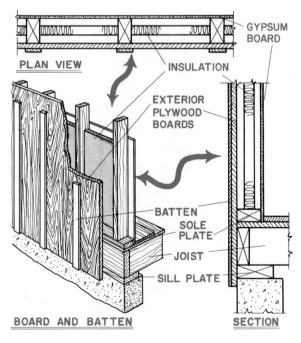

BOARD AND BATTEN

SECTION

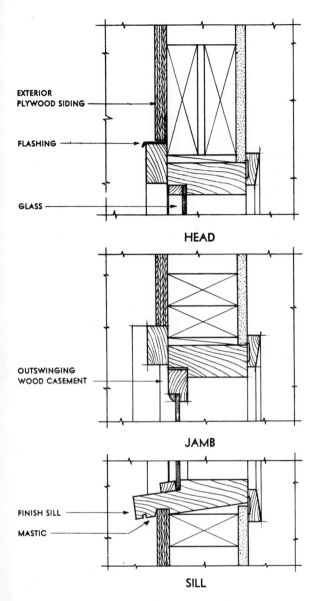

EXTERIOR PLYWOOD SIDING

FLASHING

GLASS

HEAD

OUTSWINGING WOOD CASEMENT

JAMB

FINISH SILL

MASTIC

SILL

Fig. 46–20. Head, jamb, and sill sections are most commonly used to show window-framing details.

the relationship of each material as it exists in each drawing. You should be able to visualize the pictorial drawing by studying the sectional drawings of the plan and elevation. Figure 46–18 shows the same relationship of sectional to pictorial drawings for a stucco wall. Figure 46–19 shows how a board and batten wall appears in pictorial, plan, and elevation sections.

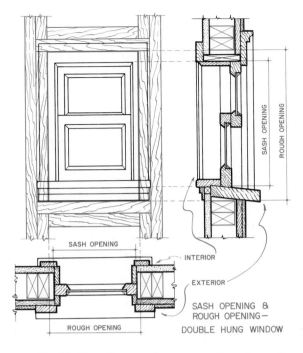

SASH OPENING

ROUGH OPENING

SASH OPENING

INTERIOR

EXTERIOR

ROUGH OPENING

SASH OPENING & ROUGH OPENING— DOUBLE HUNG WINDOW

Fig. 46–21. Details are often needed to show the rough openings for doors and windows.

▶ Window-framing Drawings

One of the most effective methods of showing window-framing details is the head, jamb, and sill sections, as described in Section Nine (Figure 46–20). Most windows are factory-made components ready for installation. Therefore, the most critical framing dimensions are those that describe the exact size of the framing opening. Window-framing drawings should include the dimensions of the rough framing-opening in addition to the dimensions of the sash openings or windows that may be found on the door and window schedule (Fig. 46–21).

Figure 46–22 shows rough stud openings and sash openings for some of the more common sizes of windows.

When fixed windows or unusual window treatments are constructed in the field or even at the factory for a specific building, complete framing details must be drawn similar to the detailed drawing shown in Fig. 46–23.

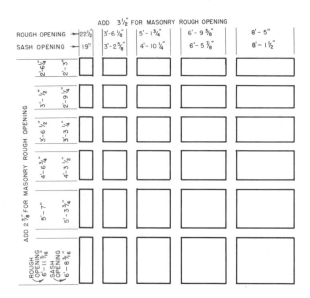

		ADD 3½" FOR MASONRY ROUGH OPENING			
ROUGH OPENING →	22½"	3'-6⅛"	5'-1¾"	6'-9⅜"	8'-5"
SASH OPENING →	19"	3'-2⅝"	4'-10¼"	6'-5⅞"	8'-1½"
2'-6¼" / 2'-3"	☐	☐	☐	☐	☐
3'-½" / 2'-9¼"	☐	☐	☐	☐	☐
3'-6½" / 3'-3¾"	☐	☐	☐	☐	☐
4'-6¾" / 4'-3½"	☐	☐	☐	☐	☐
5'-7" / 5'-3¾"	☐	☐	☐	☐	☐
ROUGH OPENING 6'-11 7/16" / SASH OPENING 6'-8 3/16"	☐	☐	☐	☐	☐

(left axis) ADD 2 7/8" FOR MASONRY ROUGH OPENING

Fig. 46–22. Rough-opening dimensions for common sizes of windows.

The more radical or unusual the deviation from standard sizes and components may be, the more complete must be the detail framing drawings that accompany the design. Figure 46–24 shows a Japanese *shoji* window assembly that would require complete detailing of the shutters, screening glass, and shoji construction. Complete construction details for the fabrication of the track and for the installation of the track in the wall would also be necessary for this type of construction.

▶ Door-framing Plans

The use of modular-component door units, as shown in Fig. 46–25, is increasing throughout the home-building industry. Maintaining accurate rough-opening dimensions for these units is most critical to their installation. Whether the door framing is conventional or of a component design, the exact position of the opening and the dimensions of the rough opening must be clearly illustrated and labeled on the framing drawing. Figure 46–26 shows some rough-opening dimensions for standard-sized doors that are used in various locations throughout a residence.

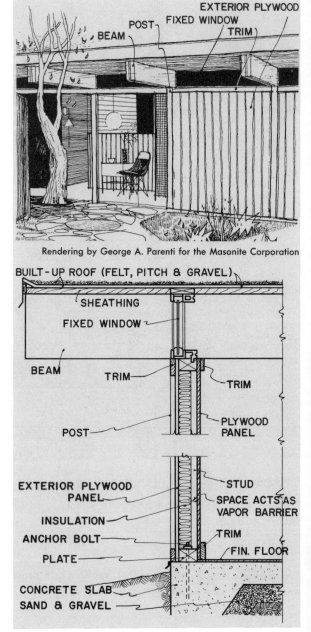

Rendering by George A. Parenti for the Masonite Corporation

Fig. 46–23. Details are always needed for fixed window construction.

Head, sill, and jamb sections, as shown in Section 9, are as effective in describing the door-framing construction as they are in showing window-framing details. Since the door extends to the floor, the relationship of the floor-framing

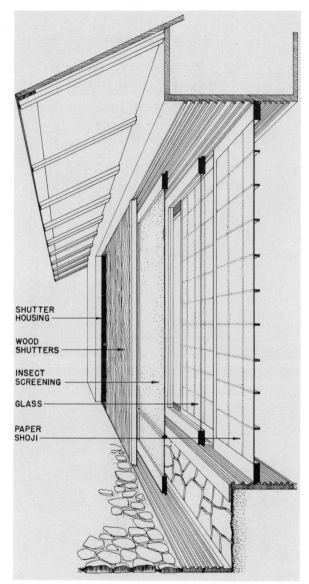

SHUTTER
HOUSING

WOOD
SHUTTERS

INSECT
SCREENING

GLASS

PAPER
SHOJI

House Beautiful

Fig. 46-24. A Japanese shoji window assembly.

system to the position of the door is critical. The method of intersecting the door and hinge with the wall framing, as shown in Fig. 46–27, is also important. Section A (head) shows the intersection of the door and the header framing. Section B (sill) shows how the door relates to the floor framing. Section C (jamb) shows how the latch side is constructed.

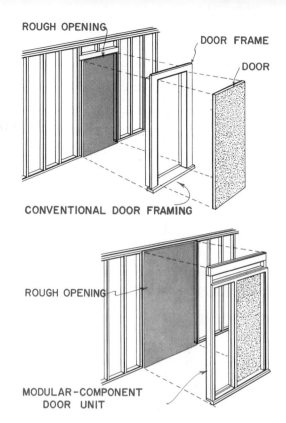

ROUGH OPENING

DOOR FRAME

DOOR

CONVENTIONAL DOOR FRAMING

ROUGH OPENING

MODULAR-COMPONENT
DOOR UNIT

Fig. 46–25. Modular-component door assembly.

Fig. 46–26. Rough-opening dimensions for standard-sized doors.

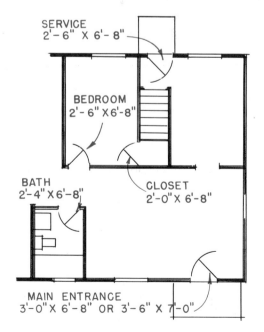

SERVICE
2'-6" X 6'-8"

BEDROOM
2'-6" X 6'-8"

BATH
2'-4" X 6'-8"

CLOSET
2'-0" X 6'-8"

MAIN ENTRANCE
3'-0" X 6'-8" OR 3'-6" X 7'-0"

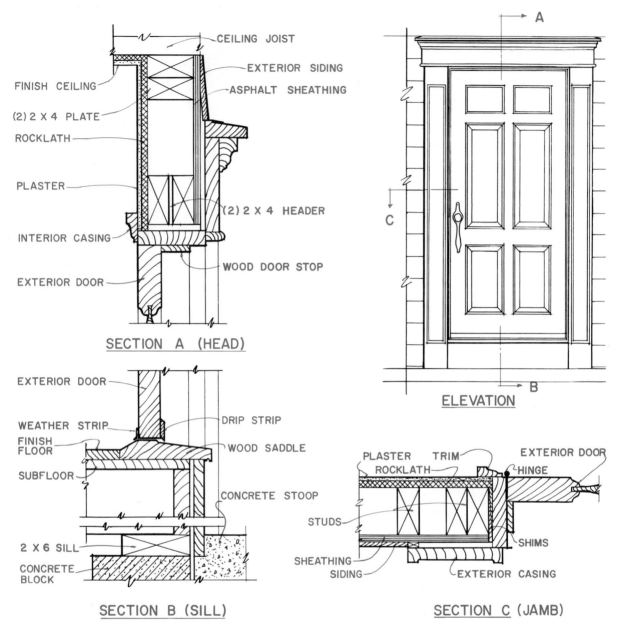

Fig. 46-27. The relationship between the door assembly and wall-framing method.

SECTION A (HEAD)

- FINISH CEILING
- (2) 2 X 4 PLATE
- ROCKLATH
- PLASTER
- INTERIOR CASING
- EXTERIOR DOOR
- CEILING JOIST
- EXTERIOR SIDING
- ASPHALT SHEATHING
- (2) 2 X 4 HEADER
- WOOD DOOR STOP

SECTION B (SILL)

- EXTERIOR DOOR
- WEATHER STRIP
- FINISH FLOOR
- SUBFLOOR
- 2 X 6 SILL
- CONCRETE BLOCK
- DRIP STRIP
- WOOD SADDLE
- CONCRETE STOOP

ELEVATION

SECTION C (JAMB)

- PLASTER TRIM
- ROCKLATH
- STUDS
- SHEATHING
- SIDING
- EXTERIOR DOOR
- HINGE
- SHIMS
- EXTERIOR CASING

Problems

1. Draw a plan section view of the walls shown in Fig. 46–28.

2. Identify the framing members shown in Fig. 46–29.

3. Draw a wall section using Fig. 46–30 as a guide. Plan to use stone veneer.

4. Prepare an elevation section of the wall shown in Fig. 46–31.

5. Prepare an exterior framing plan for the elevation shown in Fig. 29–1.

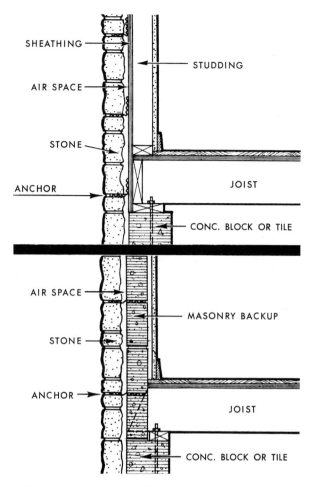

SHEATHING

STUDDING

AIR SPACE

STONE

ANCHOR

JOIST

CONC. BLOCK OR TILE

AIR SPACE

MASONRY BACKUP

STONE

ANCHOR

JOIST

CONC. BLOCK OR TILE

Fig. 46–28. Draw a plan section of these walls.

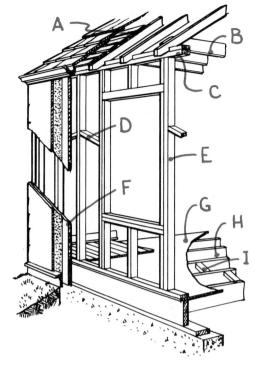

Fig. 46–29. Identify these framing members.

Fig. 46–30. Complete a sectional drawing of this wall.

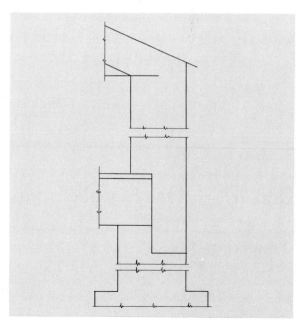

6. Draw an exploded view of the carport-post construction shown in Fig. 29–2.
7. Draw a wall-elevation section of the wall types shown in Fig. 29–3.
8. Prepare a window detail drawing for the Thermopane units shown in Fig. 29–4.
9. Prepare an exterior panel-framing plan for a home of your own design.
10. Prepare an exterior panel-framing plan for your own home.
11. Define the following terms: *framing elevation, bracing, let-in, panel elevation, removed sections, exploded view, rough opening, sash opening, sectional breaks.*

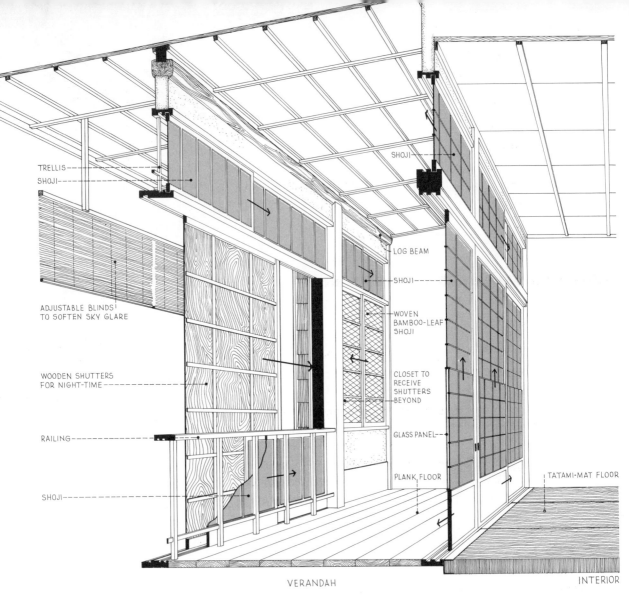

TRELLIS

SHOJI

ADJUSTABLE BLINDS
TO SOFTEN SKY GLARE

WOODEN SHUTTERS
FOR NIGHT-TIME

RAILING

SHOJI

SHOJI

LOG BEAM

SHOJI

WOVEN
BAMBOO-LEAF
SHOJI

CLOSET TO
RECEIVE
SHUTTERS
BEYOND

GLASS PANEL

PLANK FLOOR

TATAMI-MAT FLOOR

VERANDAH

INTERIOR

Fig. 46–31. Prepare an elevation section of this wall.

Unit 47. Interior - wall Framing Plans

Interior-framing drawings include plan, elevation, and pictorial drawings of partitions and wall coverings. Detail drawings of interior partitions are also prepared to show intersections between walls and ceilings, floors, windows, and doors.

▶ Partition-framing Plans

Interior partition-framing elevations are most effective in showing the construction of interior partitions. Interior partitions are projected from the partition on the floor plan in a manner similar to

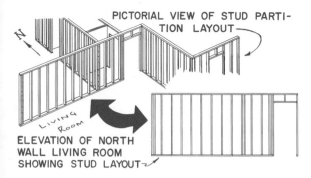

Fig. 47–1. Panel elevation of an interior wall.

the projection of exterior partitions. To ensure the correct interpretation of the partition elevation, each interior elevation drawing should include a label indicating the room and compass direction of the wall. For example, the elevation shown in Fig. 47–1 should be labeled *North Wall Living Room.* If either the room name or the compass direction is omitted, the elevation may be misinterpreted and confused with a similar wall in another room. The elevation drawing is always projected from the room it represents.

A complete study of the floor plan, elevation, plumbing diagrams, and electrical plans should be made prior to the preparation of the interior wall-framing drawings. Provision must be made in the framing drawings for soil stacks and other large plumbing facilities and for special electrical equipment (Fig. 47–2).

When a stud must be broken to accommodate an item such as the cabinets shown in Fig. 47–3, the framing drawing must show the recommended construction.

▶ Wall-covering Details

Basic types of wall-covering materials used for finished interior walls include plaster, dry-wall construction, paneling, tile, and masonry.

Plaster. Plaster is applied to interior walls by using wire lath or gypsum sheet lath, as shown in Fig. 47–4. Plaster walls are very strong and sound-absorbing. Plaster is also decay-proof and termite-proof. However, plaster walls crack easily

Fig. 47–2. Space must be allowed for plumbing and electrical equipment.

Fig. 47–3. Framing-elevation details show provisions for built-in items.

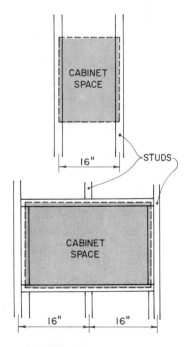

303

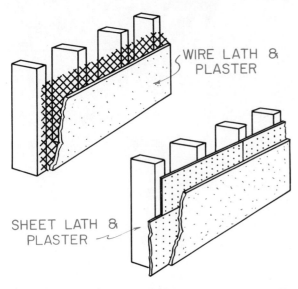

Fig. 47–4. Application of plaster to interior walls.

Fig. 47–5. Dry-wall construction.

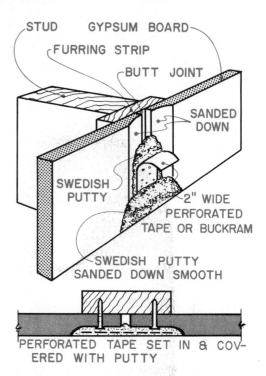

Fig. 47–6. Method of concealing dry-wall joints.

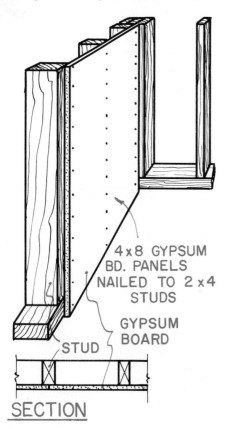

4 x 8 GYPSUM BD. PANELS NAILED TO 2 x 4 STUDS

GYPSUM BOARD

STUD

SECTION

and take months to dry. Also, installation costs are rather high.

Dry-wall construction. Materials applicable to dry-wall construction include fiber boards, gypsum wallboards, plywood, and asbestos wallboard. The most popular type of dry-wall construction is gypsum wallboards nailed directly to the studs, as shown in Fig. 47–5. When this type of construction is used, furring strips may be placed over the joints and nail holes. However, the more common practice is to camouflage the joints by sanding a depression in the wallboard and applying a perforated tape covered with Swedish putty and sanded smooth, as shown in Fig. 47–6.

Paneling. When paneling is used as an interior finish, horizontal furring strips should be placed on the studs to provide a nailing or gluing surface for the paneling (Fig. 47–7). Determining the type of joint that should be used between panels is a design problem that should be solved through the use of a separate detail, as shown in Fig. 47–8. The joint may be exposed by use of the butt joint or cross-lap joint. A series of furring strips can be used between the joints or on the outside of them.

The method of intersecting the outside corners of paneling must also be detailed. Outside corners can be intersected by mitering or overlapping and exposing the paneling. Corner boards, metal strips, or molding may be used on the intersection (Fig. 47–9).

Inside-corner intersections can be drawn as shown in Fig. 47–10.

▶ Base Intersections

The method of intersecting the finished wall materials and the floor should be detailed. The details may be a section or a pictorial drawing, as shown in Fig. 47–11. The position of the sole plate, wall-

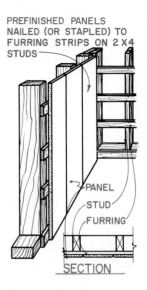

PREFINISHED PANELS NAILED (OR STAPLED) TO FURRING STRIPS ON 2 X 4 STUDS

PANEL
STUD
FURRING

SECTION

Fig. 47–7. Furring strips provide a horizontal surface for attaching paneling.

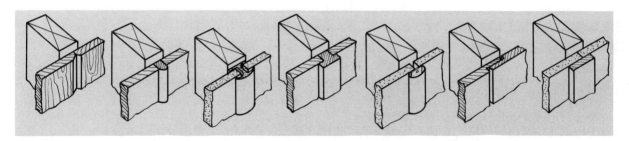

Fig. 47–8. Panel-joint details.

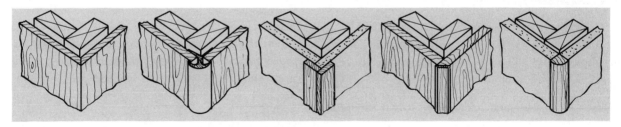

Fig. 47–9. Outside-corner panel joints.

Fig. 47–10. Inside-corner panel joints.

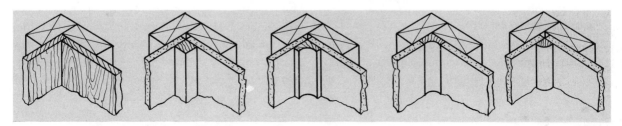

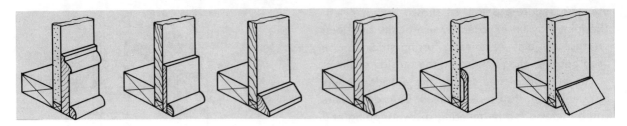

Fig. 47–11. Method of intersecting wall with floor.

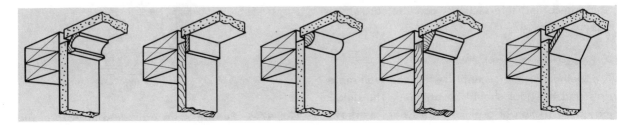

Fig. 47–12. Method of intersecting wall with ceiling.

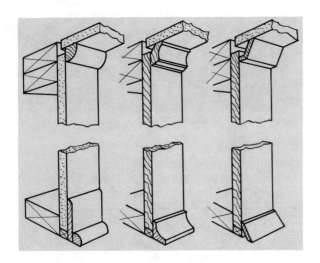

Fig. 47–13. Base and ceiling intersections should be consistent.

board or lath and plaster, baseboard, and molding should be shown.

▶ Ceiling Intersections

Details should also be prepared to show the intersection between the ceiling and the wall. Details should show the position of the top plate, wall-board-ceiling finish, and position of molding used at the intersection (Fig. 47–12). Care should be taken when designing the base treatment and ceiling-intersection treatment to ensure that the intersections are consistent in style, as shown in Fig. 47–13.

▶ Interior-door Details

Pictorial or orthographic jamb, sill, and head sections should be prepared to illustrate methods of framing used around interior doors. Figure 47–14 shows the methods of framing split-jamb, surface-mounted, bifolding, sliding-pocket, sliding-bypass, and folding-type doors. A detailed drawing need not be prepared for each door but should be prepared for each type of door used in the house and should be keyed to the door schedule for indentification. Figure 47–15 shows the relationship between a pictorial section of an interior-door jamb and the variations of this section necessary for plaster, gypsum-board, or paneled wall coverings. Details are not usually necessary for the actual construction of a door, for this is an item that is normally outlined in the specifications. However, it is important to select a proper door from

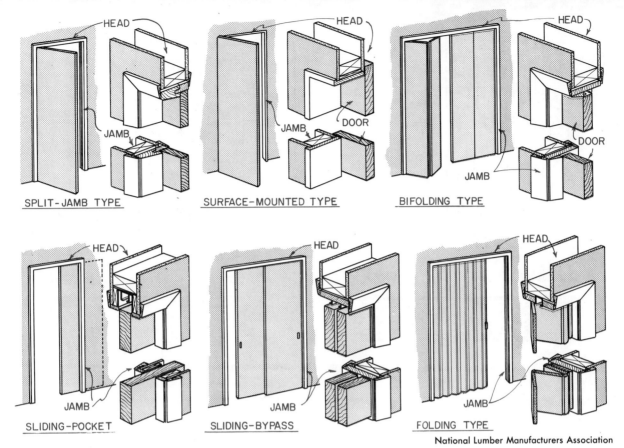

Fig. 47–14. Framing methods used for different types of interior doors.

SPLIT-JAMB TYPE   SURFACE-MOUNTED TYPE   BIFOLDING TYPE

SLIDING-POCKET   SLIDING-BYPASS   FOLDING TYPE

National Lumber Manufacturers Association

manufacturers' specifications or to prepare a detailed drawing to ensure compliance with minimum standards. Figure 47–16 shows the cutaway drawing and section of two types of hollow doors. Hollow-core doors are generally used on interior partitions.

Problems

1. Project a panel-framing elevation drawing of the south wall of bathroom #1, as shown in Fig. 28-7.
2. Draw a vertical section of the wall shown in Fig. 47-7.
3. Draw plan and elevation sections of one of the joints shown in Fig. 47-8.
4. Draw plan sections for one of the intersections shown in Fig. 47–9 and Fig. 47–10.

Fig. 47–15. Door-framing methods needed for different types of construction.

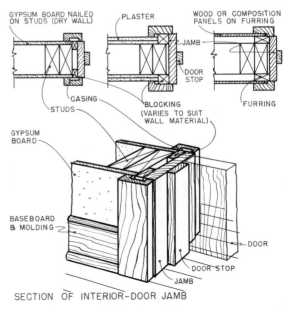

SECTION OF INTERIOR-DOOR JAMB

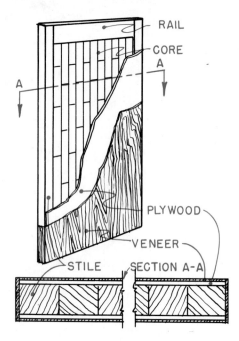

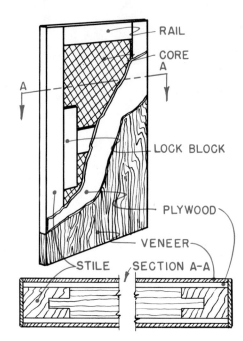

Fig. 47–16. Types of interior-door construction.

5. Draw a complete horizontal wall section of the front living room wall shown in Fig. 1–4. As part of the fireplace treatment, plan to make the entire wall brick from the fireplace to the door opening.

6. Prepare a plan section similar to the plan shown in Fig. 47–15. Show the position of brick, blocking, casing, and jamb.

7. Define the following terms: *dry wall, plaster, paneling, base detail, interior partition.*

Unit 48. Stud Layouts

A stud layout is a plan similar to a floor plan, showing the position of each wall-framing member. The stud layout is a section through each panel elevation, as shown in Fig. 48–1. The cutting-plane line for purposes of projecting the stud layout is placed approximately at the midpoint of the panel elevation. Figure 48–2 shows a stud layout which represents the framing plan of the panel.

▶ Stud Details

Stud layouts are of two types: the *complete plan*, which shows the position of all framing members on the floor plan, and the *stud detail,* which shows only the position and relationship of several studs or framing intersections. Figure 48–3 shows the relationship of a stud detail, a section through the elevation, and a pictorial framing of the same wall.

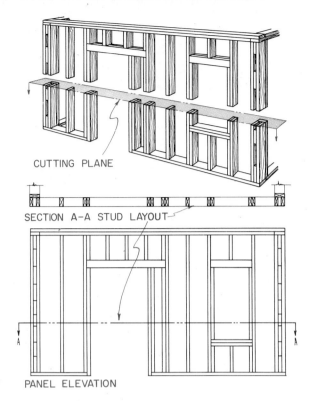

CUTTING PLANE

SECTION A-A STUD LAYOUT

PANEL ELEVATION

Fig. 48-1. The stud layout is a plan section taken through the panel elevation.

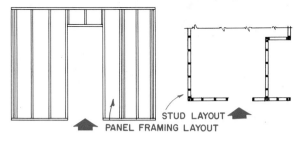

STUD LAYOUT

PANEL FRAMING LAYOUT

Fig. 48-2. The relationship of a stud layout to a panel elevation.

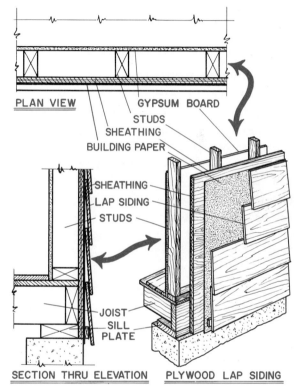

PLAN VIEW — GYPSUM BOARD

STUDS
SHEATHING
BUILDING PAPER

SHEATHING
LAP SIDING
STUDS

JOIST
SILL
PLATE

SECTION THRU ELEVATION   PLYWOOD LAP SIDING

Fig. 48-3. The stud layout is a plan view.

▶ Corner Post

The position of each stud in a corner-post layout is frequently shown in a plan view, as illustrated in Fig. 48-4. Occasionally, siding and inside-wall covering materials are shown on this plan. Preparing this type of detail without covering materials is the easiest and quickest way to show corner-post construction.

Fig. 48-4. Stud details of corner-post layout.

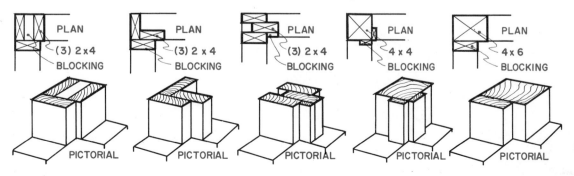

PLAN
(3) 2 x 4
BLOCKING
PICTORIAL

PLAN
(3) 2 x 4
BLOCKING
PICTORIAL

PLAN
(3) 2 x 4
BLOCKING
PICTORIAL

PLAN
4 x 4
BLOCKING
PICTORIAL

PLAN
4 x 6
BLOCKING
PICTORIAL

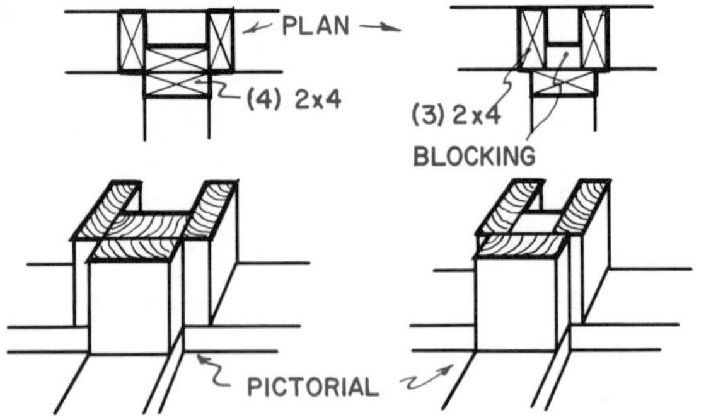

Fig. 48–5. Position of studs in a partition intersection.

➤ Partition Intersections

Details of the exact position of each stud and blocking in an intersection are shown by a plan section (Fig. 48–5). If wall coverings are shown on the detail, the complete wall structure can be drawn (Fig. 48–6). In preparing the plan section, care should be taken to show the exact position of blocking or short pieces of stud stock that may not pass through the cutting-plane line. Blocking should be labeled to prevent the possibility of identifying the blocking as a full-length stud. When laying out the position of all studs, remember that the finished dimensions of a 2 × 4 are actually 1⅝ × 3⅝. The exact dressed sizes of other rough stock are as follows:

Rough	*Dressed*
2 × 3	1⅝ × 2⅝
2 × 4	1⅝ × 3⅝
2 × 6	1⅝ × 5⅝ or 5½
2 × 8	1⅝ × 7⅝ or 7½
2 × 10	1⅝ × 9⅝ or 9½
2 × 12	1⅝ × 11⅝ or 11½
1 × 6	25/32 × 5⅝ or 5½
1 × 8	25/32 × 7⅝ or 7½

➤ Complete Plan

The main purpose of a stud layout is to show how interior partitions fit together and how studs are spaced on the plan. Figure 48–7 shows part of a stud layout. The outline of the plate and the exact position of each stud that falls on an established center (16″, 20″, or 24″) are normally identified by diagonal lines. Studs other than those that are

Fig. 48–6. Wall covering and blocking can be shown on intersection details.

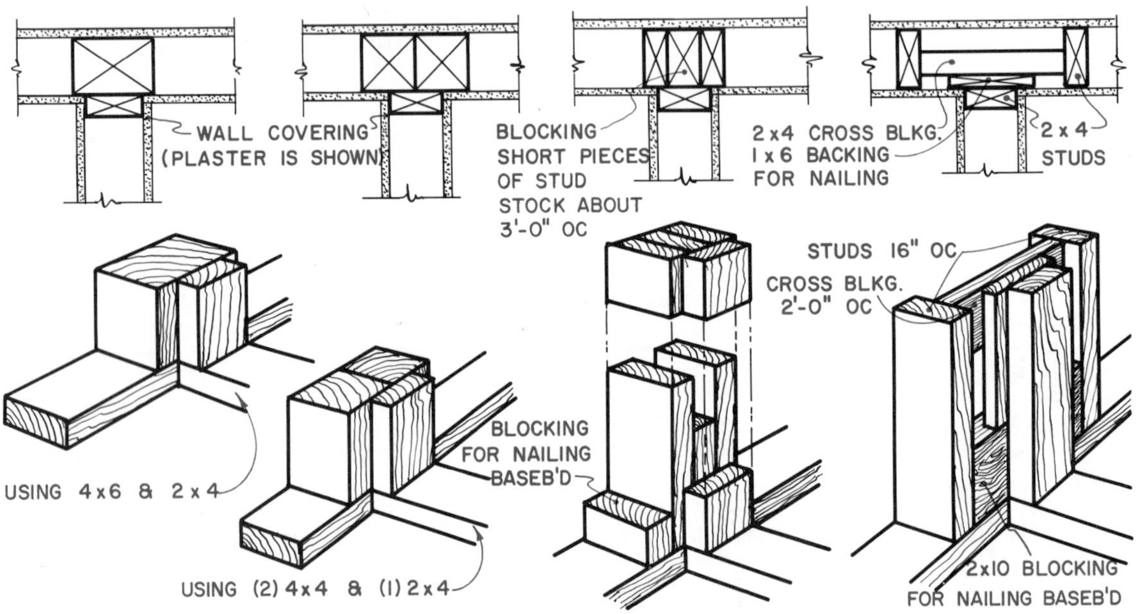

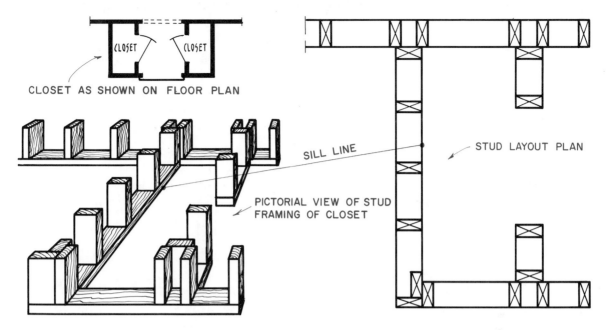

CLOSET AS SHOWN ON FLOOR PLAN

SILL LINE

STUD LAYOUT PLAN

PICTORIAL VIEW OF STUD FRAMING OF CLOSET

Fig. 48–7. The outline of the sill is shown on a stud layout.

on regular centers are shown by different symbols. Studs that are short, blocking, or different in size are identified by a different key (Fig. 48–8). Using a coding system of this type eliminates the need for dimensioning the position of each stud if it is part of the regular partitioned pattern. The practice of coding studs and other members shown on the stud plan also eliminates the need for showing detailed dimensions of each stud.

Detailed dimensions are normally shown on the key or on a separate enlarged detail.

Distances that are dimensioned on stud layout include the following:

1. Inside framing dimensions of each room
2. Framing width of the halls
3. Rough openings for doors and arches
4. Length of each partition
5. Width of partition where dimension lines pass through from room to room (This provides a double check to ensure that the room dimensions plus the partitioned dimensions add up to the overall dimension.) When a stud layout is available it is used on the job to establish partition positions.

Fig. 48–8. Stud-layout symbols.

2 x 4 STUDS 16" OC, 8' LONG

2 x 4 BLOCKING

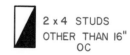

2 x 4 STUDS OTHER THAN 16" OC

2 x 2 BLOCKING

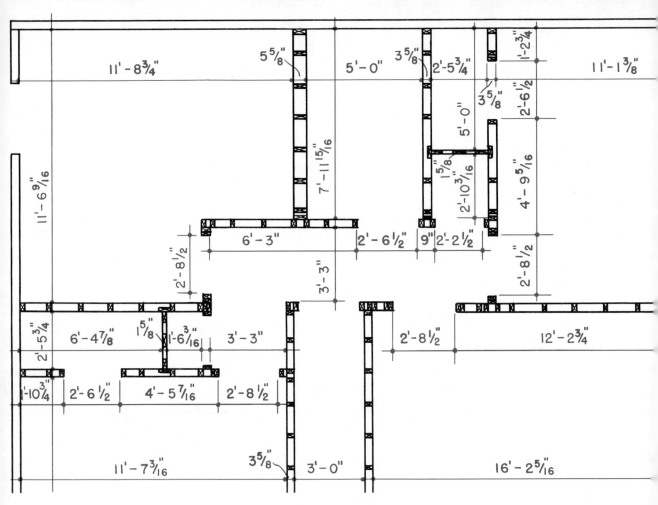

Fig. 48-9. Stud-layout dimensioning.

Figure 48-9 shows the application of these dimensional practices to a typical stud layout.

To conserve space where full partition width is not important, as between closets, studs are sometimes turned on end. This rotation should be reflected in the stud layout (Fig. 48-10).

Fig. 48-10. Studs are turned on end to conserve space.

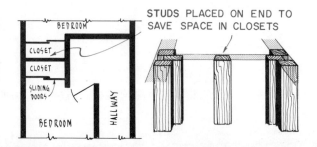

Problems

1. Prepare a stud layout for the floor plan shown in Fig. 25-4.

2. Prepare a corner-post detail for the corner posts shown in Fig. 25-7.

3. Prepare a stud layout for the home in which you now reside.

4. Prepare a stud layout ($\frac{1}{4}'' = 1'\text{-}0''$) for a home of your own design.

5. Draw a stud layout of the east living-room partition shown in Fig. 25-16.

6. Define the following terms: *stud layout, stud detail, corner post, rough lumber, dressed lumber, blocking, inside framing dimensions.*

Unit 49. Roof-framing Plans

The first man-made structure was probably a lean-to roof supported by posts. As structures became larger and more complex, the composition and shape of the roof also changed.

The main function of a roof is to provide protection from rain, snow, sun, and various degrees of temperature. The roof of a northern building is designed to withstand heavy snow loads. The thatched roof of a tropical native hut provides protection only from sun and rain.

As roof styles developed through the centuries, pitches (angles) were changed, gutters and downspouts were added for better drainage, and overhangs were extended to provide more protection from the sun. As the size of roofs changed, the size and types of material changed accordingly. In any modern residence the roof is an integral part of the design.

▶ Structural Design

The walls of the structure are given stability by their attachment to the ground and to the roof. Most buildings are not structurally sound without roofs. Walls cannot resist forces from the outside or forces from the inside unless some horizontal support (roof) is given to the upper part of the wall (Fig. 49–1).

▶ Support

The weight of the roof is normally supported by the exterior walls of the structure (Fig. 49–2). Roofs may be supported by a combination of the exterior walls plus the load-bearing partitions or beams (Fig. 49–3). In a frame or continuous-arch design, the roof is supported by direct connection with the foundation (Fig. 49–4).

▶ Loads

The structural members of a roof must be sufficiently strong to withstand the loads which bear upon it.

A STRUCTURE IS NOT COMPLETE WITHOUT A ROOF.

WALLS CANNOT RESIST FORCES—FORCE FROM OUTSIDE...

FORCES FROM INSIDE...

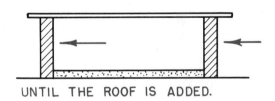

UNTIL THE ROOF IS ADDED.

Fig. 49–1. A roof adds stability to a structure.

Fig. 49–2. The weight of the roof is transmitted to outside walls.

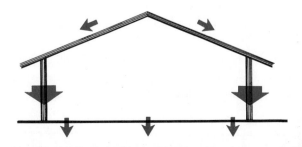

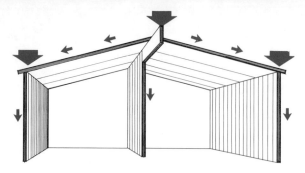

Fig. 49-3. Interior load-bearing partitions help support roofs.

Fig. 49-4. A roof can be connected directly to the foundation.

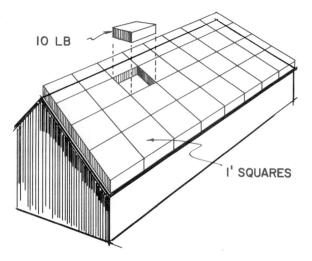

10 LB

1' SQUARES

Fig. 49-5. Roof loads are measured in pounds per square foot.

Dead loads. Dead loads that bear upon most roofs include the weight of shingles, sheathing, and rafters.

All loads are computed on the basis of pounds per square foot. The typical asphalt-shingle roof weighs approximately 10 pounds per square foot

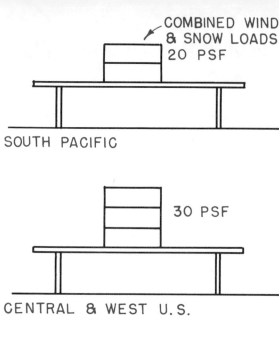

COMBINED WIND & SNOW LOADS
20 PSF

SOUTH PACIFIC

30 PSF

CENTRAL & WEST U.S.

40 PSF

NORTHEAST & NORTHWEST U.S.

Fig. 49-6. Live roof loads vary from region to region.

(Fig. 49-5), and a typical asbestos roof weighs approximately 12 pounds per square foot. A Spanish tile roof weighs 17 pounds per square foot. Thus a 40′ × 20′ (800 square feet) asphalt-shingle roof would be designed to carry an 8,000 pound load (800 square feet × 10 pounds per square foot).

Live loads. Live loads that act on the roof include wind loads and snow loads, which vary greatly from one geographical area to another. For example, the combined wind and snow loads in the South Pacific are approximately 20 pounds per square foot. In the central and western parts of the United States, these loads are 30 pounds

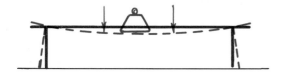

NO PITCH

NO WIND RESISTANCE — 0 PSF

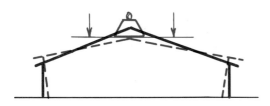

LOW PITCH

MODERATE WIND RESISTANCE — 15 PSF

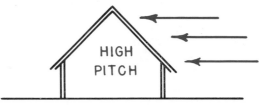
HIGH PITCH

MUCH WIND RESISTANCE — 35 PSF

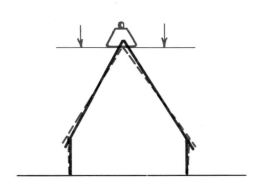

Fig. 49–7. Low-pitch roofs need heavier supports or shorter spans to withstand snow and wind loads.

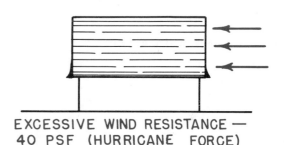
EXCESSIVE WIND RESISTANCE —
40 PSF (HURRICANE FORCE)

Fig. 49–8. High-pitch roofs contribute to high wind loads.

per square foot, and in the northeastern and northwestern parts of the United States, they are 40 pounds per square foot (Fig. 49–6).

Snow and wind loads vary greatly as the pitch of the roof is changed. Snow loads are exerted in a vertical direction; wind loads are exerted in a horizontal direction. A high-pitch roof will withstand snow loads better than a low-pitch roof (Fig. 49–7). The reverse is true of wind loads. There is virtually no wind load exerted on a flat roof, and moderate wind loads (15 pounds per square foot) are exerted on a low-pitch roof. Approximately 35 pounds per square foot is exerted on a high-pitch roof. An excessively resistant wind load is exerted on a completely vertical wall, approximately 40 pounds per square foot, which

is equivalent to hurricane force, as shown in Fig. 49–8. For all practical purposes, snow and wind loads are combined in one total live load. Live loads and dead loads are then combined in the total load acting on the roof.

▶ Size of Members

The size of all structural members used for roof framing depends on the combined loads bearing on the member and the spacing of each member. If the load is increased, either the spacing must

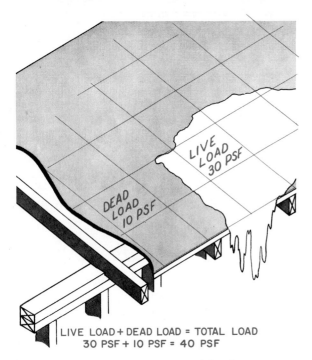

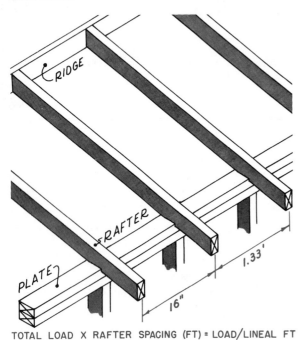

LIVE LOAD + DEAD LOAD = TOTAL LOAD
30 PSF + 10 PSF = 40 PSF

Fig. 49-9. Determining the total load per square foot.

Fig. 49-10. Determining the load per lineal foot on each rafter.

TOTAL LOAD X RAFTER SPACING (FT) = LOAD/LINEAL FT
40 PSF X 1.33 = 53 LBS / LINEAL FT

Fig. 49-11. Rafter loads are expressed in lineal feet.

be decreased or the size of the member increased to compensate for the increased load. Consequently, if the size of a member is decreased, the members must be spaced more closely or the span must be decreased. If the length of the span is increased, the size of the members must be increased or the spacing made closer.

To compute the most appropriate size of roof rafter for a given load, spacing, and span, follow these steps:

1. To determine the total load per square foot of the roof space, add the live load and the dead load (Fig. 49-9).

2. To determine the load per lineal foot on each rafter, multiply the load per square foot by the spacing of the rafters (Fig. 49-10). If rafters are spaced at 12″ intervals, then the load per square foot and the load per lineal foot will be the same. However, if the rafters are spaced at 16″ intervals, then each lineal foot of rafter must support 1 ⅓ of the load per square foot (Fig. 49-11).

3. To find the total load each rafter must support, multiply the load per lineal foot by the length of the span in feet (Fig. 49-12).

4. To compute the bending moment in inch pounds, multiply the total load supported by each rafter by the length of the span in feet by 12. Divide this figure by 8. The *bending moment* is the force needed to bend or break the rafter. When the length of the span in pounds is multiplied by

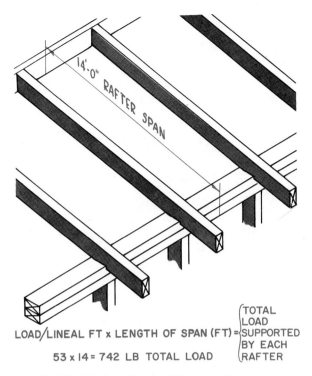

LOAD/LINEAL FT x LENGTH OF SPAN (FT) = {TOTAL LOAD SUPPORTED BY EACH RAFTER

53 x 14 = 742 LB TOTAL LOAD

Fig. 49–12. Finding the total load each rafter must support.

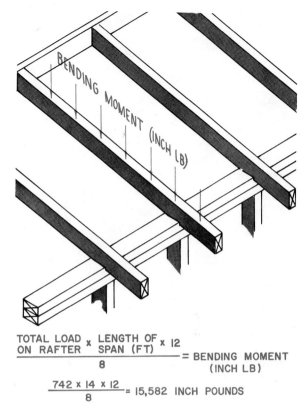

$$\frac{\text{TOTAL LOAD ON RAFTER} \times \text{LENGTH OF SPAN (FT)} \times 12}{8} = \text{BENDING MOMENT (INCH LB)}$$

$$\frac{742 \times 14 \times 12}{8} = 15{,}582 \text{ INCH POUNDS}$$

Fig. 49–13. Computing the bending moment.

the length of the span in feet, the result is expressed in foot pounds. The span must be multiplied by 12 to convert the bending moment into inch pounds (Fig. 49–13).

5. Set up the equation to determine the resisting moment. The *resisting moment* is the strength or resistance the rafter must possess to withstand the force of the bending moment. The resistance moment must therefore be equal to or greater than the bending moment of the rafter (Fig. 49–14). The resistance moment is determined by multiplying the fiber stress by the rafter width by the rafter depth squared. This figure is divided by 6. Rafter widths should be expressed in the exact dimensions of the finished lumber (Fig. 49–15). The *fiber stress* is the tendency of the fibers of the wood to bend and stress as the member is loaded. Fiber stresses range from 1,750 pounds per square inch for Southern dense pine select to 600 pounds per square inch for red spruce. Dense Douglas fir and

Fig. 49–14. The resisting moment must be equal to, or greater than, the bending moment.

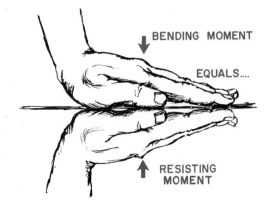

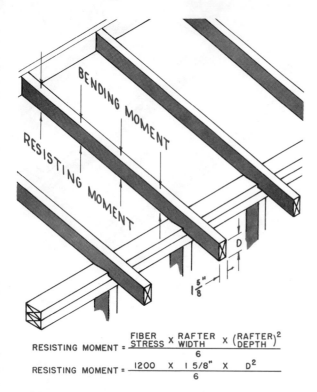

$$\text{RESISTING MOMENT} = \frac{\text{FIBER STRESS} \times \text{RAFTER WIDTH} \times (\text{RAFTER DEPTH})^2}{6}$$

$$\text{RESISTING MOMENT} = \frac{1200 \times 1\ 5/8" \times D^2}{6}$$

Fig. 49–15. Determining the resistance moment.

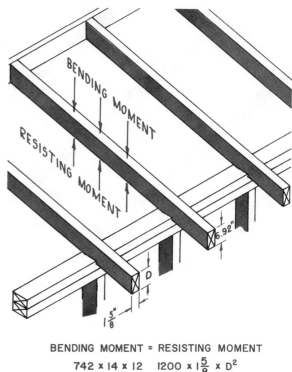

$$\text{BENDING MOMENT} = \text{RESISTING MOMENT}$$

$$\frac{742 \times 14 \times 12}{8} = \frac{1200 \times 1\frac{5}{8} \times D^2}{6}$$

$$15{,}582 = 325\ D^2$$

$$6.92 = D$$

Fig. 49–16. Combining the bending-moment and resistance-moment formulas.

Southern pine possess average fiber stresses of 1,200 pounds per square inch. The rafter depth is squared, since the strength of the member increases by squares. For example, a rafter 12″ deep is not three times as strong as a rafter 4″ deep. It is nine times as strong.

6. Since the bending moment equals the resistance moment, the formulas can be combined, as shown in Fig. 49–16. The formula can then be followed for any of the variables, preferably the depth of the rafter, since varying the depth will alter the resisting moment more than any other single factor.

Care should be taken in establishing all sizes to ensure that the sizes of materials conform to manufacturers' standards and building-code allowances. Figure 49–17 shows a typical space-span chart based on common lumber sizes and spacing. Figure 49–18 shows common truss specifications based on normal loading for residential work.

▶ Roof-framing Types

The conventional method of roof framing consists of roof rafters or trusses spaced at small intervals such as 16″ on center. These roof rafters align with the partition studs placed on the same centers (Fig. 49–19). The second method is the post and beam method or plank and beam (Fig. 49–20). The plank and beam roof consists of planks placed on longitudinal (transverse) beams. Regularly spaced posts serve as load bearers for the roof members. A *ridge beam* is the center of a gable roof, and intermittent beams directly support the roof planking. Roof planking can then be used as a ceiling and a base for roofing that will shed water. Exposed plank and beam ceilings achieve a distinctive and pleasing architectural effect.

When planks are selected for appearance, the only ceiling treatment needed is a desired finish. Longitudinal beam sizes vary with the span and spacing of the beams. Design variations of end walls are achieved by an extensive use of glass and protecting roof overhangs.

The use of larger members in post and beam construction allows the designer to plan larger open areas unobstructed by bearing partitions (Fig. 49–21).

▶ Gable Roofs

Gable roofs are constructed by the use of conventional rafters and ceiling joists usually spaced 16" on center and covered with sheathing felt and shingles (Fig. 49–22). An adaptation of this conventional method of constructing roofs is the use of roof trusses to replace the conventional rafters and ceiling joists (Fig. 49–23). Trusses provide a much more rigid roof but eliminate the use of a space between the joists and rafters for an attic or crawl-space storage. An increasingly popular type of gable construction is a prefabricated gable end, to which beams and roof sections with insulation and finishing are attached (Fig. 49–24). This is one variation of the post and beam method of roof construction.

Pitch: 5/12
Load: 40 PSF

Lumber size	Spacing, in inches	Fiber stress, 1,200 pounds, for Douglas Fir and Southern Yellow Pine
2 x 4	24	6'–6"
	20	7'–3"
	16	8'–1"
	12	9'–4"
2 x 6	24	10'–4"
	20	11'–4"
	16	12'–6"
	12	14'–2"
2 x 8	24	13'–8"
	20	15'–2"
	16	16'–6"
	12	18'–4"

Fig. 49–17. Maximum rafter spans for 5/12 pitch, 40 PSF load.

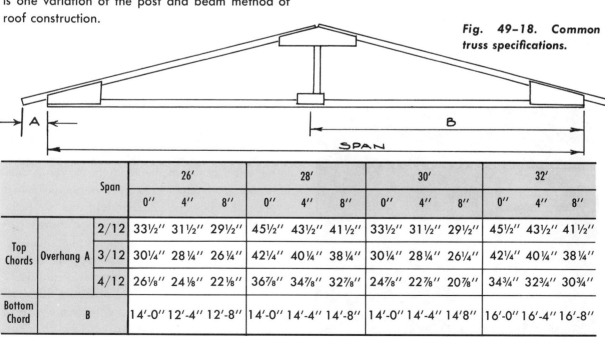

Fig. 49–18. Common truss specifications.

		Span	26'			28'			30'			32'		
			0"	4"	8"	0"	4"	8"	0"	4"	8"	0"	4"	8"
Top Chords	Overhang A	2/12	33½"	31½"	29½"	45½"	43½"	41½"	33½"	31½"	29½"	45½"	43½"	41½"
		3/12	30¼"	28¼"	26¼"	42¼"	40¼"	38¼"	30¼"	28¼"	26¼"	42¼"	40¼"	38¼"
		4/12	26⅛"	24⅛"	22⅛"	36⅞"	34⅞"	32⅞"	24⅞"	22⅞"	20⅞"	34¾"	32¾"	30¾"
Bottom Chord	B		14'-0"	12'-4"	12'-8"	14'-0"	14'-4"	14'-8"	14'-0"	14'-4"	14'8"	16'-0"	16'-4"	16'-8"

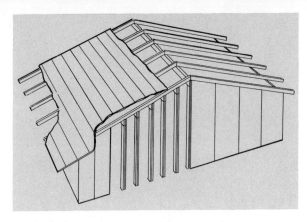

Fig. 49-19. Conventional roof framing.

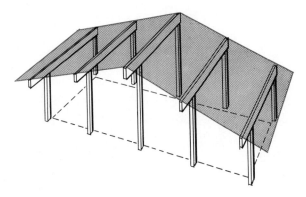

Fig. 49-20. Plank and beam framing.

Fig. 49-21. Post and beam framing allows for larger open areas.

Samuel Cabot, Inc.

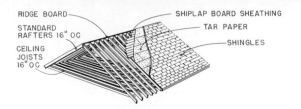

RIDGE BOARD

STANDARD RAFTERS 16" OC

CEILING JOISTS 16" OC

SHIPLAP BOARD SHEATHING

TAR PAPER

SHINGLES

Fig. 49-22. A conventionally-framed gable roof.

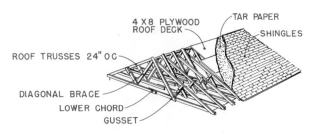

4 X 8 PLYWOOD ROOF DECK

TAR PAPER

SHINGLES

ROOF TRUSSES 24" OC

DIAGONAL BRACE

LOWER CHORD

GUSSET

Fig. 49-23. A trussed gable roof.

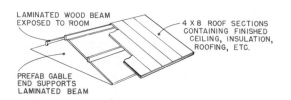

LAMINATED WOOD BEAM EXPOSED TO ROOM

4 X 8 ROOF SECTIONS CONTAINING FINISHED CEILING, INSULATION, ROOFING, ETC.

PREFAB GABLE END SUPPORTS LAMINATED BEAM

Fig. 49-24. A prefabricated post and beam gable roof.

▶ **Pitch**

A gable roof has pitch on two sides but no pitch on the ends (gable ends). The *pitch* is the angle between the top plate and the ridge board. *Rise* is the vertical distance from the top plate to the ridge. *Run* is the horizontal distance from the ridge to the top plate. The *pitch* is referred to as the *rise over the run*. In a gable roof with the ridge board in the exact center of the building, the run is one-half the span (Fig. 49-25). The run is always expressed in units of 12. Therefore, the rise is the number of inches the roof rises as it moves 12" horizontally. A 6/12 pitch means that the roof rises 6" for every 12" of horizontal distance (run).

Gable-roof pitches vary greatly. The 1/12 pitch shown in Fig. 49-25 is almost a flat roof. The 8/12 pitch however is a moderately steep roof. The angle of a roof with a 12/12 pitch is 45°.

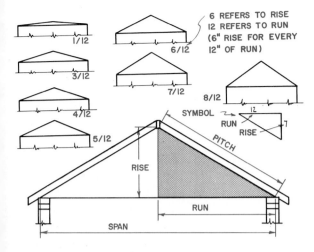

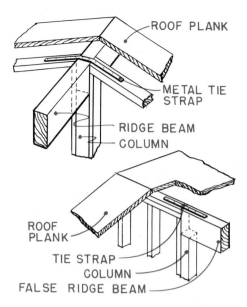

Fig. 49–25. The pitch of a roof is referred to as the rise over the run.

Fig. 49–27. Ridge-beam assemblies.

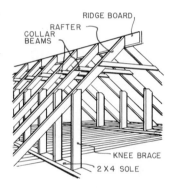

Fig. 49–26. The ridge board is the top member in the roof assembly.

▶ Ridge Beams

The ridge board or ridge beam as shown in Fig. 49–26 is the top member in the roof assembly. Rafters are fixed in their exact position by being secured to the ridge board. The ridge beam in a cathedral ceiling of post and beam construction may be part of the top plate assembly (Fig. 49–27).

▶ Gable End

The gable end is the side of the house that rises to meet the ridge (Fig. 49–28). In some cases, especially on low-pitch roofs, the entire gable-end wall from the floor to the ridge can be panelized with varying lengths of studs. However, it is more com-

mon to prepare a rectangular wall panel and erect separate studs that project from the top plate of the panel to the rafter. Sheathing and siding are then added to the entire gable end of the house. When post and beam construction is used, celestial windows in the gable end can be utilized, since studs are unnecessary on the gable end.

An increased use of windows in gable ends has necessitated the use of larger overhangs on the gable end. Gable-end lookouts can be framed from the first or second rafters on the gable plate, as shown in Fig. 49–29.

Fig. 49–28. Gable-end construction.

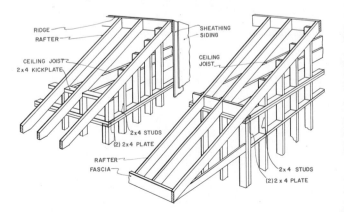

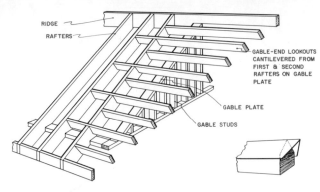

Fig. 49-29. Winged-gable lookout construction.

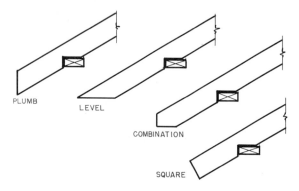

Fig. 49-30. Types of tail-rafter cuts.

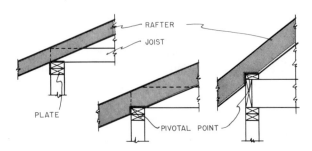

Fig. 49-31. Method of intersecting rafters and top plates.

Fig. 49-32. Large overhangs are desirable only if designed correctly.

Overhangs

Post and beam construction allows for larger overhangs since larger members are used and rafters can quite often be exposed. Several variations of cuts are used to finish the rafter end. A comparison of the plumb, level, combination, and square cuts is given in Fig. 49-30. Notice also that the rafters are notched with a *seat* (birdmouth) cut, to provide a level surface for the intersection of the rafters and top plates. The area bearing on the plate should not be less than 3″ (Fig. 49-31).

Overhangs are normally larger on the side walls than on gable ends. Overhangs should be designed to provide maximum protection from sun and rain without restricting the light and view. Figure 49-32 shows some of the difficulties in designing large overhangs. On a low-pitch roof the problem is not acute since the rise is relatively small compared with the run. But on a steep pitch roof, where the rise is large, the light might be completely shut off if the same amount of overhang were used. Furthermore, when the end of the overhang extends below the level of the window, there is no possibility of using a flat soffit. Figure 49-33 shows several alternative soffits.

Collar Beams

Collar beams provide a tie between rafters. They may be placed on every rafter or only on every other rafter. Collar beams are used to reduce the rafter stress that occurs between the top plate and the rafter cut. They also act as ceiling joists for finished attics (Fig. 49-34).

Knee Walls

Knee walls are vertical studs which project from an attic floor to the roof rafters, as shown in Fig. 49-35. Knee walls add rigidity to the rafters and also provide wall framing for finished attics.

Trusses

Figure 49-36 shows lightweight wood trusses that have become increasingly popular for homes and small buildings. Roof trusses allow complete flexibility for interior spacing. They save from approxi-

322

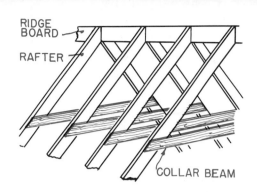

Fig. 49-34. Collar beams reduce rafter stress.

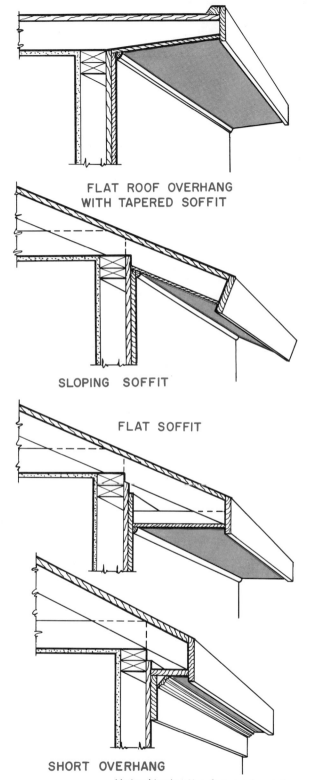

FLAT ROOF OVERHANG
WITH TAPERED SOFFIT

SLOPING SOFFIT

FLAT SOFFIT

SHORT OVERHANG

National Lumber Manufacturers Association

Fig. 49-33. Types of soffit design.

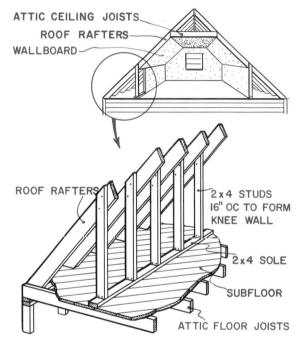

Fig. 49-35. Knee walls add rigidity to the rafters.

Fig. 49-36. Lightweight wood trusses.

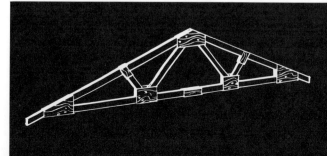

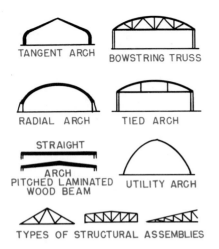

Fig. 49–37. Standard types of trusses.

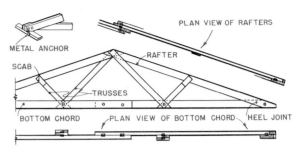

Fig. 49–39. A wood-frame truss.

mately 30 percent to 35 percent on materials, compared with the requirements of conventional framing methods. Trusses can be fabricated and erected in one-third of the time required for rafter and ceiling-joist construction. Truss construction helps to put the building under cover almost immediately. The use of trusses saves material and erection time and eliminates normal interior load-bearing partitions. Trusses save construction foundations and footings required for load-bearing partitions. Standard types of trusses are shown in Fig. 49–37. Truss-construction methods are as applicable to large steel-framed buildings (Fig. 49–38) as to small wood-framed buildings (Fig. 49–39).

▶ **Hip Roof**

Hip-roof framing is similar to gable-roof framing except that the roof slopes in two directions instead of intersecting a gable-end wall. The hip roof may be pyramid-shaped on square buildings.

Where two adjacent slopes meet, a *hip* is formed on the external angle. A *hip rafter* extends from the ridge board over the top plate to the edge of the overhang. The hip rafter performs the same function as the ridge board.

The internal angle formed by the intersection of two slopes of the roof is known as the *valley*. A valley rafter is used on the internal angle as a hip rafter is used on the external angle. Hip rafters and valley rafters are normally 2″ deeper or 1″ wider than the regular rafters, for spans up to 12′. For spans of over 12′, the rafter should be doubled in width.

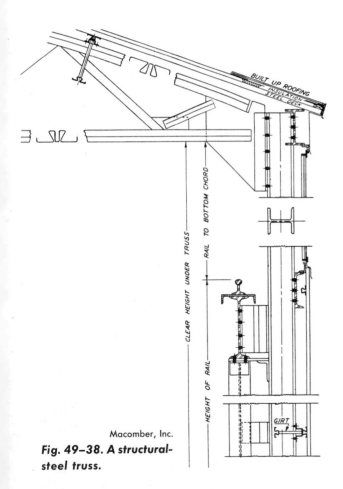

Macomber, Inc.

Fig. 49–38. A structural-steel truss.

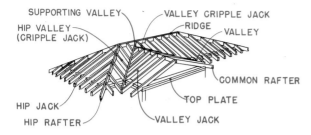

Fig. 49–40. Hip-roof construction.

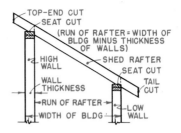

Fig. 49–41. Shed-roof framing.

Jack rafters are rafters that extend from the wall plate to the hip or valley rafter. They are always shorter than common rafters. Figure 49–40 illustrates the use of these various framing members in hip-roof construction.

▶ Shed Roof

A shed roof is a roof which slants in only one direction (a gable roof is actually two shed roofs, sloping in opposite directions). Shed-roof rafter design is the same as rafter design for gable roofs, except that the run of the rafter is the same as the span. The shed rafter differs from the common rafter in the gable roof in that the shed rafter has two seat cuts, a tail cut, and a top-end cut (Fig. 49–41).

▶ Flat Roof

A flat roof has no slope. Therefore the roof rafters must span directly from wall to wall or from wall to bearing partition. When rafters also serve as ceiling joists, the size of the rafter must be computed on the basis of both the roof load and the ceiling load.

▶ Overhang

Large overhangs are possible on flat roofs. In other words, the roof joists can be extended past the top plate far enough to provide sun protection and yet not block the view. This extension is possible because there is no slope. When overhangs are desired on all sides, *lookout rafters,* as shown in Fig. 49–42, are used to extend the overhang on the side of the building perpendicular to the rafter direction.

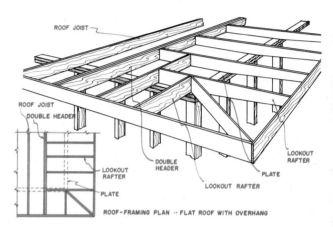

Fig. 49–42. Lookout rafters are used to extend the overhang perpendicular to the common rafters.

In post and beam construction, roof beams are used to support the roof construction. They also function as exposed ceiling beams.

▶ Drainage

Since there is no slope to a flat roof, drainage must be provided for by downspouts extending through the overhang. Flat roofs must be designed for a maximum snow load, since snow will not slide off the roof but must completely melt and drain away. A built-up roof consisting of sheathing, roofing paper, and crushed gravel can be used (Fig. 49–43). If a flat roof is so designed, a gravel stop and cant strip can be made high enough to hold water at a specific level. Water will then lie on the roof at all times and provide additional insulation.

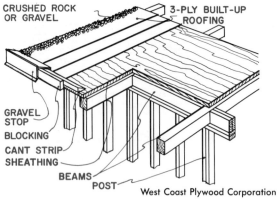

CRUSHED ROCK OR GRAVEL
3-PLY BUILT-UP ROOFING
GRAVEL STOP
BLOCKING
CANT STRIP
SHEATHING
BEAMS
POST

West Coast Plywood Corporation

Fig. 49–43. Built-up roof construction.

Fig. 49–44. Erecting a steel roof.
Ambridge, American Bridge Division of U.S. Steel

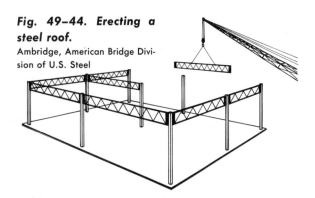

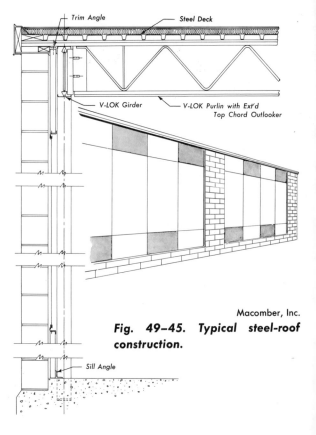

Trim Angle
Steel Deck
V-LOK Girder
V-LOK Purlin with Ext'd Top Chord Outlooker
Sill Angle

Macomber, Inc.

Fig. 49–45. Typical steel-roof construction.

▶ Steel

Steel-construction methods are especially applicable to flat roofs. The simplicity of erecting a steel roof results from the great strength of steel joints (Fig. 49–44). The crossbracing between widths of a steel *purlin* (horizontal member), as shown in Fig. 49–45, provides the purlin with a strength comparable to that of a truss.

▶ Plan Development

A *roof plan* (Fig. 49–46) is a plan view of the roof showing the outline of the roof and the major object lines indicating ridges, valleys, hips, and openings. The roof plan is not a framing plan. To develop a roof-framing plan, a roof must be stripped of its covering to expose the position of each structural member and each header (Fig. 49–47). The roof plan can be used as the basic outline for the roof-framing plan. The roof-framing plan must show the exact position and spacing of each member. Figure 49–48 shows a comparison of a roof plan and a roof-framing plan of the same roof.

▶ Single-line Plans

In the roof-framing plan shown in Fig. 49–48, each member is represented by a single line. This method of preparing roof-framing plans is acceptable when only the general relationship and center spacing are desired.

▶ Complete Plan

However, when more details concerning the exact construction of intersections and joints are needed, a plan showing the thickness of each member, as shown in Fig. 49–49, should be prepared. This type of plan is necessary to show the relative height of one member compared with another; that is,

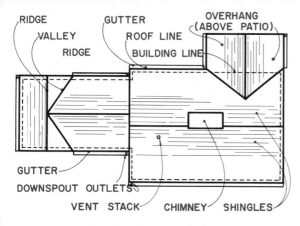

Fig. 49-46. A roof plan.

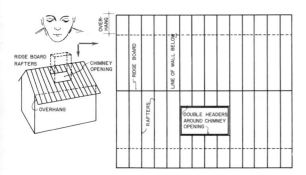

Fig. 49-47. A roof-framing plan.

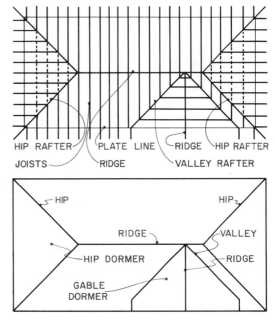

Fig. 49-48. Comparison of a roof plan (bottom) and a roof-framing plan (top).

Fig. 49-49. A roof-framing plan showing the thickness of each member.

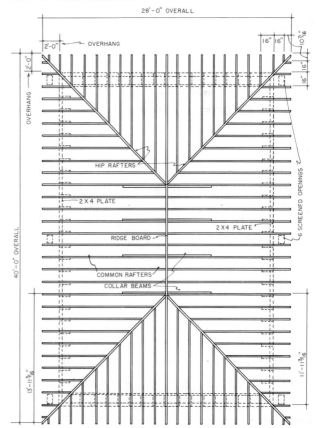

to determine whether one member passes over or under another. In this plan the width of ridge boards, rafters, headers, and plates should be shown to the exact scale.

When a complete roof-framing plan of this type cannot fully describe construction framing details, then additional removed pictorial or elevation drawings should be prepared, as shown in Fig. 49-50. A similar technique of removing details can also be used to increase the size of a particular area in detail for dimensioning purposes.

On roof-framing plans, only the outline of the top of the rafters is shown. All areas underneath, including the gable-end plate, are shown by dotted lines. When a gable-end lookout slopes, a true orthographic projection of the plan would indicate three lines—two lines for the top of the rafter and one line for the bottom. However, roof-framing

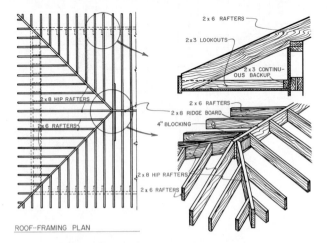

Fig. 49–50. Roof-framing plan details.

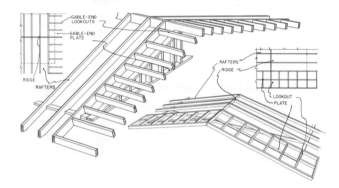

Fig. 49–51. Roof-framing plans show only the out-line of the top of each member.

plans are normally simplified to show only the out-line of the top of each member (Fig. 49–51). The angle or vertical position of any roof-framing member should be shown on a roof-framing elevation.

▶ **Dormers**

Parts of the roof-framing plan which extend above the normal plane of projection, such as dormer rafters, are drawn with dotted lines. This device indicates that the parts do not directly intersect with the other framing members shown on the plan. It is quite common to show the position of

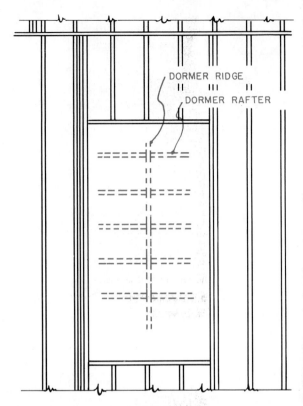

Fig. 49–52. Method of drawing dormer rafters.

dormer rafters or ridge as illustrated in Fig. 49–52. The details of intersecting the dormer-roof framing with dormer walls should be shown on roof-framing elevations or other details.

Fig. 49–53. Steel roof-framing plan areas are often identified by numbers and letters.

Macomber, Inc.

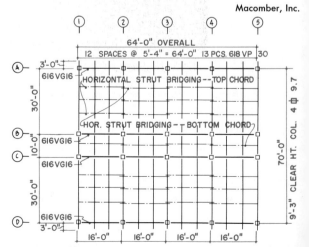

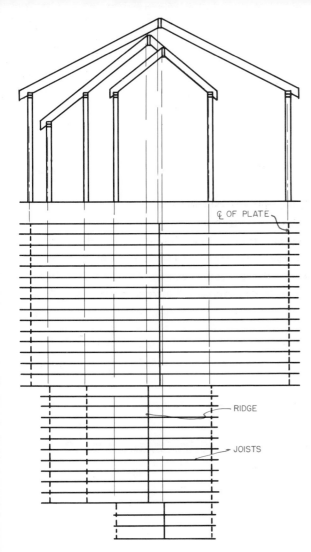

Fig. 49–54. Method of projecting roof-framing elevations.

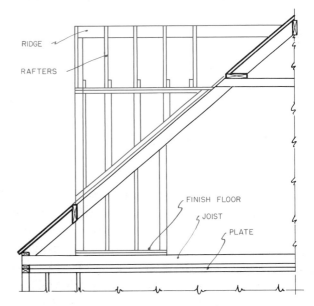

Fig. 49–55. Framing elevation of an individual dormer.

▶ **Steel**

Roof-framing plans for steel construction are prepared like those for wood construction. However, in plans for structural steel, single-line drawings are almost universally used. A complete classification of each steel member is shown on the drawing. This includes the size, type, and weight of the beams and columns. Each different type of member is shown by a different line weight, which relates to the size of the member. Structural-steel roof-framing plans frequently show *bay areas* (areas between columns) indicating the number of

spaces and the spacing of each purlin between columns. Bays are frequently shown in circles: numerically in one direction and alphabetically in the other direction (Fig. 49–53).

▶ **Roof-framing Elevations**

Roof-framing plans show horizontal relationships of members such as width, length, and horizontal spacing. In a top view (plan), you cannot show vertical dimensions such as pitch, ridge height, plate height. The transverse sections supply information of this type through one part of the structure. However, if a comparison of different heights and pitches is desired, a composite framing-elevation drawing should be prepared. This elevation can be projected from the roof-framing plan and corresponding lines on the elevation drawings, as shown in Fig. 49–54.

Dormer rafters and walls do not lie in the same plane as the remainder of the roof rafters. A framing-elevation drawing is therefore advantageous in illustrating the exact position of the dormer members and their tie-in with the common roof rafters. Figure 49–55 illustrates a side-framing elevation of an individual dormer and shows how it is structurally related to other roof-framing mem-

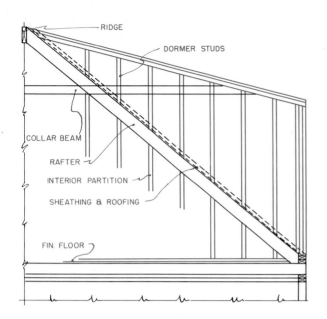

Fig. 49–56. Side-wall framing elevation of a shed dormer.

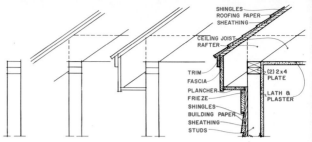

Fig. 49–57. Steps in laying out a cornice detail.

bers. Figure 49–56 shows the side-wall framing of a shed dormer, in which the position of the dormer studs is revealed by the elevation drawing.

Parts of roof-framing elevations are actually parts of transverse sections. They are used to show the basic relationship between major framing members and the roof-covering and trim details. Figure 49–57 shows the steps in laying out one of the most widely used drawings of this type, a cornice detail. Other cornice details that show the relation-

Fig. 49–58. Cornice-framing details.

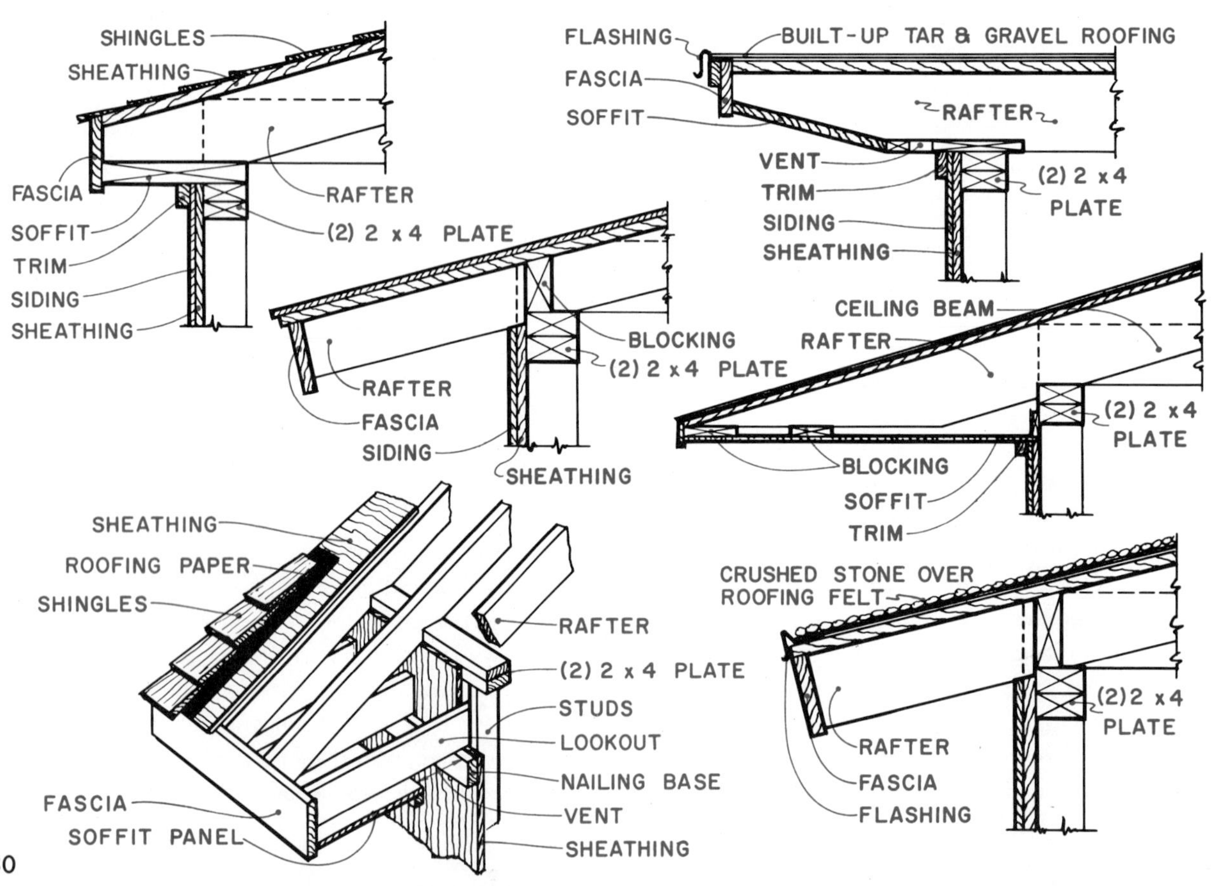

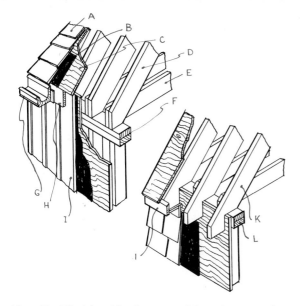

Fig. 49–59. Identify these roof-framing members.

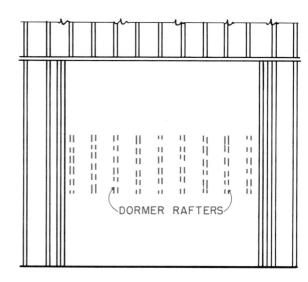

DORMER RAFTERS

Fig. 49–61. Draw a framing elevation of this dormer.

ship among roof-framing members and trim materials are shown in Fig. 49–58.

Problems

1. Identify the roof-framing members shown in Fig. 49–59.
2. Draw a roof-framing plan for the dormer shown in the roof-framing elevation in Fig. 49–60. Use the dormer shown in Fig. 49–55 as a guide.

Fig. 49–60. Draw a roof-framing plan of this dormer.

3. Draw a framing elevation of the dormer shown in Fig. 49–61. Use the dormer shown in Fig. 49–55 as a guide.
4. Identify the roof-framing members shown in Fig. 49–62.
5. Prepare a roof-framing plan of the roofs shown in Fig. 49–63.
6. Identify the framing members shown in Fig. 49–64.
7. Prepare a roof-framing plan for the house shown in Fig. 25–2A. First prepare a roof plan for a gable roof or a hip roof and project the roof-framing plan from this.

Fig. 49–62. Identify these roof-framing members.

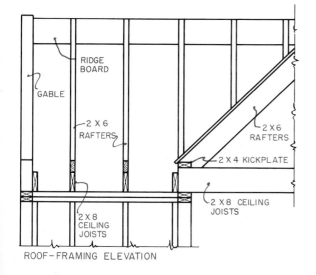

RIDGE BOARD

GABLE

2 X 6 RAFTERS

2 X 6 RAFTERS

2 X 4 KICKPLATE

2 X 8 CEILING JOISTS

2 X 8 CEILING JOISTS

ROOF-FRAMING ELEVATION

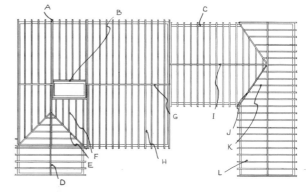

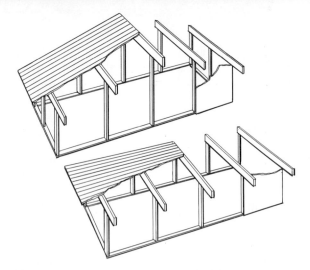

Fig. 49–63. Prepare a roof-framing plan of these roofs.

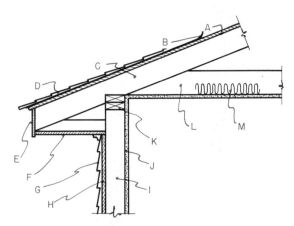

Fig. 49–64. Identify the parts of this cornice detail.

8. Prepare a roof-framing plan for the house shown in Fig. 25–14.
9. Prepare a roof-framing plan for the house shown in Fig. 25–17.
10. Prepare a roof-framing plan for your own house.
11. Prepare a roof-framing plan for a house of your own design.
12. Define the following terms: *wind load, snow load, bending moment, resisting moment, fiber stress, truss, transverse beam, gable end, rise, run, seat cut, collar beam, knee wall, valley, hip, cornice, jack, downspout, roof plan, roof-framing plan, dormer, bay.*
13. Draw a roof-framing plan for the house shown in Fig. 64–12.

Unit 50. Roof-covering Materials

Roof covering protects the building from rain, snow, wind, heat, and cold. Materials used to cover pitched roofs include wood shingles, asphalt shingles, and asbestos shingles. On heavier roofs, tile or slate may also be used. Roll roofing or other sheet material, such as galvanized iron, aluminum, copper, and tin, may also be used for flat or low-pitched roofs. A built-up roof consisting of layers of roofing-felt covered with gravel topping may also be used on low-pitched or flat roofs. If a built-up roof is used on high-pitched roofs, the gravel will weather off.

▶ Sheathing

Roof sheathing consists of 1 × 6 lumber or plywood nailed directly to the roof rafters. Sheathing adds rigidity to the roof and provides a surface for the attachment of waterproofing materials. In humid parts of the country, sheathing boards are sometimes spaced slightly apart to provide ventilation and to prevent shingle rot.

▶ Roll Roofing

Roll roofing may be used as an *underlayment* for shingles or as a finished roofing material (Fig.

SATURATED FELT SMOOTH SURFACE MINERAL SURFACE PATTERN EDGE SELVAGE

Fig. 50–1. Types of roll roofing.

50–1). Roll roofing used as an underlayment includes asphalt and saturated felt. The underlayment serves as a barrier against moisture and wind. Mineral surface and selvage roll-roofing can be used as the final roofing surface.

▶ Weight

The weight of roofing materials is important in computing dead loads. A heavier roofing surface makes the roof more permanent than does a lighter surface. Generally, heavier roofing materials last longer than lighter materials. Therefore, heavy roofing, such as strip or individual shingles, is superior. Roof-covering materials are classified by their weight per 100 square feet (100 square feet equals 1 *square*). Thus 30-pound roofing felt weighs 30 pounds per 100 square feet.

▶ Shingles

Shingles are commonly made from asphalt, asbestos, wood, tile, and slate and are available in a variety of patterns and shapes. Shingles and underlayment are overlapped when applied as shown in Fig. 50–2. Shingles are best for pitches steeper than 4/12. For pitches less than 4/12, roll roofing is better. Shingles may be laid flat or, if extra shingles are added, patterns may be produced (Fig. 50–3).

RIDGE SHINGLES

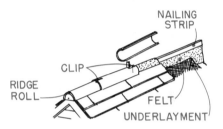

NAILING STRIP
CLIP
RIDGE ROLL
FELT UNDERLAYMENT

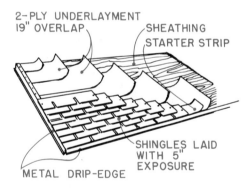

2-PLY UNDERLAYMENT 19" OVERLAP
SHEATHING
STARTER STRIP
SHINGLES LAID WITH 5" EXPOSURE
METAL DRIP-EDGE

Fig. 50–2. Method of shingle application.

Fig. 50–3. Shingle patterns.

  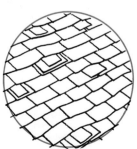

OCEAN-WAVE ROOF   SERRATED ROOF   THATCH OR STAGGERED   PYRAMID STYLE

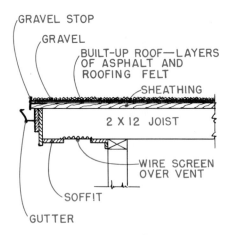

Fig. 50-4. Built-up roof construction.

▶ Built-up Roofs

Built-up roof coverings are used on flat or extremely low-pitched roofs. Because rain or snow may not be immediately expelled from these roofs, complete waterproofing is essential. Built-up roofs may have three, four, or five layers of roofing-felt, sealed with tar or asphalt, between each two coatings. The final layer of tar or asphalt is then covered with roofing gravel or a top sheet of roll roofing (Fig. 50-4).

▶ Flashing

Joints where roof-covering materials intersect at the ridge, hip, valley, chimney, and parapet joints must be flashed. *Flashing* is additional covering used on a joint to provide complete waterproofing. Roll-roofing shingles or sheet metal is used as the flashing material. For flashing hip and valley joints, shingle flashing is best; it may be attached by nails to wood strips applied over asphalt, cement, and felt underlayment (Fig. 50-5).

When sheet-metal flashing is used, watertight sheet-metal joints should be used, as shown in Fig. 50-6. Chimney flashing is frequently bonded into the mortar joint and under shingles and is caulked to provide completely waterproof joints.

▶ Gutters

Gutters are troughs designed to carry water to the downspouts, where it can be emptied into the sewer system (Fig. 50-7). The two materials used most commonly for gutters are sheet metal and wood such as red cedar and redwood (Fig. 50-8). Gutters may be built into the roof structure, as shown in the fascia-board gutter and the pole gutter in Fig. 50-9. Gutters may be made of additional sheet metal or wood attached or hung from the fascia board. All gutters should be pitched sufficiently to provide for drainage to the down-

Fig. 50-5. One method of flashing corners.

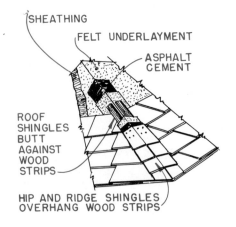

Fig. 50-6. Application of sheet-metal flashing.

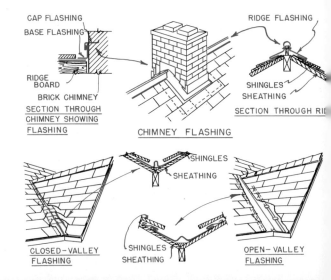

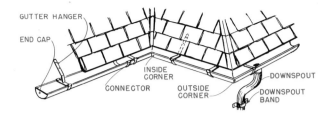

Fig. 50–7. Gutter-assembly terminology.

spout. In selecting gutters and downspouts, care must be taken to ensure that their size is adequate for the local rainfall.

▶ **Sun Screens**

The design of the roof overhang must be sufficient to provide complete protection from the direct rays of the sun. Such protection is especially important in large areas such as patios and porches. The basic problem is to block the direct rays of the sun

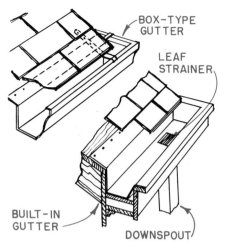

Fig. 50–8. Common types of gutters.

Fig. 50–9. Built-in gutters.

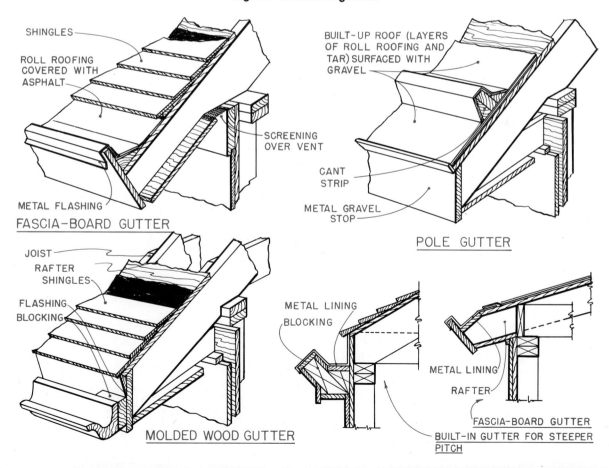

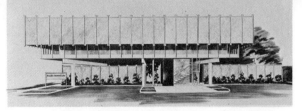

Neuhaus & Taylor; Pacific Mutual Life Insurance Company

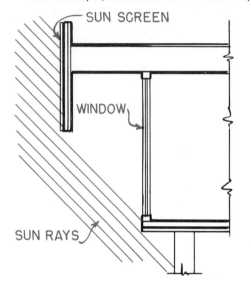

Fig. 50–10. An effective sun-screening device.

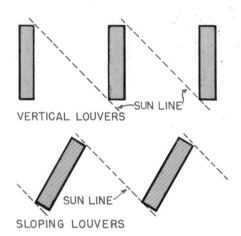

Fig. 50–11. The angle and spacing of louvers is important in sun screening.

without impairing the illumination. Often a completely solid covering would produce an area so dark that the advantages of outdoor living would be eliminated. The sunshade shown on the building in Fig. 50–10 does not completely block illumination from the window or obstruct the view. It does block the direct rays of the sun from reaching the window.

Fig. 50–12. There are numerous methods of screening out the sun's rays.

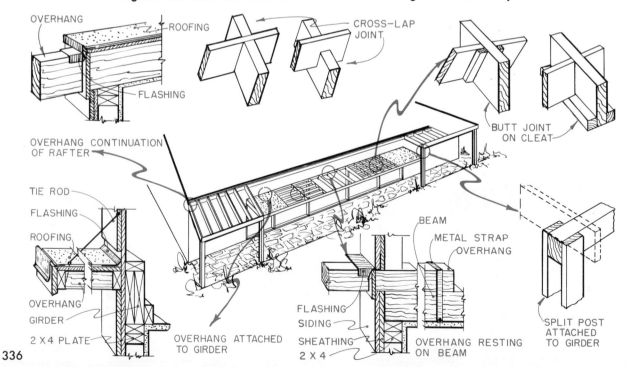

On many patios it is desirable to admit the rays of the sun when it is high and block the rays of the sun when it is lower in the sky. To accomplish this, the angle of the sun should be measured at several times during the day. The spacing and angle of louvers are then set to block the rays at the appropriate time (Fig. 50–11). There are many methods that can be used to construct sun shields of this type (Fig. 50–12). Louvers placed only in one direction will block the rays of the sun from the side perpendicular to the louvers. Louvers placed in egg-crate patterns will block the rays of the sun at all angles.

Problems

1. Name three types of roll roofing suitable for finished roof covering.
2. Name two types of roll roofing suitable for underlayment.
3. Name three shingle patterns.
4. Name the materials used in a built-up roof.
5. Sketch a roof plan for the house shown in Fig. 50–13. With a color pencil, indicate the areas to be flashed.
6. Design a sun screen for the house shown in Fig. 5–6.
7. Define these terms: roof *sheathing, roll roofing, slate, shingles, underlayment, square, roofing-felt, flashing, pole gutter, fascia board, louvers.*

Western Pine Association; National Lumber Manufacturers Association

Fig. 50–13. Indicate the areas to be flashed on a roof plan of this roof.

8. Draw flashing and gutter details for the house shown in Fig. 50–14. Also draw a section through the cornice.

Southern California Gas Co. Samuel Cabot Inc.

Fig. 50–14. Draw roof details for this house.

SECTION TWELVE. SCHEDULES AND SPECIFICATIONS

The plans and drawings of a building are documents prepared to ensure that the building will be constructed as planned. It is sometimes difficult or impossible to show on the drawings all details pertaining to the construction of a building. All features not shown on a drawing should be listed in a schedule or in the specifications.

A *schedule* is a chart of materials and products. Most plans include a window, door, and interior-finish schedule. Schedules are also prepared for exterior finishes, electrical fixtures, and plumbing fixtures. Schedules can also be prepared for equipment and furnishings specified for the building.

Specifications are lists of details and products to be included in the building. Specifications may be rather brief descriptions of the materials needed, or they may be complete specifications which list the size, manufacturer, grade, color, style, and price of each item of material to be ordered.

Unit 51. Door and Window Schedules

Door and window schedules conserve time and space on the drawing. Rather than include all the information about a door or window on the drawing, a key number or letter is attached to each door and window (Fig. 51–1). This symbol is then keyed to the door and window schedule, which includes the width, height, material, type, quantity, and other general information about each window or door (Fig. 51–2). Window schedules eliminate space consuming notes on drawings.

Figure 51–3 shows some of the basic information included in a door schedule. In addition to the information shown in chart form on the door and window schedule, the door or window design is often drawn separately and indexed to the schedule. Figure 51–4 shows exterior door designs, which may be drawn separately, thus eliminating the need for this detail on the elevation. Unless an interior wall elevation is prepared for every wall in the house, it is impossible to determine the style of interior doors from the floor-plan drawing. Figure 51–5 shows drawings of interior door styles which may be indexed to the door schedule.

Window styles are normally depicted on the elevation drawing and complete information included in the window schedule. However, to conserve time many architectural draftsmen draw a separate window detail and show only the window outline and the schedule key for that window on the elevation drawing.

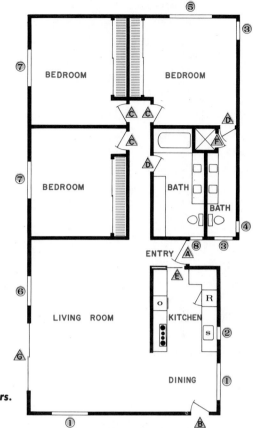

Fig. 51–1. Key numbers.

Fig. 51–2. The key symbol is indexed to a door and window schedule.

DOOR SCHEDULE

Symbol	Width	Height	Thickness	Material	Type	Screen	Quantity	Threshold	Remarks	Manufacturer
A	3'-0''	7'-0''	1¾''	Wood—Ash	Slab core	No	1	Oak	Outdoor varnish	A. D. & D. Door, Inc.
B	2'-6''	7'-0''	1¾''	Wood—Ash	Slab core	Yes	1	Oak	Oil stain	A. D. & D. Door, Inc.
C	2'-3''	6'-8''	1⅜''	Wood—Oak	Hollow core	No	3	None	Oil stain	A. D. & D. Door, Inc.
D	2'-0''	6'-8''	1⅜''	Wood—Ash	Hollow core	No	2	None	Oil stain	A. D. & D. Door, Inc.
E	2'-3''	6'-8''	1¼''	Wood—Fir	Plywood	No	1	None	Sliding door	A. D. & D. Door, Inc.
F	1'-9''	5'-6''	½''	Glass & metal	Shower door	No	1	None	Frosted glass	A. D. & D. Door, Inc.
G	4'-6''	6'-6''	½''	Glass & metal	Sliding	Yes	2	Metal	1 sliding screen	A. D. & D. Door, Inc.

WINDOW SCHEDULE

Symbol	Width	Height	Material	Type	Screen	Quantity	Remarks	Manufacturer	Catalog number
1	5'-0''	4'-0''	Aluminum	Stationary	No	2		A & B Glass Co.	18BW
2	2'-9''	3'-0''	Aluminum	Louver	Yes	1		A & B Glass Co.	23JW
3	2'-6''	3'-0''	Wood	Double Hung	Yes	2	4 Lites—2 High	A & B Glass Co.	141PW
4	1'-6''	1'-6''	Aluminum	Louver	Yes	1		Hampton Glass Co.	972BW
5	6'-0''	3'-6''	Aluminum	Louvered Sides	Yes	1		Hampton Glass Co.	417CW
6	4'-0''	6'-6''	Aluminum	Stationary	No	1		H & W Window Co.	57DH
7	5'-0''	3'-6''	Aluminum	Sliding	Yes	2	Frosted Glass	H & W Window Co.	22DH
8	1'-9''	3'-0''	Aluminum	Awning	Yes	1		H & W Window Co.	1711JB

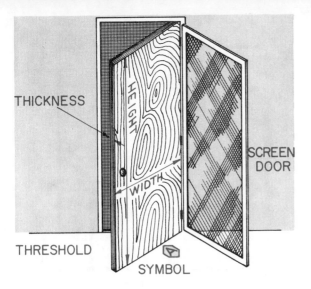

THICKNESS
HEIGHT
WIDTH
SCREEN DOOR
THRESHOLD
SYMBOL

Fig. 51-3. Basic information included on a door schedule.

FLUSH   PANEL

BLIND OR SUMMER   FRENCH OR CASEMENT

Fig. 51-5. Interior door designs.

Problems

1. Prepare a door schedule for the plan shown in Fig. 51–6.
2. Prepare a separate drawing showing the several styles of doors you would recommend for the exterior doors shown in Fig. 51–6.
3. Draw the designs you would recommend for the interior doors shown in Fig. 51–6.
4. Prepare a window schedule for the windows shown in Fig. 51–6.
5. Prepare a drawing of each of the window styles you would recommend for the windows shown in Fig. 51–6. Give the manufacturer's name and catalog number for each door and window in your schedule.
6. Prepare a door and window schedule for the windows and doors in your classroom.
7. Prepare a door and window schedule for the doors and windows in your home.
8. Define these architectural terms: *schedule, specifications, sliding window, awning window, double-hung window, panel door, flush door, french door, dutch door.*

Fig. 51-4. Exterior door designs.

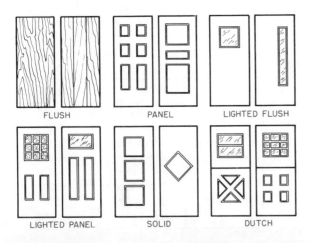

FLUSH   PANEL   LIGHTED FLUSH

LIGHTED PANEL   SOLID   DUTCH

Fig. 51-6. Prepare a door and window schedule for this plan.

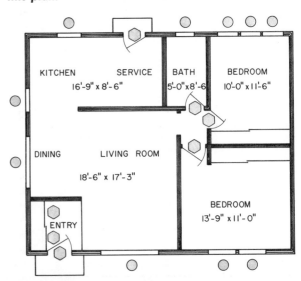

KITCHEN
16'-9" x 8'-6"

SERVICE

BATH
5'-0"x8'-6"

BEDROOM
10'-0"x11'-6"

DINING

LIVING ROOM
18'-6" x 17'-3"

BEDROOM
13'-9" x11'-0"

ENTRY

Unit 52. Finish Schedules

Many types of finishes are used on the interior and the exterior of a building.

▶ Paint Schedule

To describe the type of finish enamel, paint, and stain, and the amount of gloss and color of each finish for each room would require an exhaustive list with many duplications. A *finishing schedule* is a chart which enables the designer to condense all this information. The interior-finish schedule shown in Fig. 52–1 includes, in the horizontal column, the parts of each room and the type of finish and, in the vertical column, information pertaining to the application of the finish. The exact color classification has been noted in the appropriate

intersecting block. When a schedule of this type is used, one schedule is prepared for each room.

▶ Materials Schedule

To ensure that all floor, wall, and ceiling coverings blend with the overall decor in each room, an interior-finish schedule can be prepared with all the possible materials—slate, plaster, wood paneling, tile—listed for each part of the room in the horizontal column; the rooms are listed in the vertical column. The appropriate block can be checked for the suitable material for the ceiling, wall, wainscoting, base, and floor of each room (Fig. 52–2). When a schedule is prepared in this manner, it is easy to read and facilitates checking the color

Fig. 52–1. Paint schedule.

Rooms	Floor			Ceiling					Wall					Base					Trim					Remarks
	Floor varnish	Unfinished	Waxed	Enamel gloss	Enamel semigloss	Enamel flat	Zolotone	Stain	Enamel gloss	Enamel semigloss	Enamel flat	Zolotone	Stain	Enamel gloss	Enamel semigloss	Enamel flat	Zolotone	Stain	Enamel gloss	Enamel semigloss	Zolotone	Enamel flat	Stain	
Entry			✓					Lt Brn					Lt Brn					Lt Brn					Drk Brn	Oil stain
Hall			✓					Lt Brn		Tan					Drk Brn					Drk Brn				Oil stain
Bedroom 1						Wht					Grey				Grey					Grey				One coat primer & sealer —painted surface
Bedroom 2	✓					Wht					Lt Yel				Yel							Yel		One coat primer & sealer —painted surface
Bedroom 3		✓				Wht							Lt Brn		Drk Brn								Tan	One coat primer & sealer —painted surface
Bath 1	✓			Wht					Wht					Lt Blue					Lt Blue					Water-resistant finishes
Bath 2				Wht					Wht					Lt Blue					Lt Blue					Water-resistant finishes
Closets	✓						Brn					Brn					Brn				Brn			
Kitchen			✓		Wht				Yel					Yel					Yel					
Dining			✓				Tan			Yel					Yel				Yel					Oil stain
Living		✓					Tan						Lt Brn					Lt Brn					Lt Brn	Oil stain

Rooms	Floor										Ceiling				Wall			Wainscot					Base					Remarks
	Asphalt tile	Ceramic tile	Cork tile	Linoleum tile	Wood strip—oak	Wood sqs.—oak	Plywood Panel	Carpeting	Slate	Diato	Plaster	Wood panel	Acoustical tile	Exposed beam	Plaster	Wood panel	Wall paper	Wood	Ceramic tile	Paper	Asphalt tile	Stone veneer	Linoleum	Wood	Rubber	Tile—ceramic	Asphalt	
Entry									✓	✓		✓				✓								✓				Diato step covering
Hall			✓								✓				✓					✓				✓				
Bedroom 1					✓								✓		✓			✓									✓	Mahogany wainscot
Bedroom 2					✓								✓		✓	✓		✓									✓	Mahogany wainscot
Bedroom 3							✓	✓					✓			✓								✓				See owner for grade carpet
Bath 1		✓									✓				✓				✓						✓			Water seal tile edges
Bath 2	✓										✓				✓				✓						✓			Water seal tile edges
Kitchen			✓										✓								✓		✓					
Dining			✓											✓	✓						✓		✓					
Living							✓	✓						✓		✓						✓		✓				See owner for grade carpet

Fig. 52–2. Materials schedule.

Fig. 52–3. Fixture and appliance schedules.

APPLIANCE SCHEDULE

Room	Appliance	Type	Size	Color	Manufacturer	Model No.
Kitchen	Electric stove	Cook top	4 Burner	Yellow	Ideale Appliances	341 MG
Kitchen	Electric oven	Built-in	30″ x 24″ x 24″	Yellow	Zeidler Oven Mfg.	27 Mg
Service	Hot water heater	Gas	50 Gal	White	Oratz Water Htr.	249 KG

FIXTURE SCHEDULE

Room	Fixture	Type	Material	Manufacturer	Model Number
Living	2 Electric lights	Hanging	Brass reflectors	Hot Spark Ltd.	1037 IG
Bedroom 1	2 Spot lights	Wall bracket	Flexible neck—aluminum	Gurian & Barris Inc.	1426 SG
Baths 1 & 2	2 Electric lights	Wall bracket	Aluminum—water resistant	Marks Electrical Co.	2432 DG

scheme of each room and of the overall decor. This type of schedule condenses pages of unrelated material lists for each room into one chart, thus enabling the designer to see at a glance all the material that should be ordered for each room.

▶ Special Schedules

To ensure that appliances and fixtures will blend with the decor of each room, a separate schedule can be prepared for them (Fig. 52–3). Similar schedules are sometimes prepared for furniture and built-in components. By preparing a schedule of this type, the designer can control every aspect of the overall design, including colors, materials, and styles.

▶ Uses of Schedules

Schedules not only are useful in designing and ensuring that the finishing is completed as planned, but also are valuable as aids in ordering manufactured items, such as appliances and fixtures.

Problems

1. Make a finish schedule for Fig. 51–6.

2. Make a paint schedule for Fig. 51–6.

3. Add to each item on your schedules the name of a manufacturer and the catalog number.

4. Make an appliance schedule for Fig. 51–6.

5. Make a fixture schedule for Fig. 51–6.

6. Complete all the schedules for your own home. List the types of fixtures, finishes, and doors that you prefer.

7. Know these architectural terms: *finish schedule, trim, base, wainscot, fixture schedule, appliance schedule, zolotone, enamel, primer, sealer, asphalt tile, slate, diato, acoustical tile, veneer, ceramic tile.*

Unit 53. Specifications

Specifications are written instructions describing the basic requirements for constructing a building. Specifications describe sizes, types, and quality of building materials. The methods of construction, fabrication, or installation are also spelled out explicitly. Specifically they tell the contractor, "These are the materials you must use, and this is how you must use them, and these are the conditions under which you undertake this job." Specifications guarantee the purchaser that the contractor will deliver the building exactly as specified.

Information that cannot be conveniently included in the drawings, such as the legal responsibilities, methods of purchasing materials, and insurance requirements, is included in the specifications. In order to make an accurate construction

estimate, contractors refer to the material lists that are included in the specifications (Fig. 53–1).

Specifications help ensure that the building will be constructed according to standards that the building laws require. Specifications are used frequently by banks and federal agencies in appraising a building.

Since many specifications are similar, the use of a fill-in form is often desirable. Fill-in forms include all the major classifications included in most specifications; and the designer adds the exact size and type of material required.

The following specification outline shows the major divisions and subdivisions of a typical set of specifications. This outline does not include the exact size and type of material included under each category, as these would vary with each

LINE NO.	ITEM COLUMN NO. 2	QUANTITY & UNIT MEAS.	MATERIAL (TYPE and/or SIZE)	UNIT COST	TOTAL COST
	#1575				
1	Interior Partitions				
2		195 Pcs.	2 x 4 x 8'-0" Studs		
3		10 Pcs.	2 x 4 x 10'-0" Studs		
4		14 Pcs.	2 x 4 x 12'-0" Studs		
5		870 Lin. Ft.	2 x 4 Plates		
6		48 Lin. Ft.	2 x 6 Headers		
7		3 Pcs.	2 x 8 x 10'-0" Headers		
8		2 Pcs.	2 x 8 x 14'-0" Headers		
9		2 Pcs.	2 x 12 x 12'-0" Headers		
10		7 Pcs.	2 x 8 x 8'-0" Studs		
11		3 Pcs.	2 x 8 x 6'-0" Plates		
12					
13	Ceiling Framing				
14		26 Pcs.	2 x 6 x 12'-0" Ceiling Joist		
15					
16	Roof Framing				
17		16 Units	24'-0" 3/12 Pitch 2 x 6 Trusses		
18		76 Pcs.	2 x 6 x 16'-0" Rafters		
19		24 Pcs.	2 x 6 x 12'-0" Rake Rafters		
20		2800 Sq. Ft.	Roof Sheathing		
21		5600 Sq. Ft.	15# Felt		
22		9 Pcs.	2 x 6 x 10'-0" Rafters		
23	Balcony Framing				
24		24 Lin. Ft.	2 x 6 Joist Trimmers		
25		230 Lin. Ft.	2 x 6 S 4 S Plank Flooring		
26					
27	Roofing & Sheet Metal				
28		1 Square	Asphalt Ridge Shingles		
29		28 Squares	Asphalt Self Sealing Shingles		
30		284 Lin. Ft.	Metal Drip Edging		
31		90 Pcs.	5" x 7" Metal Drip Edging		
32		16 Lin. Ft.	Window Head Flashing		
33		24 Lin. Ft.	Roof to Wall Flashing		
34		13 Lin. Ft.	Chimney Counter Flashing		
35		140 Lbs.	Roofing Nails		
36					
37	Windows				
38		15 Single	4'-0"x3'-0" Aluminum Gliding Windows-Loose Casing		
39		4 Single	4'x80" Fixed Plate Glass - Loose Casing		
40		1 Each Right			
41		4 Left	40x24"-36" Fixed Plate Glass 3/12 Pitch		
42			Sloping Head - Loose Casing		
43		1 Each Right			
44		4 Left	26"x104"-110" Fixed Plate Glass 3/12 Pitch		
45			Sloping Head - Loose Casing		
46		2 Singles	26"x92" Fixed Plate Glass - Loose Casing		
47		1 Single	8"x80" Fixed Plate Glass - Loose Casing		
48		4 Single	4'-78" Fixed Plate Glass - Loose Casing		
49	Door Frames	1 Front	'7'-0" Rabbeted 1-3/4" 5/4 x 6" Casing		
9		1'-9"	Rabbeted 1-3/4" 5/4 x 6" Casing		
		9'	1mm" Glass Sliding Casing		

Fig. 53-1. Part of a contractor's materials list.

building. You will notice that the sequence of the outline roughly approximates the sequence of actual construction.

Specifications Outline

Owner's name and address
Contractor's name and address
Location of new structure

1. *General information*
   List of all drawings, specifications, legal documents
   Allowances of money for special orders, such as wallpaper, carpeting, fixtures
   Completion date
   Contractor's bid
   List of manufactured items bought for the job
   Guarantees for all manufactured items

2. *Legal responsibilities—contractor*
   Good workmanship
   Adherence to plans and specifications
   Fulfillment of building laws
   Purchase of materials
   Hiring and paying all workers
   Obtaining and paying for all permits
   Providing owner certificate of passed inspection
   Responsibility for correction of errors
   Responsibility for complete cleanup
   Furnish all tools and equipment
   Provide personal supervision
   Having a foreman on the job at all times
   Providing a written guarantee of work

3. *Legal responsibilities—homeowner*
   Carrying fire insurance during construction
   Paying utilities during construction
   Specifying method of payment

4. *Earthwork*
   Excavation, backfills, gradings
   Irregularities in soil
   Location of house on lot
   Clearing of lot
   Grading for water drainage
   Preparation of ground for foundation

5. *Concrete and cement work*
   Foundation sizes
   Concrete and mortar mix
   Cement, sand, and gravel
   Curing the concrete
   Finishing-off concrete flatwork
   Vapor seals and locations
   Type and size of reinforcing steel and locations
   Outside concrete work, sizes and locations
   Cleaning of masonry work
   Porches, patios, terraces, walks, driveways: sizes and locations

6. *Carpentry, rough*
   Required types of wood grades
   Maximum amount of moisture in wood
   List of construction members, sizes and amount of wood needed
   Special woods, mill work
   Nail sizes for each job

7. **Floors**
   Type, size and finish of floor
   Floor coverings

8. **Roofing**
   Type of coverings
   Amount of coverings
   Methods to bond coverings
   Color of final layer

9. **Sheet metal**
   List of flashing and sizes
   List of galvanized iron and sizes
   Protective metal paint and where to use
   Size and amount of screens for vents,
     doors, and windows

10. **Doors and windows**
    Sizes
    Material
    Type
    Quantity
    Manufacturer and model number
    Window and door trims
    Frames for screens
    Amount of window space per room
    Amount of openable window space per
      room
    Types of glass and mirrors
    Types of sashes
    Window and door frames
    Weather stripping and caulking

11. **Lath and plaster**
    Type, size, and amount of lath needed
    Type, size, and amount of wire mesh, felt
      paper, and nails
    Types of interior and exterior plaster
    Instructions of manufacturer for mixing
      and applying
    Number of coats
    Finishing between coats
    Drying

12. **Dry walls**
    Wall covering—types, sizes, manufacturer's
      model number

13. **Insulation**
    List of types, makes, sizes, model number
    Thermal or sound type
    Instructions for applying

14. **Electrical needs**
    Electrical outlets and their locations
    Electrical switches and their locations
    Wall brackets and their locations
    Ceiling outlets and their locations
    Signed certificate that electrical work has
      passed the building inspection
    Guarantee for all parts
    List of all electrical parts with name, type,
      size, color, model number, and lamp
      wattage
    Locations for television outlet and aerial,
      telephone outlet, main switches, panel
      board, circuits, and meter
    Size of wire used for wiring
    Number of circuits

15. **Plumbing**
    List of fixtures with make, color, style,
      manufacturer, and catalog number
    List of type and size of plumbing lines—
      gas, water, and waste
    Vent pipes and sizes
    Inspection slips on plumbing
    Guarantees for plumbing
    Instructions for installing and connecting
      pipelines

16. **Heating and air conditioning**
    List of all equipment with make, style, color,
      manufacturer's name, catalog number
    Guarantee for all equipment
    Signed equipment inspection certificate
    List and location of all sheet metal work
      for heat ducts
    List of fuels, outlets, exhausts, and registers
    Types of insulation and location for heating
      and air-conditioning units

17. **Stone and brickwork**
    List and location of all stone and brickwork
      (fireplace, chimney, retaining walls)

Concrete and mortar mix

Reinforcing steel

Type, size, and name of manufacturer of any synthetic stone

18. *Built-ins*

List of all built-ins to be constructed on the job

Dimensions

Types of materials

List of all manufactured objects to be built-in

Model

Make

Color

Catalog number

Manufacturer

19. *Ceramic tile*

List of types, sizes, colors, manufacturers, catalog numbers

Mortar mix

20. *Painting*

List of paints to be used—type, color, manufacturer's name, catalog number

Preparation of painted surface

Number of coats and preparation of each

Instructions for stained surfaces or special finishes (type of finish, color, manufacturer, and catalog number)

21. *Finish hardware*

List of hardware—type, make, material, color, manufacturer's name, catalog number

22. *Exterior*

List of types of finishes for each exterior wall

Instructions for each type

Color, manufacturer, and catalog number

23. *Miscellaneous*

List and location of all blacktop areas

Problems

1. Make a specifications list for a single garage.
2. Make a specifications list for Fig. 51–6.
3. Obtain a specifications list from a set of plans.
4. Define these terms: *specifications, guarantee, documents, contractor.*

Home Planners, Inc.

Fig. 53–2. Sketch a floor plan for this house and make a list of specifications.

SECTION THIRTEEN. BUILDING CODES

A building code is a collection of laws listed in book or pamphlet form for a given community. It outlines restrictions which will maintain minimum standards set up by the Building Department of the community for safeguarding life and health. These laws help to control design, construction, materials, maintenance, location of structure, use of structure by the occupants, quality of materials, and use of materials. To stay within the law, designers and builders must observe the code.

Before anything is built, altered, or repaired, a building permit must be obtained from the Building Department. This permit ensures the appearance of an inspector to inspect the work. The inspections for a house are on plans, grading of land, excavations, foundation forms, foundations, carpentry, plumbing, heating, ventilation, and electrical work.

Building laws have lessened the loss of life and property from earthquakes, storms, and fires. The homeowner knows that when his home is finished, it will be a secure and well-constructed dwelling.

It will be free from shoddy materials and poor workmanship. He knows that his home will have a good resale value and that he will be able to obtain a mortgage loan on it (see Unit 71).

Other advantages of the building codes are that they allow an amateur craftsman to build his own home by supplying all the engineering information necessary for building a family dwelling. Since he does not need a complete version of the building code, many communities print a condensed copy for the family dwelling.

The codes of some communities are better than others because the laws are continually being revised to keep pace with new types of construction and materials. These codes accept any material and method of construction that does the job safely. Using newer methods may save the owner money through efficiency of construction.

Building codes also vary in different communities because of the geographical differences in our country. However, a problem arises concerning such differences. The codes vary in their make-up as well as in their methods of construction, which leads to confusion among builders. A method of construction used in one community is barred in another because of a different interpretation of the law. What is needed is a uniform code that has a simple interpretation of each law. Each community would have this law adjusted to fit the physical conditions of the area. For example, the foundation footings need to be deep in the ground in cold climates. It must be below the frost line where the earth does not freeze. In warm climates there is no need for such depth. The law concerning foundation footings should be stated and cataloged in the same way in all building codes, except that the specification for distance beneath the ground should vary according to the community. Required sizes, classifications and types of materials are shown in building codes.

Unit 54. Required Sizes

Each municipality formulates its own building code requirements. Building codes are necessary to ensure that substandard, unsafe, and unattractive buildings are not built in the area. Building codes also help to regulate the types of structures that can be built in a specific area by zoning areas as residential, commercial, and industrial. Size restrictions are a vital part of every code.

Fig. 54–1. Common items controlled by building codes.

ROOF CONSTRUCTION

CEILING HEIGHT
LINTELS
ELECTRICAL EQUIPMENT
WALLS & PARTITIONS
WINDOW AREAS
ROOM AREAS

WOOD FLOORS

CONCRETE MIX
FOUNDATION

STEEL REINFORCEMENTS

PERMITS & FEES
REQUIRED DRAWINGS
PROPERTY DESCRIP.
ZONING
PROPERTY LOCATION

MORTAR MIX
BRICK SIZE

FIREPLACE

GAS LINES
WATER LINES
GIRDERS
SANITATION
JOISTS
HEATING & AIR CONDITIONING

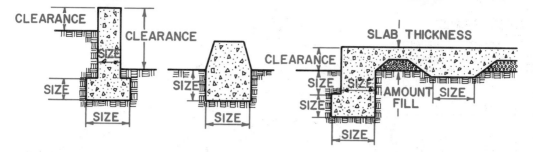

Fig. 54–2. Size, clearance, and composition of foundations are determined by building codes.

Building code information is presented in printed material, charts, sectional drawings, specifications, and pictorial drawings (Fig. 54–1). Building codes also contain regulations pertaining to building permits, fees, inspection requirements, drawings, property location, zoning, and general legal implications connected with building.

Some of the more common items included in family dwelling building codes are as follows:

Minimum room sizes
Ceiling heights
Window areas
Foundations (Fig. 54–2)
Retaining walls
Concrete mix
Girders (Fig. 54–3)

Joists (Fig. 54–4)
Walls and partitions
Lintels (Fig. 54–5)
Wood floors
Concrete blocks
Steel reinforcing
Fireplaces
Chimneys
Roof construction (Fig. 54–6)
Stairways
Electrical equipment
Gas piping
Heating
Air conditioning
Plumbing
Sanitation
Garages

GIRDER SPANS

GIRDER SIZE	GIRDER SPACING	SUPPORTING WALLS	NO WALL SUPPORT
4 X 4	6'	3'-6"	4'-0"
	8'	3'-0"	3'-6"
4 X 6	6'	5'-6"	6'-6"
	8'	4'-6"	5'-6"
4 X 8	6'	7'-0"	8'-6"
	8'	6'-0"	7'-6"

Fig. 54–3. Girder size and spacing are prescribed by building codes.

349

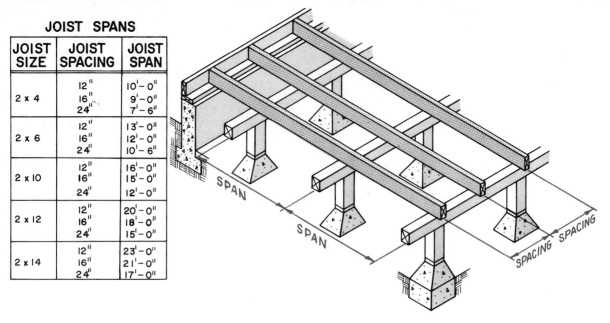

JOIST SPANS

JOIST SIZE	JOIST SPACING	JOIST SPAN
2 x 4	12"	10'-0"
	16"	9'-0"
	24"	7'-6"
2 x 6	12"	13'-0"
	16"	12'-0"
	24"	10'-6"
2 x 10	12"	16'-0"
	16"	15'-0"
	24"	12'-0"
2 x 12	12"	20'-0"
	16"	18'-0"
	24"	15'-0"
2 x 14	12"	23'-0"
	16"	21'-0"
	24"	17'-0"

Fig. 54-4. The size and spacing of joists are outlined in building codes.

Problems

1. Determine the distance between the posts shown in Fig. 54-3, using the building code of your community.

2. Sketch the joists shown in Fig. 54-4. Dimension them according to the building code in your community.

3. Draw Fig. 54-2 and put in the T foundation members according to the building laws of your community.

4. From study of your building code, what other parts of construction can be added to the list of building requirements in this unit?

Fig. 54-5. The size and span of lintels are outlined in building codes.

LINTEL SPANS

SUPPORTING ROOF & CEILING ONLY		SUPPORTING FLOOR, ROOF & CEILING ONLY	
SIZE	SPAN	SIZE	SPAN
4 x 4	3'-0"	4 x 4	3'-6"
4 x 6	4'-0"	4 x 6	5'-0"
4 x 8	6'-0"	4 x 8	5'-6"
4 x 10	8'-0"	4 x 10	7'-0"
4 x 12	9'-0"	4 x 12	8'-0"
4 x 14	10'-0"	4 x 14	9'-0"
4 x 16	12'-0"	4 x 16	10'-0"

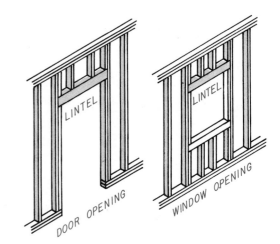

350

5. Does your building code permit the use of pre-fabricated materials?
6. Know these architectural terms: *building code, building permit, cutaway view, legal description, zoning.*

SIZE	RAFTER SPACING	SPAN·ROOF PITCH LESS THAN 4:12	SPAN·ROOF PITCH MORE THAN 4:12
2 X 4	12"	9'-0"	10'-0"
	16"	8'-0"	8'-6"
	24"	6'-6"	7'-0"
	32"	5'-6"	6'-0"
2 X 6	12"	14'-0"	16'-0"
	16"	12'-6"	13'-6"
	24"	10'-6"	11'-0"
	32"	9'-0"	9'-6"
2 X 8	12"	19'-0"	21'-6"
	16"	17'-0"	18'-6"
	24"	13'-6"	15'-0"
	32"	11'-6"	13'-0"
2 X 10	12"	23'-0"	25'-0"
	16"	21'-0"	22'-6"
	24"	17'-6"	19'-0"
	32"	15'-0"	16'-6"

SIZE	JOIST SPACING	SPAN
2 X 4	12"	10'-0"
	16"	9'-0"
	24"	8'-0"
2 X 6	12"	16'-0"
	16"	14'-6"
	24"	12'-6"
2 X 8	12"	21'-6"
	16"	19'-6"
	24"	17'-0"

Fig. 54–6. Material, size, type, spacing, and pitch of roofs are determined by building codes.

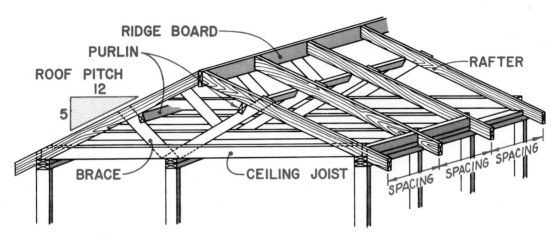

Unit 55. Building Loads

The weight of all the materials used in the construction of a building, including all permanent structures and fixtures, constitutes the *dead weight* of a building. All movable items, such as the occupants and furniture, are the *live weight*. The total weight of the live load plus that of the dead load is called the *building load.*

▶ **Maximum Allowances**

The maximum amount of load permissible for each type of structure is always listed in the building code. The size of the various structural members to support the various loads is also included in the code.

When material-size regulations are compiled for the building codes, they are computed on the basis of maximum allowable loads. Engineers who are drawing up the code determine the correct size of construction members for carrying a maximum load. A safety factor is then added to the size of the materials to eliminate any possibility of building failure.

Structural sizes required by building codes not only provide for the support of all weight in a vertical direction but also allow for all possible horizontal loads, such as winds and earthquakes (Fig. 55–1).

▶ **Live Loads**

Live loads include the weight of any movable object on the floors, roofs, or ceilings. Live loads acting on floors include persons and furniture. Live

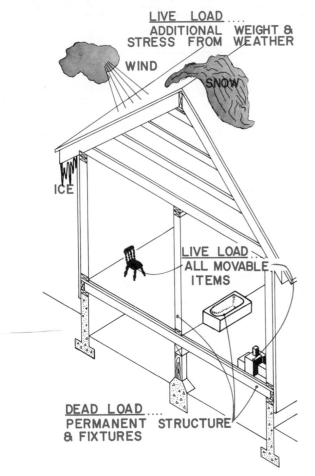

LIVE LOAD....
ADDITIONAL WEIGHT &
STRESS FROM WEATHER

WIND

SNOW

ICE

LIVE LOAD....
ALL MOVABLE
ITEMS

DEAD LOAD....
PERMANENT STRUCTURE
& FIXTURES

Fig. 55-1. Building codes help ensure that the structure will resist and support all loads.

Fig. 55-2. The horizontal load acting on exterior walls is greater than the load acting on interior walls.

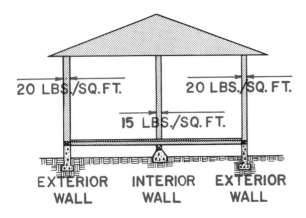

20 LBS./SQ.FT.   20 LBS./SQ.FT.

15 LBS./SQ.FT.

EXTERIOR   INTERIOR   EXTERIOR
WALL   WALL   WALL

loads acting on roofs include wind and snow loads. Live loads acting on walls are wind loads. Lateral loads from earthquakes may also be considered.

Because of the additional wind load that acts on exterior walls, the horizontal load acting on exterior walls is considerably greater than the horizontal load acting on the interior walls (Fig. 55-2). Most exterior walls must be designed to withstand a load of 20 pounds per square foot, whereas interior walls need withstand only a load of 15 pounds per square foot. The type of exterior-wall sheathing differs greatly in its ability to withstand horizontal loads (Fig. 55-3). Figure 55-3 shows that horizontal sheathing will withstand only 1,021 pounds per square foot. Diagonal sheathing will withstand 1,907 pounds per square foot, and insulation-board sheathing will withstand up to 2,179 pounds per square foot.

▶ Dead Loads

A building must be designed to support its own weight (dead load). Building codes specify the size and type of materials that are used in foundations to support maximum live loads. The size and spacing and type of materials used in walls that support the roof load is also specified. Loads become greater as the distance from the footing diminishes. For example, the load on the attic shown in Fig. 55-4 is only 25 pounds per square foot, whereas the load on the first floor is 45 pounds per square foot. However, the typical floor load for an average room will vary from 30 to 40 pounds per square foot.

Roof loads are comparatively light, but vary according to the pitch of the roof. Flat roofs offer less resistance to loads than do pitch roofs. Low-pitched roofs—those below 3/12 pitch—must often be designed to support wind and snow loads of 20 pounds per square foot. High-pitched roofs—those over 3/12 pitch—need be designed to support only 15 pounds per square foot. Since these loads, especially snow loads, vary greatly from one part of the country to another, local building codes establish the amount of load a roof must be designed to support at any given pitch (Fig. 55-5).

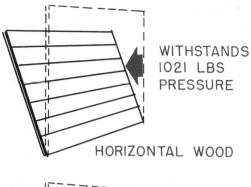

WITHSTANDS
1021 LBS
PRESSURE

HORIZONTAL WOOD

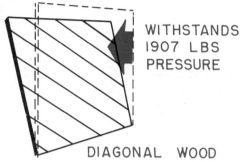

WITHSTANDS
1907 LBS
PRESSURE

DIAGONAL WOOD

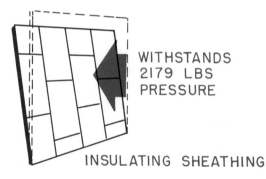

WITHSTANDS
2179 LBS
PRESSURE

INSULATING SHEATHING

Fig. 55-3. Ability of sheathing to resist horizontal loads.

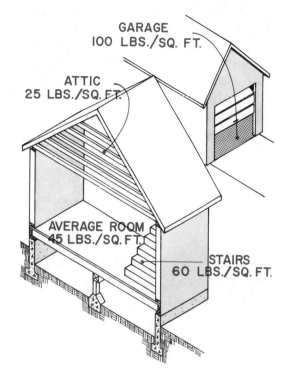

GARAGE
100 LBS./SQ. FT.

ATTIC
25 LBS./SQ. FT.

AVERAGE ROOM
45 LBS./SQ. FT.

STAIRS
60 LBS. FT.

Fig. 55-4. Loads increase closer to the foundation.

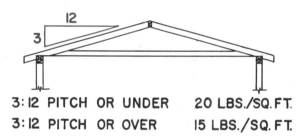

3:12 PITCH OR UNDER   20 LBS./SQ.FT.
3:12 PITCH OR OVER   15 LBS./SQ.FT.

Fig. 55-5. Roofs must be designed to support load limits established by local building codes.

Problems

1. List 20 items used in the construction of a home that are part of the dead load.
2. List 20 objects that are part of the live load.
3. Why is load specified in pounds per square foot?
4. Why is a low-pitched roof constructed to support more weight per square foot than a roof of steeper pitch?
5. If a room has 600 square feet, how much load should it be designed to support?
6. An exterior wall is 8' high and 30' long and is sheathed with diagonal sheathing. How much vertical load will the entire wall support?
7. Define these terms: *maximum allowance, live loads, dead loads, building load, wind load, snow load.*

General Electric Company;
Douglas Fir Plywood Association

SECTION FOURTEEN. ELECTRICAL PLANS

Electricity is the major source of power for the home. Electricity cooks, washes, cleans, heats, air-conditions, lights, preserves, and entertains. But the finest home is not practical if the unseen wiring is not adequate to bring power to the appliances and lighting fixtures. The most important problem in planning the electrical wiring system is to keep up with all the new requirements for power.

Unit 56. Lighting

Seeing involves three things: the eyes, the object, and the light (Fig. 56–1). Planning to light the home involves these three questions: How much light is needed? What is the best quality of light? How should this light be distributed?

▶ Types of Light

Candles, oil and gas lamps were once the major source of light (Fig. 56–2). Today's major source of light in the home comes from the incandescent lamp and the fluorescent lamp.

Incandescent lighting. Incandescent lamps are shown in Fig. 56–3. A filament inside the bulb provides a small, concentrated glow of light when an electric current heats the filament to the glowing point. Following are some of the many types of incandescent bulbs:

Inside-frosted bulbs to spread out the light
White bulbs for softer light for exposed bulbs
Silver-bowl bulbs that direct the light upward
Outdoor projector bulbs for spotlight or floodlight

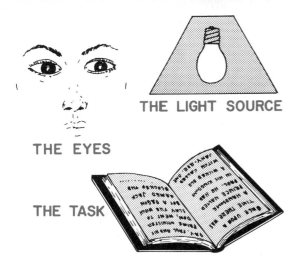

THE LIGHT SOURCE

THE EYES

THE TASK

Fig. 56-1. Lighting needs vary according to three factors.

Colored bulbs for decorative effects
Sun-lamp bulbs for sun tanning
Infrared bulbs for instant heat
Reflector bulbs that are used to display with a spot or floodlight
Outdoor yellow bulbs that do not attract insects
Night-light bulbs

Fluorescent lighting. Fluorescent lamps (Fig. 56-4) give an unbroken line of light, a uniform glareless light which is ideal for large working areas. Fluorescent lamps give more light per watt than incandescent lamps and last as much as seven times longer.

In the fluorescent lamp, current flows through mercury vapor inside the tube and activates the light-giving properties of the coating inside the tube.

Fig. 56-2. Light sources of yesterday.

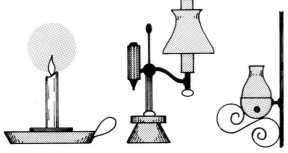

CANDLE LIGHT   KEROSENE   GAS LIGHT
                 OR OIL LIGHT

General Electric Company

Fig. 56-3. Uses of the incandescent bulb.

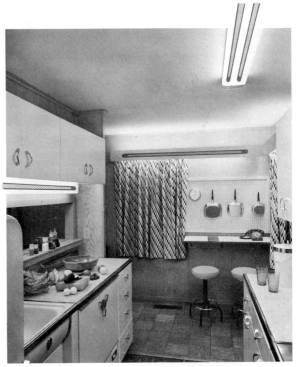

General Electric Company

Fig. 56-4. Uses of fluorescent tubes.

▶ Light Measurements

You can read in bright sunlight or in a dimly lit room because your eyes are adaptable to varying intensities of light (Fig. 56-5). However, you must be given enough time to adjust slowly to different light levels. Sudden extreme changes of light cause great discomfort.

LOW LIGHT LEVEL   HIGH LIGHT LEVEL

Fig. 56–5. Eyes will adjust to extreme intensities of light.

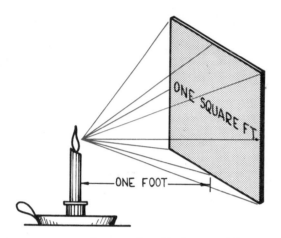

Fig. 56–6. One footcandle of light (candela) is the amount of light thrown on one square foot of surface one foot away.

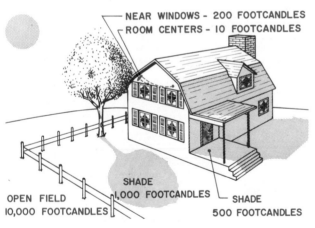

NEAR WINDOWS - 200 FOOTCANDLES
ROOM CENTERS - 10 FOOTCANDLES

OPEN FIELD
10,000 FOOTCANDLES

SHADE
1,000 FOOTCANDLES

SHADE
500 FOOTCANDLES

Fig. 56–7. Light distribution on a sunny day.

Fig. 56–8. Methods of light dispersement.

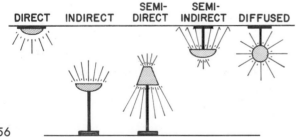

DIRECT   INDIRECT   SEMI-DIRECT   SEMI-INDIRECT   DIFFUSED

Light is measured in units called *footcandles*. A footcandle is the amount of light a candle throws on an object 1' away (Fig. 56–6). Ten footcandles is the amount of light that ten candles throw on a surface 1' away. A 75-watt bulb provides 30 footcandles of light at a distance of 3'. It provides 20 footcandles at a distance of 6'.

On a clear summer day the sun delivers 10,000 footcandles of light to the earth (Fig. 56–7). This is found at the beaches and in open fields. In the shade of a tree there will be 1,000 footcandles. In the shade on an open porch there will be 500 footcandles. Inside the house a few feet from the window there will be 200 footcandles; and in the center of the house, 10 footcandles.

Accepted light levels for various living activities are as follows:

10–20 footcandles: casual visual tasks, card playing, conversation, television, listening to music

20–30 footcandles: easy reading, sewing, knitting, house cleaning

30–50 footcandles: reading newspapers, doing kitchen and laundry work, typing

50–70 footcandles: prolonged reading, machine sewing, hobbies, homework

70–200 footcandles: prolonged detailed tasks such as fine sewing, reading fine print, drafting

▶ Dispersal of Light

After the necessary amount of light is known, the method of spreading, or dispersing, the light through the rooms must be determined.

Types of lighting. There are five types of lighting dispersement (Fig. 56–8): direct, indirect, semi-direct, semi-indirect, and diffused. *Direct* light shines directly on an object from the light source. *Indirect* light is reflected from large surfaces. *Semi-direct* light shines mainly down as direct light, but a small portion of it is directed upward as indirect light. *Diffused* light is spread evenly in all directions.

Reflectance. All objects absorb and reflect light. Some white surfaces reflect 94 percent of the light. Some black surfaces reflect 2 percent of the light. The rest of the light is absorbed. The proper amount of reflectance is obtained by the color and type

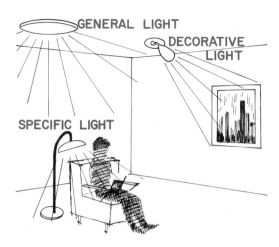

Fig. 56-9. Three types of lighting.

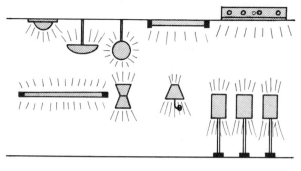

Fig. 56-10. Types of general lighting.

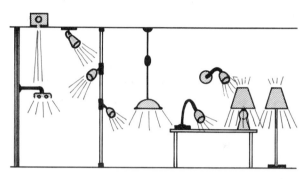

Fig. 56-11. Types of specific lighting.

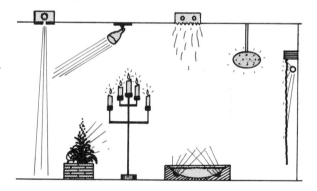

Fig. 56-12. Decorative lighting.

of finish. The amounts of reflectance that are recommended are from 60 percent to 90 percent for the ceiling, from 35 to 60 percent for the walls, and from 15 to 35 percent for the floor.

All surfaces in a room will act as a secondary source of light when the light is reflected. Glare can be eliminated from this secondary source of light by having a dull, or matte, finish on surfaces and by avoiding strong beams of light and strong contrasts of light. Eliminating excessive glare is essential in designing adequate lighting.

▶ **Lighting Methods**

Good lighting in a home depends upon three methods (Fig. 56-9). *General lighting* spreads an even, low level light throughout a room. *Specific (local) lighting* directs light to an area used for a specific visual task. *Decorative lighting* makes use of lights to develop different moods and to accent objects for interest.

General lighting. General lighting is achieved by reflecting light from the ceiling. This light, which should be diffused and without glare, can be produced by many portable lamps, ceiling fixtures, or long lengths of light on the walls (Fig. 56-10). In the living and sleeping areas the intensity of general lighting should be between 5 and 10 footcandles. A higher level of general lighting should be used in the service area and bathrooms.

Specific lighting. Specific (local) lighting (Fig. 56-11) for a particular visual task is directed into the area in which the task will be done. The specific light in a room will add to the general lighting level.

Decorative lighting. Decorative lighting (Fig. 56-12) is used for atmosphere and interest when activities do not require much light. Bright lights are stimulating; low levels of lighting are quieting. Decorative lighting strives for unusual effects. Some

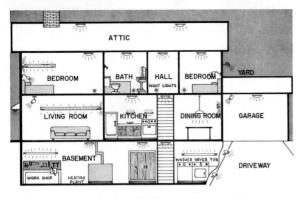

Fig. 56–13. Locations of lighting fixtures throughout the home.

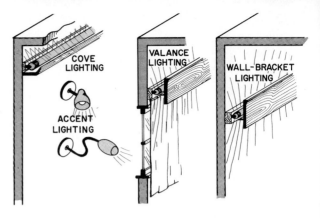

Fig. 56–15. Types of wall fixtures.

of these can be obtained with candlelight, lights behind draperies, lights under planters, lights in the bottoms of ponds, controlled lights with a dimmer switch, and different types of cover materials over floor lights and spotlights.

▶ Electrical Fixtures

The average two-bedroom home should have between 24 and 35 light fixtures (Fig. 56–13). It should also have from 16 to 20 floor, table, or wall lamps. Yet most homes average only one-third of the fixtures they should have for quality lighting.

Light fixtures fall into three groups: ceiling fixtures (Fig. 56–14), wall fixtures (Fig. 56–15), and portable plug-ins (Fig. 56–16).

A *valance* is a long source of light over a window. Its light illuminates the wall and draperies for the spacious effect that daylight gives a room.

A *wall bracket* balances the light of a valance. It gives an upward and downward wash of light difficult to obtain on an inner wall.

A *cornice* is attached to the wall and can be used with or without drapes. All light from this fixture is directed downward, to give an impression of height to the room.

Lamps provide light needed for a seeing task. The bottom of the shade must be below the level of the eyes doing the visual task (Fig. 56–17). The source of light for a lamp should be a short distance at one side of the work area.

▶ Illumination Planning

Following are general rules to observe when planning the lighting of each room.

The kitchen (Fig. 56–18) requires a high level of general lighting from ceiling fixtures. Specific

Fig. 56–14. Types of ceiling fixtures.

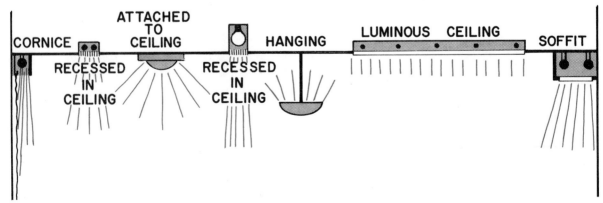

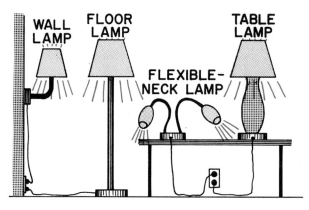

Fig. 56-16. Portable plug-in lamps.

General Electric Company

Fig. 56-18. Kitchen lighting.

lighting for all work areas, range, sink, tables, and counters is also recommended.

The bathroom (Fig. 56-19) requires a high level of general lighting from ceiling fixtures. The shower and water closet, if compartmented, should have a recessed, vaporproof light. The mirror should have lights on two sides.

The living room (Fig. 56-20) requires a low level of general lighting but should have specific lighting for areas for reading and other visual tasks. Decorative lighting should be used.

The bedroom (Fig. 56-21) requires a low level of general lighting but should have specific lighting for reading in bed and on both sides of the dressing-table mirror. The dressing area requires

General Electric Company

Fig. 56-19. Bathroom lighting.

Fig. 56-17. The bottom of a lamp shade should be lower than the eyes.

Fig. 56-20. Living-room lighting.

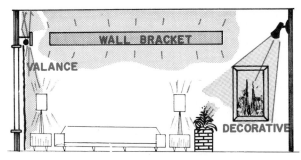

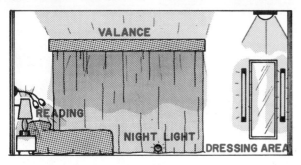

Fig. 56-21. Bedroom lighting.

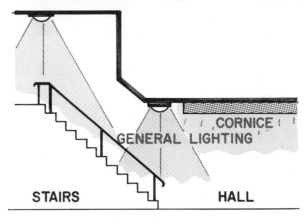

Fig. 56-24. Traffic-area lighting.

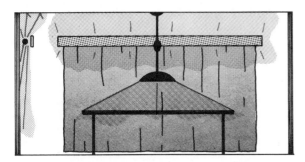

Fig. 56-22. Dining room lighting.

Fig. 56-23. Entry lighting.

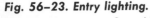

General Electric Company

a high level of general lighting. Children's bedrooms require a high level of general lighting. Closets should have a fixture placed high at the front.

The dining area (Fig. 56-22) requires a low level of general lighting, with local lighting over the dining table.

The entrance and foyer (Fig. 56-23) require a high level of general and decorative lighting.

Traffic areas (Fig. 56-24) require a high level of general lighting for safety.

Reading and desk areas require a high level of general light and specific light that is diffused and glareless. There should be no shadows (Fig. 56-25).

Television viewing (Fig. 56-26) requires a very low level of general lighting. Television should not be viewed in the dark because the strong contrast of dark room and bright screen is tiring to the eyes.

Fig. 56-25. Lighting for reading and studying.

Fig. 56-26. Lighting for television viewing.

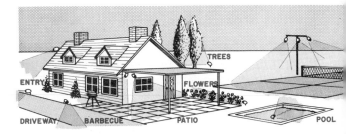

Fig. 56-27. Outdoor lighting.

Outdoor lighting (Fig. 56–27) is accomplished by waterproof floodlights and spotlights. Extensive outdoor lighting will provide convenience, beauty, and safety. Areas which could be illuminated are the landscaping, game areas, barbecue area, patio, garden, front of picture window, pools, and driveways.

Outdoor lights should not shine directly on windows. Lights near the windows should be placed above the windows to eliminate the glare. Ground lights should be shielded by bushes to keep them from shining into the windows (Fig. 56–28).

Fig. 56-28. Outdoor lights should be shielded from windows.

Problems

1. List several artificial light sources.
2. List several natural light sources.
3. List several methods to obtain general lighting.
4. List several sources for specific lighting.
5. List several methods for decorative lighting.
6. On a floor plan of your home, show the lighting as it now exists.
7. On a floor plan of your home, show how you would plan the lighting.
8. Plan the lighting for the floor plan in Fig. 56–29.
9. Plan the lighting for the floor plan in Fig. 51–1.
10. Know these terms: *incandescent bulb, fluorescent tube, filament, footcandle, direct light, indirect light, semidirect light, diffused light, reflectance, valance lighting, wall bracket lighting, cornice lighting.*

Fig. 56-29. Locate lighting fixtures in this apartment.

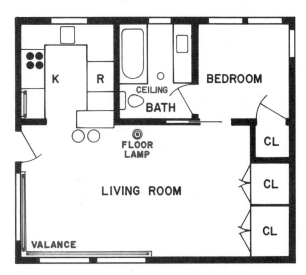

Unit 57. Electricity in the Home

An average home has 45 different electrical appliances, and the number is increasing. In addition to the new appliances, the existing ones are being improved to provide higher standards of performance. The resulting demands for additional power make it necessary to have larger wiring systems for safety and convenience. Electrical appliances cannot effectively serve the homemaker unless the wiring system that supplies the power is adequate.

Electrical power is generated by a utility company and sent through wires to the home by means of a transmission line system (Fig. 57–1). The correct amount of electricity sent over the wires is regulated by transformers.

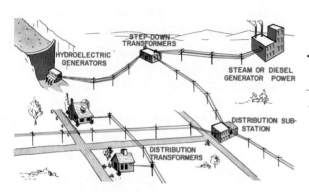

Fig. 57–1. Sources of electrical power for the home.

▶ **Wiring Terms**

Understanding the electrical system of the home begins with the basic terms used in home wiring.

Voltage is an electrical pressure that is produced by a generator. It is this pressure that makes the electricity move from the generator to the home. Electrical power can also come from small generators, batteries, photoelectric cells that convert light energy to electrical energy, and a thermocouple of two different metals that generate a low voltage when heated.

Ampere is the unit by which the electricity that passes through a wire is measured. The number of amperes determines the size of wire and fuses that should be used in the wiring system.

Watt is the unit by which the amount of electricity needed for the operation of an electric appliance is measured. The wattage can be obtained by multiplying the amperage by the voltage (Fig. 57–2). Watts measure the amount of electric power used.

A *kilowatt* is 1,000 watts.

A *kilowatthour* is 1,000 watts used per hour. A *watthour* is 1 watt used for one hour. To keep units smaller, the utility companies charge by

Fig. 57–3. A simple electric circuit.

Fig. 57–2. Properties of electric circuits.

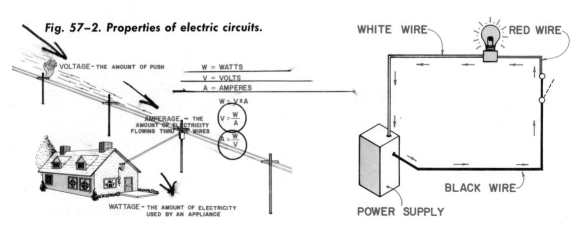

every 1,000 watthours, or 1 kilowatthour. The total kilowatthours used determines the amount of the electricity bill.

A *circuit* is a path for electricity to follow from the power supply to the source and back to the power supply (Fig. 57–3).

A *conduit* is a pipe containing the wires that connect the lights and convenience outlets throughout the house. The conduits may be flexible or rigid, depending on where they are to be used (Fig. 57–4).

Electric current is the moving electricity that is carried by a wire. By applying an electrical pressure (voltage) with a generator, the *electrons* (negative electrical charge) are forced along a wire to an appliance that will use the power. Current is measured in amperes.

Overloading occurs if too much current moves through the wires leading to the electrical appliances. In this condition the wires will become overheated. Proper wiring design and installation will minimize the chance of fire.

Resistance is an electrical friction that tends to prevent electrical current from passing through wires. All materials have some resistance to electricity. Materials that offer little resistance are *conductors*. Copper is one of the best conductors. Materials that offer great resistance are *noncon-*

ductors, or *insulators*. Glass, rubber, and many plastics are excellent insulators.

A *short circuit* will occur when a faulty appliance or exposed wires touch a conductor. The wires heat rapidly and cause a fire.

Service is all the equipment used to bring the electricity to the home from the power lines.

▶ Source

The electrical power is brought to the home by the service entrance wires. The size of the service entrance wires determines the amount of electricity that can enter the wiring system safely. The heavy service wires are connected to the watthour meter (Fig. 57–5), then to the service entrance equipment, with the same heavy wire (Fig. 57–6). At the service entrance equipment is a distribution panel (Fig. 57–7) that sends the electricity throughout the house with branch circuits (Fig. 57–8).

Between the meter and the branch circuit box is a main fuse or circuit breaker. If too much current is drawn from the outside source and heats

Fig. 57–5. The watthour meter records the amount of electricity used.

Los Angeles Dept. of Water & Power

Fig. 57–4. A conduit is a hard shield which protects electric wires.

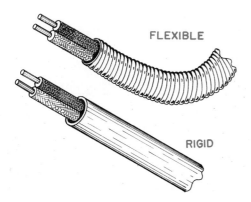

FLEXIBLE

RIGID

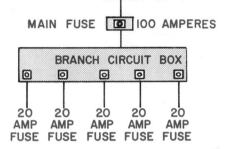

Fig. 57–8. The branch circuit box.

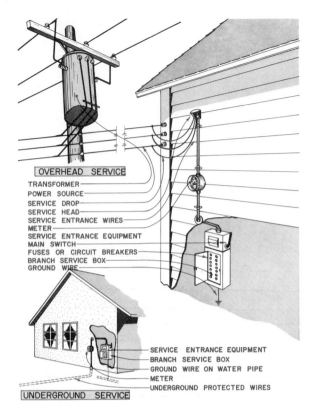

Fig. 57–6. Service entrance equipment.

Fig. 57–7. The branch circuit distribution panel.

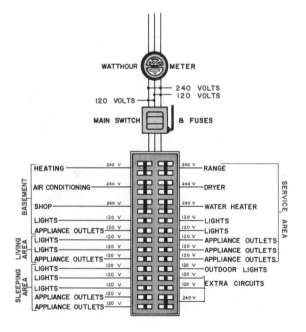

the wires, the fuse will burn out (Fig. 57–9). If there is a circuit breaker instead of a fuse, it will trip itself and open the circuit. In addition to the protection of the main source of power, each branch circuit is protected with fuses. Branch circuits become hot when too many appliances draw too much current. The fuse then "blows" or the circuit breaker "trips." Fuses may be tampered with by unknowing people who bypass the fuse with a penny or insert too large a fuse for the branch circuit, allowing the wires to grow too hot for safety. Before replacing a burned-out fuse, one should turn off the power switch and remove the cause of overloading or short circuit.

▶ **Branch Circuits**

Each branch circuit delivers electricity to one or more outlets. It is necessary to divide the electricity that enters the house into branch circuits so that one line will not have to carry all the power. If the whole house were on one circuit, a short circuit or an overloading would leave the entire house without power.

The size of the service entrance wires determines the total amount of electricity the home can use at one time. The homeowner should plan for more power than needed at the time of building, to allow for future demands from new and improved appliances.

Electricity is delivered at pressures of about 120 volts and 240 volts. Major electrical appliances,

364

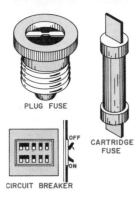

Fig. 57–9. Fuses and circuit breakers provide safety from fires.

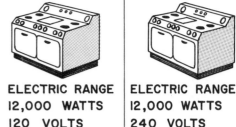

Fig. 57–10. Two identical ranges may use a different number of amperes on different power lines.

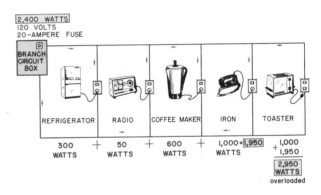

Fig. 57–11. Drawing too much current will overload a circuit.

such as the electric range, water heater, clothes dryer, and large air conditioners are usually operated on a 240-volt system. Higher voltage systems are used where the power requirements are high, in order to reduce the number of amperes, and therefore the size of wire, in these circuits (Fig. 57–10).

To determine the size of service entrance wires needed, the homeowner should know how much current will be needed. In the older-style home, a 60-ampere electric service was sufficient. Today the size should be selected from the following guidance list for homes:

100-ampere service: appliance circuits, lighting circuits, electric cooking, electric water heater, electric laundry. 100 amperes @ 120 volts = 12,000 watts. 100 amperes @ 240 volts = 24,000 watts.

150-ampere service: appliance circuits, lighting circuits, electric cooking, electric water heater, electric laundry, electric heating, air conditioning for small home. 150 amperes @ 120 volts = 18,000 watts. 150 amperes @ 240 volts = 36,000 watts.

200-ampere service: appliance circuits, lighting circuits, electric cooking, electric water heater, electric laundry, electric heating, air conditioning for large home. 200 amperes @ 120 volts = 24,000 watts. 200 amperes @ 240 volts = 48,000 watts.

To plan the size of a branch circuit, add all the wattages of the appliances to be placed on the circuit. The total wattage determines the size of

the wire and fuses or circuit breakers (Fig. 57–11). A 120-volt circuit has one fuse. A 240-volt circuit has two fuses.

The wires of the branch circuits are smaller than the wires of the service entrance. Minimum requirements for branch circuit wires in many areas still are a No. 14 wire with a 15-ampere fuse for safe delivery up to 1,800 watts. It is more convenient and less expensive to use a No. 12 wire with a 20-ampere fuse for safe delivery of 2,400 watts. The smaller wires create heat which wastes power.

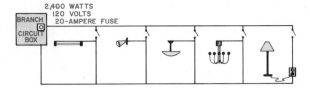

Fig. 57-12. A typical lighting circuit.

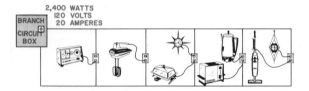

Fig. 57-13. A small-appliance circuit.

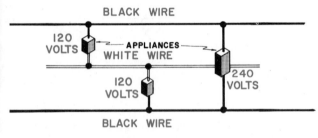

Fig. 57-14. Method of obtaining 120 volts or 220 volts from a three-wire system.

Fig. 57-15. Individual circuits.

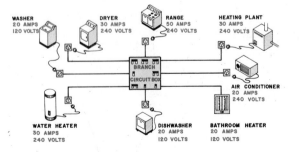

▶ Types of Branch Circuits

The branch circuits are divided into three groups.

Lighting Circuits (Fig. 57–12) provide for the lighting outlets in the home. Multiple lights in one room should be on different circuits. If one fuse blows, the room will not be in darkness. Use a No. 12 wire with a 20-ampere fuse for 2,400 watts for lighting circuits. Lighting requires about 6,000 watts of power. Have a minimum of four 15-ampere fuse circuits for 1,800 watts each, or three 20-ampere fuse circuits for 2,400 watts each.

Small-appliance circuits serve only convenience outlets (Fig. 57–13). Use No. 12 wire with a 20-ampere fuse for 2,400 watts on each circuit. For more power, use a double-branch circuit with three wires and two fuses for 240 volts. With a 20-ampere fuse, this circuit will safely carry up to 4,800 watts (Fig. 57–14).

Individual circuits serve one piece of electrical equipment (Fig. 57–15). Appliances that require individual circuits are the electric range, automatic heating units, water heater, clothes dryer, air conditioner, built-in electric heater, shop bench, and large motor-driven appliances such as washers, disposals, and dishwashers. When a motor starts, it needs an extra surge of power. This is called the *starting load*.

Allow extra circuits and outlets for future addition of appliances. Well-planned wiring gives more power throughout the home for appliances, and makes the lighting more efficient.

The chart in Fig. 57–16 shows acceptable electrical loads and circuits for residential wiring systems.

Problems

1. Figure 57–17 represents a four-circuit system for a one-bedroom apartment. Draw the floor plan to ¼″ scale. List the rooms on each circuit; draw all lighting outlets; draw all convenience outlets; draw all special outlets; draw all circuits; and label the wire size, the line voltage, the maximum watts on each circuit, and the fuse size.

Fig. 57-16. Load requirements for electrical appliances.

	Typical Connected Watts	Volts	Wires	Circuit Breaker or Fuse	Outlets on Circuit	Outlet	Notes
				KITCHEN			
Range	12000	120/240	3 #6	50A.	1	Special Purpose	Use of more than one outlet is not recommended.
Oven (Built in)	4500	120/240	3 #10	30A.	1	Special Purpose	May be direct connected.
Range top	6000	120/240	3 #10	30A.	1	Special Purpose	May be direct connected.
Range top	3300	120/240	3 #12	20A.	1	Special Purpose	May be direct connected.
Dishwasher	1200	120	2 #12	20A.	1	Parallel Grounding	These appliances may be direct connected on a single circuit. Grounded receptacles required, otherwise.
Waste disposer	300	120	2 #12	20A.	1	Parallel Grounding	These appliances may be direct connected on a single circuit. Grounded receptacles required, otherwise.
Broiler	1500	120	2 #12	20A.	1 or more	Parallel Grounding Parallel	Heavy duty appliances regularly used at one location should have a separate circuit. Only one such unit should be attached to a single circuit at the same time.
Fryer	1300	120	2 #12	20A.	1 or more	Parallel Grounding Parallel	Heavy duty appliances regularly used at one location should have a separate circuit. Only one such unit should be attached to a single circuit at the same time.
Coffeemaker	1000	120	2 #12	20A.	1 or more	Parallel Grounding Parallel	Heavy duty appliances regularly used at one location should have a separate circuit. Only one such unit should be attached to a single circuit at the same time.
Refrigerator	300	120	2 #12	20A.	1 or more	Parallel Grounding Parallel	Separate circuit serving only refrigerator and freezer is recommended.
Freezer	350	120	2 #12	20A.	1 or more	Parallel Grounding Parallel	Separate circuit serving only refrigerator and freezer is recommended.
				LAUNDRY			
Washing machine	1200	120	2 #12	20A.	1 or more	Parallel Grounding	Grounding type receptacle required. Separate circuit is recommended.
Dryer	5000	120/240	3 #10	30A.	1	Special Purpose	Appliance may be direct connected—must be grounded.
Ironer	1650	120	2 #12	20A.	1 or more	Parallel Grounding	
Hand iron	1000	120	2 #12	20A.	1 or more	Parallel	Consider possible use in other locations.
Water heater	3000					Special Purpose	Consult utility company for load requirements.

	Typical Connected Watts	Volts	Wires	Circuit Breaker or Fuse	Outlets on Circuit	Outlet	Notes
LIVING AREAS							
Workshop	1500	120	2 #12	20A.	1 or more	Parallel Grounding	Separate circuit recommended.
Portable heater	1300	120	2 #12	20A.	1	Parallel	Should not be connected to circuit serving other heavy duty loads.
Television	300	120	2 #12	20A.	1 or more	Parallel	Should not be connected to circuit serving appliances.
Portable lighting	1200	120	2 #12	20A.	1 or more	Parallel	Provide one circuit for each 500 sq. ft. Divided receptacle may be switch controlled.
FIXED UTILITIES							
Fixed lighting	1200	120	2 #12	20A.			Provide at least one circuit for each 1200 watts of fixed lighting.
Air conditioner ¾ hp	1200	120	2 #12	20A.	1	Parallel Grounding	Consider 4 kw 3-wire circuits to all window or console type air conditioners. Outlets may then be adapted to individual 120- or 240-volt machines. Connection to general purpose or appliance circuits is not recommended.
Central air conditioner	5000	240				Special Purpose	Consult manufacturer for recommended connections.
Heat pump	*14000	240				Special Purpose	Consult manufacturer for recommended connections.
Sump pump	300	120	2 #12	20A.	1 or more	Parallel Grounding	May be direct connected.
Heating plant	600	120	2 #12	20A.	1		Direct connected. Some local codes require separate circuit.
Fixed bathroom heater	1500	120	2 #12	20A.	1		Direct connected.
Attic fan	300	120	2 #12	20A.	1 or more	Parallel Grounding	May be direct connected. Individual circuit is recommended.

* Maximum connected load (range varies from 6000 to 14000 depending on season).

McGraw-Hill, Inc.

Fig. 57–17. Complete the four circuits by sketching outlets and fixtures.

Fig. 57–18. Complete the circuits for this home.

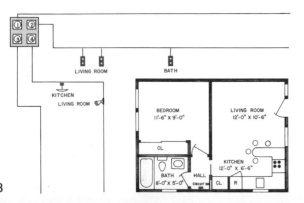

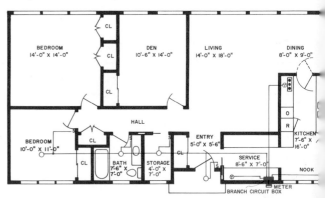

2. What circuits would you add to Fig. 57–17 for future use?

3. Draw Fig. 57–18 and complete the electrical plan. Show all the circuits and label each type. Label the voltage, wattage, wire size and fuse size for each circuit.

4. Define these terms: *wiring system, generator, transformer, voltage, battery, photoelectric cell,* *light energy, thermocouple, ampere, watts, circuit, electric current, electrons, overloading, short circuit, conductor, resistance, nonconductor, transmission line system, insulators, kilowatt, kilowatthour, conduit, service entrance, service meter, distribution panel, branch circuits, main fuse, plug fuse, circuit breaker, power switch, cartridge fuse, outlet, lighting circuit, small-appliance circuit, individual circuit, starting load.*

Unit 58. Planning with Electricity

Wiring methods are controlled by building codes. The job of wiring is performed by licensed electricians. However, the wiring plans for a building are prepared by the architect. For large structures a consulting electrical contractor may aid in the preparation of the final plans. Electrical plans must include information concerning the type and location of all switches, fixtures, and controls.

▶ **Planning Rules**

Basic rules to follow when planning the electrical system are listed below.

1. The main source of light in a room should be controlled by a wall switch located on the latch side of the room's entrance. It should not be necessary to walk into a dark room to find the light switch (Fig. 58–1).

2. Electrical outlets (except in the kitchen) should average one for every 6' of wall space.

3. Electrical outlets in the kitchen should average one for every 4' of wall space.

4. Walls between doors should have an outlet, regardless of the size of the wall space (Fig. 58–2).

5. Each room should have in the ceiling or wall a light outlet that will be a major source of light for the whole room (Fig. 58–3).

6. Each room should have adequate lighting for all visual tasks.

Fig. 58–1. The light switch should be conveniently located near a door.

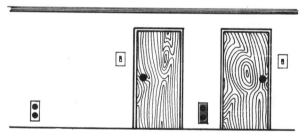

Fig. 58–2. Wall spaces between doors should have a convenience outlet.

Fig. 58–3. A switch by a door should control the main source of light.

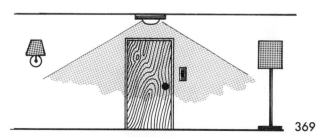

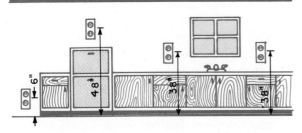

Fig. 58-4. The height of all outlets should be noted on wall elevations or in the specifications.

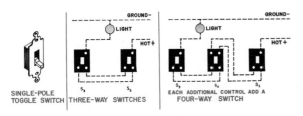

Fig. 58-5. Types of switching controls.

7. Each room should have at least one easy-to-reach outlet for the vacuum cleaner or other appliances which are often used.

8. Not all the lights in one room should be on the same circuit.

9. List the height of all outlets in the house (Fig. 58-4) on the plans.

Fig. 58-6. Three-way switching for stair lights.

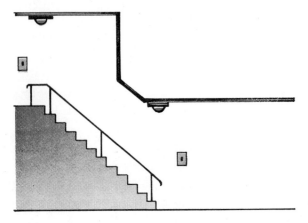

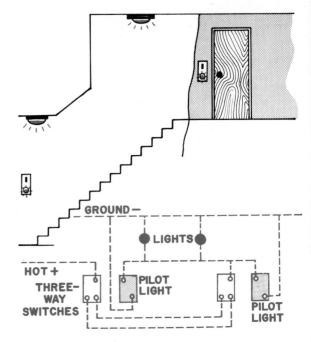

Fig. 58-7. Three-way switches for pilot lights.

▶ Switch Location

Switches should be located according to the following guides.

1. Plan what switches are needed for all lights and electrical equipment. Toggle switches are available in several different types: single-pole, double-pole, three-way, and four-way (Fig. 58-5).

2. Show location and height of switches.

3. Select the type of switches, type of switch-plate cover, and type of finish.

4. If there are only lamps in a room, the entry switch should control the outlet into which the lamps are plugged.

5. Lights for stairways and halls must be controlled from both ends (Fig. 58-6).

6. Bedroom lights should be controlled from bedside and entrance with a three-way switch.

7. Outside lights must be controlled with a three-way switch from the garage and from the exit of the house.

8. Basement lights should be controlled by a switch and a pilot light in the house at the head of the basement stairs (Fig. 58-7).

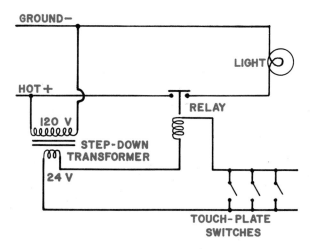

Fig. 58-8. Low-voltage control system.

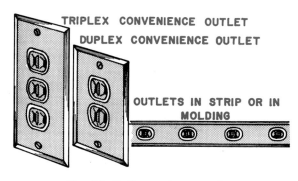

Fig. 58-9. Convenience outlets.

9. Install wall switches in preference to pull-string switches in closets.

10. Describe all special controls to be used.

▶ Special Controls

Special controls make appliances and lighting systems more efficient. Some special controls for electrical equipment include the following:

Mercury switches are silent, shockproof, easy to wire and install, and last longer than the old type switch.

Automatic cycle controls, as on washers, can be installed on appliances to make them perform their functions on a time cycle.

Photoelectric cells control switching at a wave of the hand.

Automatic controls adjust heating and cooling systems.

Clock thermostats adjust heating units for day and night.

Aquastats keep water heated to selected temperatures.

Dimmers control intensity of light.

Time switches control lights or watering systems.

Safety alarm systems activate a bell when a circuit on a door or window is broken.

Master switches control switching throughout the home from one location.

Low-voltage switching systems (Fig. 58-8) provide economical long runs.

The low-voltage method of switching offers convenience and flexibility. A *relay* isolates all switches from the 120-volt system. The voltage from the switch to the appliance is only 24 volts. At the appliance a *magnetic-controlled switch* opens the full 120 volts to the appliance. The magnetic-controlled switch is more commonly called a *touch switch.* The low, 24-volt system permits long runs of inexpensive wiring that is easy to install and safe to use. This makes it ideal for master-control switching from one location in the house.

▶ Electrical Outlets

There are several types of electrical outlets. The *convenience outlet* (Fig. 58-9) is the plug-in, receptacle, type. It is available in single, double, triple, or strip outlets.

Lighting outlets (Fig. 58-10) are for the connection of lampholders, surface-mounted fixtures, flush or recessed fixtures, and all other types of lighting fixtures.

The *special-purpose outlet* (Fig. 58-11) is the connection point of a circuit for one special piece of equipment.

The wires that hook up the whole electric system are installed during the construction of the building, in conduits in the walls, floors, and ceilings. In a finished house, the entire system is hidden (Fig. 58-12). The conventional wiring method with conduits is the most common system. This consists of

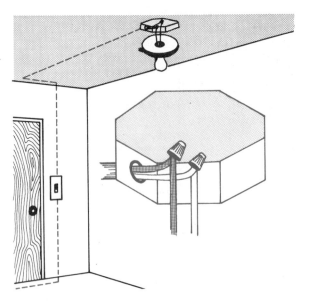

Fig. 58-10. Ceiling lighting outlets.

Los Angeles Dept. of Water & Power

Fig. 58-12. Conduits should be installed before wall coverings are attached.

the *black wire* (hot wire) from the circuit box to the switch. The wire from the switch to the appliance is called the *red wire*. The wire returning to the branch circuit box is the *white wire* (neutral wire) (Fig. 58-13). If the wire is too long or too small, there will be a voltage drop because of the wire's resistance. Another cause of voltage drop is the drawing of too much electricity from the branch circuit. This will cause heating appliances such as toasters, irons, and electric heaters to work inefficiently. Motor-driven appliances will overwork and possibly burn out.

▶ **Electrical Working Drawings**

Complete electrical plans will ensure the installation of electrical equipment and wiring exactly as planned. If electrical plans are incomplete and sketchy, the completeness of the installation is largely dependent upon the judgment of the electrician. The designer should not rely upon the electrician to design the electrical system, but only to install it.

Preparing the electrical plan. After the basic floor plan is drawn, the designer should determine the exact position of all appliances and lighting

Fig. 58-11. Special-purpose outlets.

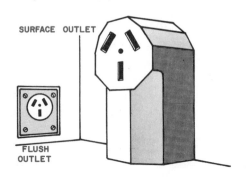

SURFACE OUTLET

FLUSH OUTLET

Fig. 58-13. Convenience-outlet wiring.

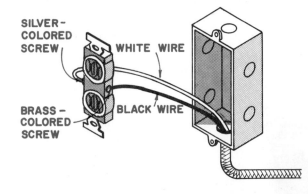

SILVER-COLORED SCREW

WHITE WIRE

BLACK WIRE

BRASS-COLORED SCREW

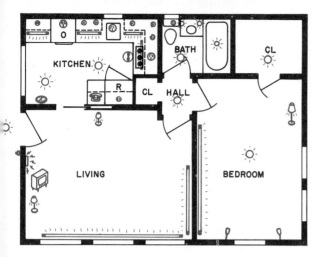

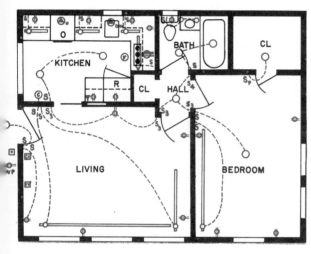

Fig. 58–14. Sequence of planning home wiring.

General Outlets

○ Lighting Outlet

⊡ Ceiling Lighting Outlet for recessed fixture. (Outline shows shape of fixture.)

Continuous Wireway for Fluorescent Lighting on ceiling, in coves, cornices, etc. (Extend rectangle to show length of installation.)

Ⓛ Lighting Outlet with Lamp Holder

Ⓛ_PS Lighting Outlet with Lamp Holder and Pull Switch

Ⓕ Fan Outlet

Ⓙ Junction Box

Ⓓ Drop-Cord Equipped Outlet

Ⓒ Clock Outlet

To indicate wall installation of above outlets, place circle near wall and connect with line as shown for clock outlet.

Convenience Outlets

⊖ Duplex Convenience Outlet

⊖_3 Triplex Convenience Outlet (Substitute other numbers for other variations in number of plug positions.)

⊖ Duplex Convenience Outlet — Split Wired

⊖_GR Duplex Convenience Outlet for Grounding-Type Plugs

⊖_WP Weatherproof Convenience Outlet

Multi-Outlet Assembly (Extend arrows to limits of installation. Use appropriate symbol to indicate type of outlet. Also indicate spacing of outlets as X inches.)

⊖_S Combination Switch and Convenience Outlet

⊖_R Combination Radio and Convenience Outlet

⊙ Floor Outlet

⊖ Range Outlet

▲ Special-Purpose Outlet. Use subscript letters to indicate function. DW-Dishwasher, CD-Clothes Dryer, etc.

Switch Outlets

S Single-Pole Switch

S_3 Three-Way Switch

S_4 Four-Way Switch

S_D Automatic Door Switch

S_P Switch and Pilot Light

S_WP Weatherproof Switch

S_2 Double-Pole Switch

Low-Voltage and Remote-Control Switching Systems

S Switch for Low-Voltage Relay Systems

MS Master Switch for Low-Voltage Relay Systems

○_R Relay-Equipped Lighting Outlet

----- Low-Voltage Relay System Wiring

Auxiliary Systems

● Push Button

▽ Buzzer

◗ Bell

◖ Combination Bell-Buzzer

CH Chime

◇ Annunciator

D Electric Door Opener

M Maid's Signal Plug

T Interconnection Box

Bell-Ringing Transformer

▶ Outside Telephone

▷ Interconnecting Telephone

R Radio Outlet

TV Television Outlet

Miscellaneous

▨ Service Panel

▬ Distribution Panel

----- Switch Leg Indication. Connects outlets with control points.

○_a,b ⊖_a,b ▲_a,b □_a,b Special Outlets. Any standard symbol given above may be used with the addition of subscript letters to designate some special variation of standard equipment for a particular architectural plan. When so used, the variation should be explained in the Key of Symbols and, if necessary, in the specifications.

Edison Electrical Institute (ASA standard Z32.9)

Fig. 58–15. Electrical symbols for residential wiring plans.

fixtures on the plan, as shown in Fig. 58–14. The exact position of switches and outlets to accommodate these appliances and fixtures should be determined. Next, the electrical symbols representing the switches, outlets, and electrical devices should be drawn on the floor plan. A line is then drawn from each switch to the connecting fixture. Figure 58–15 shows the electrical symbols used for residential wiring plans. The exact position of each wire is determined by the electrician. The designer indicates only the position of the fixture and the switch and the connecting line.

Figure 58–16 shows a typical electrical plan of a residence. The architectural method as shown in Fig. 58–17 is used on this plan because of its simplicity. Compare the architectural method with the true wiring diagram and you will see that it would be virtually impossible to complete a true wiring diagram for the entire structure.

Room wiring diagrams. Figures 58–18 through 58–27 show some typical wiring diagrams of various rooms in the home. Refer to the symbols shown in Fig. 58–15 to identify the various symbols. You will notice you can trace the control of each fixture to a switch. You will notice how much more involved the electrical appliances for the kitchen and laundry are than those in the other rooms in the house. Notice also the use of three-way and four-way switches in halls and other traffic areas to provide flexibility and control.

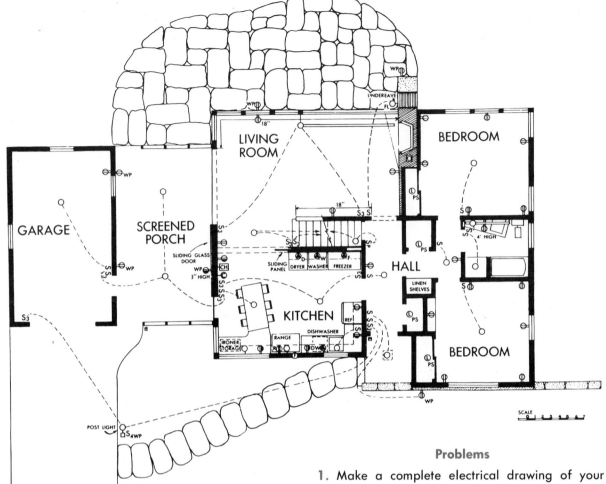

Fig. 58–16. A floor plan complete with electrical symbols.

Fig. 58–17. Architectural wiring plans do not show the position of each separate wire.

TRUE WIRING DIAGRAM

WHITE WIRE

BLACK WIRE

ARCHITECTURAL METHOD

Problems

1. Make a complete electrical drawing of your classroom.

2. Complete with symbols an electrical plan of your home.

3. Complete the electrical plan for Fig. 58–28.

4. Complete the electrical plan for Fig. 58–29.

5. Go to a store and compile a list of new lighting fixtures, and fixtures and parts of the wiring system.

6. Define these terms: *switch, outlet, toggle switch, single-pole switch, double-pole switch, three-way switch, four-way switch, switch plate, switch and pilot light, mercury switch, automatic cycle control, photoelectric cells, clock thermostats, aquastats, dimmers, time switch, master control switch, low-voltage switching system, hot wire, black wire, red wire, white wire, neutral wire, strip outlets, special-purpose outlets, convenience outlets, lighting outlets.*

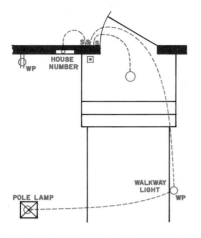

Fig. 58–18. Wiring plan for an entrance.

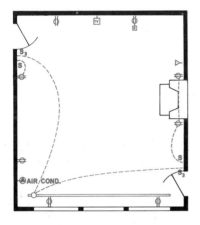

Fig. 58–19. Wiring plan for a living room.

Fig. 58–20. Wiring plan for a dining room.

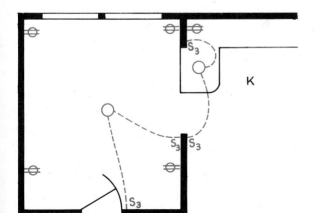

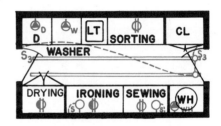

Fig. 58–21. Wiring plan for a kitchen.

Fig. 58–22. Wiring plan for a utility room.

Fig. 58–23. Wiring plan for a bathroom.

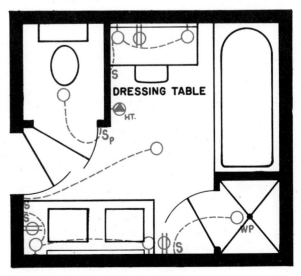

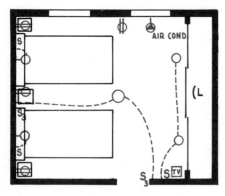

Fig. 58-24. Wiring plan for a bedroom.

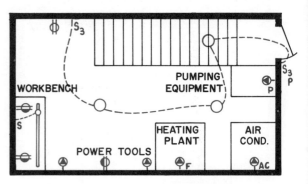

Fig. 58-27. Wiring plan for a basement.

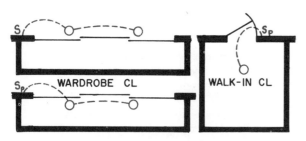

Fig. 58-25. Wiring plan for closets.

Fig. 58-26. Wiring plan for hall and stairs.

Fig. 58-28. Complete a wiring plan for this floor plan.

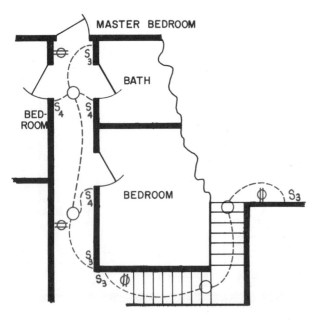

Fig. 58-29. Add electrical symbols to this floor plan.

SECTION FIFTEEN. AIR-CONDITIONING PLANS

Comfort requires more than having enough control to keep warm in the winter and cool in the summer. True comfort means a correct temperature, a correct amount of moisture in the air (humidity), and clean, fresh, odorless air. The achievement of this ideal comfort, or air conditioning, is achieved through the use of a heating system, a cooling system, air filters, and humidifiers.

Unit 59. Air-conditioning Methods

Many different systems can be used to heat and cool a building. The effective use of insulation, ventilation, roof overhang, caulking, weather stripping, and solar orientation helps to increase the efficiency of the air-conditioning system (Fig. 59-1).

▶ **Heat Transfer**

Heat is transferred from a warm to a cool surface by three methods: radiation, convection, and conduction.

Fig. 59-1. Many factors affect the efficiency of air-conditioning systems.

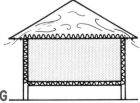

- VENTILATION
- INSULATION
- ROOF OVERHANG
- CAULKING
- WEATHER STRIPPING
- ORIENTATION TO SUN

Fig. 59–2. Radiation is one method of heat transfer.

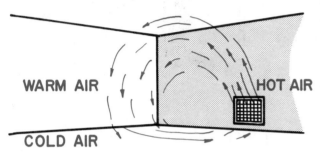

WARM AIR   HOT AIR

COLD AIR

Fig. 59–3. Heating by convection.

Fig. 59–4. Heating by conduction.

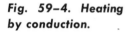

Radiation. In radiation, heat flows to a cooler surface through space in the same way in which light travels. The air is not warm but the cooler object it strikes becomes warm. The object, in turn, warms the air that surrounds it (Fig. 59–2).

Convection. In convection, a warm surface heats the air about it. The warmed air rises and cool air moves in to take its place, causing a convection current (Fig. 59–3).

Conduction. In conduction, heat moves through a solid material. The denser the material, the better it will conduct heat. For example, iron conducts heat better than wood (Fig. 59–4).

▶ Insulation

Insulation is a material used to stop the transfer of heat. Thus, insulation can be used to limit the area to be heated or cooled; it helps keep heat inside the house in the winter and outside in the summer.

Without insulation, a heating or cooling system must work harder to overcome the loss of warm air or cool air through the walls, floors, and ceilings. Full insulation—6″ in the roof, 3″ in the walls, and 2″ in the floors—can save 40 percent of the heating and cooling costs (Fig. 59–5).

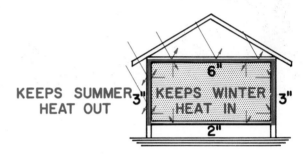

KEEPS SUMMER HEAT OUT   6″   KEEPS WINTER HEAT IN   3″   3″   2″

Fig. 59–5. Insulation stops or retards the transfer of heat.

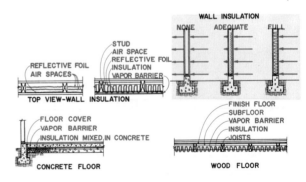

Fig. 59–6. Types of wall and floor insulation.

Fig. 59–7. Ceiling and roof insulation.

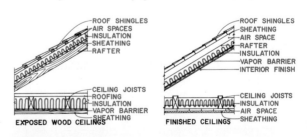

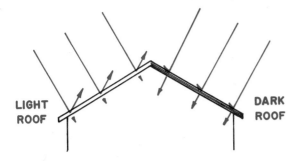

Fig. 59-8. Roofs should reflect some heat.

construction (Fig. 59-11). *Fill-type insulation* is loose insulation poured on attic floors or blown into the walls.

All insulation materials should include a vapor barrier to prevent moisture from condensing inside the building (Fig. 59-12). A vapor barrier may be

Properly insulating walls and floors, as shown in Fig. 59-6, alone can reduce 25 percent of the heat transfer.

▶ Roof

Because most roofs cannot be sheltered from the sun, 40 percent of all heat transfer is through the roof. Six-inch insulation with an area for ventilation above the insulation, as shown in Fig. 59-7, is most effective. The use of light-colored roofs also helps in reflecting the heat and preventing the absorption of excessive heat (Fig. 59-8).

▶ Windows and Doors

Windows alone can allow 25 percent of the heat within a house to transfer to the outside. Some deterrents to this transfer are the use of large roof overhangs, trees and shrubbery, drapes, and window blinds. Double-paned glass is also effective (Fig. 59-9).

In an imperfectly constructed house, cracks around doors, windows, and fireplaces can combine to make a hole of sufficient size to lose all internal heat in less than an hour. Weather stripping and caulking can prevent this heat loss.

▶ Insulation Materials

Insulation is available in different forms. *Blanket insulation* consists of flexible sheets. *Batt* insulation is a flexible roll of insulation. Both blanket insulation and batt insulation are usually covered with reflective foil vapor barriers on each side (Fig. 59-10). *Rigid board insulations* are thin sheets that are used for controlling heat flow and for dry-wall

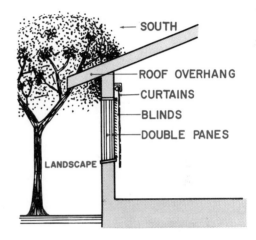

Fig. 59-9. Deterrents to heat transfer.

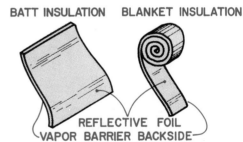

Fig. 59-10. Types of insulation.

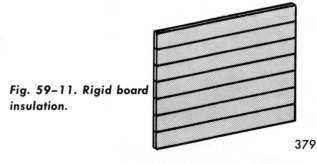

Fig. 59-11. Rigid board insulation.

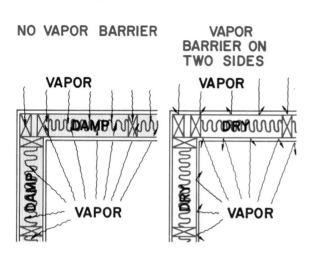

NO VAPOR BARRIER

VAPOR BARRIER ON TWO SIDES

Fig. 59–12. Vapor barriers prevent condensation.

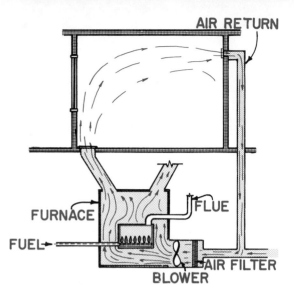

Fig. 59–14. Warm air heating system.

made of thin plastic sheets, asphalt paper, or aluminum foil.

▶ Heating Systems

The two most flexible types of heating systems are perimeter heating and radiant heating (Fig. 59–13).

Perimeter heating. In perimeter heating, the heat outlets are located on the outside walls of the rooms. The heat rises and covers the coldest areas in the house. In this system the main loss of the heat is through the windows and outside walls. Warm air rises, passes across the ceiling, and returns in an *air return* while still warm. Baseboards, convectors, and radiators can be used to project the heat in the perimeter system.

Radiant heating. Radiant heating functions by heating an area of the wall, ceiling, or floor. These

Fig. 59–13. Two types of heating systems.

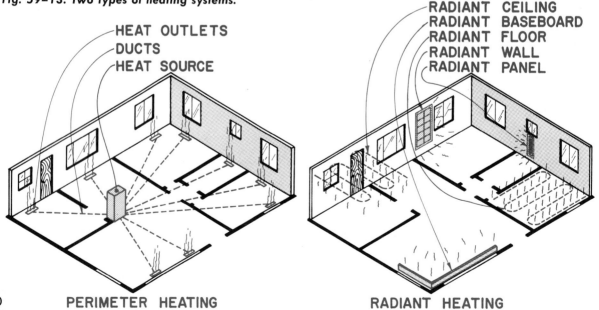

HEAT OUTLETS
DUCTS
HEAT SOURCE

PERIMETER HEATING

RADIANT CEILING
RADIANT BASEBOARD
RADIANT FLOOR
RADIANT WALL
RADIANT PANEL

RADIANT HEATING

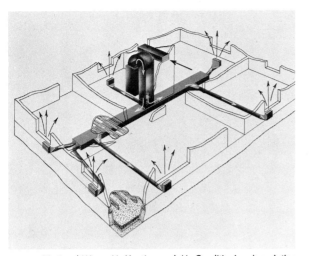

National Warm Air Heating and Air Conditioning Association

Fig. 59–15. Air ducts distribute heated air.

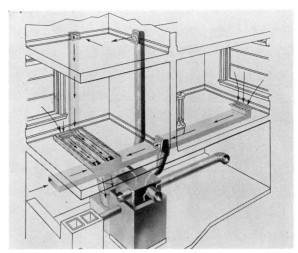

National Warm Air Heating and Air Conditioning Association

Fig. 59–16. Distribution of the air supply.

warm surfaces in turn radiate heat to cooler objects. The heating surfaces may be lined with pipes containing hot water or hot air, or with electric resistance wires covered with plastic.

▶ Heating Devices

Devices that produce the heat used in the various heating systems include the following types: warm air units, hot water units, steam units, electrical units, solar heating.

Warm air units. In a warm air unit the air is heated in a furnace (Fig. 59–14). Air ducts distribute the heated air to outlets throughout the house (Fig. 59–15). The air supply can be taken from the outside, from the furnace room, or from return-air ducts in heated rooms (Fig. 59–16). Warm air units can operate either by gravity or by forced air. Warm air (often called *hot air*) provides almost instant heat. Air filters and humidity control can be combined with the heating unit, and the cooling system can use the same ducts as the heating system, if the ducts are rustproof.

Hot water units. A hot water unit uses a boiler to heat water and a water pump to send the heated water to radiators, thin tubes, convectors, or baseboards (Fig. 59–17). Forcing the water through the pipes with a pump is faster than allow-

ing gravity to make it flow (Fig. 59–18). If a radiant heating system is used with a hot water unit, hot water pipes are placed either in the ceiling or in the floor, as shown in Fig. 59–19. The ceiling is the best location for radiant heating since furniture and rugs may restrict the distribution of heat from the floor. The balance of hot water and cold water lines in a hot water unit is shown in Fig. 59–20. Hot water heating provides even heat. It keeps heat in the outlets longer than warm air units, and it uses a smaller boiler and pipe. Maintenance for the most part involves keeping an adequate supply of hot water.

Fig. 59–17. Hot water unit.

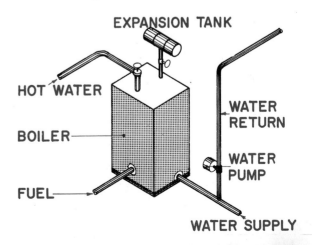

EXPANSION TANK

HOT WATER

BOILER

FUEL

WATER RETURN

WATER PUMP

WATER SUPPLY

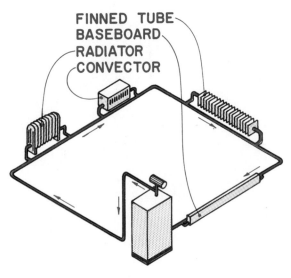

FINNED TUBE
BASEBOARD
RADIATOR
CONVECTOR

Fig. 59-18. A hot water system.

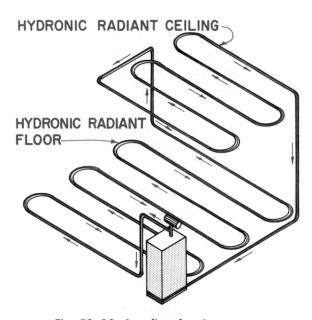

HYDRONIC RADIANT CEILING

HYDRONIC RADIANT
FLOOR

Fig. 59-19. A radiant heating system.

Steam units. The steam heating unit operates by or through a boiler used to make steam. The steam is then transported by pipes to radiators or convectors and baseboards which give off the heat. The steam condenses to water, which returns to the boiler to be reheated to steam. The boiler must always be located below the level of the rooms

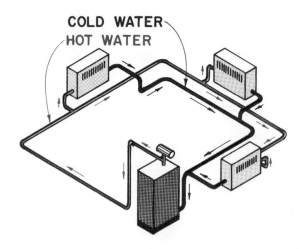

COLD WATER
HOT WATER

Fig. 59-20. Hot and cold water distribution in a hot water system.

being heated. For this reason, steam heat is generally not used for residences but for larger buildings.

Electric heat. Electric heat is produced when electricity passes through resistance wires. This heat is radiated or blown or fan-blown (convection). Resistance wires can be placed in panel heaters built into the wall or ceiling (Fig. 59-21) or placed in baseboards or set in plaster to heat the walls, ceilings, or floors. Electric heaters use very little space and require no air for combustion. Electric heat is therefore very clean. It requires no storage or fuel and no duct work.

Complete ventilation and humidity control should accompany electric heat, since it provides no air circulation, thus tending to be dry (Fig. 59-22).

Another application of the use of electricity and air conditioning is the heat pump. The *heat pump* is a year-round air conditioner. In winter it takes the heat from the outside and pumps it into the house. There is always some heat in the air regardless of the temperature. In summer the pump is reversed and the heat in the house is pumped outside. Thus the pump works like a reversible refrigerator (Fig. 59-23).

Solar heat. Solar heating is simply the use of the sun to its fullest possible extent to help the heating system. The key to solar heating is the

Fig. 59–21. Resistance wires can be placed in the ceiling for radiant heat.

relationship between the roof overhangs and large englassed areas on the south side of the building. Overhangs should be designed so that the summer sun, which is more directly overhead, is blocked off and the winter sun, which is lower on the southern horizon, is allowed to heat the large window area (Fig. 59–24). Summer control on the east and west sides of the building can also be provided through the use of protective window coverings and trees and shrubbery. In summer the trees provide shade and in winter they lose their leaves and allow the sun to enter the house (Fig. 59–25).

▶ Thermostat

A thermostatic control keeps the house at a constant temperature regardless of the loss of heat and the temperature outside. Thermostatic controls may be used with any heating system. The automatic thermostat control should be located on an interior wall away from any sources of heat or cold such as fireplaces or windows. Larger homes may require zoning controls in which two or more separate heating areas work on separate thermostats (Fig. 59–26). One advantage of electrical heating is the fact that each room may be thermostatically controlled. This is especially important in regulating the temperature of children's rooms.

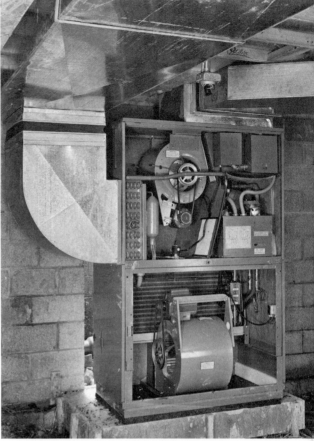

Fig. 59–22. A heat pump.

Fig. 59–23. The operation of a heat pump.

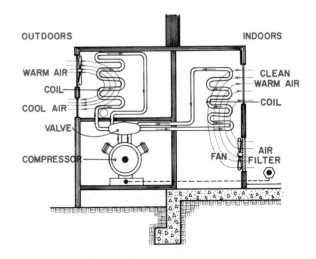

OUTDOORS   INDOORS

WARM AIR
COIL
COOL AIR
VALVE
COMPRESSOR

CLEAN
WARM AIR
COIL

FAN   AIR
FILTER

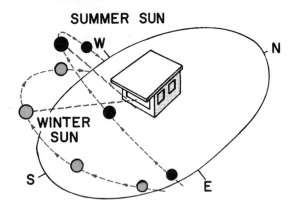

Fig. 59-24. Solar heat should be used to its greatest possible advantage.

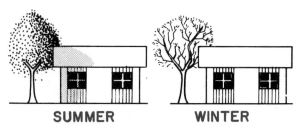

Fig. 59-25. Trees provide shade in summer and allow sun to enter the house in the winter.

▶ Cooling

A building is air-conditioned by removing the heat. Heat can be transferred in one direction only, from the warmer object to the cooler object. Therefore, to cool a building comfortably, the central air-conditioning system absorbs the heat from the house and transfers it to a liquid refrigerant, usually freon.

Fig. 59-26. Large homes may require zoning controls.

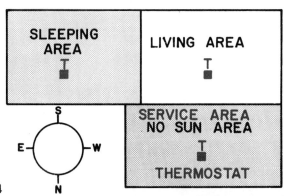

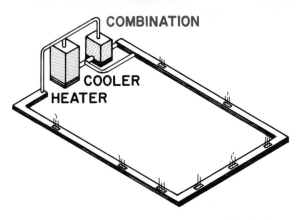

Fig. 59-27. A cooling unit can be part of the heating unit.

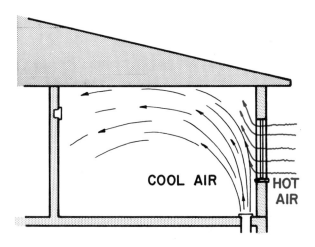

Fig. 59-28. Circulation of cool air.

▶ Cooling Units

The cooling unit can be part of the heating unit and use the blower and vent. In this arrangement, the cooling unit can also use the perimeter ducts (Fig. 59-27). In this system the cool air rises against the warm walls in the summer and cools the house, as shown in Fig. 59-28. The cooling system can also be separate from the heating system (Fig. 59-29).

▶ Air-conditioning Capacity

The size of air-conditioning equipment is usually rated in *tons of refrigeration*. A *ton of refrigeration* is equal to the amount of cooling that would be produced by melting 1 ton of ice in 24 hours (Fig. 59-30). This amount is equivalent to removing

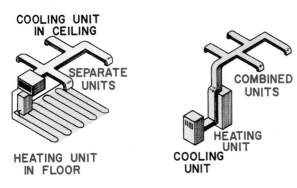

Fig. 59–29. Heating and cooling units may be either separate or combined.

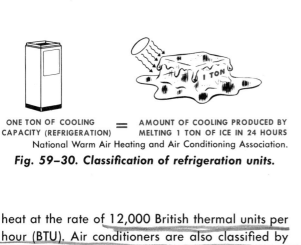

ONE TON OF COOLING CAPACITY (REFRIGERATION) = AMOUNT OF COOLING PRODUCED BY MELTING 1 TON OF ICE IN 24 HOURS
National Warm Air Heating and Air Conditioning Association.

Fig. 59–30. Classification of refrigeration units.

heat at the rate of 12,000 British thermal units per hour (BTU). Air conditioners are also classified by British thermal units. A British thermal unit represents the quantity of heat required to raise the temperature of 1 pound of water 1° Fahrenheit.

The average small home can be comfortably cooled with central air-conditioning units of 2- or 3-ton capacities. A 2-ton unit extracts 24,000 BTU per hour. A 3-ton unit extracts 36,000 BTU per hour. Larger homes may require a 5-ton unit which can remove 60,000 BTU per hour.

Because 1 horsepower of electricity is needed per ton of refrigeration, air-conditioning equipment is sometimes referred to by the number of horsepower used to drive the unit.

▶ Humidity Control

The proper amount of moisture in the air is important for good air conditioning. Excessive moisture in the home comes from many sources, such as cooking, cleaning, and washing, and from the outside air. To remove excessive moisture from the air,

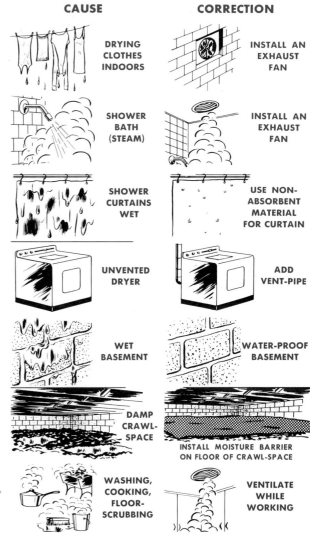

CAUSE — CORRECTION

DRYING CLOTHES INDOORS — INSTALL AN EXHAUST FAN

SHOWER BATH (STEAM) — INSTALL AN EXHAUST FAN

SHOWER CURTAINS WET — USE NON-ABSORBENT MATERIAL FOR CURTAIN

UNVENTED DRYER — ADD VENT-PIPE

WET BASEMENT — WATER-PROOF BASEMENT

DAMP CRAWL-SPACE — INSTALL MOISTURE BARRIER ON FLOOR OF CRAWL-SPACE

WASHING, COOKING, FLOOR-SCRUBBING — VENTILATE WHILE WORKING

National Warm Air Heating and Air Conditioning Association

Fig. 59–31. Methods of controlling excessive moisture in the home.

adequate ventilation and a humidification system is necessary (Fig. 59–31). A *humidification system* takes the moisture from the damp air and passes it over cold coils. When the moisture-ladened air passes over these coils, it deposits excess moisture on the coils by condensation. Conversely, if the air is too dry, the humidification system adds moisture to the air. A device used only to remove the humidity from the air is known as a *dehumidifier*. A device used only to add humidity to the air is a *humidifier*. Portable units can be used to humidify or dehumidify special areas.

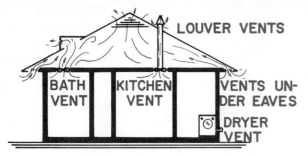

Fig. 59-32. *Effective ventilation helps control moisture.*

▶ Ventilation

Ventilation is necessary to keep fresh air circulating. In the summer it circulates warm and damp air out of the house. Effective ventilation also controls moisture and keeps air relatively dry (Fig. 59-32). The simplest type of ventilation system is cross-ventilation through open windows. However, exhaust fans should be provided in the kitchen, bathroom and attic to remove moisture and warm air. Since large appliances tend to raise the heat of the house by 15 percent, vents also should be provided.

Fig. 59-33. *Locate the position of heating outlets on this plan.*

Fig. 59-34. *Locate the position of all duct work for a forced-air perimeter system on this plan.*

Problems

1. Sketch the floor plan shown in Fig. 59-33. Sketch a warm air heating unit in the most appropriate location and locate the outlets for this system.
2. Sketch the floor plan shown in Fig. 59-34. Indicate the thermostatic zones for this house by using different colored pencils to shade the areas.
3. Sketch the house shown in Fig. 59-34. Locate the position of all duct work for a forced warm-air perimeter system.
4. Define these terms: *air conditioning, humidity, air filter, humidifier, humidification, radiation, convection, conduction, insulation, perimeter, radiant heating, warm air, hot water, steam, electric heating, thermostat, solar heating, BTU capacity, tons of refrigeration.*

Unit 60. Air-conditioning Symbols

Heating and ventilating equipment is drawn on floor plans, as shown in Fig. 60–1. Symbols show the location and type of equipment, and also the movement of hot and cold air.

The location of horizontal ducts on a heating and ventilating duct plan is shown by outlining the position of the ducts. Since vertical ducts pass through the plane of projection, diagonal lines are used to indicate the position of vertical ducts. The flow of air through the ducts can be easily traced.

The direction of air flow is shown by an arrow pointing in the direction of the air flow (Fig. 60–2).

Air flow emanating from the heating-cooling unit is shown by an arrow pointing out from the diffusers. Return air is indicated by an arrow pointing into the duct.

In preparing heating and ventilating duct plans for multiple-story buildings, the position of second-story ducts can be determined by placing the second-floor plan on top of the floor plan.

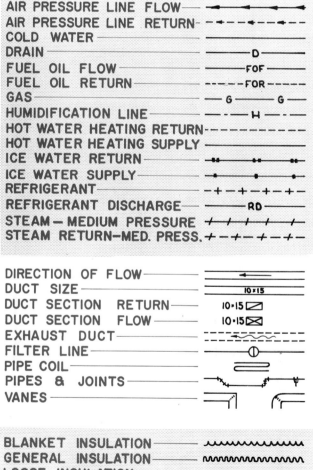

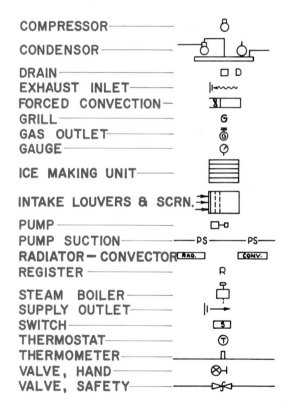

Fig. 60–1. Heating and ventilating symbols used on floor plans.

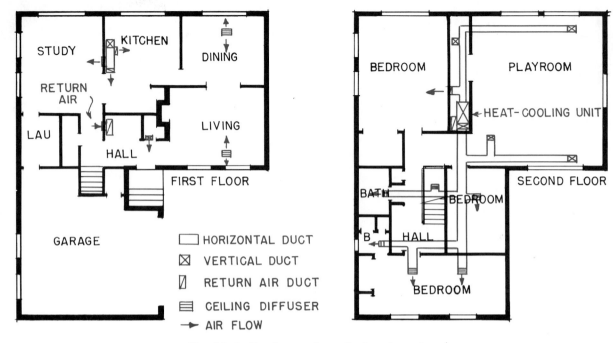

Fig. 60-2. Heating and ventilating duct plan.

Problems

1. Draw a floor plan and insert those symbols which apply to your heating unit.

2. Draw a floor plan and insert the symbols which apply to your complete air-conditioning unit.

3. What type of heating unit is best for your community? Consider the weather and the price of fuel.

4. What type of cooling system is best for your community?

5. Would a separate or a combined heating and cooling unit be more satisfactory in your home?

6. Draw an air-conditioning plan for the house shown in Fig. 60-3.

7. Define these terms: *duct, diffusers, return air, air flow.*

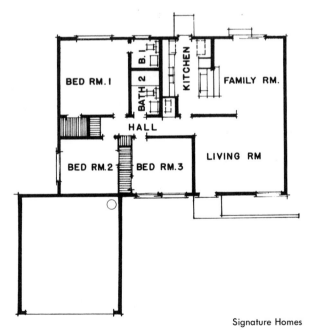

Signature Homes

Fig. 60-3. Add heating and ventilating symbols to this plan.

SECTION SIXTEEN. PLUMBING DIAGRAMS

Plumbing refers to the water supply and drainage of waste water and sewage. A plumbing system consists of supply pipes that carry fresh water under pressure from a public water supply or individual wells to fixtures. The water is then disposed of through pipes which carry waste to the disposal system by gravity drainage.

Prefabricated plumbing walls installed at the factory save the builder installation time by having part of the labor done on an assembly line. If fixtures are placed close together, many feet of pipelines can be saved. The kitchen and bathrooms can also be placed back to back or over each other (in a two-story house) to eliminate long runs of pipe. However, it is important to put the kitchen and bathrooms where they would be most convenient, even if they are at opposite ends of the house.

Unit 61. Plumbing Lines

Two types of plumbing lines (pipes)—water supply lines and waste lines—(Fig. 61–1) carry the water to and from the fixtures.

▶ Water Supply

Fresh water is brought in to all plumbing fixtures under pressure. This water is supplied from a public water supply or from private wells. Because the water is under pressure, the pipes may be run in any convenient direction after leaving the main control valve (Fig. 61–2).

Water lines require a shutoff valve at the property line and at the foundation of the house. The water meter is located at the shutoff valve near the house. The size of all water supply lines for a house range from ¾″ to 1″. Each fixture has a

Fig. 61-1. Plumbing lines are of two types, water supply lines and waste lines.

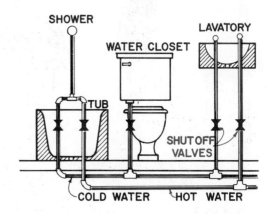

Fig. 61-3. Each fixture should have a shutoff valve.

Fig. 61-2. Position of basic plumbing lines.

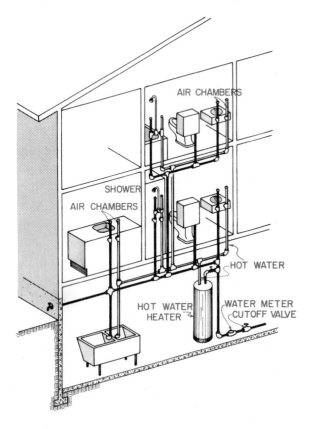

shutoff valve on the pipe to allow repairs (Fig. 61-3).

All fixtures have a free-flowing supply of water if the lines are the correct size. Lines that are too small cause a whistling as the water flows through at high speeds. Air-cushion chambers stop hammering noises caused by closing valves (Fig. 61-4). Too many changes of direction of pipe cause friction that reduces the water pressure.

Hot water is obtained by routing cold water through a water heater (Fig. 61-5). The hot water is then directed, under pressure, to all fixtures needing it. The hot water valve is on the left of the fixture as you face it. Placing insulation around hot water lines conserves hot water and makes a saving on heating bills.

▶ **Waste Lines**

Waste water is discharged through the disposal system by gravity drainage (Fig. 61-7). All pipes in this system must slant down toward the main disposal so that the weight of the waste will cause it to flow toward the main disposal system and away from the house. Because of the gravity flow, the waste lines that run to the city sewage system must be much larger than the water supply lines, in which there is pressure (Fig. 61-6).

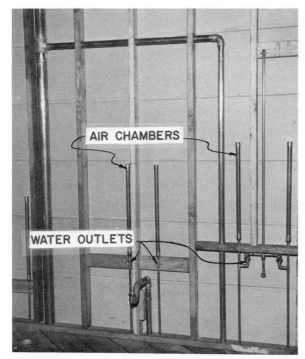

Mueller Brass Company

Fig. 61-4. Air-cushion chambers stop hammering noises.

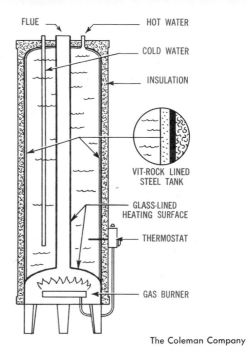

The Coleman Company

Fig. 61-5. Rock-lined steel hot water heater.

Fig. 61-6. Waste lines must be larger than water supply lines.

In the house, the waste lines are concealed in the walls and under floors. The vertical lines are called *stacks,* and the horizontal lines are called *branches.* Also needed are the *vents* for circulation of air. Vents permit sewer gases to escape through the roof to the outside, equalizing air pressure in the drainage system. The *fixture traps* stop the gases from entering the house. Each fixture must have a separate seal to prevent backflow of sewer gas into the house. The fixture traps are exposed for easy maintenance. The trap for the water closet is built into it.

The flow of waste water starts at the fixture trap. It flows through the fixture branches to the soil stack. It continues through the house drain, house sewer and finally reaches the main sewer.

Waste stacks carry only water waste. The lines taking the wastes from the water closet are called the *soil lines.* Because of the solid waste materials, soil lines are the largest in the system. Each time the soil lines are used, they are flushed.

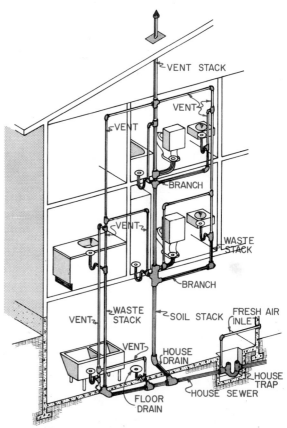

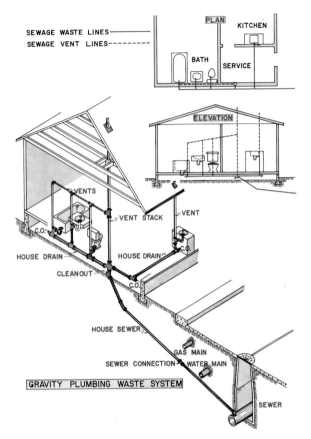

Fig. 61-7. Waste is discharged through gravity drainage.

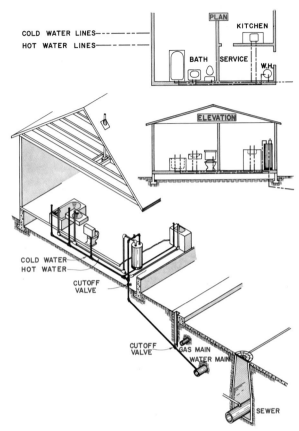

Fig. 61-8. Pressure plumbing and supply system.

The fresh water supply pipes are wet pipes, full of water under pressure at all times. The waste and soil pipes are wet pipes having water in them only when waste water is being disposed of. The vent-pipe system is composed of dry pipes which never have water in them.

Figure 61-8 shows the plumbing and supply system. The systems are usually shown on a pictorial drawing, elevation, or plan. Figures 61-9 and 61-10 show the working drawings for a bathroom.

▶ Septic System

When a city sewer is not available, a private sewer, called a *septic system,* must be used (Fig. 61-11). The septic system converts waste solids into liquid by bacterial action. The house wastes go to a septic tank buried outside. The lighter part of the liquid flows out of the septic tank into the *drainage field,* which is made up of porous pipes spread over an area to allow distribution of water (Fig. 61-12).

The size of the septic system varies according to the number of occupants of the house. The size of the lines and the distance of the septic tank and drainage field from the house depend on the building codes of the community.

Problems

1. Make a sketch of Fig. 61-13 and add the water supply system, using the proper plumbing symbols. Use examples in Figs. 61-9 and 61-10.

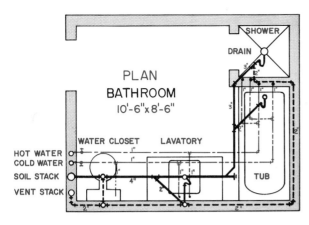

Fig. 61-9. Schematic plan of bathroom plumbing lines.

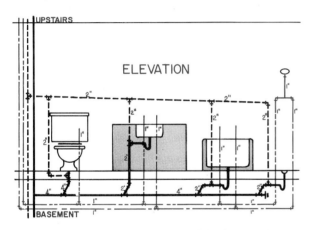

Fig. 61-10. Schematic elevation of bathroom plumbing lines.

Fig. 61-11. A septic system.

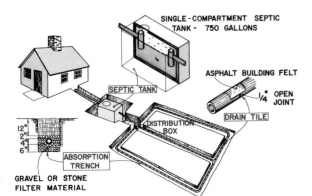

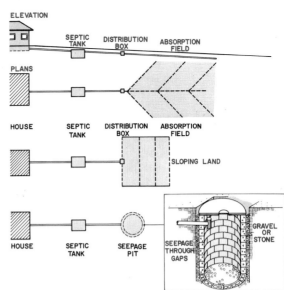

Fig. 61-12. Types of drainage fields.

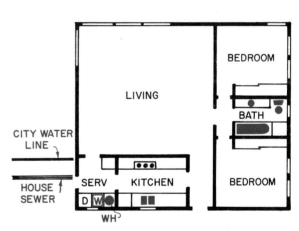

Fig. 61-13. Add water supply lines to this plan.

Fig. 61-14. Add plumbing symbols to this plan.

2. Make a sketch of Fig. 61–14 and indicate a water supply system, using the proper plumbing symbols.

3. Add the waste lines to the sketch you made for Problem 2.

4. Know these terms: *gravity drainage, stack, branch, vent, fixture trap, soil stack, house drain, house sewer, waste stack, septic system, septic tank, drainage field, shut-off valve, air chambers, waste lines.*

Unit 62. Plumbing Fixtures

Plumbing fixtures are available in a variety of sizes, colors, and materials. Since they are used continually for many years, durability is extremely important. Good fixtures are more convenient than poorer ones and require fewer repairs. The following fixtures represent the most common types available in each area.

▶ Bathroom Fixtures

Bathroom fixtures are divided into four types, as follows:

Water closets: tank and bowl in one piece, separate tank and bowl, wall-hung tank and bowl

Showers (Fig. 62–1): prefabricated, built on the job, placed over bathtub

Bathtubs (Fig. 62–2): recessed, square, free-standing, sunken

Lavatories (Fig. 62–3): wall-hung, cabinet, built-in counter-top, corner

▶ Kitchen Fixtures

Kitchen fixtures are divided into five types, as follows:

Sinks (Fig. 62–4): counter, double, sink and drainboard unit

Laundry tubs: single, double, triple

Dishwashers (Fig. 62–5): in sink, built-in, free-standing

Hot water heater: electric, gas

Washing machine (Fig. 62–6): top-loading, front-loading, wringer-type

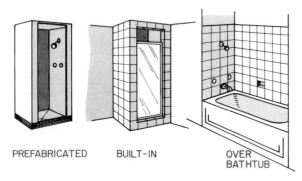

PREFABRICATED   BUILT-IN   OVER BATHTUB

Fig. 62–1. Types of showers.

Fig. 62–2. Types of bathtubs.

WALL-HUNG   CABINET   COUNTER TOP   CORNER

Fig. 62–3. Types of lavatories.

Fig. 62–4. Types of sinks.

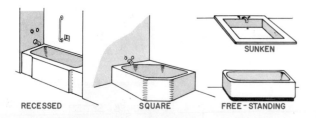

RECESSED   SQUARE   SUNKEN   FREE-STANDING

COUNTER TOP   DOUBLE SINK   SINK & DRAINBOARD

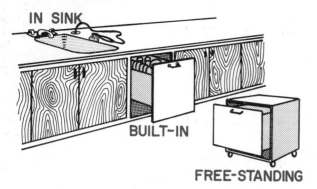

Fig. 62–5. Types of dishwashers.

Fig. 62–6. Types of washing machines.

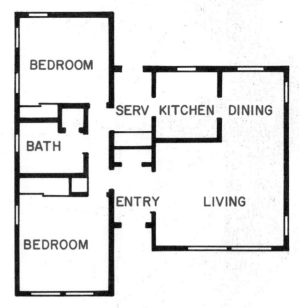

Fig. 62–7. Add plumbing fixtures and lines to this plan.

Fig. 62–8. Add plumbing lines to this plan.

Problems

1. Make a sketch to show the positions of the plumbing fixtures on the plan shown in Fig. 62–7 (water closet, shower, bathtub, lavatories, sinks, laundry tub, dishwasher, water heater, and washing machine).

2. Add the plumbing lines to the plan shown in Fig. 62–7.

3. Add the plumbing fixtures and lines to the plan shown in Fig. 62–8.

4. From your building code, give the sizes of the plumbing lines to be used in the plan shown in Fig. 62–7.

5. Define these terms: *plumbing fixture, water closet, wall-hung water closet, drainboard.*

SECTION SEVENTEEN. MODULAR COMPONENT PLANS

Industrial automation methods have enabled manufacturers to produce high quality and low-priced products more quickly than ever before. However, the home-building industry, which has constructed over 33 million homes for American families, has not industrialized or standardized production methods to any great degree. Construction methods used in the homebuilding industry continue to contribute to excessive waste of materials and time on the job.

However, to standardize and automate more fully the home-building industry, lumber manufacturers have developed a program of coordinating dimensional standards and components on standard structural parts such as windows, doors, and trusses. Standardization of these components enables the part to fit into the plan for any home designed according to a standard modular component.

Using a coordinated system of dimensioning for these components results in the most efficient use of materials and time. The National Lumber Manufacturers Association, in conjunction with Richard B. Pollman, Architectural Consultant for Home Planners, Inc., has developed modular dimensional standards for design and fabrication to help standardize components in the building industry. The system is called *Unicom*. The Unicom method of construction permits faster planning and erection of houses, to the benefit of both builder and home buyer.[1]

The name *Unicom* means "uniform manufacture of components." Unlimited design flexibility provided by Unicom methods facilitates the design of houses in conformity with accepted requirements of the housing market in all regions. Design flexibility is maintained by adhering to simple principles and moderate restrictions of modular design.

[1]All the illustrations in Section 17 courtesy of Home Planner, Inc. and the National Lumber Manufacturers Association.

Unit 63. Modular System of Designing

The Unicom method of designing includes the use of modular components and the preparation of plans to a modular dimensional standard. Using this method, the designer must think of the home as a series of component parts. These component parts may be standard factory-made components or built on the job site. In either case, plans are prepared to be consistent with the size of these components. Plans must also be interchangeable and consistent with the Unicom method of dimensioning. Without this dimensional standard the use of modular component parts is of no value (Fig. 63–1).

▶ Advantages

The Unicom method is applicable to on-site or shop fabrication and is based on standard lumber sizes. Thus it may be used effectively by large builders or by the custom builder who erects only a few homes each year (Fig. 63–2).

Homes may be erected completely with factory-made parts (Fig. 63–3), or the house may be framed conventionally, or a combination method may be used. Faster planning and erection of the house benefit both builder and home buyer. This system makes possible the more efficient use of materials, thus reducing waste in conventional home construction.

Building inventory costs are cut because of the number of elements needed for maximum design flexibility. This saves considerable time. It also reduces the number of items that must be kept on inventory. Perhaps the most important advantage of the Unicom system is that it makes possible the use of modern mass-production techniques. These techniques provide great accuracy in the construction of components and superior quality control in their fabrication.

▶ Designing with Modular Grids

The coordination of modular components with the system of modular dimensions utilizes all three dimensions—length, width, and height. The overall width and length dimensions are most critical in the planning process, as shown in Fig. 63–4. The

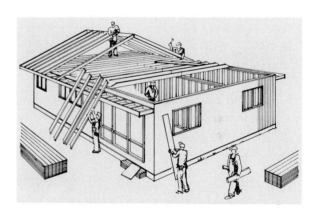

Fig. 63–2. On-site fabrication.

Fig. 63–1. Component parts may be factory-made or produced on the job site.

Fig. 63–3. Shop-fabricated components.

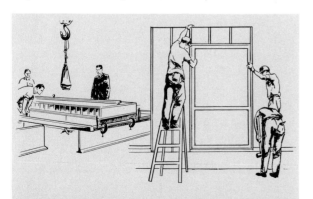

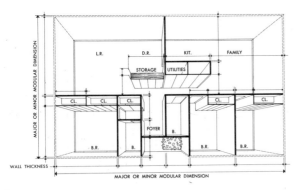

Fig. 63-4. The overall length and width must be modular dimensions.

modular planning grid—a horizontal plane divided into equal spaces in length and width—provides the basic control for the modular coordination system. The entire grid, shown in Fig. 63-5, is divided into equal spaces of 4″, 16″, 24″, and 48″. Composite dimensions are therefore all multiples of 4″. The 16″ unit is used in multiples for wall, window, and door panels to provide an increment small enough for flexible planning and optimum inventory of these components.

Increments of 24″ and 48″ are used for overall dimensions of the house. The 24″ module is called the *minor module*. The 48″ module is called the *major module*. Figure 63-7 shows the use of the major and minor modules in establishing basic

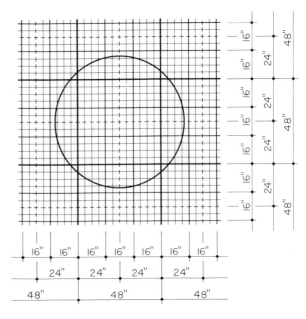

Fig. 63-5. Modular-component grid.

modular house length and width. Figure 63-6 shows the use of the 16″ module in designing locations for window and door component panels.

Since the Unicom method does not require the wall, floor, and roof elements to be tied to a large fixed panel size, there is no need for the designer to adhere to a fixed 4′ or larger increment in planning.

Fig. 63-6. Modular-component door and windows.

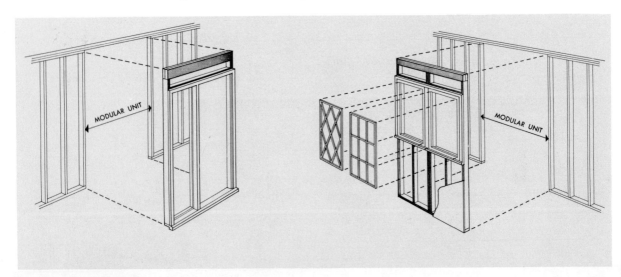

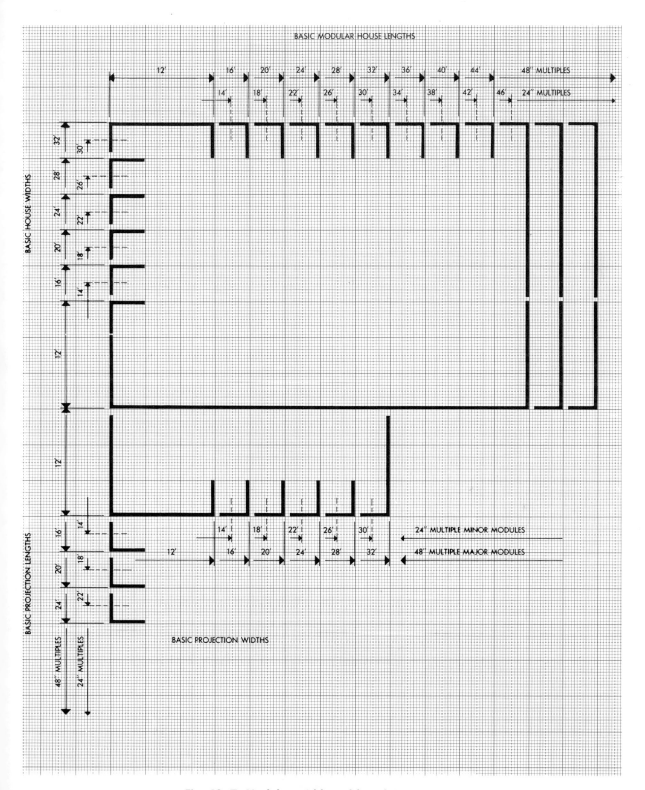

Fig. 63–7. Modular width and length increments.

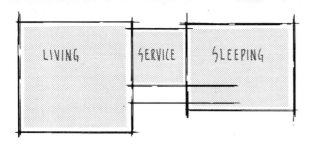

Fig. 63-8. Initial planning for modular construction is the same as in designing conventional buildings.

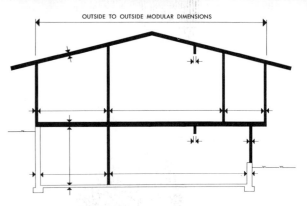

Fig. 63-10. The sum of the wall thicknesses must be subtracted from the overall modular dimension to obtain the net inside dimension.

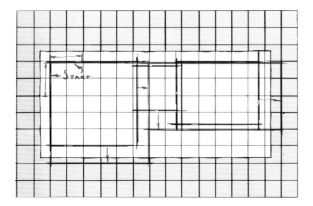

Fig. 63-9. Nonmodular dimensions must be converted to the nearest module.

(Fig. 63-9). Each square on the grid represents the basic 4″ module. Standard 16″ modules are represented by the intermediate heavy lines. Major 48″ module lines are indicated by the heaviest lines. Minor 24″ modules are represented by dotted lines. By employing modular dimensions in multiples of 2′ or 4′ for house exteriors, fractional spans for floor and roof framing are eliminated.

Variations in the thickness of exterior and partition walls interfere with true modular dimensioning; therefore, the total thicknesses of all of these walls must be subtracted from the overall modular dimension to obtain the net inside dimension, as shown in Fig. 63-10. Also nonmodular dimensions created by existing building laws or built-in equipment must be incorporated in the modular coordination system (Fig. 63-11). This end is accomplished

▶ Preparing the Modular Plan

When the basic floor-plan design is completed (Fig. 63-8), the plan should be sketched or drawn on the Unicom modular grid and all nonmodular dimensions converted to the nearest modular size

Fig. 63-11. Nonmodular dimensions must be incorporated into the Unicom system.

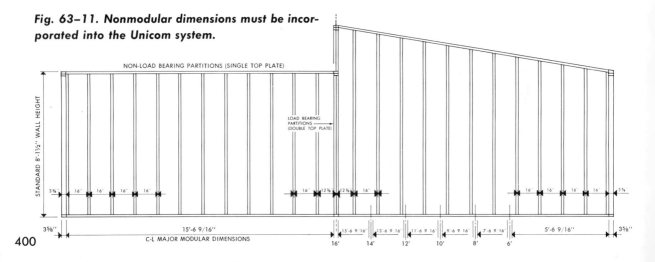

by dimensioning conventionally the nonmodular distances where they exist.

After the overall dimensions are established and nonmodular dimensions incorporated in the plan, the panels for exterior doors, and windows and for exterior walls should be established on the 16″ module, as shown in Fig. 63–12. The precise location of wall openings on the 16″ module also eliminates the extra wall framing commonly encountered in nonmodular home planning; and the

Fig. 63–12. Doors, windows, and panels should be located on the 16″ module.

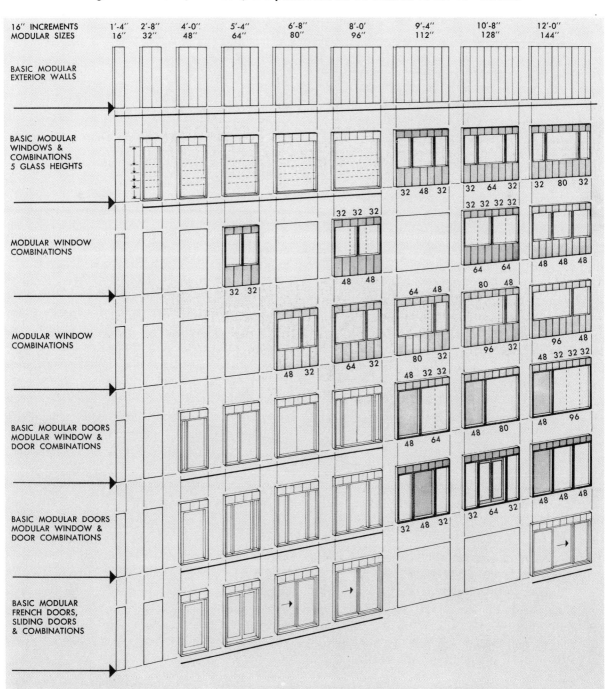

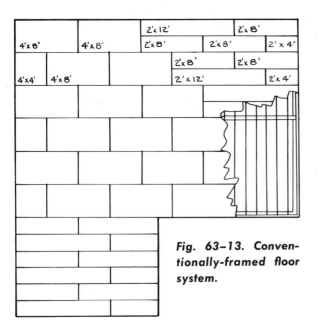

4'x8'	4'x8'	2'x12'		2'x8'	
		2'x8'	2'x8'	2'x8'	2'x4'
4'x4'	4'x8'	2'x8'	2'x8'		
		2'x12'		2'x8'	2'x4'

Fig. 63–13. Conventionally-framed floor system.

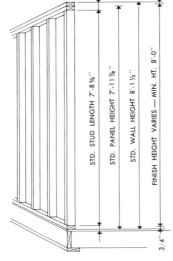

STD. STUD LENGTH 7'-8⅝"

STD. PANEL HEIGHT 7'-11⅞"

STD. WALL HEIGHT 8'-1½"

FINISH HEIGHT VARIES — MIN. HT. 8'-0"

¾"

¾"

Fig. 63–14. Framing dimensions that produce an 8' finished ceiling height.

16" spacing of structural members increases design flexibility by one-third, compared with spacing at the 24" minor module.

Conventionally framed platform floor systems (Fig. 63–13) provide the most flexible method of floor framing for the variety of design conditions encountered with the Unicom system. Modular sizes of floor sheathing materials are economically applied to the modular spacing of floor joists.

X	Exterior-wall panels
XC	Full-corner exterior-wall panels
XCBM	Cantilever-beam exterior-wall corner panels
XCA	Cut-back corner exterior-wall panels
RP	Roof panels
FP	Floor panels
P	Interior partition panel
WC	Casement window panels
WD	Double-hung window panels
WS	Sliding window panels
WAF	Fixed-awning window panels
WP	Fixed picture-window panels
WPP	Full-height, fixed, picture-window panels
GG	Glass gable panels
D	Door panels with one door
2D	Door panels with two doors
DS	Door panels with one side light
2DS2	Door panels with two doors and two side lights
DS2	Door panels with two side lights
DSL	Sliding door panels
DA	Garage door panels

Fig. 63–15. Abbreviations used to identify components.

As previously stated, the Unicom method is based on modular coordination of all three dimensions—width, length, and height. Although width and length are the most critical dimensions, standard heights are necessary to eliminate much waste and to ensure the proper fitting of components. A standard height of 8'-1½" for exterior-wall components allows for floor- and ceiling-finish applications with a combined thickness of 1½". The result is a standard 8' finished ceiling height, as shown in Fig. 63–14.

▶ **Identification System**

A complete system of short-form identification for separate pieces and fabricated components simplifies the practical use of the modular coordination system of building. Figure 63–15 shows some of the abbreviations used to identify components. In most cases, the basic identifying letter or combination is directly associated with the element. For example, J stands for joist and R stands for rafter.

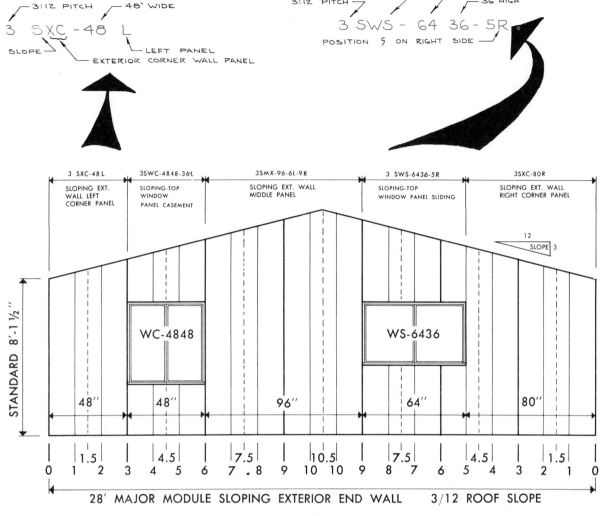

Fig. 63–16. *The use of code numbers in describing components.*

The shorthand has been extended to include complete descriptions of wall panels, including information pertaining to the slope, window style and position, as shown in Fig. 63–16.

Problems

1. Resketch the plan shown in Fig. 63–17 on modular grid paper and convert all nonmodular dimensions to the nearest modular size.

2. Identify the following terms: *Unicom, modular components, modular planning grid, minor module, major module, nonmodular dimensions, modular dimensions, 16" module.*

Fig. 63–17. *Convert this plan to Unicom standards.*

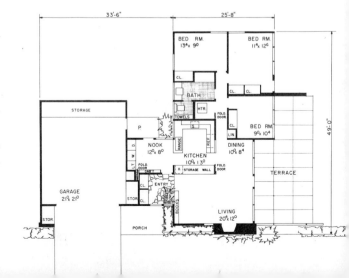

Unit 64. Drawing Modular Plans

The floor plan shown in Fig. 64–1 has been fitted on the modular grid, and the designer has thus properly established the modular relationship of the foundation, floors, walls, windows, doors, partitions, and roof. Establishing the dimensions and components precisely on the 16″, 24″, and 48″ spaces of the modular grid assures accurate fitting of components when the house is constructed.

Fig. 64–1. Floor plan fitted on a modular grid.

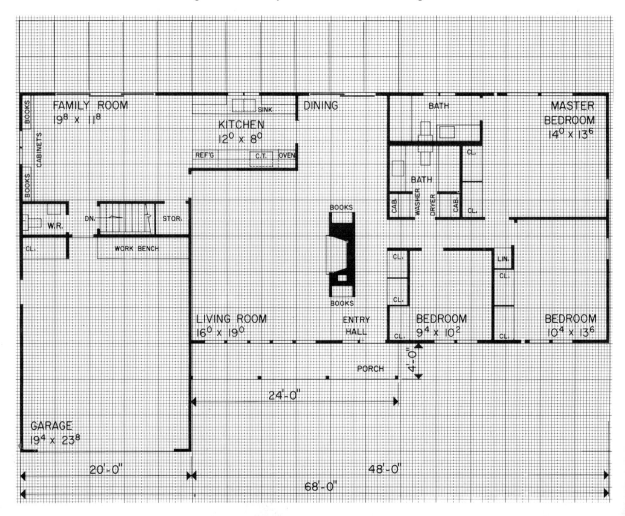

▶ Component Floor Plans

After completing the basic floor plan, a detailed component plan for fabrication and erection is prepared. Standard symbols are used to identify wall, window, door, and partition components by type and size (Fig. 64–2). The erection sequence for site assembly is also designated on this plan by ER 1, ER 2, and so on. This basic component floor plan for erection contains all basic dimensions necessary for layout work on the floor platform. Interior partitions may then be erected in varying sequences.

▶ Elevation Component Drawings

Just as the component floor plan for erection is prepared from the floor plan shown in Fig. 64–1, the elevation component drawings are prepared from standard elevations projected from the floor plan, as shown in Fig. 64–3. Elevation component drawings closely resemble conventional panel-

framing elevations, except that wall, window, door, and roof components are identified and shown in their proper relationship, complete with standard Unicom nomenclature and erection sequences. Figure 64–4 shows the component elevation drawings prepared from standard elevations shown in Fig. 64–3.

▶ Framing Plans

From the basic floor plan, a floor-framing plan, as shown in Fig. 64–5, is projected and dimensioned according to Unicom standards. Notice the precise rhythm of the 16″, on-center floor joists and the 48″ modular dimensions of the house perimeter. The advantage of designing to these standards is shown in the floor-sheathing plan shown in Fig. 64–6. Waste occurs only in cutting at the stair-well and fireplace openings.

The roof-framing plan shown in Fig. 64–7 is prepared like the floor-framing plan. Modular

Fig. 64–2. Symbols are used to identify components on the floor plan.

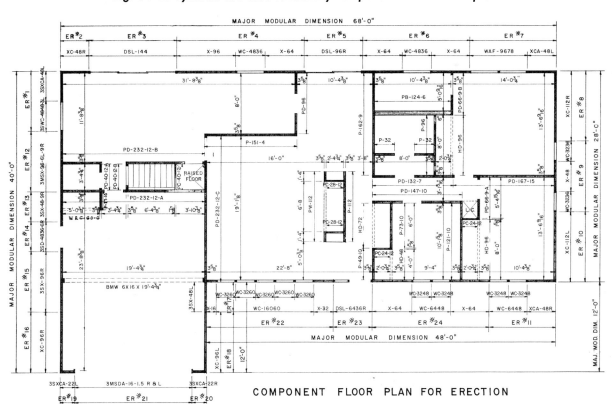

COMPONENT FLOOR PLAN FOR ERECTION

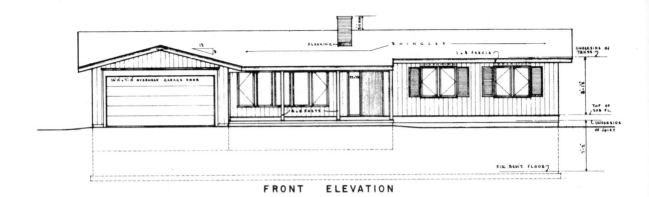

FRONT ELEVATION

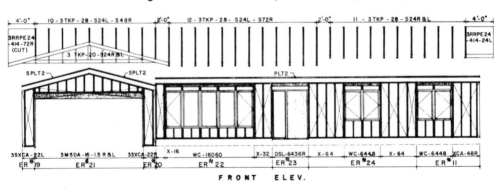

LEFT SIDE ELEVATION   RIGHT SIDE ELEVATION

Fig. 64-3. Elevation component drawings are prepared from conventional elevations.

Fig. 64-4. Elevation component framing drawing.

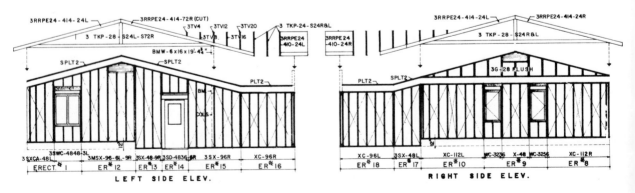

FRONT ELEV.

LEFT SIDE ELEV.   RIGHT SIDE ELEV.

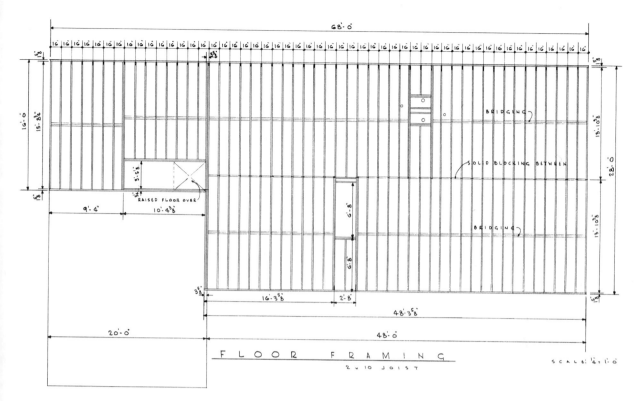

Fig. 64–5. Modular floor-framing plan.

Fig. 64–6. Modular floor-sheathing plan.

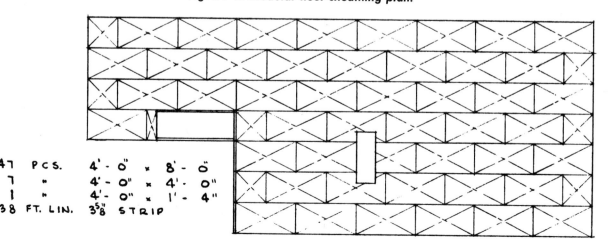

47 PCS. 4'-0" x 8'-0"
7 " 4'-0" x 4'-0"
1 " 4'-0" x 1'-4"
38 FT. LIN. 3⅝" STRIP

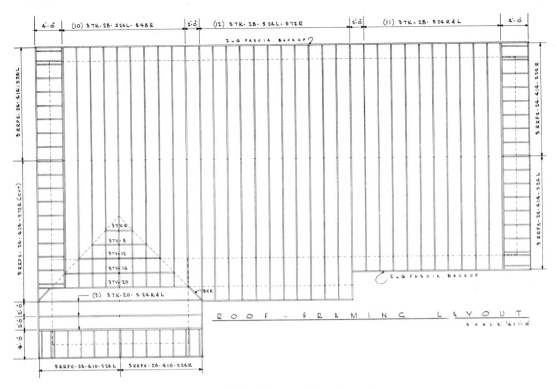

Fig. 64–7. Modular roof-framing plan.

Fig. 64–8. Modular roof-sheathing plan.

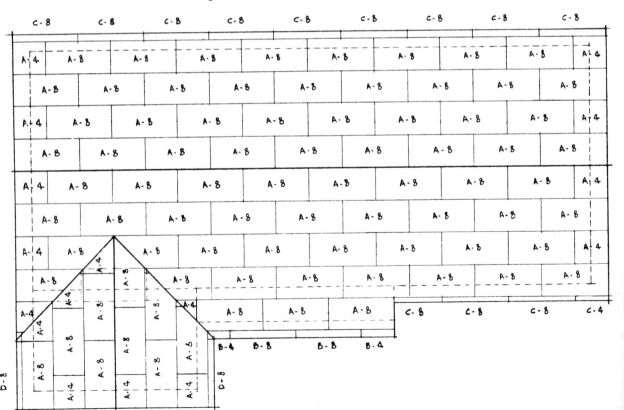

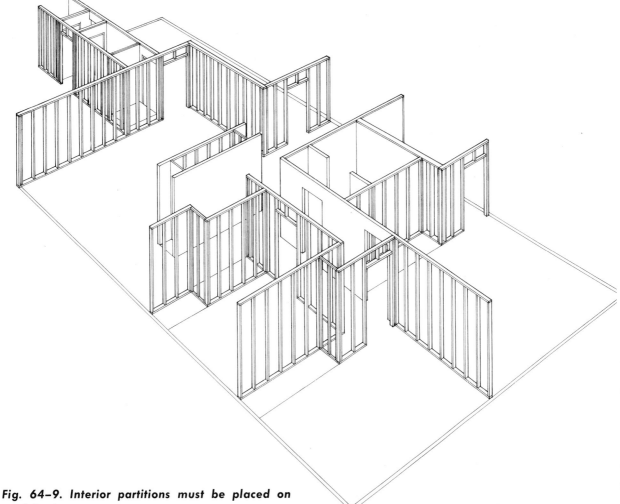

Fig. 64–9. Interior partitions must be placed on modular increments.

dimensions and panel code numbers are indicated on this plan. Figure 64–8 illustrates the simplicity of controlled modular standards in effecting economies in the use of materials.

▶ Interior Partition Components

Partitions function as interior space separators for room privacy, traffic control, and storage. Their aesthetic value depends on decorative surface materials, doors, and trim designs. Partitions are a maze of intersecting planes which may carry the roof and ceiling loads, depending on the roof design. The illustration in Fig. 64–9 shows the partitions from the plan in Fig. 64–1 placed by modular standards. Interior panel elevation drawings, as shown in Fig. 64–10, reveal some of the complexities of modular design of interior partitions. Partitions must fit between the basic exterior modular increments with allowance for exterior wall thicknesses. Space must be provided for intersecting partitions with backup members, proper door placement, vertical and horizontal plumbing runs, medicine cabinets, closets, fireplaces, and flexible room arrangements with varying designs. The partition shown in Fig. 64–10 illustrates the method of dimensioning partitions to relate effectively modular and nonmodular dimensions. In addition to the dimensional designations, the identification code for the panel is also included on the partition drawing.

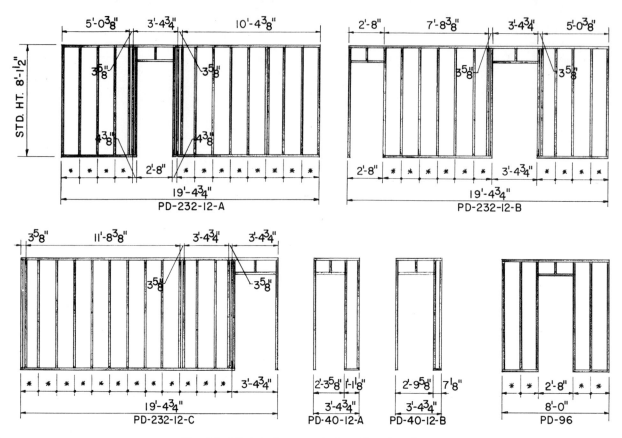

Fig. 64–10. Interior-panel elevation drawings.

Fig. 64–11. Plans for all components of the structure must be consistent with Unicom standards.

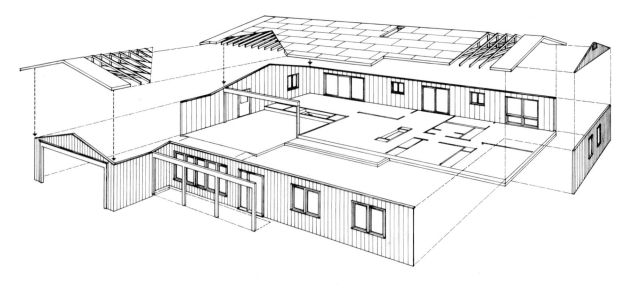

Many more modular drawings are needed to describe completely a Unicom plan in every detail. Just as in structures of conventional design, the more detailed the drawings are, the better the chance of achieving the desired outcome. Other plans which may become part of the complete Unicom design include transverse sections, truss and gable component drawings, roof-overhang details, and detailed drawings of many nonstandard components. Figure 64–11 shows the relationship of basic components in a house designed by the modular system. With the Unicom method, all other basic house types may be designed and engineered in the same manner.

Problems

1. Prepare a component floor plan for the floor plan shown in Fig. 64–12.

2. Prepare an elevation component drawing for the front elevation of the house shown in Fig. 64–13.

3. Prepare a floor-framing plan for the house shown in Fig. 64–12 and dimension it according to Unicom standards.

4. Prepare a roof-framing plan of the floor plan shown in Fig. 64–12 and dimension it to modular standards.

5. Identify the following terms: component floor plan, elevation component drawing, Unicom, modular increment.

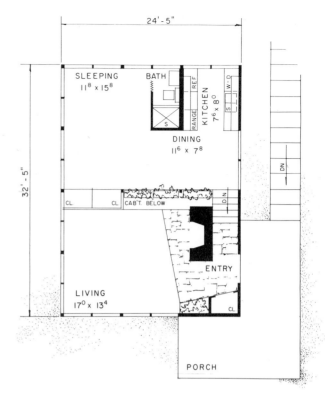

Fig. 64–12. Prepare a component floor plan of this house.

Fig. 64–13. Prepare a component elevation drawing of the front elevation.

Fig. 64–14. Many components were used in the construction of the Pan Am Building.

PART IV

Creative Architectural Drafting and Design

It is difficult to design creatively in any
medium unless you are familiar with the
properties of materials and the drafting and
design procedures and techniques. Once you have
learned the fundamentals of area planning and the
techniques employed in preparing basic architectural
drawings and technical architectural plans, you are
better equipped to express creatively the fundamental principles, concepts, skills, and ideas
you have developed throughout your study of
architectural drafting and design.
In part IV you will be exposed to the broader
horizons of architectural design and you will be
provided with exercises that will stimulate and
develop creative architectural activities.

Raymond International, Inc.

SECTION EIGHTEEN. THEORY OF DESIGN

The architect, designer, and draftsman must at various times possess the structural inventiveness of an engineer and the artistic imagination of the sculptor.

Revolutionary advances in our technology provide a great stimulus for architectural design; constant changes in our culture must be successfully reflected in our architecture.

In this section you will be given an opportunity to express some of your ideas, to experiment with the new materials, to try new ideas, and to acquire a respect and a feeling for architectural creativity.

Unit 65. Architectural Styles

Architectural styles have evolved through the years as a result of new developments in building materials and new demands of the culture. Styles of the past reflect the culture of the past. Styles of the present reflect our current living habits and needs. Architectural styles of the future will be largely determined by advancements in technology and changes in our living habits.

Our architectural heritage is largely derived from European (Fig. 65–1) and early American architecture although the oriental influence has become significant.

▶ European Styles
The English, French, Italians, and Spanish have had the most significant influence on our architecture.

English architecture. The English Tudor type of architecture originated in England during the fifteenth century. Tudor homes featured high-pitched gable roofs, small windows, shallow dormers, Norman towers, and tall chimneys which extended high above the roof line.

The Elizabethan, or half-timbered, style is an adaptation of the Tudor style. It is characterized by the use of mortar set between timbers.

French architecture. French provincial architecture was brought to this continent when the French settled Quebec. French provincial architecture can be identified by the mansard roof, which was developed by the French architect François Mansard. On the French provincial home this roof is high-pitched, with steep slopes and rounded dormer windows projecting from the sides.

Southern European architecture. Spanish architecture was brought to this country by Spanish colonials who settled the Southwest. Spanish architecture is characterized by low-pitched roofs of ceramic tile and stucco exterior walls. A distinguishing feature of almost every Spanish home is a courtyard patio. Two-story Spanish homes contain open balconies enclosed in grillwork. One-story Spanish homes were the forerunners of the present ranch-style homes that first developed in southern California.

Italian architecture is very similar to Spanish architecture. One distinguishing feature is the use of columns and arches at a loggia entrance, and windows of balconies opening onto a loggia roof. The use of classical mouldings around first-floor windows also helps to distinguish the Italian style from the Spanish.

► **Early American**

Early colonists came to the New World from many different cultures and were familiar with many different styles of architecture.

New England. The colonists who settled the New England coastal areas were influenced largely by English styles of architecture. Lack of materials, time, and equipment greatly simplified their adaptation of these styles (Fig. 65–2). One of the most

British Travel Association

Fig. 65–1. European architecture.

Fig. 65–2. New England colonial home.

Fig. 65–3. Southern colonial home.

popular of the New England styles was the *Cape Cod.* This is a one-and-one-half story, gabled-roof house with dormers, a central front entrance, a large central chimney, and exterior walls of clapboard or bevel siding. Double-hung windows are fixed with shutters, and the floor plan is symmetrical.

Dutch colonial. Gambrel roofs characterized many small farm buildings in Germany. A *gambrel roof* is a double-pitched roof with projecting overhangs. Many of the German settlers who later settled New York and Pennsylvania made the gambrel roof a part of the Dutch colonial style of architecture.

Southern colonial. When the early settlers migrated to the South, warmer climates and outdoor living activities led them to develop the colonial style of architecture. As the house became the center of plantation living, the size was increased and often a second story was added. Two-story columns were used to support the front-roof overhang and the symmetrical gabled roof (Fig. 65–3).

Ranch style. As settlers moved West, architectural styles were changed to meet their needs. The availability of more space eliminated the need for second floors. This same amount of space could then be spread horizontally rather than vertically, which resulted in a rambling plan. The Spanish influence also led to the popularization of the Western ranch, which utilized a U-shaped plan with a patio in the center.

Victorian. The Industrial Revolution in this country provided architects and builders with machinery and equipment which could be used to construct very intricate millwork items. Since living habits had changed little, this new-found technology was turned to adding to the building. Intricate finials, lintels, parapets, balconies and cornices were added to structures (Fig. 65–4). Ornate aspects of Victorian architecture (gingerbread) were designed into our homes until recent years.

Only a few architects who were practicing at the turn of the century attempted to functionalize architecture during that period. Frank Lloyd Wright and Louis Sullivan were the most notable of these architects.

▶ **The Present**

Louis Sullivan wrote, "Our architecture reflects us as truly as a mirror." Modern architecture is now reflecting our freedom, our functionalism, and our technological advances. Modern architects are working to achieve even more functionalism, freedom, and technological refinements in the art and science of architecture.

Functionalism. Louis Sullivan's "form follows function" concept has now been accepted by most modern architects. It has so permeated architectural thought that few items can find their way into

Fig. 65–4. A home in the Victorian style of architecture.

Fig. 65–5. The relationship between architecture and sculpture.

an architectural design without performing some specific function. Most modernists feel this is the line of distinction between architecture and sculpture (Fig. 65–5). Architecture must perform a function; a piece of sculpture does not. It may exist and be admired for its aesthetic qualities alone.

The concept of functionalism in architecture has led to extreme applications of simplicity in design (Fig. 65–6). Simplicity and functionalism complement each other.

Freedom. Freedom of expression, freedom in the use of space, and structural freedom in design characterize modern architecture (Fig. 65–7). Le Corbusier is one of the leading exponents of freedom in architectural design. His five points of modern architecture include: free-standing support, independence of the wall from the frame, the free plan (open plan), the free façade, and a roof garden.

Le Corbusier felt that we must no longer challenge nature with our architecture but rather work with nature.

Eduardo Torroja, the most outstanding architect in the field of reinforced concrete, has worked with this medium because of its great ability to provide a structure with beauty, fluid continuity, and freedom. An engineer or architect should free himself from the use of traditional building materials and methods in all situations. Complete freedom of expression can be achieved only by using materials that are more flexible and that allow the architect

Fig. 65–6. Extreme simplicity of design.

Fig. 65–7. David Wright residence.

Frank Lloyd Wright, architect; Guerrero Photo

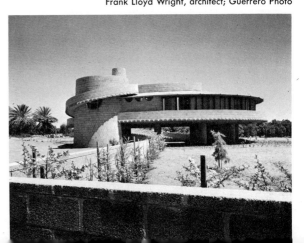

Knoll Associates, Inc.

Fig. 65–8. Furniture design is frequently a part of complete architectural planning.

Fig. 65–9. Trans World Airlines Terminal at the John F. Kennedy International Airport.

Trans World Airlines Photo

to express his ideas with more freedom and independence.

Relationships. Relating the areas of the structure to each other and to its environment have become well-established principles of modern architecture.

Eero Saarinen advanced the importance of relationships in stating, ''Always design a thing by considering it in its next largest context—a dish on a table, a table in a room, a room in a house, a house in a neighborhood, a neighborhood in a city.'' Saarinen practiced this concept. His designing pursuits have included the design of furniture as well as buildings (Fig. 65–8). His designs for the TWA Terminal at the Kennedy International Airport (Fig. 65–9), the General Motors Technical Center, and the Dulles International Terminal (Fig. 65–10) were created with great freedom in the use of space.

Oscar Niemeyer, the designer of Brasilia, operates on the premise that architectural freedom should be expressed through a conquest of space. Brasilia is a classic example of relating large areas to each other. It is the only city in the world that has been designed to be built at one time. Hence, space could be controlled without the hazards of evolution that normally accompany the growth of cities (Fig. 65–11).

Technology. Our technological advances now allow us to build larger structures of lighter materials (Fig. 65–12), to erect buildings faster, and to design the utmost in structural safety into buildings. Ludwig Mies van der Rohe, the architect of steel, believed that when technology reaches its full development in any culture, it immediately transcends into architecture.

Fig. 65–10. Dulles International Terminal.

Molitor Photo

Fig. 65–11. Brasilia is a planned city.

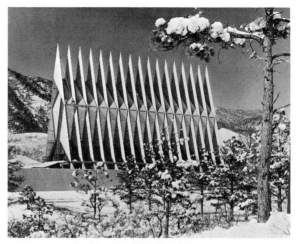

Fig. 65–12. Lighter materials can now be used to build larger structures.

Technological advancement has developed a need for more specialization in architecture and in building, and hence a need for greater coordination. Walter Gropius advances the belief that more and more an architect must become a coordinator —a coordinator of teamwork activities of the structural engineer, the electrical engineer, the acoustical engineer, and the sociologist. The design of large structures and centers is becoming extremely complex, and all these persons are needed to arrive at a good conception of the final design. As our technology becomes more complex, no one person can perform all these functions (Fig. 65–13). The coordinator must bring unity to architecture in combining art and technology, for one without the other is ineffective.

Our technology has brought improvement. It has also brought chaos. Speed and traffic congestion contribute to the restlessness of congested areas. Minoru Yamasaki feels that we need architecture to put our lives in balance and that our buildings must provide serenity and quiet.

The romanticists. Many architects favor the attempt to bring back to architecture some of the traditional elements of ornament that have been a part of the great classic monuments of the past.

Fig. 65–13. The architect's job of designing structures is becoming more complex.

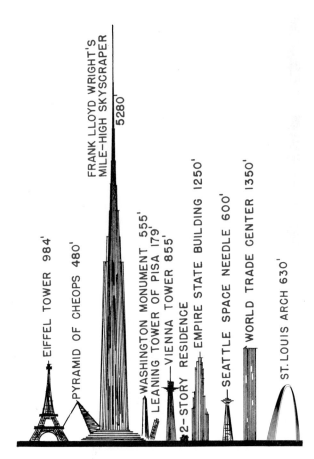

Fig. 65-15. *A comparison of the sizes of some of the major structures of the world.*

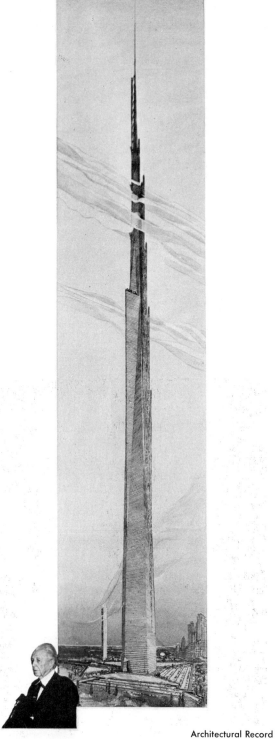

Architectural Record

Fig. 65-14. Frank Lloyd Wright's proposed mile-high skyscraper.

Edward D. Stone, designer of the United States Embassy building in New Delhi and our Brussels World's Fair building, is one of the leading exponents of this romanticism. However, he favors utilization of new materials and new methods, such as the concrete grill.

▶ The Future

No one can accurately predict what the future of architecture will bring. The future will certainly be related to the development of new materials, new construction methods, and the sociological changes we undergo.

Size. The technological explosion should enable us to build in sizes heretofore impossible. Figure

Fig. 65–16. Buckminster Fuller's proposed Manhattan geodesic dome.

65–14 shows Frank Lloyd Wright's proposal for a mile-high skyscraper. Ten such structures, Wright said, would take care of the working office staff of all New York City. Six would suffice for Chicago. The structure's tremendous weight would not rest on a flat surface, as with conventional buildings, but would be distributed equally around a deep-sunk taproot, a sharp wedge descending approximately a thousand feet (one-fifth of the structure's height) into solid bedrock. The proposed skyscraper would tower far above such existing structures as the Empire State Building, the Eiffel Tower, the Washington Monument, and the Great Pyramid, as shown in Fig. 65–15.

Who can say what will be possible? The prospect of building a geodesic dome over central Manhattan as shown in Fig. 65–16 certainly seems impossible, but an orbital flight around the earth or to the moon seemed impossible a few years ago.

Within the span of a lifetime we have advanced from the horse and buggy era to the space age.

Location. In the future we should be capable of building structures on locations that would now be unthought of. The house perched on the rim of the Grand Canyon shown in Fig. 65–17 may not be entirely practical for typical home life, but it is within the realm of technical possibility at the present time.

Advancements in transportation methods and refinement in the engineering of structures will make even more locations feasible.

Shapes. For centuries we have been hampered in our architectural development through the use and overuse of the square and the cube as the basis for our structures. We are just now entering into a fuller realization of the possibilities of utilizing other shapes such as the triangle, the pyramid, the circle, and the sphere. The development of stronger,

Fig. 65–17. Advancements in technology have opened up endless possibilities in utilizing new locations.

Ford Motor Company

Fig. 65–18. A supermarket of the future.

Engineering News-Record

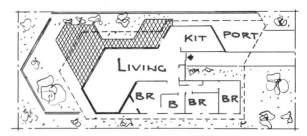

Robert Le Ricolais; Roebling, Inc.

Fig. 65–19. Model of a 30-story high cosomorama.

more versatile materials and new construction techniques should enable us to construct buildings that are completely functional without reference to any basic geometric form. The supermarket of the future shown in Fig. 65–18 utilizes a revolutionary new concept in fully automated marketing. The model of the 30-story high cosomorama shown in Fig. 65–19 is based on the principle of the suspension system and will simulate space travel.

Even the basic shapes of floor plans should be more diversified with the development of new and more flexible building materials, as shown in Fig. 65–20. Frank Lloyd Wright demonstrated for 60 years that interior space can be much richer and much more interesting than a box. When you see any corner of a square room, without looking around you know what the remainder of the room is like. Not so when the squareness is removed. Frank Lloyd Wright constantly attempted to avoid the box and to accomplish his goal of greater freedom and less static space. Even today more diversified shapes are finding their way into the architectural scene, as shown by the 600' space needle in Fig. 65–21.

Components. The development of new components should enable us to design and build custom-designed structures that can be erected on the site

Fig. 65–20. Flexibilities achieved by altering the normal rectangular floor-plan pattern.

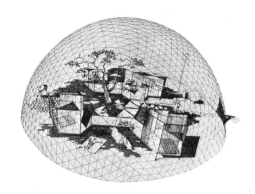

Fig. 65-22. Buckminster Fuller's Garden of Eden.

with the use of large and small components. This practice would practically eliminate on-the-job construction work. Construction would then merely be the assembly of the component parts in a unique design, just as an automobile is constructed of many different, interchangeable parts. What our houses will look like in 10, 20, 30, or 100 years is an interesting question to ponder. Figure 65–22 shows Robert Buckminster Fuller's concept of the Garden of Eden. It is not a house; it is controlled environment. Indeed, houses as we now know them may become museum pieces, or only illustrations of architectural history.

Morley Studios

Fig. 65-21. Seattle's 600'-high space needle.

Fig. 65-23. Redevelopment of Pittsburgh's Golden Triangle.

Newman Schmidt and John R. Shrader Photo

Population mobility. With increased mobility of the population, custom designing becomes more and more difficult. Building for resale becomes more and more important. Therefore, designs that will permit the rearranging of partitions and fixtures may be developed to meet the unique needs of the housholder.

With more leisure time anticipated in the future, more emphasis will be placed on recreational activities within or about the home.

The city. The team approach to the design of commercial buildings such as hotels, motels, air terminals, and schools will be intensified in the future. The importance of planning whole cities, or at least whole sections of cities, based on sociological needs, will become more and more evident. With growing suburbanization and exurbanization, cities are now in need of complete redevelopment (Fig. 65–23).

The role of the architect as a coordinator in these activities will be increased, and the relationship between art and technology will be refined to enable all types of buildings, including industrial plants, to be not only technically appropriate but aesthetically acceptable. Frank Lloyd Wright, writing *In the Cause of Architecture,* made this prophecy for the future: "The work shall grow more truly simple; more expressive with fewer lines, fewer forms; more articulate with less labor; more plastic; more fluent, although more coherent; more organic." Figure 65–24 illustrates this concept.

Problems

1. Name three advancements we might expect in the field of architecture in the next ten years.
2. What effect will the mobility of our population have on the future of architecture?
3. What effect does the team approach have on the design of commercial buildings?
4. Sketch your ideas for a house of the future.

Fig. 65–24. Proposed World Trade Center.

Balthazar Korab

Unit 66. Design Process

Design activities may be formal or informal. *Informal design* occurs when the product is made by the designer without the use of a plan. *Formal design* involves the complete preparation of a set of working drawings and the use of the working drawings in constructing the product. Buildings are designed formally; that is, a complete set of working drawings is prepared before the actual construction begins. Therefore, the major design activity in architectural work occurs during the preparation of sketches, plans, and detailed drawings.

National Concrete Masonry Association

Fig. 66–1. This design breaks down the barrier between the inside and the outside of the house.

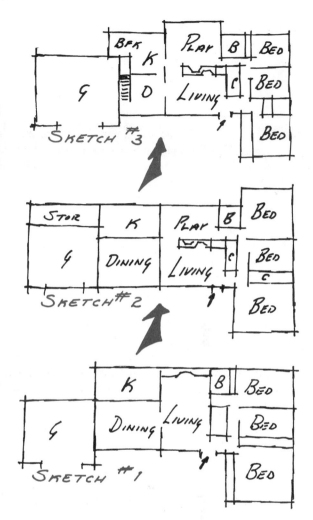

Fig. 66–2. Sketches are used to revise and alter the plan.

▶ Creative Design

The building should be designed creatively. In other words, the design should be an expression of the ideas of the creator. The designer of the building shown in Fig. 66–1 expressed his love of nature when he designed the structure, for he made every attempt to relate and combine the internal and external parts of the design.

Ideas in the creative stage may be recorded by sketching basic images and revising these sketches until the basic ideas are crystallized. First sketches rarely produce a finished design. Usually many revisions are necessary.

Many designers make a habit of never throwing away a sketch. They resketch the problem on successive sheets of paper (usually a pad of graph paper). Often the fifth sketch may reveal the solution to a problem in the tenth sketch. The ideas may not be combined in a functional design until perhaps twenty or thirty sketches have been made.

Until you become familiar with standard building-material sizes and furniture requirements, you should use the template method of design, as outlined in Unit 24. Sketches may then be used to revise and alter the plan until the final design is achieved (Fig. 66–2).

▶ Technical Design

A basic idea, regardless of how creative and imaginative, is useless unless the design can be successfully transformed into the final product. Technical designing involves the transfer of basic sketches into architectural working drawings.

Every useful building must perform a specific function, and every part of the structure should be designed to perform a specific function. The retractable roof on Pittsburgh's Civic Auditorium is designed to perform a dual function (Fig. 66–3).

425

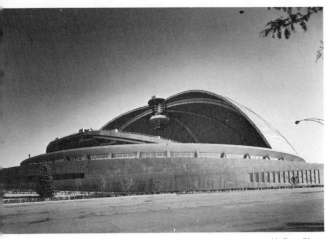

Fig. 66-3. Pittsburgh's Civic Auditorium.

Fig. 66-5. Rocket-assembly building.

It provides an open air theater in good weather and provides protection from the elements during inclement weather.

▶ Aesthetic Design

Today's buildings not only must be functional but must be aesthetically designed as well. The term *aesthetic* refers to beauty. When the appearance

Fig. 66-4. Open and projecting form.

of a building appeals to our senses, it is beautiful. Thus beauty is the aesthetic part of design. Today the aesthetic part of design is an important factor.

▶ Elements of Design

Every building should contain the six basic elements of design in some combination. These basic elements are form, space, light and shadow, texture, line, and color.

Form. The form of the building is its mass or shape. The form may appear closed and solid, or closed and volume-containing. It may be open and projecting, as shown in the building in Fig. 66-4. The form of a structure should be determined by its function. The rocket-assembly building shown in Fig. 66-5 was designed only for the assembly of the Saturn C-5 moon rocket.

Space. Space surrounds form and is contained within it. The design can create a feeling of space; it should not create the impression that every form is surrounded by other forms and those forms by other forms.

Light and shadow. Light reflects from the surface of a form, and shadows appear in areas the light cannot reach. Light and shadow both give a sense of depth to the building. Areas around windows and doors, and areas under roof overhangs appear darker, since these parts are shadowed.

United Nations Photo

Fig. 66-6. Light and shadow are used to create an impressive effect.

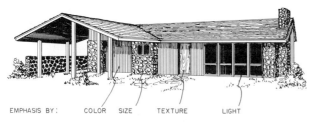

EMPHASIS BY: COLOR   SIZE   TEXTURE   LIGHT

Fig. 66-7. Do not include too many different textures.

The relationship of light and dark areas should be planned accordingly. The designer of the room shown in Fig. 66-6 has used the element of light and shadow to create an impressive effect.

Texture. Building materials such as concrete, stone, and brick have rough and dull surfaces. Others, such as glass, aluminum, and plastics are relatively smooth. A balance between these two types of textures should be striven for in every building. The designer must be careful not to include too many different textures of a similar nature. For this reason, brick and stone are usually not combined (Fig. 66-7).

Line. The elements of line can produce a sense of movement within the object, or a greater sense of length or height. The lines of the building shown in Fig. 66-8 emphasize the horizontal aspects of

S. C. Johnson & Son

Fig. 66-8. Horizontal line emphasis.

this design. The major lines of most buildings include the ground line, eave line, roof line, and the pattern of any other large areas within the building, such as the window lines.

Color. Color is either an inherent part of the material or must be added to the material by painting, spraying, or dyeing. If possible, the natural color of building materials should be used. In using color, the designer should create his scheme to emphasize one color and to add contrasting colors for variety. The use of too many colors is as objectionable as an insufficient use of color.

Bold colors, such as red, tend to advance. Pale colors (pastels) tend to recede (Fig. 66-9).

▶ Principles of Design

The basic principles of design show how the designer uses the elements of design in creating a building. The six basic principles of design are unity, repetition, rhythm, variety, emphasis, and balance.

Fig. 66-9. Bold colors advance; pale colors recede.

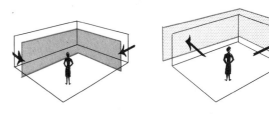

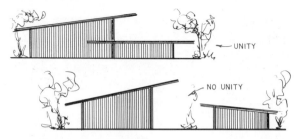

Fig. 66–10. Consistent lines help achieve unity.

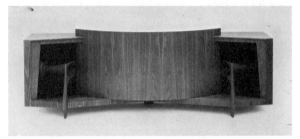

James B. Lansing Sound, Inc.

Fig. 66–11. Dark speaker areas contrast well with the light-textured wood surface of this stereophonic reproducer.

Fig. 66–12. Emphasis is provided by the chimney.

Unity. Unity is the sense of wholeness in the design. Every building should appear complete. No parts should appear as appendages or afterthoughts. In the building in Fig. 66–10, the designer has achieved unity through the use of a consistent line, which transcends several parts of the building.

Repetition. Unity is often achieved through repetition. Curved lines, spaces, and textures are repeated throughout the design to tie the structure together aesthetically and to achieve unity.

United Airlines Photo

Fig. 66–13. A formally balanced house.

Rhythm. When lines, planes, and surface treatments are repeated in a regular sequence, a sense of rhythm is achieved.

Variety. Without variety, a building may become dull and tiresome to the viewer. Too much rhythm, too much repetition, too much unity ruin a sense of variety. Light, shadow, and color are used to achieve variety. The light-textured surface of the wood makes a good contrast to the dark speaker area in the stereophonic reproducer shown in Fig. 66–11. Variety is also achieved in the form of this reproducer. The mass of the curved front, the vertical lines and the delicately-turned legs, create considerable variety of form.

Emphasis. The principle of emphasis is used by the designer to draw attention to any given area of his subject. Emphasis may be achieved by color, form, texture, or line. The chimney in the building shown in Fig. 66–12 is emphasized by form and texture. It is larger than any other area in the building. It is also of a different texture from any other

Fig. 66–14. An informally balanced house.

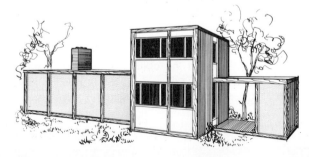

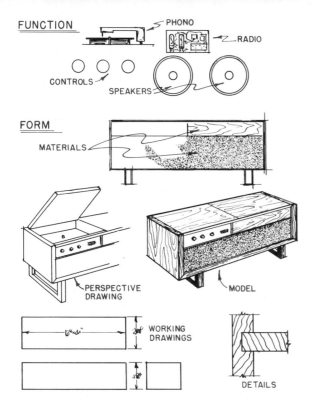

Southern California Gas Company

Fig. 66–17. Provide more emphasis in this design.

Southern California Gas Company

Fig. 66–18. Improve the light and shadow patterns of this house.

Fig. 66–15. Progressive steps in the development of a design.

part of the building. These features also create emphasis in light and color, since the sun will strike and reflect from the surface differently.

Balance. Balance is the achievement of equilibrium in design. Buildings may be *formally* balanced if they are symmetrical (Fig. 66–13). Buildings are *informally* balanced if there is variety in the space relationship and yet a distribution of space, form, line, color, and light and shade. The building shown in Fig. 66–14 is informally balanced.

Fig. 66–16. Convert the front elevation to a formally balanced elevation.

New Homes Guide

▶ Design Sequence

Proceeding logically from a basic idea to a final design is often a long process. Rough ideas are recorded in sketches. The sketches are refined and changed. The basic form is established. Elements of light and shadow, texture, line, and color are combined in the most appropriate relationship.

The effects of unity, repetition, rhythm, variety, emphasis, and balance must be achieved without sacrificing the functional or technical aspect of the design. Figure 66–15 shows major steps in the progression of a design from a basic idea to the final design.

Problems

1. Sketch the front elevation of the house shown in Fig. 66–16. Convert the front-elevation design to a formally balanced elevation.
2. Sketch the house shown in Fig. 66–17 to provide more emphasis on one phase of the design.

3. Sketch the house shown in Fig. 66–18 to improve the light and shadow patterns and to provide more unity of texture and line in the design.

4. List the major color you would use to decorate each room in your home. List two supporting colors you would use for contrast or variety.

5. Follow the steps shown in Fig. 66–15 to achieve a creative design of your own.

6. Define these terms: *technical design, creative design, aesthetic, informal design, formal design, function, form, space, light, shadow, texture, line, color, beauty, repetition, variety, emphasis, informal balance, formal balance.*

Unit 67. Orientation

The orientation of a building is the relationship of the building to its environment. The building must be suitably oriented to the site, the lot, the sun, and the prevailing winds (Fig. 67–1). A well-oriented home is designed to take full advantage of the good features of these exterior conditions (Fig. 67–2).

▶ Solar Orientation

A structure should be oriented to provide maximum control and utilization of the rays of the sun. Solar orientation is becoming increasingly important with the extensive use of larger glass areas. In the Northern Hemisphere the south and west sides of a structure are warmer than the east and north sides. The north side is always cooler because it is shaded (Fig. 67–3). The south side of the building has almost constant exposure to the sun.

Ideally the building should be oriented to absorb as much winter heat as possible and to repel excessive summer heat.

Overhang protection. The angle of the sun differs in summer and in winter (Fig. 67–4). Roof overhangs should therefore be designed with the length and angle that will shade the window in summer and allow the sun to enter during winter months. (See Unit 49).

Room locations. Rooms should be located either to absorb the heat of the sun through glass or to be *baffled,* or walled from the heat of the sun. Rooms should also be located so that they can make

Fig. 67–1. A building must be oriented to the lot and site.

Fig. 67–2. All exterior conditions must be considered.

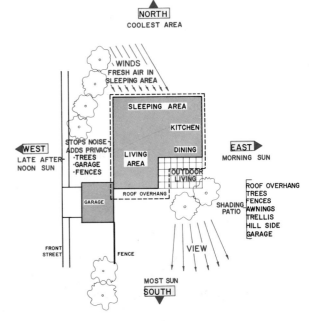

the maximum utilization of light from the sun. Generally sunshine should be available in the kitchen in mornings and should reach the living areas in the afternoon. Kitchens and dining rooms placed on the south or east side of the house are desirable. Living areas placed on the south or west side of the house to obtain afternoon exposure are usually desirable. The north side is the most appropriate side for placing sleeping areas, since it provides the greatest darkness in the morning and evening for sleeping, and is also the coolest side. North light is consistent and has little glare.

▶ Wind

In some areas, wind or heavy breezes may be menacing to outdoor living activities. Efforts should be made to preserve large trees. Trees not only are effective as wind baffles but provide necessary shade. Prevailing winds can be baffled also by the use of shelters and shrubbery.

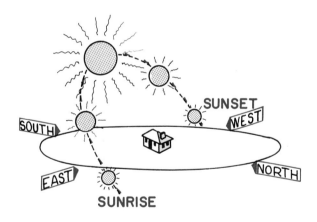

Fig. 67-3. The north side is always shaded.

Fig. 67-4. Sun angles in the summer, fall, and winter.

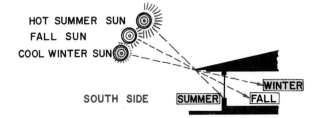

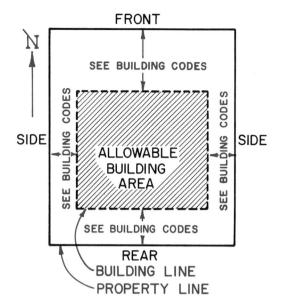

Fig. 67-5. The position of a building is restricted by building codes.

▶ Noise

Insulation will help reduce excessive noise from the outside. However, locating rooms requiring quiet on the side away from the source of noise is also effective.

▶ Lot

The size of the lot affects the flexibility of choice in locating the house. Building codes restrict the placement of the house on the lot. Some building codes require that the house be placed no closer than 10' to the property line. Other codes require a distance of 50' or more. Building codes also restrict the distance from the house to the street (Fig. 67-5). A line drawn parallel to the property line on all sides represents the *building line*. The area within the building line is the area in which the building can be located (Fig. 67-6). On small lots, there is often little flexibility in orienting the home. On larger lots, the possibility of using a variety of positions is greater.

Lots may be divided into three areas according to function: the private area, the public area, and the service area (Fig. 67-7). The private area includes the house and outdoor living space. A

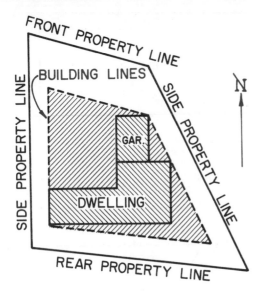

Fig. 67-6. Permissible building area.

Fig. 67-7. The three areas of a lot are the public area, the private area, and the service area.

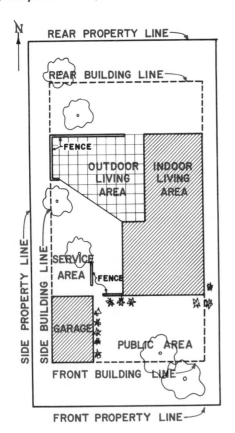

Architectural Forum; Hedrich-Blessing Photo

Fig. 67-8. Frank Lloyd Wright always sought to relate a building structurally and aesthetically to the site.

southern exposure is usually desirable for the outdoor living area.

The public area is the area of the lot viewed from the street. This area is usually at the front of the house and should provide off-street parking and access to the main entrance.

The service area of the lot should be adjacent to the service area of the home. The placement of the home on the lot determines the relative size and relationship of these areas.

▶ Relationship of House to Site

A lot may be hilly, rugged, and rocky, or it may be smooth and level. Whatever the shape of the terrain, the house should be designed as an integral part of the site. It should not appear as an appendix to the land. It should appear as a desirable, functional improvement of the site.

Frank Lloyd Wright probably did more than any other architect to popularize and intensify the desirability of relating the home structurally and aesthetically to the site. He called this principle *organic architecture*. One of the most profound examples of organic architecture is "Falling

Water," at Bear Run, Pennsylvania (Fig. 67–8). The bold use of the site, with cantilevered decks extending over a waterfall, produces a dramatic effect that has rarely if ever been equaled. Cantilevered slabs are anchored in the hillside, relating the building structurally and aesthetically to its setting.

Figure 67–9 shows another house that has been effectively related to the contour of the lot. In this case the relationship is developed and reinforced by the use of materials related to the site, and by cantilevered wood decks that project over the slope of the lot and provide shelter for the first level.

A house may be compatible with one lot and site and yet appear out of place in another location. Split-level homes, for example, are designed for sloping lots where an entrance can be provided on each level, and each level is used functionally to its maximum. The placement of the split-level home on a flat lot does not utilize the house or the lot effectively. If complete integration of indoor

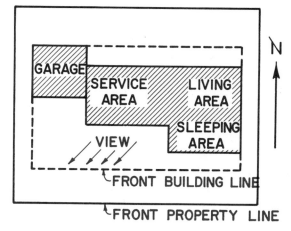

Fig. 67–10. Reorient this house.

and outdoor living areas is to be achieved, a house and lot must be designed as part of the same plan.

Problems

1. Sketch the house shown in Fig. 67–10. Change the north arrow to indicate a more desirable orientation.

Fig. 67–9. A house effectively related to the contour of the land.

Architectural Record, Elliott Erwitt Photo

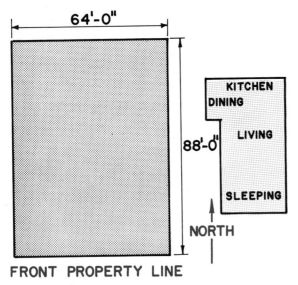

Fig. 67-11. Locate this house on the lot.

Fig. 67-12. Place this house and garage on the lot.

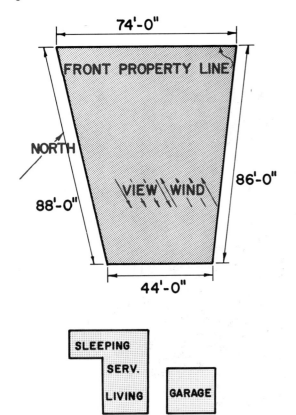

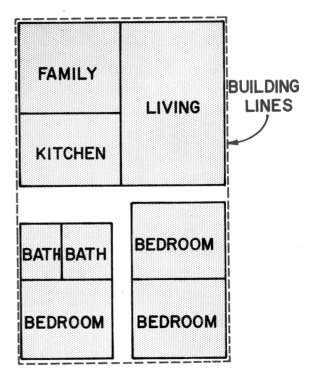

Fig. 67-13. Locate this house on a 100' × 100' lot.

Fig. 67-14. Reorient this house.

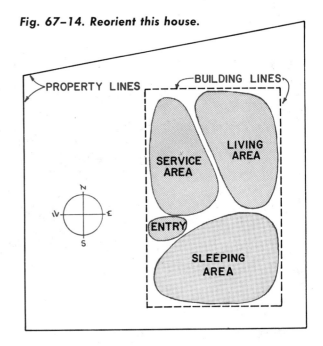

2. Sketch the property shown in Fig. 67–11. Prepare a template of the house to the same scale and place it on the property in the most desirable location.

3. Sketch the lot layout shown in Fig. 67–12. Place templates of the house and garage on this lot in the most desirable position. Also sketch the position of driveways, walks, and other landscape features you would add to this design. Sketch adjacent lots and show their key landscape features.

4. Prepare templates of the rooms in Fig. 67–13. Combine these in a workable floor plan and place the templates on a 100′ × 100′ level lot.

5. Change the points of the compass shown in Fig. 67–14 to provide a more desirable orientation of the house.

6. Define the following terms: *solar orientation, site, lot, overhang, wind baffle, building line, public area, private area, service area, organic architecture, split level.*

Unit 68. New Materials

Advancements in technology have developed new and better materials and methods for building construction. Longer life and easier maintenance are two distinguishing characteristics of many new products.

Many new materials are not really new. They are old materials used in new applications. For example, glass is not a new material, but new developments in glass manufacture have enabled architects to design complete walls of glass that are structurally sound (Fig. 68–1).

▶ **Aluminum**

Aluminum is a lightweight, durable metal that is being used increasingly by architects. It is available in sheets and structural shapes. Since it is light-

Fig. 68–1. Complete walls of glass are now possible.

Nestlé Alimentana

Fig. 68–2. Gold anodized aluminum is used on the Pittsburgh Hilton.

Hilton Hotel Corp.

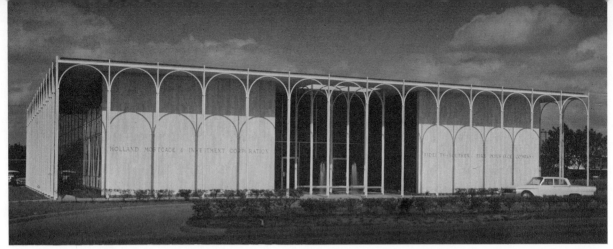

Neuhaus & Taylor, architects

Fig. 68-3. The use of aluminum structural shapes.

weight, it is an excellent metal to be used for walls and roofs. The Pittsburgh Hilton Hotel, for example, uses gold anodized aluminum for walls and mullions (Fig. 68-2).

Aluminum structural shapes provide the architect with considerable flexibility in designing columns and grillwork in a variety of shapes and forms (Fig. 68-3).

Because of aluminum's light weight, durability, and ease of maintenance, it is especially applicable to the design of portable structures, as shown in Fig. 68-4.

As production methods and flexibility increase, the cost of aluminum for architectural residential work may decrease greatly.

▶ **Glass**

The use of glass in building construction has increased immensely in the last decade. Not long ago, common window glass and mirrors were the only practical applications of glass in home building. Today structural glass, glass blocks, and corrugated glass are used in many sizes, shapes, colors, and textures.

Structural glass. Structural glass is plate glass, usually of a deep color, with one side polished. It provides a sanitary, wear-resistant surface. Dirt and moisture cannot penetrate it. Structural glass is easily maintained and never fades. It is used for counter tops, walls, wall panels, door fronts, window stools, stall partitions, and ceilings.

Fig. 68-4. An aluminum portable structure.

Aluminum Company of America

Fig. 68-5. The use of frosted glass panels.

American-Saint Gobain Corp.

Glass blocks. Glass blocks are two pieces of plate glass with an air space between them. Blocks are usually 3⅞" thick and can be used to construct a solid insulated wall. Glass-block walls provide privacy yet allow light to enter.

Corrugated glass. Corrugated glass and frosted glass panels (Fig. 68–5) are also used effectively to provide privacy without shutting off the source of light.

Window walls. Exterior window-wall units which consist of two sheets of glass separated by an air space provide sufficient insulation from heat and cold.

▶ Wood

Wood is one of the oldest materials used in building construction, yet the development of new structural wood forms using plywood and other laminates has revolutionized the structural use of wood.

Improved production techniques and bonding agents have opened new horizons for the application of plywoods. Thin sheets can now be bonded together to almost any desired thickness. Glued laminated arches and beams now offer the designer unlimited opportunity to span extremely long distances without the use of intermediate supports (Fig. 68–6). Laminated beams (Fig. 68–7) and laminated arches (Fig. 68–8) are constructed in numerous shapes and sizes. Arches have been constructed with a span of 242' and a rise of 74'.

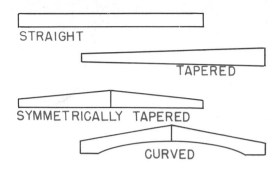

Fig. 68–7. Laminated beams.

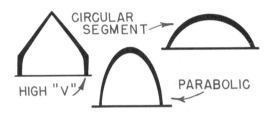

Fig. 68–8. Laminated arches.

The manufacture of fabricated plywood components, such as stressed skin panels, box beams, curved panels, and folded plate roofs, have increased the use of plywood structural systems.

Stressed skin panels are constructed of plywood and seasoned lumber. The simple framing and the plywood skin act as a unit to resist loads. Glued joints transmit the shear stresses, making it possible for the structure to act as one piece. Stressed skin panels (Fig. 68–9) are used in floors, walls, and roofs.

Box beams consist of one or more vertical plywood webs laminated to seasoned lumber flanges. Vertical lumber spacers separate the flanges at intervals along the beam's length to distribute the concentrated loads and prevent web buckling (Fig. 68–10). Large beams can span distances up to 120'.

Curved panels are constructed in three types: the sandwich, or honeycomb paper-core, panel;

Fig. 68–6. Glued laminated arches.

Southern Pine Association

437

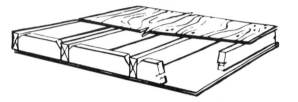

Fig. 68–9. Stressed skin panels.

the hollow-stressed end panel; and the solid-core panel. The arching action of these panels (Fig. 68–11) permits the spanning of great distances with a relatively thin cross section.

Fig. 68–10. Box beams.

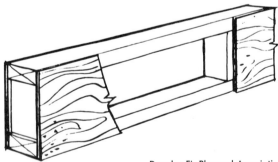

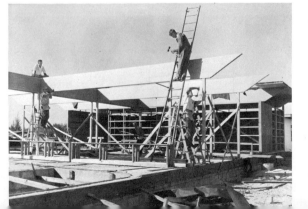

Folded plate roofs are thin skins of plywood reinforced by purlins to form shell structures that can utilize the strength of plywood. The use of folded plate roofs eliminates trusses and other roof members. The tilted plates lean against one another, acting as giant V-shaped beams supported by walls or columns.

By combining the use of all these components, the architect can design a structure that is in perfect structural equilibrium and lightweight in materials. The design of the structure shown in Fig. 68–12A can be compared to the action of the gymnast in Fig. 68–12B. The arms of the gymnast compare with the footer and pier of the structure. The cantilevered section of the structure must be as rigid as the legs of the gymnast. The intersections between the roof, the cantilevered arm, and the footer are all controlled and held in the state of equilibrium by plywood panels. These panels can be compared to the shoulders of the gymnast which keep him in a rigid, fixed position, falling neither forward nor backward.

▶ Concrete

Pouring concrete into forms is certainly not new to the building industry. But the preparation of concrete building components away from the site is

Fig. 68–11. Curved sandwich panels.

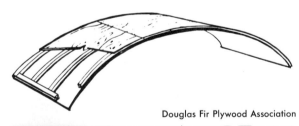

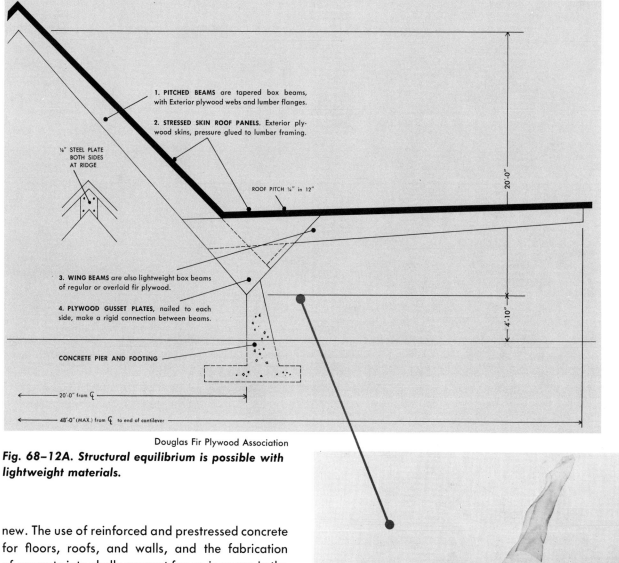

1. **PITCHED BEAMS** are tapered box beams, with Exterior plywood webs and lumber flanges.

2. **STRESSED SKIN ROOF PANELS.** Exterior plywood skins, pressure glued to lumber framing.

⅛" STEEL PLATE BOTH SIDES AT RIDGE

ROOF PITCH ¼" in 12"

3. **WING BEAMS** are also lightweight box beams of regular or overlaid fir plywood.

4. **PLYWOOD GUSSET PLATES**, nailed to each side, make a rigid connection between beams.

CONCRETE PIER AND FOOTING

20'-0" from ℄

48'-0" (MAX.) from ℄ to end of cantilever

20'-0"

4'-10"

Douglas Fir Plywood Association

Fig. 68-12A. *Structural equilibrium is possible with lightweight materials.*

new. The use of reinforced and prestressed concrete for floors, roofs, and walls, and the fabrication of concrete into shells account for an increase in the use of concrete as a building medium. For example, the New York Telephone Company building in Manhattan uses $10' \times 10'$ concrete slabs that are $1'$ thick to protect sensitive electronic equipment from the effects of radiation and other outside disturbances (Fig. 68-13).

Prestressed concrete. When a beam carries a load, it bends and its center sags lower than the ends. The bottom fibers are stretched and the top fibers are compressed. Concrete can be prestressed to eliminate sag. In prestressing concrete, steel wires are strung through the concrete beam. The wires are stretched and anchored at the ends of

Jack Eismont, gymnast

Fig. 68-12B. *The position of the gymnast can be compared to a building.*

Fig. 68–13. The use of concrete to reduce radiation.

Fig. 68–14. The principle of prestressing concrete.

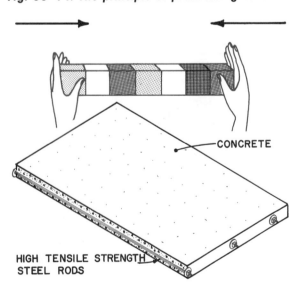

CONCRETE

HIGH TENSILE STRENGTH
STEEL RODS

the beam. When the concrete is hard, the protruding wires spring back to their original shape outside the beam because the stress is relieved here. This return to their original shape acts as a wedge to hold the wires bonded to the concrete. The wires inside are held under stress.

Prestressing can be compared to holding a row of blocks or books between your hands. As long as sufficient pressure can be exerted, as shown in Fig. 68–14, no sag can occur. The use of prestressed concrete prevents cracks because concrete is always in compression. Prestressing permits less depth of beams as related to the span. Prestressed concrete has remarkable elastic properties and develops considerable resistance to shear stresses.

Precast concrete. Precast concrete is concrete that has been poured into molds prior to its use

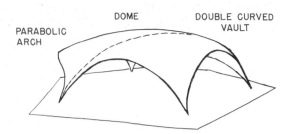

PARABOLIC ARCH   DOME   DOUBLE CURVED VAULT

Fig. 68–15. A concrete shell.

in construction. When high stresses will not be incurred, precasting without prestressing will suffice.

Reinforced concrete. Reinforced concrete is precast concrete with steel reinforcing rods inserted for stability and rigidity. The rods are not placed under stress as are the wires in prestressed concrete. Reinforced concrete slabs are used extensively for floor systems where short spans make prestressing unnecessary.

Concrete shells. Concrete shells are curved, thin sheets of concrete usually poured or sprayed on some material, such as steel rods, that provides temporary rigidity until the concrete hardens (Fig. 68–15). One of the latest innovations in the design and construction of concrete shells is the use of reinforcing mats that are flat on the ground. The struc-

Fig. 68–16. Model of the framework for a concrete-lift building.

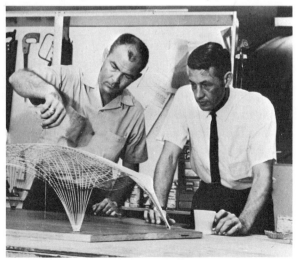

Fig. 68–17. Concrete-shell construction used on the TWA Terminal at the John F. Kennedy International Airport.

ture is then lifted into the desired position, as shown in the model in Fig. 68–16. The mat is then sprayed with a coating of concrete which holds the steel rods in place after the concrete solidifies. Concrete-shell construction is becoming increasingly popular in the design of air terminals, auditoriums, and gymnasiums (Fig. 68–17).

Concrete blocks. Concrete blocks have been used for years for foundation construction and for solid concrete walls. An adaptation of the concrete block is a concrete grill which is now gaining wide acceptance. Concrete grillwork provides protection from heat and from the glare of the sun during the day. It provides some degree of privacy at night. Concrete blocks are cast into many different shapes and can be assembled in various patterns (Fig. 68–18).

As stronger materials are developed more varied blocks will be produced to provide more flexibility in placement and design.

Fig. 68–18. Concrete grillwork.

Fig. 68–20. A building design using precast concrete slabs, large girders, and glass partitions.

Fig. 68–19. The stainless-steel arch rising over St. Louis.

▶ Steel

Steel has classically been used for the framework of large buildings but was always hidden from view in the final design. Steel can now be used for both its structural and its aesthetic qualities. For example, the simple lean strength and beauty of stainless steel is revealed in the 630'-high arch rising over the original site of St. Louis, Missouri (Fig. 68–19).

With the development of each new building material or practice, the utilization of other building materials becomes more practical. For example, the building shown in Fig. 68–20 has floors which are carried by rods suspended from giant rafters. The four exterior columns which are faced with prestressed concrete result in a large, column-free interior. This type of construction would have been impossible before the development of precast concrete slabs and large girders. The development and manufacture of large glass partitions were also necessary for this design. As larger materials are developed more design flexibility will be possible.

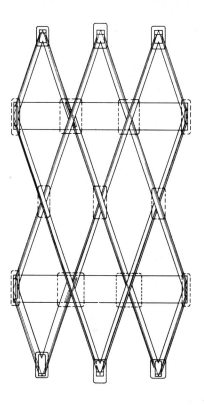

United States Steel; Curtis & Davis, architects

Fig. 68–21. The use of an exposed curtain-wall steel frame.

The 13-story IBM Building in Pittsburgh is an excellent example of the versatility of steel. Unlike conventional curtain-wall construction, in which the wall is applied to a steel frame, the IBM Building exposes its structural steel frame. The steel framework illustrated in Fig. 68–21 will carry all wind and wall loads. A central core in the building will carry all interior loads. In conventional post and beam buildings, a skeleton frame of vertical columns and horizontal beams carries all loads, and independent curtains of metal and glass are applied to it. The design of the IBM Building eliminates all vertical columns from the skin to the core. The truss walls direct all building loads around the structure and downward to concentrate on two points of contact on each side of the base.

▶ **Plastics**

The use of plastics in the building industry has increased in recent years. The development of vinyls and other laminates gives the architect increased flexibility in designing with permanent, wear-resistant, easily maintained materials. The possibilities for the use of plastics range from coating on wallpaper and insulation to the application of Dacron to the "radome" Telstar Earth Station (Fig. 68–22). This 13-story, 2-acre expanse of fabric is the world's largest earthbound inflated structure. It not only illustrates the possible uses of plastics as building material, but emphasizes the limitless horizons in the use of all building materials and methods in the future.

Problems

1. Name the major building materials used in the building shown in Fig. 68–23. Make a sketch of the elevation of this building and label the materials.

2. Sketch a transverse cross section of the building shown in Fig. 68–24. Show how you think the building is structurally supported, and label the type of material used for the major support.

Fig. 68–22. The 13-story "Radome" Telstar Earth Station.

Fig. 68–23. Name the building materials used in the Allen M. Scaife Hall of Engineering.

Fig. 68–24. Sketch a transverse section of this building. Indicate how you think it is structurally supported.

3. Sketch two elevations of the building shown in Fig. 68–25. Label the materials used. Sketch a transverse section of this same building, showing the means of support of the cantilevered areas.

4. Define these terms: *aluminum, structural glass, glass block, corrugated glass, laminates, stressed skin panel, box beams, laminated beams, curved panels, sandwich core, folded plate roof, prestressed, precast, reinforced concrete, shell.*

Fig. 68–25. Sketch two elevations of this building. List the materials used.

General Motors Corporation; Engineering News-Record

SECTION NINETEEN. METHODS OF CHECKING

The appropriateness of the size and layout should be completely checked by the architect, designer, builder, and occupant before a completed architectural plan is used for actual construction purposes. The technical authenticity of the drawing should first be checked by the draftsman and/or by a checker. He should be certain that all dimensions and symbols are correct and that each detail drawing agrees with the basic plan.

It is sometimes difficult for the layman to interpret engineering and architectural drawings adequately.

For this reason, it is sometimes advisable to construct an architectural model which represents more closely the appearance of the finished building or groups of buildings.

Another concept that is sometimes difficult for the layman to grasp is the relationship of the size of rooms to the furniture and equipment that will actually be placed in these rooms. Checking the adequacy of room size can be done by placing furniture, equipment, and even people in the rooms through the use of templates.

Unit 69. Architectural Models

The use of an architectural model is the only way actually to see the finished design in all three dimensions. A model is also the only representation that can be viewed from any angle.

▶ Function

Models may be used in planning cities or parts of city redevelopments, as shown in Fig. 69–1. Models are often used to check the design of large com-

Fig. 69–1. Models may be used for planning cities.

The appropriateness of size and layout can be seen better on a model than through any other device. The relationship to other objects, such as people, cars, trees, and other buildings, becomes more apparent when the structure is viewed in three-dimensional form. For these reasons, it is advisable to include within the overall model as many scale models of furniture, equipment, cars, and people, as possible. Fig. 69–4 shows a model with cutaway walls revealing the relationship among furnishings, room size, and layout. It is sometimes advisable to prepare basic outline blocks representing adjacent buildings in order to compare their relative size and position with those of the building being designed (Fig. 69–1). The model can also be used to design effectively or to check the color scheme of the entire house or of individual rooms since the entire house can be seen at a glance.

Some models are prepared to check only the structural qualities of the building. The architect shown in Fig. 69–5 is discussing a better way to frame a house he has designed. When a structural model of this type is prepared, balsa wood strips are used to represent sills, studs, rafters, and beams. These structural members are prepared to the exact scale of the model, and the balsa wood

mercial buildings, as shown in Fig. 69–2; or they may be used to check the design of a residence (Fig. 69–3).

Fig. 69–2. Models are often used to check the design of commercial buildings.

Fig. 69–3. The use of a model to check the design of a home.

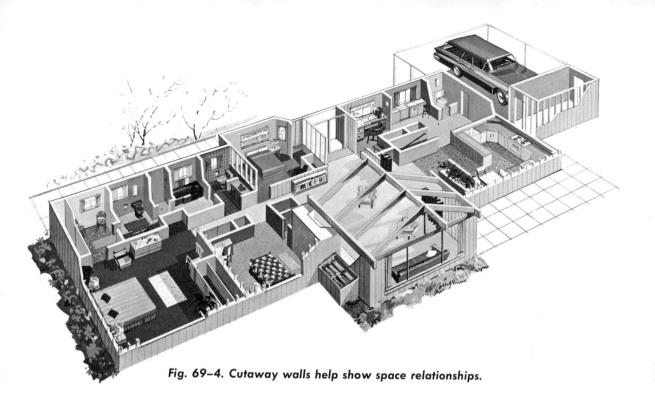

Fig. 69-4. Cutaway walls help show space relationships.

members are attached together with modelmakers' glue or with small pins, to approximate the methods used in nailing the full-sized house. Pre-cut model lumber is often used.

▶ Model Construction

Since the materials used in full-size buildings are too large for model construction, they must be simulated by other materials and other products. For example, coarse sandpaper may be used to simulate a built-up gravel roof. Sponges may be used to simulate trees, and green flocking may be used for grass. In addition to such substitute materials, a great variety of commercially prepared model materials are now available. The chart shown in Fig. 69-6 shows some of the special materials used to make various parts of architectural models.

Methods of constructing models vary greatly, just as methods of constructing full-sized structures vary, according to the building materials used. Nevertheless, the following procedures represent the normal sequence of constructing models, even

though some of the techniques may vary with the use of different materials.

1. A floor plan and elevation outline should be prepared to the size to which the model will

Fig. 69-5. The use of a model to check structural qualities.

Southern Pine Association

Part	Model Materials	Methods of Construction
Walls	Soft wood; cardboard	Cut wall to exact dimensions of elevations. Allow for over-lapping of joints at corners. Have wall thicknesses 6'' to scale.
Roofs	Thin, stiff cardboard; paint-colored sand; sandpaper; wood pieces	Cut out roof patterns and assembly. For sand or gravel roof, paint with slow-drying enamel the color of roof. Sprinkle on sand. For shingle roof, cut sandpaper or thin wood pieces, and glue on as if laying shingle roof.
Brick & stone	Commercially-printed paper	Glue paper in place; or cut grooves in wood, and paint color of bricks or stones.
Wood paneling	Commercially-printed paper; 1/32'' veneer wood	Glue paper in place; with veneer wood, rule on black lines for strip effect, and glue in place. Mahogany veneer equals redwood.
Stucco	Plaster of Paris	Mix and dab on with brush.
Windows & doors	Preformed plastic; wood strips and clear plastic	Purchase ready-made windows to scale in model store; or frame openings with wood strips and glue in clear plastic for windows or wood panel for door.
Floors	Flocked carpet; commer-cially-printed paper; 1/32'' veneer wood	Paint area with slow-drying colored enamel, and apply flock, removing excess when dry. With paper, glue in place. With veneer, rule on black lines for strip effect, and glue in place.
Furniture	Cardboard, nails, flock, wood, clay	Fashion furniture to scale. Paint and flock to give effect of material.
Site areas	3/4'' wood slab, wire screen, paper mâché	Build up hilly areas with sticks and wire. Place paper mâché over wire.
Grass	Green enamel paint and flock	Paint grass area. Apply flock, removing excess when dry.
Trees & bushes	Sponge; lichen	Grind up sponges and paint different shades of green. Use small pieces for bushes. Glue small pieces to tree twigs for trees. Lichen may be purchased in model stores and used in the same manner as sponges.
Autos & people	Toys and miniatures	If time permits, carve from soft wood.

Fig. 69–6. Materials used on architectural models.

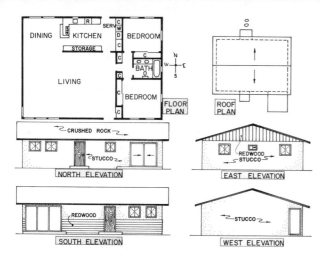

Fig. 69-7. Models should be built from floor plans and elevations.

be built (Fig. 69–7). Small structures such as houses can be built conveniently at the scale ½″ = 1'-0″. Larger structures such as commercial office buildings should be built to the scale ¼″ = 1'-0″ or even smaller.

2. The contour of the lot should be developed, as shown in Fig. 69–8.

3. Glue or trace the floor-plan outline on a ¼″ pad, and tack or glue this pad to a base, as shown in Fig. 69–9.

4. Cut exterior walls from balsa wood or heavy cardboard. Carefully cut out the openings for windows and doors with a razor blade, as shown in Fig. 69–10. When cutting side walls, cut them long to allow overlapping of the front and back walls.

Fig. 69-8. Developing the contour of a lot.

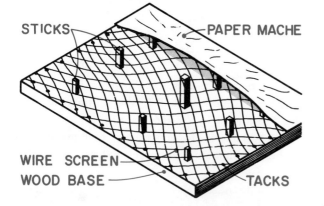

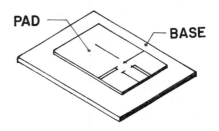

Fig. 69-9. A pad attached to a base.

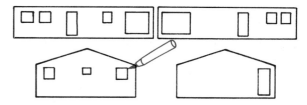

Fig. 69-10. Cut-outs of exterior walls.

5. Glue small strips of wood or paper around the windows to represent framing and trim, as shown in Fig. 69–11. Glue clear plastic inside the window openings to represent window glass and cover the joint with trim. Cut out doors and hang them on the door openings, using transparent tape, as shown in Fig. 69–12. Add siding materials to the exterior of the wall panels to simulate the materials that will be used on the house, as shown in Fig. 69–13.

6. Glue the exterior walls to the pad and to each other at the corners (Fig. 69–14).

Fig. 69-11. Small strips of wood or paper can represent framing and trim around windows and doors.

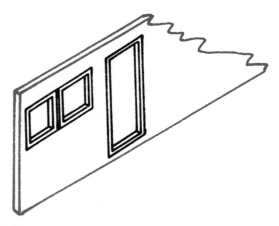

449

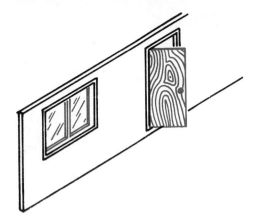

Fig. 69–12. Doors can be hung with transparent tape.

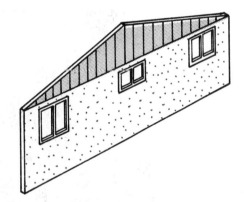

Fig. 69–13. Siding materials are added to the exterior panels.

Fig. 69–14. Exterior walls are glued to the pad.

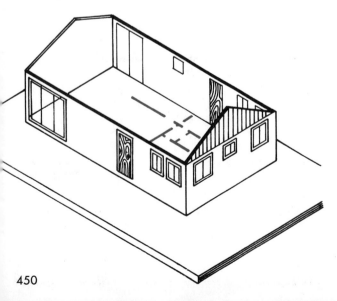

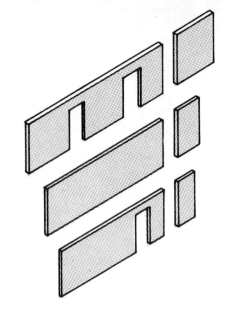

Fig. 69–15. Openings in interior walls are cut out.

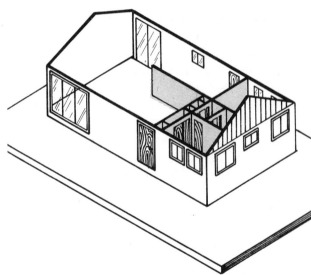

Fig. 69–16. Interior walls are glued to exterior walls and to the pad.

7. Cut out openings in interior walls for doors, arches, and fireplaces, as shown in Fig. 69–15.

8. Glue interior walls to the partition lines of the floor plan (Fig. 69–16).

9. Add interior fixtures such as built-in cabinets, kitchen equipment, bathroom fixtures. Paint the

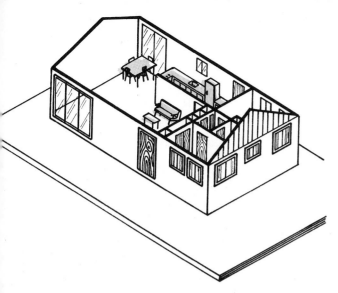

Fig. 69-17. Furniture, fixtures, and color schemes are added.

Fig. 69-18. Roof sections are joined and braced.

interior surfaces to determine the color scheme and add furniture if desired (Fig. 69-17).

10. Cut out roof parts, join roof parts together, and brace them so that the roof will lift off. Add material to simulate the roof treatment on the exterior of the roof (Fig. 69-18).

11. Add landscaping features such as trees, shrubs, grass, patios, walkways, and outdoor furniture to add to the authentic appearance of the model (Fig. 69-19).

SCALE 1/4"= 1'-0"
GREEN FLOCK
MAHOGANY VENEER
GROUND-UP SPONGE
SANDPAPER ROOF
PAPER PRINTED BRICK

Fig. 69-19. Landscaping features are added.

Problems

1. Construct a model similar to the one shown in Fig. 69-17.

2. Construct a model of your own home. Make any design adjustments you would recommend in the basic plan.

3. Construct a model of a home you have designed.

4. Construct a model of the home shown in Fig. 28-1.

5. Define these terms: *scale model, structural model, balsa wood, flocking.*

Fig. 69-20. Make a model of this plan.

Unit 70. Template Checking

Room sizes often appear adequate on the floor plan, but when furniture is placed in the rooms, the occupants may find them too small or proportioned incorrectly. After the house is built, it is too late to change the sizes of most rooms. Therefore, extreme care should be taken in the planning stage to ensure that the plan as designed will accommodate the furniture, fixtures, and traffic anticipated for each area.

▶ Template Preparation

One method of determining the adequacy of room sizes and proportions is to prepare templates of each piece of furniture and equipment that will be placed in the room. These templates should be on the same scale as the floor plan. Placing the templates on the floor plan (Fig. 70–1) will show graphically how much floor space is occupied by each piece of furniture. The home planner can determine whether there is sufficient traffic space around the furniture, whether the room must be enlarged, whether the proportions should be changed or whether, as a last resort, smaller items of furniture should be procured.

The placement of the templates on the plan in Fig. 70–2 indicates that some rearrangement or adjustment should be made in the furniture placement in Bedroom No. 3, and that the dining room might be inadequate if the table is expanded.

Checking by templates can be significant only if the templates are carefully prepared to the same scale as the floor plan and if the actual furniture dimensions are used in the preparation of the templates. Figure 70–3 shows some typical furniture sizes that may be used in the preparation of templates for checking purposes. The floor-plan design can be checked much more quickly by the template method than it can by a model. Furthermore, if templates are used while the plan is still in the sketching stage, adjustments can be made easily and rooms rearranged to produce a more desirable plan.

Fig. 70–1. Placing templates on a floor plan.

Fig. 70–2. Space requirements can be determined by placing furniture templates on the floor plans.

Southern California Gas Company

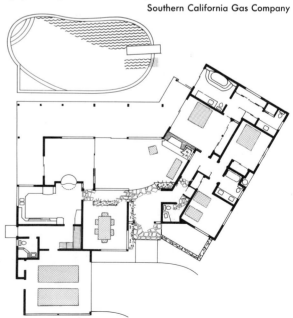

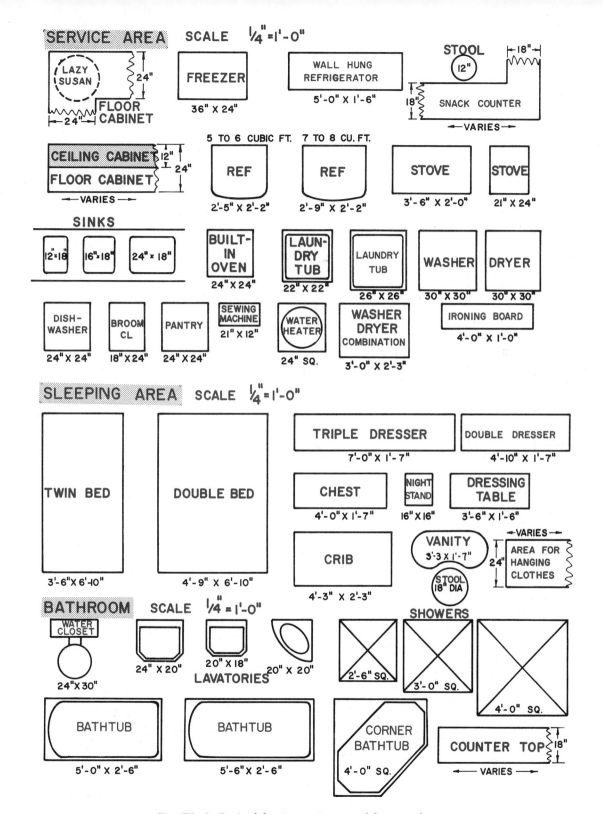

Fig. 70–3. Typical furniture sizes used for templates.

453

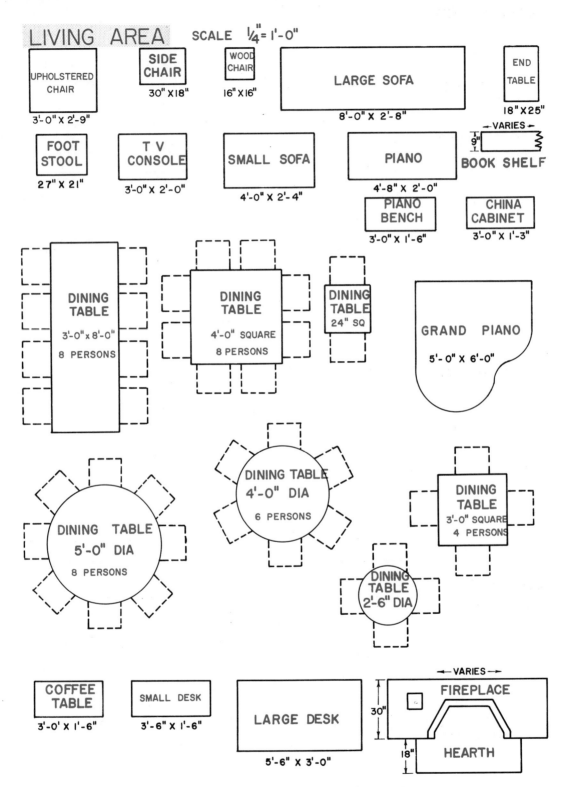

Fig. 70–3. Typical furniture sizes used for templates.

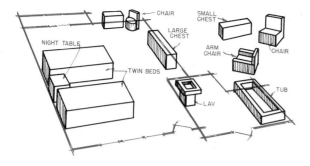

Fig. 70-4. Three-dimensional templates.

▶ Three-dimensional Templates

The template method of checking room sizes does not reveal the three-dimensional aspect of space planning as a model does. One compromise between the model method and the template method of checking drawings is the preparation of three-dimensional templates. Three-dimensional templates have not only width and length but also height, as shown in Fig. 70-4. This method of checking is essentially the same as placing furniture on a model, except that the walls do not exist and adjustments can be made much more easily. Figure 70-5 shows the height of typical pieces of furniture for use in preparing three-dimensional templates. These dimensions are typical and may vary slightly with different manufacturers.

Fig. 70-5. Height of typical pieces of furniture.

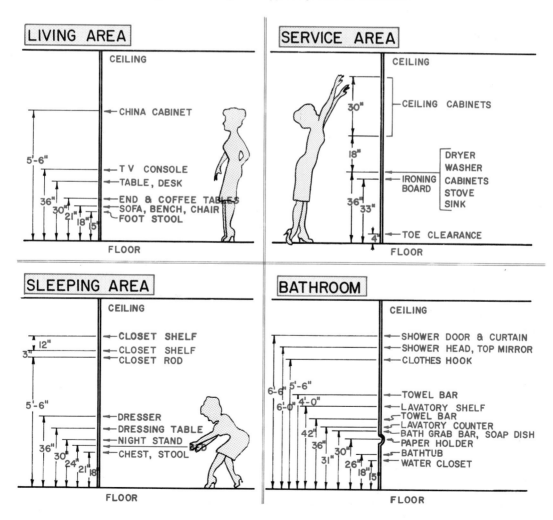

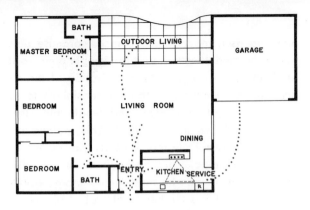

Fig. 70-6. Checking traffic patterns.

▶ Traffic Patterns

A well-designed structure must provide for efficient and smooth circulation of traffic. Traffic patterns must be controlled, and yet sufficient space must be allowed for adequate passage and flexibility in the traffic pattern. Rooms should not be used as hallways or access areas to other rooms. Any room should be accessible from the front entrance or the service entrance without the necessity of passing through other rooms. The length of halls should be minimized because halls provide only traffic access and do not contribute livable space.

Fig. 70-7. Checklist for traffic patterns.

	Excellent	Fair	Poor	Distance
Service circulation				
• Service door to kitchen	X			5'
• Service door to living area	X			12'
• Service door to bathroom			X	30'
• Service door to bedrooms			X	36'
• Kitchen to bathrooms		X		14'
• Paths around work triangle			X	
Guest's circulation				
• Front door to closet	X			3'
• Front door to living room	X			10'
• Front door to bathroom	X			16'
• Front door to outdoor living		X		33'
• Living room to bathroom	X			8'
Occupants' circulation				
• Front door to kitchen	X			6'
• Kitchen to bedrooms		X		15' to 35'
• Kitchen to children's play area		X		15'
• Kitchen to children's sleeping area		X		17'
• Bedrooms to bathrooms	X			4' to 10'
• Outdoor living area to bathroom			X	25'
• Living room to outdoor living area	X			3'

One method of checking the traffic pattern is to use a scale drawing and trace, with a pencil, the movements of your daily routine, as shown in Fig. 70–6. If you prepare a template of a person (an overhead view of yourself with arms outstretched), you will be able to determine the effectiveness of the traffic pattern as it relates to the size of each room and the layout of the entire plan. Figure 70–7 is a checklist of traffic-pattern adequacies.

▶ Technical Checking

The draftsman should always check dimensions, labels, and symbols before the drawing is removed from the board. He should also make a more formal check of these factors on a print prepared for checking purposes (check print). After the draftsman has made this check, another draftsman, architect, or checker should also scrutinize the drawing for dimensional accuracy, proper labeling, and correctness of symbols.

One of the most effective methods of checking architectural drawings is the use of a colored pencil,

as shown in Fig. 70–8. A checker draws a line through each dimension, label, and symbol as it is checked. Otherwise he may find himself rechecking the same dimensions and missing many others. Many architectural offices use a color-coding system to indicate the checker's reaction to the drawing. In one system a yellow pencil is used for checking items that are correct, a red pencil for checking errors, and a blue pencil for marking recommended changes.

Regardless of the checking method used, one of the most important items to check on architectural drawings is the correctness of dimensions. Dimensioning errors cause more difficulty on the construction job than any other single factor relating to architectural drawings. Dimensions must be added to ensure that they total the overall dimension. Interior dimensions must be added to ensure that they agree with the exterior dimensions.

▶ Plan Agreement

An important relationship that must be very carefully checked on architectural drawings is the

Fig. 70–8. Checking architectural drawings with a colored pencil.

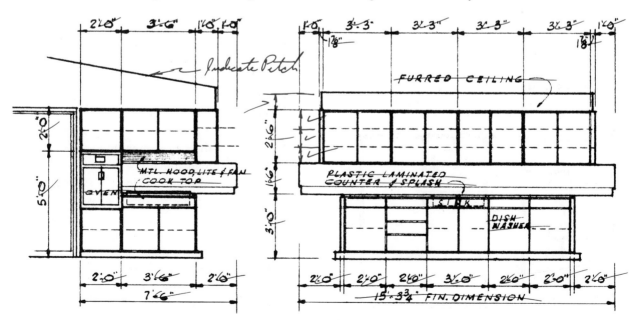

Fig. 70–9. Rearrange this plan to improve the traffic pattern.

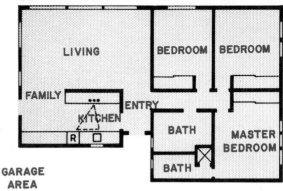

Fig. 70–11. Redesign this plan to produce a better traffic pattern.

agreement of plans with each other. The design and dimensions of the floor plan must be compared with the design and dimensions of the elevation. The floor plan must also be compared with the

Fig. 70–10. Check the adequacy of these rooms with templates.

foundation to ensure complete alignment on the perimeter, over the beams, and through the chimney. The foundation plan must also be compared with the elevation. Sectional drawings and all details must be compared with the floor-plan and elevation drawing to which they relate. It is therefore mandatory that a complete system of checking be established and carefully followed in the preparation of all architectural plans.

Problems

1. Prepare a set of templates, using Fig. 70–3 as a guide. Sketch the floor plan of your own home and check its adequacy with these templates.
2. Use the templates you have prepared to check a floor plan of your own design.
3. Check the traffic pattern of the plan shown in Fig. 70–9. What recommendations would you make to improve the traffic pattern?
4. Sketch the plan shown in Fig. 70–10 and determine the adequacy of room sizes by the use of templates.
5. Redesign the plan shown in Fig. 70–11 to produce a better traffic pattern.
6. Define these architectural terms: *template, two-dimensional template, three-dimensional template, traffic pattern, checker, check print.*

Donald A. Wexler, architect; Bernard Perlin, engineer

SECTION TWENTY. COST ANALYSIS

Architects would welcome the opportunity to design a structure free from financial limitations. Such a condition, however, rarely exists. Budgets are the necessary framework within which architects must design most buildings, ranging from the smallest residence to the largest office building. There is of course more flexibility in some budgets than in others, but in every design problem the designer must strive to create a design that will provide optimum facilities and keep within his budget.

Unit 71. Building Costs

Approximately 40 percent of the cost of the average home is for materials. Labor costs account for another 40 percent. The remaining 20 percent is taken up by the price of the lot. As labor and material costs rise, the cost of homes increases proportionately.

▶ Total Cost

Many factors influence the total cost of the house. The location of the site is extremely important. An identical house built on an identical lot can vary several thousand dollars in cost, depending on whether it is located in a city, in a suburb, or in

Labor $12,000 (40%)	Materials $12,000 (40%)	Lot $6,000 (20%)
plans and specs	building permits	average city lot
utilities installation	insurance	
survey	drain tiling	
excavating, grading	concrete materials	
foundation work	paving materials	
paving	rough lumber	
sodding	millwork and trim	
rough carpentry	sash and doors	
finish carpentry	screens	
window installation	windows	
glazing	cabinets	
door installation	counter tops	
sanding floors	hardwood floors	
finishing floors	roofing materials	
roofing	sheet metal	
plumbing	iron and steel	
heating	lath and plaster	
air conditioning	dry wall material	
sewer connection	plumbing fixtures	
masonry	plumbing lines	
two-car garage	heating plant	
closed-in porch	air conditioner	
hardware installation	shower door	
electrical	masonry materials	
insulation	two-car garage	
weatherproofing	closed-in porch	
painting	rough hardware	
sheet-metal work	finish hardware	
sprinkling system	electrical fixtures	
landscaping	electrical wiring	
basement	lighting fixtures	
fences	insulation	
clean-up	weather-stripping	
fixture installation	caulking	
	shades and blinds	
	linoleum	
	tile	
	paints	
	sprinkling system	
	landscaping	
	fence and trellis materials	
	fireplace materials	
	floor covers	
	composition	

Fig. 71–1. Approximate cost breakdown for a $30,000 home.

the country. Labor costs also vary greatly from one part of the country to another and from urban to rural areas (Fig. 71–1). Normally labor costs are lower in rural areas. The third important variable contributing to the difference in housing costs is the cost of materials. Material costs vary greatly, depending upon whether materials indigenous to the region are used for the structure. In some areas, brick is a relatively inexpensive building material. In other parts of the country, a brick home may be one of the most expensive. Climate also has some effect on the cost of building. In moderate climates many costs can be eliminated by exclusion of expensive insulation, heating plants, and frost-deep foundations. In other climates air conditioning is mandatory.

▶ Estimating Costs

There are two basic methods of determining the cost of a house. One is adding the total cost of all the materials to the hourly rate for labor multiplied by the anticipated number of hours it will take to build the home. The cost of the lot, landscaping, and various architects' and surveyors' fees must also be added to this figure. This process involves much computation and adequate techniques for estimating construction costs.

Two quicker, rule-of-thumb methods for estimating the cost of the house are the square-foot method and the cubic-foot method. These methods are not as accurate as itemizing the cost of all materials, labor, and other items. However, they do provide a quick estimate for speculative purposes.

Square-foot method. In general, the cost of the average home ranges from $10 to $20 per square foot of floor space, depending on the geographical location (Fig. 71–2). Each local office of the Federal Housing Administration can supply current estimating information peculiar to the locale.

Cubic-foot method. The cubic-foot method of estimating is slightly more accurate than the square-foot method and is more appropriate for multiple-story dwellings (Fig. 71–3).

Building materials method. The square-foot and cubic-foot methods are at best rough estimates.

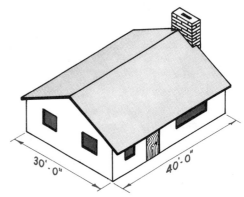

CONSTRUCTION COST = $ 15 PER SQ FT
SQUARE FOOTAGE = 30 X 40 = 1200 SQ FT
COST = 1200 X 15 = $ 18,000

Fig. 71–2. The square-foot method of determining costs.

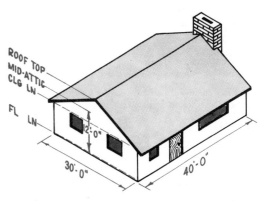

CONSTRUCTION COST = $ .75 PER CUBIC FT
CUBIC VOLUME = FLOOR AREA X HEIGHT
CUBIC VOLUME = 1200 X 12
CUBIC VOLUME = 14,400 CU FT
COST = 14,400 X .75 = $ 10,800

Fig. 71–3. The cubic-foot method of determining cost.

The final cost of a building will depend upon the quality of building materials used. Figure 71–4 shows the percentage of total cost of each material in a typical building. A 2,000-square-foot home constructed with inexpensive materials may vary in cost several thousand dollars from a 2,000-square-foot home constructed with more expensive materials.

Principal Items	Cost	Percentage of Total Cost
Excavation and site improvements	$ 65,524	4.45%
Foundations	107,101	7.28
Structural frame	140,080	9.52
Cement finish	80,018	5.44
Exterior masonry	96,776	6.58
Interior partitions	71,956	4.89
Carpentry and millwork	71,184	4.84
Sash and glazing	70,213	4.77
Roofing	36,374	2.47
Insulation	33,562	2.28
Waterproofing and dampproofing	1,700	0.12
Metal lath, furring, and plastering	52,424	3.56
Hollow metal work	16,730	1.14
Miscellaneous iron and ornamental metal	27,955	1.90
Tile, terrazzo, and marble	22,068	1.50
Floor covering	15,284	1.04
Painting	25,154	1.71
Finish hardware	22,825	1.55
Acoustical ceilings	53,040	3.60
Plumbing	109,335	7.43
Heating, ventilating, and air conditioning	220,585	14.99
Electrical work and light fixtures	131,560	8.94
TOTAL	$1,471,448	100%

Engineering News-Record

Fig. 71-4. A method of determining cost of a commercial building by computing the cost of building materials.

Lots. The cost of the lot and landscaping must be added to the total cost of the materials.

The cost of residential lots in the United States varies considerably, as does the cost of landscaping a typical residence (Fig. 71–5). Other costs in addition to the cost of the home must also be considered. These include service charges, title search, insurance costs, and transfer taxes. These are called *closing costs*. Figure 71–6 shows a breakdown of typical closing costs.

The lawyer's, architect's, and surveyor's fees are sometimes included in the closing costs. Lawyers' fees range between $75 and $200, and surveys cost between $35 and $75. Architects usually work on a 5 percent commission basis—7 percent if they supervise construction in addition to designing.

▶ Cutting Costs

Some construction methods and material utilization that may greatly affect the ultimate cost of the home are listed as follows:

1. Square or rectangular homes are less expensive to build than irregular-shaped homes.

2. It is less expensive to build on a flat lot than on a sloping or hillside lot.

3. Using locally manufactured or produced materials cuts costs greatly.

4. Using stock materials and stock sizes of components takes advantage of mass-production cost reductions.

5. Using materials that can be quickly installed cuts labor costs. Prefabricating large sections or panels eliminates much time on the site.

Fine grading	$ .03 per sq ft
Site clean-up	12.00 per hour
Medium trees	
15 gal container	35.00
20" box container	85.00
Small trees and shrubs	
5 gal container	7.00
1 gal container	2.00
1 qt container	.65
Redwood header boards	.50 per lineal ft
Boulders—24" to 36"	15.00 each
Crushed rock	.15 per sq ft
Ground cover	
Ivy	.08 per sq ft
Ice plant	.08 per sq ft
Strawberry	.08 per sq ft
Lawns	
Top quality	.11 per sq ft
Medium	.08 per sq ft
Inexpensive	.06 per sq ft

Fig. 71–5. Cost of landscaping.

Loan Charges	$250
(Mortgage Service Charge) (Loan Origination Fee) (Points on Loan)	
Notary Fee	2
Recording Deed of Trust	5
Recording Deed	3
Title Search	75
Title Insurance	100
Household Insurance	100
Appraisal Fee	15
Credit Report	15
Federal Revenue Stamps	15
State Revenue Stamps	15
Conveyancing Fee	20
Lawyers Fee	200
Survey	35

Fig. 71–6. Closing costs for a $30,000 home.

6. Using prefinished materials saves labor costs.

7. Using prehung doors cuts considerable time from the finishing process.

8. Designing the home with a minimum amount of hall space increases the usable square footage and provides more living space for the cost.

9. Using prefabricated fireboxes for fireplaces cuts installation costs.

10. Investigation of existing building codes before beginning construction, to eliminate unnecessary changes as construction proceeds.

11. Refraining from changing the design or any aspect of the plans after construction begins.

12. Minimizing special jobs or custom built items.

13. Designing the house for short plumbing lines.

14. Insulating to save heating and cooling costs.

Problems

1. At $15 a square foot, how much will the home shown in Fig. 25–8, cost?

2. At $1.00 per cubic foot, how much will the home shown in Fig. 26–2. cost?

3. Resketch the elevation of the building shown in Fig. 29–14. Substitute building materials that will reduce the cost of this home.

4. Resketch the plan shown in Fig. 6–1 to reduce the cost.

5. Compute the cost of your present home based on the existing cost per square foot or cubic foot in your area.

6. Define these architectural terms: *real-estate survey, square footage, cubic footage.*

Unit 72. Financing

Few people can accumulate sufficient funds to pay for the entire cost of the home at one time. Therefore, most home buyers pay a percentage—10, 20, or 30 percent—at the time of occupancy, and arrange a loan (mortgage) for the balance.

▶ Mortgage

A mortgage is obtained from a mortgage company, bank, savings and loan association, or insurance company. The lending institution pays for the house, and through the mortgage loan agreement collects this amount from the home buyer over a long period of time: 10, 20, or even 30 years.

Fig. 72–1. Payments on a $10,000 mortgage at 5% interest.

Time in years	Monthly payments	Number of payments	Total cost
10	$106.07	120	$12,728.40
15	79.08	180	14,234.40
20	66.00	240	15,840.00
25	58.46	300	17,538.00
30	54.00	360	19,440.00

▶ Interest

In addition to paying back the lending institution the exact cost of the house, the home owner must also pay for the services of the institution. Payment is in the form of a percentage of the total cost of the home and is known as *interest*. Normal interest rates range from 4 to 8 percent. Rates of 5 and 6 percent, however, are the most common. The interest rate increases with the length of time needed to pay back the loan. On a long-term loan—for example, 30 years—the monthly payments will be smaller but the overall cost will be much greater because the interest is higher. A long-term loan can, over the life of the loan, accumulate 100 percent interest.

A comparison of the time factor, amount of payment, and number of payments on a $10,000 loan at 5 percent interest is shown in Fig. 72–1. Figure 72–2 shows similar information for a $20,000 loan, and Fig. 72–3 shows the same information for a $30,000 loan.

▶ Taxes

In addition to the principal (amount paid back that is credited to the payment for the house), and the interest, the taxes on the house must be added to the total cost of the home. Taxes on residential property vary greatly. Taxes on a $20,000 home

Fig. 72–2. Payments on a $20,000 mortgage at 5% interest.

Time in years	Monthly payments	Number of payments	Total cost
10	$212.14	120	$25,456.80
15	158.16	180	28,468.80
20	132.00	240	31,680.00
25	116.92	300	35,076.00
30	107.37	360	38,653.20

Fig. 72–3. Payments on a $30,000 mortgage at 5% interest.

Time in years	Monthly payments	Number of payments	Total cost
10	$318.21	120	$38,185.20
15	237.24	180	42,703.20
20	198.00	240	47,520.00
25	175.38	300	52,614.00
30	162.00	360	58,320.00

TYPE OF INSURANCE	$10,000 HOME	$20,000 HOME	$50,000 HOME
Minimum coverage Fire Public liability	$100	$200	$315
Average coverage Fire Public liability Property damage Theft	$135	$235	$350
Maximum coverage Fire Public liability Property damage Theft Medical Personal liability Landscape insurance Wind Flood Earthquake	$250	$350	$450

Fig. 72–4. Insurance rates per three year period.

in most residential suburban communities range between $300 and $800 per year.

▶ **Insurance**

The purchase of a home is a large investment and must be insured for the protection of the home buyer and for the protection of the lending institution. Insurance rates vary greatly, depending on the cost of the home, location, type of construction and availability of fire fighting equipment (Fig. 72–4). The home should be insured against fire, public liability, property damage, vandalism, natural destruction, and accidents to trespassers and workers.

▶ **Budgets**

Since most household budgets are established on a monthly basis, the monthly payments needed to purchase and maintain a residence are more significant than the total cost of the home. Monthly payments are broken into four categories: principal, interest, taxes, and insurance (PITI). Figure 72–5 shows the amortization for a 10-year, 20-year, and 30-year loan.

The prospective home buyer and builder should consider the following factors before selecting a particular institution for a mortgage. He should

Fig. 72–5. Principal, interest, taxes, and insurance costs ($20,000 loan at 5% interest).

PAYMENT BREAKDOWN	10 YEAR LOAN—AMORTIZATION $212.14			20 YEAR LOAN—AMORTIZATION $132			30 YEAR LOAN—AMORTIZATION $107.37		
	First payment	5th year payment	Last payment	First payment	10th year payment	Last payment	First payment	15th year payment	Last payment
Principal	$128.81	$165.30	$211.14	$48.67	$80.15	$131.00	$24.04	$50.81	$106.37
Interest	83.33	46.84	1.00	83.33	51.85	1.00	83.33	56.56	1.00
Taxes	40.00	40.00	40.00	40.00	40.00	40.00	40.00	40.00	40.00
Insurance	10.00	10.00	10.00	10.00	10.00	10.00	10.00	10.00	10.00
Total monthly payment	$262.14	$262.14	$262.14	$182.00	$182.00	$182.00	$157.37	$157.37	$157.37

know the interest rate, the number of years needed to repay, prepayment penalties, total amount of monthly payment, conditions of approval, placement fees, amount of down payment required, service fees, and closing fees. Typical closing costs on a home would include lawyers' fees, transfer taxes, escrow deposit, insurance, and survey fees.

▶ Salary and Home Costs

If the home buyer considers the purchase or the building of a home as an investment, he should take steps to ensure the maximum return on his investment. If the home buyer purchases a home that costs considerably less than he can afford, he is not investing adequately. On the other hand, if the home buyer attempts to buy a home that is more expensive than he can afford, his payments will become a drain on the family budget and undue sacrifices will have to be made to compensate.

Family budgets vary greatly, and a house that may be a burden for one person to purchase may be quite suitable for another, even if the two owners are earning the same relative salary. In general, the cost of the house should not exceed twice the annual income.

Problems

1. What is the cost of the home you could afford if you were earning $5,000 a year? $10,000 a year? $15,000 a year?

2. You purchase a home valued at $24,000 and make a 10 percent down payment. Your interest rate is 5½ percent. What amount of interest will you pay over the life of a 25-year mortgage?

3. What will be your total monthly payment on an $18,000 home if you have made a 5 percent down payment and are paying an interest rate of 5¼ percent? Your yearly taxes are $600 and your insurance is $72.

4. Define these terms: *interest, principal, escrow, mortgage, closing costs, taxes, insurance.*

5. What would your monthly mortgage payment be if you bought the house shown in Fig. 72–6 for $15. per sq. ft. Your interest is 6% for 25 years. You make a 9% down payment of the total price. Your closing costs total $1000. Width is 24 feet, length is 48 feet.

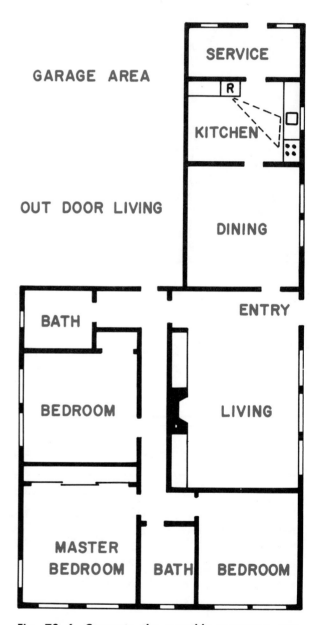

Fig. 72–6. Compute the monthly mortgage payments for this house.

INDEX